# Practical Guide to Azure Cognitive Services

Leverage the power of Azure OpenAI to optimize operations, reduce costs, and deliver cutting-edge AI solutions

**Chris Seferlis**

**Christopher Nellis**

**Andy Roberts**

BIRMINGHAM—MUMBAI

# Practical Guide to Azure Cognitive Services

**Group Product Manager**: Ali Abidi

**Publishing Product Manager**: Ali Abidi

**Senior Editor**: David Sugarman

**Content Development Editor**: Priyanka Soam

**Technical Editor**: Rahul Limbachiya

**Copy Editor**: Safis Editing

**Project Coordinator**: Farheen Fathima

**Proofreader**: Safis Editing

**Indexer**: Hemangini Bari

**Production Designer**: Alishon Mendonca

**Marketing Coordinator**: Shifa Ansari and Vinishka Kalra

First published: April 2023

Production reference: 2050523

Published by Packt Publishing Ltd.

Livery Place

35 Livery Street

Birmingham

B3 2PB, UK.

ISBN 978-1-80181-291-7

www.packtpub.com

*Writing this book has been a very difficult yet rewarding process. I want to thank my colleagues and friends who continued to motivate, advise, and encourage me to keep going. I appreciate our editors, and colleagues for their guidance and reviews throughout the process. Many hours of family time were sacrificed to complete this book and will not be forgotten. Most of all, Kristen, Cora and Thea, thank you for dealing with my writer's block, stress and frustration while providing continuous love and support.*

*- Chris Seferlis*

# Contributors

## About the authors

**Chris Seferlis** is a technology strategist at Microsoft. He has over 20 years of experience working in IT and using technology to accomplish business objectives. He has an MBA from UMass, is a part-time professor at Boston University, and brings a mix of business acumen and practical technology solutions.

**Christopher Nellis** is a senior infrastructure engineer and is experienced in deploying large-scale infrastructure for organizations. He has a passion for automation and MLOps and enjoys working with people to solve problems and make things better.

**Andy Roberts** is a seasoned data and AI architect. His career has included roles such as developer, DBA, architect, project lead, and pre-sales, always revolving around data. He is experienced in acquiring, shaping, moving, protecting, and using data to predict future outcomes, and processing them efficiently.

## About the reviewer

**Sumit Garg** is a product manager at Azure Cognitive Search, Microsoft. Sumit has over 17 years of experience in tech. He started as a developer and consultant and moved on to product management in the last decade. He has worked extensively with B2B PaaS and SaaS products. In his free time, Sumit likes to travel and is a big fan of print. He is an amateur runner and intends to run a marathon someday.

# Table of Contents

# Part 3: Other Cognitive Services That Will Help Your Company Optimize Operations

# 14

# Using Language Services in Chat Bots and Beyond

# 15

# Surveying Our Progress

## 16

## Appendix – Azure OpenAI Overview

## Index

## Other Books You May Enjoy

# Preface

Azure Cognitive Services is a set of pre-built AI solution APIs that can be leveraged from existing applications, allowing customers to take advantage of Microsoft's award-winning vision, speech, text, and decision AI capabilities. Developers working with Azure Cognitive Services will be able to get hands-on with this practical guide and deploy AI solutions. The book provides industry-specific examples of implementations to get you into production in no time. You'll begin with an overview of how Azure Cognitive Services have been categorized and the benefits of embracing AI solutions for practical business applications. Next, we'll dive into Ocean Smart, a technically advanced seafood distributor that has adopted all the benefits the Azure platform has to offer by using Cognitive Services to attain operational efficiencies and predictive capabilities. Later, you'll learn how they implemented the Vision capabilities for quality control, Forms Recognizer to streamline supply chain nuances, Language Understanding to improve their customer service, Cognitive Search for a next-generation knowledge mining solution, and so on. By the end of this book, you will be able to implement various Cognitive Services solutions that will help you to drive efficiencies, reduce costs, and improve the customer experience at your organization.

## Who is this book for?

The readership for this book includes technology leaders, data scientists, and software engineers looking to implement Azure Cognitive Services with sample use cases derived from success stories. Experience with Python will be required, as well as an overall understanding of the Azure portal, and related services such as Azure Data Lake Storage and Azure Functions are also needed to get the best from this book.

## What this book covers

*Chapter 1, How Azure AI Changed Ocean Smart*, will give a brief overview of Ocean Smart, a fictitious company, with real-world examples of how Azure Cognitive Services digitally transformed the company to achieve operational excellence. From there, we'll give an overview of Azure Cognitive Services, ways to consider costs in terms of ROI and TCO implications, and some architectural considerations to reference from the whole Azure deployment.

*Chapter 2, Why Azure Cognitive Services?*, will give a history of Azure Cognitive Services, with an overview of the intent in developing these services, the focus areas that Cognitive Services targets, and the investments Microsoft is making in the services. At the end of this chapter, you will understand what services have been developed and why, as well as gain an understanding of what to expect from future enhancements.

*Chapter 3, Architectural and Cost Optimization Considerations*, offers an overview of how Cognitive Services are costed, with examples of workloads that Ocean Smart developed for estimation purposes. We will also talk about ways Ocean Smart was able to optimize its Azure architecture and deployments to save costs and reduce complexity for the entire set of solutions it deployed. We will also describe aspects of data ingestion as part of the overall development process. At the end of this chapter, you will better understand what common architectures exist for deployments of cognitive services.

*Chapter 4, Deriving Value from Knowledge Mining Solutions in Azure*, describes briefly the history of knowledge mining solutions and their purpose. We will then compare the additional functions and features that can be added with Azure AI, using example solutions, and see what value they provide to enhance traditional deployments, allowing for enhanced searches and the analysis of stored documents, reducing significant time spent tagging and describing documents inputted by humans. By invoking Cognitive Search and other Cognitive Services, we'll discuss how there tremendous amounts of information were uncovered across the whole document library at Ocean Smart.

*Chapter 5, Azure Cognitive Search Overview and Implementation*, offers an overview of Azure Cognitive Search, how it works with related Azure services, how the product is built architecturally, and how it was deployed for Ocean Smart. This chapter will introduce the search mechanism and how related services such as OCR, key phrase extraction, and named entity recognition help staff at Ocean Smart more quickly answer questions they have about their documents and data.

*Chapter 6, Exploring Further Azure Cognitive Services for Successful KM Solutions*, provides an overview of other Cognitive Services Ocean Smart used that are commonly combined with Azure Cognitive Search to build a fully comprehensive knowledge mining solution. We will look at how technologies such as OCR and image recognition have increased in effectiveness to add considerable value to traditional knowledge mining solutions, as well as the services that can be used for enhancement.

*Chapter 7, Pulling It All Together for a Complete KM Solution*, provides step-by-step instructions on how Ocean Smart deployed a complete knowledge mining solution in Azure, including related Cognitive Services and how they're all integrated. The related web services that call the APIs for execution will also be covered, in order to apply additional context on how all of the components work together.

*Chapter 8, Decluttering Paperwork with Form Recognizer*, offers an overview of the Forms Recognizer service, deployment considerations, and tools to accompany the service, which Ocean Smart used to optimize processes. We will describe the differences between prebuilt and custom form types for the accurate extraction of data from forms within their organization. This will serve as a foundation to streamline operations that currently require human intervention but can be automated with a high level of confidence with Forms Recognizer.

*Chapter 9, Identifying Problems with Anomaly Detector*, discusses how Ocean Smart uses the univariate and multivariate Anomaly Detector Cognitive Service to identify areas of concern in the organization and processes by analyzing data for anomalous activity. These activities can be related to quality concerns, security concerns, or equipment failures within the organization, which can cost significant amounts of money.

*Chapter 10, Streamlining the Quality Control Process with Custom Vision*, explores how Ocean Smart puts many of its species of seafood products through a rigorous quality control process, identifying irregular products before they are packaged and shipped to their customers. This process uses the Custom Vision service to identify the color, shape, size, and more information about the products for comparison with expected information about the species, which is produced with notification capabilities for production supervisors to take action.

*Chapter 11, Deploying a Content Moderator*, explains how, by using the Content Moderator service, Ocean Smart can ensure that all website content is published without the potential to offend any consumers of the related material on blogs, social media, and the customer service portal. These postings can take the form of text, images, and video, and deployment saves human inspectors significant time and effort.

*Chapter 12, Using Personalizer to Cater to Your Audience*, explores how Ocean Smart was able to use the Personalizer service to build capabilities into its sales portal and make it a mainstay, including the ability to relate, couple, and recommend products and services to customers through e-commerce platforms. We will go through the development process, cover reinforcement learning, and configure the Personalizer loop and improvements to the deployed service.

*Chapter 13, Improving Customer Experience with Speech to Text*, delves into how a great customer experience is becoming more and more critical for successful businesses in this climate of on-demand everything. If a person has a poor experience with a company, they're sure to let the world know as quickly as possible, using as many social media outlets as possible. Because of this, Ocean Smart wanted a better system to improve how customer calls were handled, setting a precedent for training customer service representatives. This chapter will describe how, by using Azure Speech services to capture customer call transcripts, Ocean Smart was able to dramatically improve the experience for its customers.

*Chapter 14, Using Language Services in Chat Bots and Beyond*, explains how to further improve the customer experience. Ocean Smart deployed a chatbot within their website to help customers get support or find what they need. To make the chat bot more effective, they deployed the Language Understanding and Translator Cognitive Services, which helps any customer enter a question in any of the supported languages and receive logical answers and receive support for their questions without any human intervention, only being directed to a human if necessary.

*Chapter 15, Surveying Our Progress*, gives an overview of how Ocean Smart was able to dramatically improve operational efficiencies by deploying Cognitive Services and the great accomplishments made. We will also explore future projects that can be undertaken to further take advantage of what this advanced technological suite offers.

*Chapter 16, Appendix – Azure OpenAI Overview*, provides a baseline understanding of the OpenAI API services in Azure. We will explore the various APIs and models, as well as their use cases within organizations. Finally, we will discuss where we feel AI is going and where enhancements can be made, and dispel some misconceptions about the services.

# To get the most out of this book

When you get started with your own workloads, using the various chapters as a reference, there are several areas you will want to have experience with. First, for a user new to Azure, you will want to have a good understanding of navigating the portal, how subscriptions are organized, and ways to control costs. Although it is not required to pass the exam, using the Microsoft AZ-900 exam preparation material will give you a good foundation for best practices. You will also want to have a minimum of Contributor permissions to be able to freely deploy resources as required. The following is a list of other tools that will be used commonly to complete the work:

| Base application | Operating system requirements |
| --- | --- |
| Visual Studio Code with Azure extensions | Windows, macOS, or Linux |
| Azure data tools with Azure extensions | Windows, macOS, or Linux |
| Python versions specific to each service | Windows, macOS, or Linux |

Each of the preceding tools is free to download and easy to find with a simple search online. There are situations where having the full version of Visual Studio may offer more capabilities than the free tools listed here, so it may be advantageous to check with your organization whether you can be assigned a license.

**If you are using the digital version of this book, we advise you to type the code yourself or access the code from the book's GitHub repository (a link is available in the next section). Doing so will help you avoid any potential errors related to the copying and pasting of code.**

# Download the example code files

You can download the example code files for this book from GitHub at `https://github.com/PacktPublishing/Practical-Guide-to-Azure-Cognitive-Services`. If there's an update to the code, it will be updated in the GitHub repository.

We also have other code bundles from our rich catalog of books and videos available at `https://github.com/PacktPublishing/`. Check them out!

# Conventions used

There are a number of text conventions used throughout this book.

`Code in text`: Indicates code words in text, database table names, folder names, filenames, file extensions, pathnames, dummy URLs, user input, and Twitter handles. Here is an example: "The demo app will also require a script to run when the container is executed. Create a file called `docker-entrypoint.sh` with the following contents."

A block of code is set as follows:

```
#!/bin/bash
python manage.py collectstatic --noinput
python manage.py migrate
python manage.py createsuperuser --noinput
```

When we wish to draw your attention to a particular part of a code block, the relevant lines or items are set in bold:

```
pipenv install azure-ai-formrecognizer
```

Any command-line input or output is written as follows:

```
az cognitiveservices account keys list \
--name OceanSmartCh14ContentModerator \
--resource-group Chapter14
```

**Bold**: Indicates a new term, an important word, or words that you see on screen. For instance, words in menus or dialog boxes appear in **bold**. Here is an example: "After you remind the user not to send personal information to a bot, repeat the dialog by adding **Dialog Management -> Repeat this dialog.**"

> **Tips or important notes**
> Appear like this.

# Get in touch

Feedback from our readers is always welcome.

**General feedback**: If you have questions about any aspect of this book, email us at customercare@ packtpub.com and mention the book title in the subject of your message.

**Errata**: Although we have taken every care to ensure the accuracy of our content, mistakes do happen. If you have found a mistake in this book, we would be grateful if you would report this to us. Please visit www.packtpub.com/support/errata and fill in the form.

**Piracy**: If you come across any illegal copies of our works in any form on the internet, we would be grateful if you would provide us with the location address or website name. Please contact us at copyright@packt.com with a link to the material.

**If you are interested in becoming an author**: If there is a topic that you have expertise in and you are interested in either writing or contributing to a book, please visit authors.packtpub.com.

## Reviews

Please leave a review. Once you have read and used this book, why not leave a review on the site that you purchased it from? Potential readers can then see and use your unbiased opinion to make purchase decisions, we at Packt can understand what you think about our products, and our authors can see your feedback on their book. Thank you!

For more information about Packt, please visit `packtpub.com`.

## Share Your Thoughts

Once you've read *Practical Guide to Azure Cognitive Services*, we'd love to hear your thoughts! Scan the QR code below to go straight to the Amazon review page for this book and share your feedback.

`https://packt.link/r/1-801-81291-8`

Your review is important to us and the tech community and will help us make sure we're delivering excellent quality content.

# Download a free PDF copy of this book

Thanks for purchasing this book!

Do you like to read on the go but are unable to carry your print books everywhere?

Is your eBook purchase not compatible with the device of your choice?

Don't worry, now with every Packt book you get a DRM-free PDF version of that book at no cost.

Read anywhere, any place, on any device. Search, copy, and paste code from your favorite technical books directly into your application.

The perks don't stop there, you can get exclusive access to discounts, newsletters, and great free content in your inbox daily

Follow these simple steps to get the benefits:

1. Scan the QR code or visit the link below

https://packt.link/free-ebook/9781801812917

2. Submit your proof of purchase
3. That's it! We'll send your free PDF and other benefits to your email directly

# Part 1:
# Ocean Smart –
# an AI Success Story

In this part, you will understand how Ocean Smart successfully deployed Azure Cognitive Services with cost-effective implementations on the Azure AI platform and the impact it has had on operational efficiencies and the bottom line.

This section has the following chapters:

# 1

# How Azure AI Changed Ocean Smart

This book is intended to teach you how to apply Azure Cognitive Services to everyday business opportunities where some efficiency can be gained, some cost can be saved, or some unknown or misunderstood insight can be unveiled. We will start with a brief introduction of why and how Azure Cognitive Services is helping with those processes.

Next, we will give an overview of our fictitious seafood company, *Ocean Smart*. The operational challenges that are outlined are based on the authors' experience working in the seafood industry for over 15 years in various capacities as consultants, technicians, developers, process improvers, and an executive. The examples provided, however, could be applied to many organizations, whether they are manufacturing companies or not. Of course, some of the examples are specific to manufacturing but can be applied to many different examples across various industries and verticals.

From there, we will take the examples provided and develop a plan for evaluating and building a case to present what the **return on investment** (ROI) and **total cost of ownership** (TCO) will be to implement these types of solutions. This will be done with guidance on ideating ways to create insight around the value of the implementations—in other words, what efficiency can be gained, how much cost can be saved, or how many insights can be brought forward in tangible examples. These examples can then be presented to the key stakeholders and project sponsors in your organization to get their approval to move ahead with the project.

These examples, of course, will be applied differently at every organization as there are variable values related to building each example that will be different depending on the industry, country, or even region of the country in which you reside.

Wrapping up the chapter, we will look at some architectural guidelines based on successfully implemented use cases that align with the examples we present later in the book to get a taste of which other services will be deployed as part of the overall solution and technologies that will accompany the Cognitive Services you will be configuring in each of the use cases.

We'll go through the following sections:

- Choosing Azure Cognitive Services
- The *Ocean Smart* story
- Building your case: calculating ROI and TCO

## Choosing Azure Cognitive Services

**Artificial intelligence** (**AI**) is not exactly a new topic of discussion: we have always desired computers that are able to do more for us. In the tools we use every day, AI is present. Whether you are using your smartphone's virtual assistant or recommendations it is making to you based on the patterns it has cataloged from your activities, you are using AI. For instance, I do my grocery shopping on Sunday mornings, and my phone knows where I am going and tells me how long it will take to get there. This is becoming more pervasive in our lives every day, whether using our phone, computer, thermostat, sprinkler system, or the far too many more applications to mention. Unless you are willing to up and move "off the grid", AI is here to stay, so you had better get used to it!

Many organizations are looking to employ AI to help streamline operations and help their businesses be even better at what they are already good at. With this in mind, Microsoft created Azure Cognitive Services as a quick and easy way to implement AI for deployment in a multitude of ways. By giving customers the ability to implement cognitive services and connect to them various applications the business is using, it helps streamline the process of taking advantage of what AI can do for an organization.

As we go through the book and provide samples and solutions, keep an eye out for areas where we see the most improvement. The reason behind this is likely to be a better design choice than building a solution from scratch. The development of these products took many years and cannot be replicated in a reasonably timely fashion. Of course, there will always be unique situations that cannot be satisfied with "canned" software products, but the heart of the conversation of this book is building value for your business in both a cost-effective and a timely manner.

Now, let's get started by looking at our fictional scenario: *Ocean Smart*.

# The Ocean Smart story

*Ocean Smart* is a fictitious seafood procuring, processing, distribution, and retailing company with locations scattered throughout the **United States** (**US**) and Canada that specializes in quality lobster, scallops, clams, crab, and various species of fish. Depending on the type of product and the medium by which customers would procure the product, they may go to their local supermarket to purchase live lobster, clams or crabs, fresh scallops or fish, and even "value-added" products that use any combination of the raw materials that can be processed into some sort of seafood pie, frozen and breaded fillets of fish, or a seafood medley to be served over rice or pasta. This encompasses the retail outlets from which a standard purchaser could buy a product to make a meal at home; however, it is just the beginning of where *Ocean Smart*-produced products may go. As we go deeper into the book, we will discuss how *Ocean Smart* is able to take advantage of Azure Cognitive Services to streamline operations; improve **quality control** (**QC**), customer support, engagement, and services; and predict what intermediate customers (distributors and wholesalers) and end customers will purchase.

The company was founded in the early 1980s when there was not a whole lot of regulation in the industry, and standards were dramatically different from company to company. This meant that the quality of seafood provided ranged widely depending on the source and how the product was handled in transit. *Ocean Smart* is just as much a success story in the world of logistics as it is in the other areas of expertise and quality standards achieved over time. This section will serve as an overview of company operations for how products are procured right through to how they are sold to end consumers and includes how the company strives to keep customers happy. We will see an overview of each of the areas in which Azure Cognitive Services has been able to help streamline operations and the other results *Ocean Smart* has realized because of these implementations.

As *Ocean Smart* decides it wants to use AI to improve operations, it evaluates the ability to build its own solutions by creating **machine learning** (**ML**) models and developing code. The company is able to wrap around those ML models and create **development-operations** (**DevOps**) and **ML-operations** (**MLOps**) practices to ensure standardization. It even goes as far as to compare public cloud vendors in what their offerings are regarding data science and related tools. What the company finds is that there is significant overhead—personnel, training, and much more—required to build all these types of solutions from scratch. Plus, there is a need to have in-house experts on business operations as well as data scientists who could either work with those experts directly or have at least some specific domain knowledge to be able to work independently to build the solutions. As a result of this discovery, *Ocean Smart* decides that it will be dramatically easier to use Azure Cognitive Services because of the service's ability to quickly and easily plug into any software that is running within the organization via the **application programming interfaces** (**APIs**) that are provided. This also helps the company to take advantage of the award-winning ML models that are already developed and deployed by Microsoft researchers, many of which have or are remarkably close to human parity, leading in many of the categories that all tools available in the space are compared against. The company wants to be able to compare how close to a human a machine can get in recognizing the same types of patterns, whether they be in vision, speech, text, or other areas of interest.

Now, let's take a look at a quick overview of some of the operations of the company and areas where Azure Cognitive Services can help streamline operations.

## Dealing with paperwork using Knowledge Mining

Today, the company consists of boats for fishing, wharves for receiving products from its own and other fishermen, trucks for transportation of products, live, fresh, or frozen at sea, production facilities for processing of seafood, short-term holding facilities for keeping the product alive, and cold-storage facilities for longer-term storage of the products after processing into a consumable form. Each step of this process requires paperwork, comprising the following:

- Purchase receipt of the product off the boat
- Trucking paperwork, customs documents, and cost receipts for transportation
- Storage facility receiving and shipping documents
- Receiving documents at production facilities containing critical date code and weight information
- Paperwork required to capture information related to disassembly of the product and downstream production
- Shipping paperwork for transport to a storage facility or customer
- Sales information about the product when sold
- Quality reports of samples, protein levels, bacterial concerns, and so on

And this is just an idea of the amount of paperwork related to each transaction to ensure the safety of the consumers who will ultimately end up eating the product. Of course, there are also the regulatory requirements that need to be satisfied for the US **Food and Drug Administration (FDA)** and other governing bodies, who will want all traceability information about the products from source to table with accompanying paperwork.

When we see a glut of documents of any kind, but especially ones from a variety of sources including both typed and handwritten text, as well as documents containing images and other areas of analysis, it immediately becomes a great use case for a **knowledge mining** solution. Traditional knowledge mining or document management solutions are great for collecting documents, capturing some detail from within them, and adding tags and references to later be able to pull some details from the documents. However, when using Azure Cognitive Search with related cognitive services, the information that can be unlocked brings the solution to a whole different category of enterprise search. It really is the next-generation engine for relating documents, finding tone in the documents, and gathering significant details of everything that is contained within.

A knowledge mining solution is a large undertaking but produces tremendous value for the companies who are willing to take the time and implement the solution so that it spans the entire organization and becomes a resource for all. The following diagram shows a sample architecture containing some of the services that will be used alongside the Cognitive Search functions, which we will elaborate further on in the second part of the book:

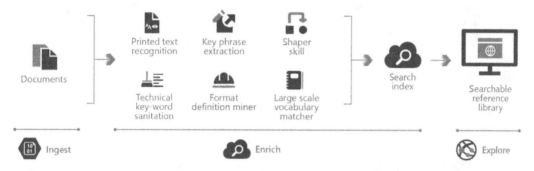

Figure 1.1 – Knowledge mining sample architecture

Next, we are going to use Form Recognizer to process financial documents.

## Using Form Recognizer to process financial documents

Another area we will focus on is process- and expense-related documents for automatic processing using the **Form Recognizer cognitive service**. Form Recognizer allows us to capture relevant details in these documents that we can then store in a database or elsewhere for further use—for instance, processing an invoice using an accounts payable system and feeding the appropriate data we capture into the fields required, with appropriate validation steps along the way. This also helps develop an ML model in the background that can be trained to provide more accurate model training over time.

The Form Recognizer cognitive service offers the ability to streamline how documents, forms, receipts, and other assets are processed within an organization and is a key component in how **robotic process automation (RPA)** systems are implemented for optimized operations. Some common uses of these technologies are listed here:

- Expense report processing
- Accounts payable/accounts receivable approvals
- Other uses where data needs to be extracted from a form and feeds a system downstream

The following diagram shows a sample architecture using Form Recognizer, some related cognitive services, and other Azure services commonly deployed together to build a full solution:

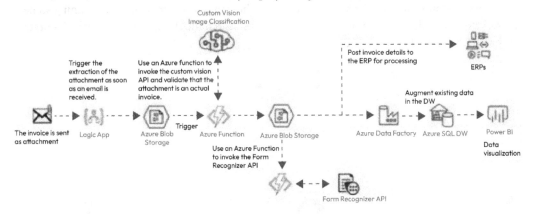

Figure 1.2 – Form Recognizer sample architecture

The next service we will discuss will help you to understand anomalous behavior among processes in your network.

## Using Anomaly Detector for discovering abnormalities

The operations at *Ocean Smart* are complex, and overhead costs are incredibly significant, especially when it comes to the product market being among the most volatile in the whole food industry. The supply is limited to what is caught, and much more challenging to produce than a traditional farm-raised product such as cattle, pork, chicken, and other land-based animals. Ironically, the industry does not follow the traditional economic models of supply and demand. The independent fishermen are resistant to any one organization, or a small group of organizations, having control of market prices, so buying in greater volume does not necessarily mean buying prices can be reduced as a result. In a very cutthroat industry, relationships matter, but do not necessarily guarantee preference when it comes to purchasing power.

Natural disasters can wreak havoc on the entire industry and can cause significant cost fluctuations for the end consumer. Even today, you can walk into many seafood restaurants throughout the world and find seafood prices marked as *Market*. This volatility also causes challenges in planning what will be produced and sold at the manufacturing stage of the overall process and what can be promised to distributors. When it comes to finished goods, in whatever form (fresh, frozen, or live), however, there is much opportunity to take advantage of pricing based on supply and demand. The process by which purchase prices are settled can depend on which distributor has which product. There is a weekly, and sometimes daily even, tug of war in the industry between buyers and sellers to determine product pricing that requires significant visibility into which product is moving where and how much of each type is available. As the details have been captured over time regarding the settled prices, fishers, product type, product quality, product region, time of year, and more details, we could use the **Anomaly Detector service** to test if one of our parameters is somehow out of a "normal" range.

The Anomaly Detector service monitors all the data being collected and calls out areas of concern to the procurement team, giving them the ability to accept the anomaly and provide feedback to the system. Again, this will improve an ML model that has been developed over time or allow the team to go in a different direction with the transaction.

The following diagram provides a sample architecture for Anomaly Detector and other common services in Azure used alongside it for building a solution.

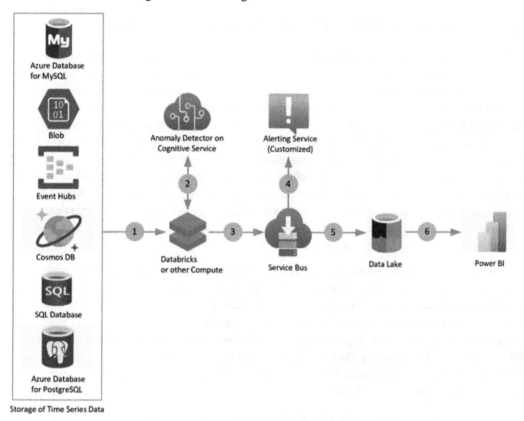

Figure 1.3 – Anomaly Detector sample architecture

The process pictured in the preceding diagram in a simplified version is outlined here:

1.  Data is ingested from some source in Azure.

2.  Some compute—in this case, Azure Databricks—is used to manipulate and prepare the data and serve it to the Anomaly Detector service for monitoring.

3.  When anomalous behavior is detected, an event is triggered and sent to Azure Service Bus for further action.

4.  An alert is sent to appropriate parties for follow-up action using the service of the developer's choosing.

5.  The output of the data is then logged in **Azure Data Lake Storage** (**ADLS**).

6.  Power BI is used to visualize the results of the logged data.

Next, we are going to discuss how human sight can be augmented using the Computer Vision service.

## Using Computer Vision to detect product quality issues early

After procurement, the manufacturing (or **production** process, as it is commonly known in the industry) is when the raw materials are disassembled, filleted, prepared, or enhanced by adding seasonings or breading, then cooked, frozen, and packed for distribution. A key part of this process is determining the quality of the product while it is being produced. Simply put, we take the incoming weight of the product and the cost of procurement, including landing the product at a production facility, do whatever production is to be performed to add further value to the product, and understand the overall cost of goods sold as a basis for what the selling price will be. Knowing that the selling price will fluctuate depending on demand and seasonality means that we need to take considerable care when setting these prices. Of course, each of the parts has a different value, similarly to the beef industry where various parts of the animal have different values (Filet mignon is highly sought after compared to chuck steak) so, for instance, the tail of a lobster is valued significantly higher and generates more saleable product than the legs of that same lobster.

As an example, the cost of a pound of tail meat would be four to five times the cost of a pound of leg meat to a grocery store. Because of the value assigned to each of the parts, it is critical to know if the product is somehow damaged upon procurement or within the production process. A tail missing a flipper or having an obvious crack is not going to be sold at the full price but will not be thrown out either. It will either be put in a "B-grade" batch or pushed to a different location to be processed in a different way— perhaps cooking. On the other hand, if a leg were to be crushed, cracked, or similar, it would likely just be thrown away because it is not worth salvaging. This is true for many of the varieties of saleable products, and each will be handled in a way that responds to their market value.

A process for capturing quality issues at the production level will significantly help avoid downstream customer complaints and returns, meaning the product would need to be destroyed and *Ocean Smart* needs to provide a refund to the customer. As a result, we will employ the **Custom Vision cognitive service** to capture potential quality issues that get past initial QC testers. By capturing images of lobster tails or irregular scallops prior to packaging, and alerting key personnel to the concern, the downstream losses can be avoided in the future.

The Computer Vision API gives the ability to handle images in several ways. Here are just a few examples of how the service can be used:

- Classifying images based on the content and aligning with similar images
- Grabbing data from screenshots or images captured for cataloging event-related information
- Comparing captured images from cameras and comparing against "known good" images for QC purposes

The Computer Vision service has ML models already developed for image classification and other uses but we can also use Custom Vision for training and deploying custom ML models to compare against.

The following diagram shows a sample architecture of the Custom Vision service and a simplified flow of how the service processes images it receives and compares or other activities downstream:

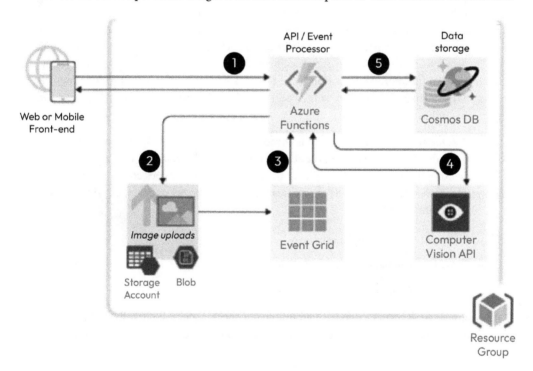

Figure 1.4 – Computer Vision sample architecture

Next, we are going to discuss how to protect corporate internet services from inappropriate content being displayed.

## Applying Content Moderator to avoid the posting of inappropriate material

Once all goods are produced, they are ready for sale to a distributor, restaurant, grocery chain, fish market, via direct sales through a website, or another outlet. *Ocean Smart* is concerned about having a recognizable brand to consumers, and it typically runs various social campaigns and has a modern, interactive website, plus other marketing materials that will help make the brand stand out to consumers. But this comes with the caveat that the company maintains its reputation for quality. If a review of *Ocean Smart*'s product is published in a forum somewhere or on a social networking website, positive or negative, it is important for the sales and marketing teams to be aware. The last thing the team wants to hear is that the public thinks poorly of their product or the **Chief Executive Officer (CEO)** comes to them with negative publicity. The company needs to be very aware of any situations that could enhance or serve as a detriment to the *Ocean Smart* family of brands in the market. All these channels need to be monitored for content as well as responded to in a timely manner to avoid any escalation of a negative situation. With data that is collected from social media outlets and review websites, we can use the **Text Analytics cognitive service** to gauge sentiment analysis in positive, neutral, or negative form, then build in automated responses as well as information being reported to customer services for appropriate action to be taken. We can also use the **Content Moderator cognitive service** to ensure no inappropriate content can be published to any of the *Ocean Smart* digital platforms or brand websites.

The Content Moderator cognitive service has three key areas that can help to moderate content: images, text, and video. The intent behind the service is to ensure that content does not get displayed on a website or other digital outlet where one of the preceding media types could be consumed by an inappropriate audience. When it is deployed, several other services can be expected to be used as part of the architecture, as follows:

- Event Hubs will capture live data streams.
- Azure Functions will parse text and content.
- Azure web services will host the application.

The architecture shown in the following diagram gives a good overview of the flow of information when the Content Moderator service is deployed for the protection of a regional chat service online:

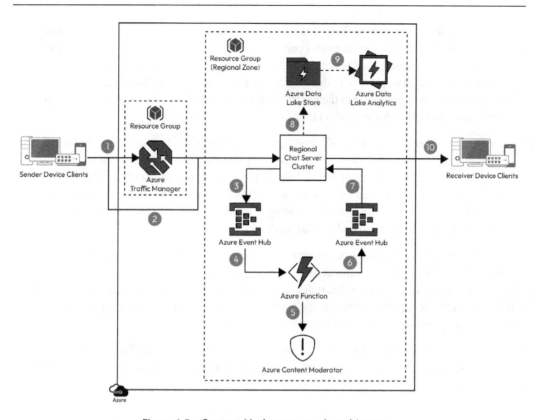

Figure 1.5 – Content Moderator sample architecture

Next, we're going to discuss a service that companies can deploy on their website for making personal recommendations to customers.

## Using the Personalizer service for product recommendations

The end consumer of a product is not generally known by the team on the production floor except perhaps by the type of packaging that is being used. There are several ways a product can be packed, depending on if it is going to a distributor who will then sell the product to a restaurant, chain of restaurants, or another type of food producer. There are also products that are specifically packaged for optimal display in retail outlets such as grocery stores, fish markets, and specialty stores where the product is much more visible and presented in a way that will try to entice a consumer, as with most retail packaging.

Customers can order the product of their choice directly from *Ocean Smart* through its e-commerce website. As a customer makes purchases and patterns are determined, the website can either make recommendations for previously purchased products or suggestions for comparable items the customer may like based on their history. There is also a capability that allows for additional recommendations when the customer puts a product into their "cart" such as a marinade or additional product from the store that might pair well with the product they have already added to their cart.

The Azure **Personalizer service** is a useful tool for just this type of application. Whether looking to make recommendations for other projects or to show commonly paired products that are purchased together by customers, the Personalizer service helps to build those recommendations. The service will improve its accuracy over time, and more of a user profile is built about the consumer of the content. Also included with the service are tools for building a "mock" scenario that could be presented to a user of the site, leading to an improved recommendation.

The Personalizer cognitive service is a resource that helps organizations to align products or make recommendations for location placement on screen. These recommendations are based on optimal positioning backed by an ML model that is developed over time and offers the ability to improve the model with a feedback capability. Because the service is embedded within a web application, many of the services required will be a part of a traditional website deployment.

The architecture in the following diagram gives an overview of how the Personalizer service is used to add recommendations in real time based on what a customer has chosen to add to their cart or explored on the website:

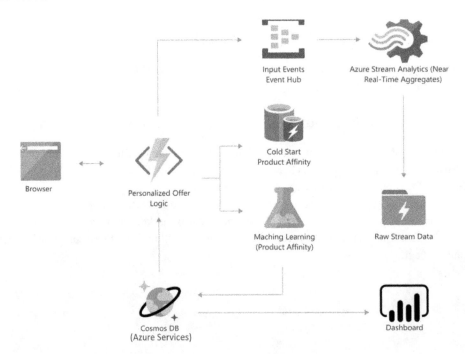

Figure 1.6 – Sample Personalizer service architecture

By implementing the Personalizer service, there was a 15% increase in profit from website sales at *Ocean Smart* due to the paired items that were offered and new items the customer had not purchased in the past when these were suggested. This increase in profit also drove the direct sales teams to start making similar suggestions when making sales to their customers to also increase sales. We will discuss this in more detail in *Chapter 12, Using Personalizer to Cater to Your Audience.*

Next, we will explore some of the options and capabilities you have when applying Speech cognitive services to your organization.

## Applying Speech services for call center improvements

With any quality product being sold, there needs to be a reputation for backing that product with quality customer service. In the case of *Ocean Smart*, if a customer has a poor experience with one of its products and they contact customer services for some sort of resolution, there are several ways they can approach this. The website has a "contact us" form where a user can leave feedback for the team. There is a need to route the feedback to the correct employee or team for handling the feedback in the appropriate manner, but most important is how communication is handled where a customer complains about the quality of the product directly. Another more likely way customers will complain is by calling customer services directly.

As has become standard for corporations, *Ocean Smart* has an automated attendant phone system that helps to triage and route the nature of calls coming in. An example of this could be the following:

- "If you would like to let us know that your experience with our product is not quite what you expected, press 1, or say 'issue with product'."
- "If you would like to tell us how great our product is, press 2, or say 'this product is great'."
- "If you would like to make a suggestion, press 3, 'I'd like to make a suggestion'."

Each of these responses, whether verbally or through the keypad, will then route the call to a team/person or, depending on the time of day, for example, route the call to a voicemail box that is likely to be emailed to a team/person for handling during normal business hours. Using **Speech cognitive services**, the system also recognizes several different languages to help customers who do not speak English fluently, further enhancing the customer service experience. There has been considerable care in the way these types of concerns can be expressed so that customers feel as though they are being heard by the company and that the company will make it right. *Ocean Smart* is using the following services together to build a "call center" reference architecture:

- Speech-to-text
- **Language Understanding Intelligent Service (LUIS)**
- Text-to-speech
- Sentiment
- Translator

By employing this group of services, *Ocean Smart* can greatly enhance the customer service experience and maintain brand loyalty.

The Speech services can be applied to a host of activities related to the translation of speech, speech-to-text, text-to-speech, and language recognition activities such as keyword, speaker, and intent from recorded or real-time audio. There are many existing use cases for how speech services can be used, so the example later in *Part 3, The other Cognitive Services that will help your company optimize operations,* of this book will cover a call center reference architecture for improving the customer service experience.

The following diagram shows a common architecture deployed when working with the Speech services for transcribing call center activities into a text-readable format. These files are stored in Blob storage for use with later activities such as sentiment analysis, translation, and other related services downstream:

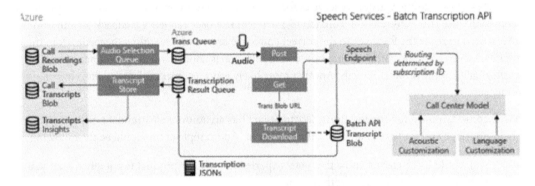

Figure 1.7 – Speech services sample architecture

LUIS is used to take natural language and process it to literally put words into action. Rudimentary versions of this service involve calling an automated phone system and being prompted "*Say yes or no*", for example. Depending on the response, the caller is then prompted to respond to the next question as the flow of information continues within the automated system until the caller is routed to the correct person, department, answering service, and so on. The following diagram shows a reference architecture representative of a solution that can be used to deploy an intelligent chatbot with related LUIS services:

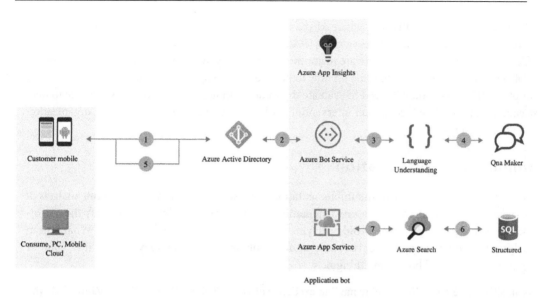

Figure 1.8 – LUIS sample architecture

Next, let's look at how we can calculate ROI

## Building your case: calculating ROI and TCO

When you are considering an AI workload in your business, there are many factors you must consider as part of the process. This section of the book will give you some helpful hints as you strive to deploy solutions to do the following:

- Recognize areas where you may be able to take advantage of AI easier than in other areas by understanding the complexity of deployment of each of the solutions.

- Calculate the ROI, because we all know that we have a boss who will want to know what it is going to take to recoup what is spent on this project.

- An overview of what you can expect your TCO to be when the solution is fully deployed, and calculating cost growth as your solution grows.

- How to pull all the necessary information together to ensure you have a complete solution that will bring value to your business and make you an AI hero!.

When we begin to discuss the areas where AI and cognitive services can be of benefit to an organization, we really need to put on our **business analyst (BA)** hat. Or, perhaps a BA has already started the process of identifying key areas where there are major inefficiencies in your organization. Each chapter of the book will include some helpful hints on how to be sure you are optimizing the services for cost and simplicity. That said, you will need to evaluate the value of implementing a cognitive service to help streamline a process, reduce human intervention, or be able to outline the benefit your organization will receive as a result.

## Building your justification

There are costs associated with the implementation of these services, and without a full analysis of what the TCO and ROI are for the implementation, it may be very challenging to justify the out-of-pocket expenses required. Try to avoid deploying technology for the sake of technology. What I mean by this is that too many technologists really want to embrace new technology because it is "cool" or "exciting" to learn and build something new.

As an alternative scenario, you may have an executive or key stakeholder from your organization who really thinks that by implementing "x" technology, the business will be greatly enhanced. This is a dangerous scenario to have to deal with when it comes to your career at your organization, and you will have to be very careful with how you proceed. In reality, there may not be much value for the use case they are pursuing, or the data available for the use case isn't clean, accurate, or good enough. In situations such as these, you will have to decide whether it is worth your reputation to push back, or even go forward with, such an implementation.

To avoid the possible fallout from a failure, it is advisable that you build your TCO and ROI models with as little conjecture as possible. Break down the use case into simple math with parameters that can help you justify your position either way. Present your findings to the stakeholder and state your position. Let that person then make a decision on whether to proceed, hopefully reducing the pressure on you and the team you are working with.

In either case, you need to get a starting point for how to build these models. Here are some thoughts on ways to get started with the data you will need for doing so using a Form Recognizer scenario to automate the accounts payable process. Be sure to work with someone in finance or accounting to understand what the average overhead is of one of these individuals to build a baseline of your averages:

- How much, on average, does an accounts payable clerk cost the company per hour?

- How much time, on average, gets spent per week on manually entering the details of that accounts payable transaction into whatever system is being used for paying vendors?

- Is there already a process for capturing forms in a digital format, such as scanning to a repository? This could add additional costs to your calculation if there is not, or if equipment is required for such a process to be implemented.

- What are the costs required to insert data into the system, and with how much confidence can it be inserted? Are you getting handwritten slips, as in the seafood industry, making it harder to be accurate, or is everything typed?

- Is there already an **electronic data interchange** (**EDI**) process in place, and the only human intervention required is validation? Find your alternate scenarios and boil costs down in the same way so that you are sure to capture the full picture.

- What is the risk or cost if payment of an incorrect amount is made or it is made to the wrong vendor? Many of these systems can be built with very high accuracy; however, they are not completely infallible, so knowing what the downstream effects are as a result may need to be factored in.

- What is the cost of the development time required to build the solution? Can you put together a sample project plan with approximate timelines to evaluate development expenses?

- What will the solution cost the organization after it is implemented? There will be recurring costs, which we will cover in each chapter, that will need to be factored in.

- Do you have clean enough data to build an ML model to run against when processing invoices for payment? Good, clean data is critical for any deployment of AI in any scenario.

This list should provide a good starting point for where you can begin to evaluate what will be required when building out your cost models. Work through the costs and the savings to build the complete model and understand how long it will take to recoup the costs that are required to the point where you start to save the company money. Is it 3 months or 3 years? That break-even point can be a critical point that helps your solution float or sink, so be sure to have a trusted advisor look at your completed analysis.

## Proving out your solution

After a complete evaluation, if you still feel it makes sense to push forward with building the solution, you will also likely have to build a **proof of concept** (**PoC**) for demonstration. Microsoft provides many tutorials for getting started with the technology through their documentation and GitHub, or you can use the solution we provide as your baseline with relevant documents for demonstration.

You have built your models, checked them with another trustworthy source, built a PoC, and tested your demonstration, so now, it is showtime. Be mindful—there is certainly no exact science to building a perfect presentation for management, as each team will have its own priorities. However, the goal is to try to make sure that you are as prepared as possible to be able to start one of these projects and build in some alternatives or answer those curveball questions that come at us when we are being challenged. The steps in the preceding list should hopefully prepare you for these challenges and will hopefully help you avoid chasing after a solution that won't provide as much value to the organization as you or the stakeholders originally thought.

Of course, there is always the possibility that the budget may not be available for any investment. If we believe there is still a compelling case to be made and it is worth pursuing, this is when we should flip the conversation to "*this is how much revenue we believe can be expected as a result of implementing these solutions*", if this is feasible. There is certainly a softer side of this conversation, as sometimes we need to evaluate best-case scenarios where maximum value can be achieved, without having the hard data to back it up. If "selling" your solution isn't one of your core skills, enlist a teammate, friend, advisor, or sponsor that you trust and see if they are willing to join your crusade of helping your company be more efficient. With time, the technology will improve and the costs will decrease for implementation, so maybe it is best, instead, to wait for the next budget cycle, possibly? Use your best judgment on how to have the most impact on your organization.

## Summary

In this chapter, we have seen an introduction to *Ocean Smart*, with some of the reasons it is using AI for optimizing operations, improving the customer experience, and increasing sales. We also discussed why the company chose to build solutions using cognitive services rather than building applications from scratch, and why it is enhancing the ML models over time for better accuracy. We wanted to give an overview of the types of scenarios that are common in many organizations where cognitive services can be quickly and easily implemented for almost immediate business value. Of course, not all of the solutions will be identical to what you are facing in your organization, but the intent is to give you the ability to get an understanding of how the technology works for each of the scenarios and tailor this to your own situation.

In *Chapter 2, Why Azure Cognitive Services?*, we will elaborate further on the Azure cognitive services we have briefly discussed in the prior section, with more detailed examples and use cases for each service that are commonly helping organizations.

# 2
# Why Azure Cognitive Services?

The Azure Cognitive Services suite of tools will help your organization quickly implement **artificial intelligence (AI)** solutions to do the following:

- Improve operational efficiencies by reducing the touchpoints within workflows that require human intervention with the use of robotic process automation and related activities.

- Provide predictive capabilities, helping to drive supply chain efficiencies in either reducing unneeded stock overages or avoiding stock outages that would drive customers to a competitor.

- Augment human capabilities in the way of quality standards and transactional interactions where large volumes of information are being handled, oftentimes too quickly for a human to monitor all the details efficiently.

- Improve the customer experience by automating services that would traditionally require human intervention, using chatbots embedded into applications customers interface with, and monitoring call center activities. This is for identifying areas of improvement by a customer service representative and improving communication overall by using real-time translation services when there is a language barrier.

This list is just a sample of all the ways that AI can be incorporated to help improve the bottom line for organizations and, downstream from that, help individuals who patronize those organizations to better use the services offered. In this chapter, we are going to discuss briefly how Microsoft got started with Cognitive Services. From there, we will give a complete overview of the five different categories that the specific services fall into and some quick explanations of what the services are commonly used for. Finally, we will look at what investments are being made in the services, as well as a preview of what is on the roadmap for new services and enhancements for existing services we can expect in the coming year.

These are the areas we'll cover:

- Exploring the history of Azure Cognitive Services
- Exploring Azure Cognitive Services
- Reviewing past and future investments

# Exploring the history of Azure Cognitive Services

There are countless cases of AI being implemented within organizations or broader society at large, and the overall topic of AI is really nothing new. Since the mid-1950s, scientists have been working on various ways to replicate the inner workings of the human brain to teach computers how to "think" on their own and perform tasks with the same efficiency as humans. Through many starts and stops of funding and support, progress has been made with various methodologies. With the introduction of cloud computing in the late 2000s with virtually limitless amounts of processing power, memory, optical networks, and solid-state disk drives, applications of AI have exploded for both corporate and personal use within software, smartphones, and many other uses.

Today, the three major public cloud vendors are **Amazon Web Services** (**AWS**), **Microsoft Azure**, and **Google Cloud Platform** (**GCP**). They are listed in order of market share in terms of revenue, with smaller providers owning a much smaller percentage of overall usage. Each of these major vendors has its own flavor of services and offerings around the topic of AI. Microsoft Azure, originally named Windows Azure, was announced in 2008 and became available in 2010 for companies to begin moving computing workloads from traditional datacenters and network operations centers. Azure provides **Software as a Service** (**SaaS**), **Platform as a Service** (**PaaS**), and **Infrastructure as a Service** (**IaaS**) offerings to help companies remove the requirement of deploying, maintaining, and purchasing physical hardware for hosting various software applications. Each of the public clouds embraced one of the areas to start—for instance, AWS started with serverless and PaaS options, whereas Azure started with IaaS options to help customers better embrace a hybrid strategy with moving to the cloud.

This strategy, and a later entry into the public cloud space by Microsoft, gave Amazon a leg up in the race to bring customer-centered AI workloads to the cloud. Today, Microsoft classifies AI into two broad categories: **Azure Machine Learning Services** and **Azure Cognitive Services**. Azure Cognitive Services was initially known as "Project Oxford" and was designed to be a set of **machine learning** (**ML**)-based **application programming interfaces** (**APIs**) that would enable developers to quickly add AI capabilities to their applications. The services were developed to leverage the deep ML investments Microsoft made and started in the areas of language understanding, speech recognition, image understanding, and face recognition. As time passed, the categories we will describe throughout this chapter were created and services added to each category. Essentially, the ML services are broken down into four main services to serve a broad selection of consumers, as follows:

- Azure Machine Learning Studio
- Azure Automated Machine Learning

- **Azure Data Science Virtual Machine (Azure DSVM)**
- Jupyter Notebooks for writing ML code

With this foundation of building ML models that are trained and retrained, Microsoft Research was able to build core models that evolved into Azure Cognitive Services. Cognitive Services is categorized into four main categories and **Search**, which is handled separately, as described here:

- **Decision**—Services that are designed to help augment the human decision process for faster responses, such as aligning similar items or items commonly paired, detecting anomalous activity, and detecting content that could be offensive to a consumer of that content.

- **Speech**—Services that can help a user understand speech with translation capabilities, speaker identification, converting digital text to spoken words, and transcribing words that are being spoken into digital text.

- **Vision**—Services that help analyze images for more detail even than the human eye can provide, facial recognition capabilities, and special custom vision training with a provided ML model.

- **Language**—Services that allow language translation, understanding natural language patterns in text, analysis of provided text for understanding the tone or context of that text, and **question and answer (Q&A)** capabilities to easily answer a question based on a dictionary of answers provided.

- **Search**—We will have a valuable solution that pairs Azure Cognitive Search and related cognitive services as part of the knowledge mining coverage in *Part 2: Deploying Next-Generation Knowledge Mining Solutions with Azure Cognitive Search* of the book. The Bing search engine, Microsoft's product for internet searching, and related services won't be covered in this book, but you should be aware of them.

Within each of these areas, individual cognitive services are developed with underlying ML models. These models have been refined over time to help simplify the process of deploying AI to applications by connecting to the cognitive service via an API. These ML models have gone so far as to be used in "human parity" contests designed to compare solution providers, where Microsoft has won top awards in several categories. These contests are designed to showcase how close exactly a computer can get to mimicking human senses' capabilities for sight, hearing, and speech.

Each of the services has independently achieved very high marks when it comes to its ability to directly mimic individual human senses. However, these services are still a long way away from being able to replace human functions. An example of this would be feeding a bunch of images of cats into a system and training that application to identify the various types of cats. We could even determine what the species of cat was, whether it was a wild cat or domesticated cat, and so on. An ML model could be trained and retrained to the point where 999,999 times out of 1,000,000, it could accurately describe the cat. However, if we were to request the same model to identify a cat with an auditory "meow," the model could not and would be unable to determine that the photo and sound together indicate a cat. On the other hand, if we assume a human has two of their core senses, sight and hearing, at least working partially, it wouldn't be a difficult task for that person to know the animal is a cat.

In the coming years, I believe there will be a massive evolution of pairing these senses for cooperative processing of that information, but currently, each of the services is handled independently. We will see this evolution in the form of more intelligent robots and other similar uses, as we are already seeing significant advances in this space. However, I believe that the suggestion that true original thought by artificial beings is even further off from becoming a reality.

Depending on the service, each can be implemented in a variety of ways, from directly within the Azure portal to **containerizing** the services. A container is a purpose-built environment with its own operating systems—commonly Linux, with Windows support increasing—that only has a few applications installed to support the activity of the container. A common implementation of a container occurs when a development team wants to be able to quickly change portions of code within a larger application; they can do so by having that portion contained in its own code base. This allows for quick swapping of code with minimal downtime, so as to not have to compile and redeploy the entire code base of an application.

In order to deploy to a container, the application must be able to send telemetry information to Azure for billing and patching reasons but offers a flexible solution for some, but not all, of the services. Using a container can also benefit customers who need to develop their cognitive service in their on-premises datacenter or a similar location (for reasons such as proximity to data) while keeping their code bases the same, no matter where the container is deployed.

The remainder of this chapter will dig into each of the cognitive services at the time of writing, in each of the categories specified previously. From there, we will discuss some of the investments that are being made in the technologies as well as where features of each are being deprecated.

## Exploring Azure Cognitive Services

In this section, we will outline each of the services and the categories they fall into. Each of the services is built with the intent of helping to alleviate the requirement to build such a feature into an existing application and all the cost and time implications as a result. Many of the services help to enhance the solution they are being tied to, and some can add revenue to the top line of your organization.

So, without further ado, let's jump in!

### Decision

The first category we will explore when discussing Azure Cognitive Services is the Decision category. When we think about the Decision category, we should focus on how Microsoft describes the category function as "*Build apps that surface recommendations for informed and efficient decision-making.*"

The Decision category is the most recent category added by Microsoft as they continue to invest in the Cognitive Services suite of tools. This category was developed to help identify a specific recommendation to enable smarter and faster decisions to be made. When we unpack that a bit, the goal here is to be able to augment a customer website with these prebuilt capabilities. They have been developed for common needs for customers looking to add value to their customer experience or strategically increase revenue by offering options that customers may add to an order. An example of this is **Content Moderator**, a service used to help identify if inappropriate or offensive content has been posted to a public-facing service. We will elaborate later in the chapter on exactly what enables you to decide if something should be classified as inappropriate or offensive.

As with the title of the category, *Decision*, these services allow for an interpretation of activity, but not just in websites. With the **Anomaly Detector** service, we are looking for anomalous behavior in a pattern of traffic or stream of data in order to avoid larger problems. The interpretation is to help augment normal logging processes and reactions to detect irregularities, for further action to take place and to investigate what the irregularity might be. In the case of user interaction, an example might be a need to offer additional products and services. This would previously be surfaced after the fact, therefore lowering the chances of a sale, or can be used at the point of purchase as an accompaniment.

### Personalizer service

The **Personalizer service** is mostly used in the context of an e-commerce website where goods and services are sold. The service API allows the website to capture information about the activity of a user who is shopping on the website. It then adds that data to the larger dataset used to train an ML model to better understand and predict user behavior.

I've intentionally drawn out an elaborate example of this service to represent the logic behind adding this type of service for effect, but future examples won't be as verbose. The following example of how the Personalizer service works adapts the old *Marketing 101* example of "beer and diapers" at the grocery store at 5:30 P.M. on a customer's way back from work with a new baby at home. The only difference is that we're imagining it happening on a website:

1. Man "A" visits a website and purchases beer, diapers, and maybe a few other items while there.

2. Over time, the products that are purchased are cataloged and analyzed.

3. After analysis, it is determined that a larger portion of men, through customer profiling, buy beer and diapers together. These two seemingly unrelated products were highlighted as being purchased more often than any two other unrelated products together.

4. Man "B" visits the website, after this product correlation has been determined, and is shopping for beer, eventually placing it in his shopping cart.

5. Because we know that Man "A" and many other examples of Man "A" also purchased diapers as part of their transaction, the Personalizer service suggests that Man "B" might also want diapers.

6.  This recommendation shows up on the screen at the checkout screen, or even sometimes immediately as the beer is added to the shopping cart, with some sort of modular window or popup.

7.  Given the customer profiling and analysis, we know that the majority of male visitors will buy both items at the same time. As such, the likelihood of Man "B" adding the diapers to his cart is significantly higher than him putting another random item recommendation in his cart.

At *Ocean Smart*, as we'll later describe fully, this example is used for all kinds of recommendations on its e-commerce website, such as pairing lobster tails and scallops with a cedar plank for placing on your grill, with a marinade or cocktail sauce on the side. This recommendation would start when a user places the lobster tails in their cart; the Personalizer engine reacts to that choice. This is very similar to the checkout aisle of your favorite grocery store. The stores know you are stuck looking at the candy, snacks, and magazines while you're waiting to check out and leave the store. The longer you wait in that line, the more likely you are to make an impulsive decision and find out just who your favorite celebrity is now dating. Ocean Smart knows you're already shopping for food, and by adding options such as "for just $10 more you can pair those lobster tails with some delicious scallops" or "Do you need butter to draw and taste the sweet lobster and butter flavor together?", they know you are significantly more likely to buy the paired items.

Another common use of the Personalizer service is for the placement of **advertisements** (**ads**) within a website. Over time, as ads are shown to users in various locations, the telemetry behind clicks in locations reveals the more effective location for those ads. The information is collected over time and placed in a dataset that is eventually used to train an ML model to determine the effectiveness of types of ads and their placement. As this occurs, a profile about a user is built on the person's computer that captures information about that specific user. As a more comprehensive collection of data about the user is developed, more targeted ads about the user's behavior are presented. Each person is different, and as we get to know more about that person, we can react more appropriately to their behavior and predict what will be most effective in that effort.

This type of ML model is built using **reinforcement learning** (**RL**), which creates a feedback loop and allows the service to learn and improve over time as more data is captured and personalized recommendations are marked as effective or not. This works as part of the ML model being retrained and making more accurate predictions as a result.

### Anomaly Detector

The **Anomaly Detector** service was designed to help with scenarios where data is being streamed from one place to another and, as you might expect from the name, it detects anomalies in that data stream over time. This service is most effectively used when we have data captured over time and can establish certain patterns in that data. The service can then notify a specified point of contact of any activity that falls outside the range of "normal" behavior. Initially started as a monitoring system for a single stream of data called **Univariate**, Microsoft has more recently added the **Multivariate** feature, which can monitor multiple streams of data. The reason for adding this ability to monitor multiple streams is that a single stream of data alone may be normal, but combined with one or more streams of data, collectively they may trigger anomalous warnings that require attention. The ML model that underlies the service has the ability to adjust to changes in patterns over time that are *not* anomalous to ensure adaptive learning. Further, depending on the type of data and patterns of data that you are attempting to detect anomalies within, data can be looked at in real time or in batches—for example, in seasonal data pattern detection.

In order to get started with the service, we first need to provide a base dataset for training the ML model that will be used to detect anomalies. The service builds the model with some basic input from whoever is using the service and tapping into the API, so no ML experience is required. However, information around normal versus anomalous data and some semblance of time-related detail are required to build that base model.

A common use for the Anomaly Detector service is real-time monitoring of industrial equipment, called **predictive maintenance**. Industrial equipment is very costly to purchase and requires significant maintenance to perform optimally. Predictive maintenance is commonly used to help prevent downtime in a production environment. The equipment can be monitored, commonly using **Internet of Things (IoT)** devices that are connected to the equipment. These IoT devices are deployed specifically to help with monitoring elements such as cycles, vibrations, lubrication, and many other areas that can lead to degraded performance. When specific areas are in need of service, signals can be sent to a maintenance team, and they can be corrected in non-production hours. There are certain scenarios, however, where a collection of signals is sent from various devices that could lead to a catastrophic failure, taking the machine offline and causing equipment downtime. Downtime for manufacturing organizations leads to significant productivity (and, potentially, revenue) loss. Consider a large manufacturer that has promised its customer a certain volume of goods by a certain date. Now, consider if a critical piece of equipment were to fail during the processing of that production run, and has to be down for several days or even weeks due to a part being needed. Often, manufacturers will have some required guarantees tied to contracts with customers about the timeliness of shipments, the volume of products, and so on. Because there are often financial milestones tied to the production of those goods, downtime on the shop floor can cause significant losses for that organization.

By deploying a service such as Anomaly Detector, those organizations can monitor that real-time data stream from those IoT devices, look at all the signals from the IoT devices, and act more quickly to avoid that costly downtime.

### Content Moderator

The majority of organizations have adopted digital services to help build brand awareness around what they offer. The services range from websites specific to the parent company, often around specific brands or **business units (BUs)**, to various social media outlets to help customers connect with appropriate individuals at the organization. For each digital medium an organization deploys its brand to, there are generally a few options for customers to be able to post information about the products, too. Many companies want their customers to share their experiences with their products or services. In theory, this should serve as a great testimonial for the organization as they are able to share real people using real products for real reasons. Unfortunately, the reality can go far beyond the simple sharing of customer experiences and can lead to these services being used for malicious purposes.

Imagine, if you will, someone who has a not-so-positive experience with a product or service. Those same outlets are available for that customer to post their dissatisfaction about the company, products, or services as for satisfied customers. Taking this scenario, imagine that the same dissatisfied customer wants to express their dissatisfaction in a not-so-appropriate way. That person posts audio, image, or video content to one of these outlets that isn't suitable for children or, even worse, depicts horrific scenes, language, and other unmentionable situations. Unfortunately, this scenario can be (and has been) carried out more times than we'd like to mention and can be very unsettling for the unfortunate consumer of this content. As the internet and websites were gaining in popularity, the process of ensuring this type of content never made it public became overwhelming. The challenge was that it required human intervention to ensure the content wasn't posted, but with the volume of content that is uploaded to the internet, this is simply overwhelming. I won't attempt to quantify how much content is uploaded on a minute-by-minute basis, let alone day by day, because it is constantly growing, but suffice it to say, it is a lot of content! **Content Moderator** was developed for just these types of scenarios.

Content Moderator was developed to be a filtering mechanism to ensure that this inappropriate content never makes it to a point where it can be consumed by a public audience. The service sits in line with the code that is used to post the content and uses an ML model that is trained and retrained to help filter the content. By using the API, the service will analyze the content being uploaded for inappropriate content, such as language and other potentially offensive material. In recent years, with the massive growth and adoption of social media, the ability to thwart this type of content has taken center stage for a number of examples beyond simply having curse words in forums. We have seen a significant number of scenarios where content is posted by extremist groups, political advocates, and many other situations, making it more and more difficult to police. The Content Moderator service, fortunately, can constantly be trained and retrained to adapt to all different situations where this type of content should be blocked.

Next, we are going to jump into the **speech services** category to discuss how to enhance your applications with various speech capabilities reaching near human parity in terms of accuracy.

## Speech

The ability to capture human speech and put it into digital formats is nothing new. As PCs became predominant in the mid-1990s in offices and households, there was a desire to be able to use speech to capture text and use it fully for commands. Just think of how much quicker and easier it is to be able to speak into a microphone and put your thoughts on paper or assist those who are unable to type at all. Some of this book, in fact, will be from transcribed text as I speak into my Macintosh computer using its built-in Speech-to-Text capabilities. So many practical use cases over the years have been highlighted that it is easy to come up with simple examples, such as the one I just detailed. However, the biggest challenge up until recent years has been the ability to capture speech accurately enough, and in such a way that it is much less of a requirement to touch the keyboard and edit text when we misspeak or want to change a thought.

It doesn't stop there, though—there is so much more that can and will be done with speech. In recent years, with the explosion of smartphones and tablets being mobile in nature, we have extremely fast and capable computers everywhere we go. These computers also have special processing chips that enhance these services and are transforming the world as a result. Of course, they are still not perfect and will require a reboot now and again when our favorite device assistant is not quite performing as expected. Apple's **Siri**, Amazon's **Alexa**, Microsoft's **Cortana**, and similar services all offer these capabilities and have become standard on devices and computers.

A real challenge has been to do the opposite, however. Reading text off a screen with a computer-generated voice seems to never be quite the same experience as discussions with a human, or having a human read to us such as with an audiobook. The voice quality is choppy, frequently mispronouncing words and missing inflection in the words and sentence structure, all with a robotic voice. Again, with advancements in technology and processing power, this is a rapidly changing landscape, and services such as the speech cognitive service are closer and closer to sounding like a real human.

In the following sections, we are going to discuss how these services are being leveraged to make customer applications more capable and enhance those customer solutions, as well as simplify some previously challenging situations.

## Speech-to-Text

The **Speech-to-Text** component of the **Speech** category is one of the most mature offerings of its type. Because there is a long history of tools that have been developed over the years for capturing speech in a digitized form, we won't dive too deeply into this category. This service is a pointed case where Microsoft uses its own products and services, as speech-to-Text is used within the Cortana service and Microsoft Office products. The service is frequently coupled with other cognitive services that can be used in conjunction to greatly enhance a customer product with services such as chatbots. The service is enhanced beyond simple speech recognition to be able to enhance the capabilities with **Customization**, allowing the filtering out of ambient noise or adapting to a custom dictionary to recognize specific industry-related dialog.

## Text-to-Speech

As referenced in the opening to this section, text-to-speech tools have a history of a robotic feel to them where the speech pattern and voice inflection are barely comprehendible. Many voice actors have made a healthy living from their ability to clearly articulate words on a page into a microphone, but they may have reason to start worrying about their future prospects in that line of work. The ability to align words from speech is quickly becoming more and more natural-sounding, helping a variety of people for a variety of reasons, such as the following:

- For accessibility purposes, text-to-speech can help the vision-impaired to "read" documents, emails, text messages, and so forth.

- For workers on the go who want to catch up on emails or text messages on their way to the office, tools such as Microsoft Outlook and most smartphones have the ability to read emails and text messages aloud so as not to distract the driver.

- When I'm wearing my Apple AirPods with my Apple iPhone connected and a text message comes in, I am prompted to hear the message and, after listening, given the ability to respond, reversing the flow of communication from text-to-speech to Speech-to-Text.

These are just a few examples of the opportunities to use this type of service to enhance text and make it more accessible for all. The differentiator for the Azure Text-to-Speech service is that it uses **prosody prediction**, using **deep neural networks** (**DNNs**) developed by Microsoft Research that match patterns of stress and intonation to overcome the traditional limitations of text-to-speech services. The service also uses **Speech Synthesis Markup Language** (**SSML**) to help with fine-tuning the speech output when transcribing from text. SSML is used to help bring the robotic element out of the speech that is produced by allowing the developer to do the following:

- Adjust the pitch of the voice

- Add pauses for a more natural flow of the audio

- Fine-tune how words are pronounced

- Speed up or slow down the speaking rate

- Increase or lower the volume of the audio

- Change the voice used and the speaking styles they're spoken in

As you can see from the preceding list, by deploying these services, you are able to greatly enhance the robotic voice of old and tailor your text-to-speech capabilities to your audience of choice.

### Speech Translation

Translating from one language to another is an area of speech that has also seen significant advancement in recent years. The most common internet browser and word processing applications have the ability to simply copy and paste text for translation capabilities. With the Speech Translation service, we are now able to take these capabilities to a much more comprehensive level by giving access to translating words in semi-real time into text or back into an audio format. As services such as this are adopted, we are seeing applications on devices that allow travelers to capture voice and offer a translation on their screen, or even translate to a language of their choice.

When using the Speech Translation service for consumer needs, when a consumer is traveling to France, for instance, it is relatively reasonable to assume the language being spoken is French. However, in situations where the language being spoken is not necessarily known, in high tourist or multi-cultural areas, for example, the Speech Translation service allows for up to 10 defined input languages at a time to help identify the language and specify which language we would want the output to be in. Depending on the type of implementation and features used in the service, there are up to 60 different languages supported.

## *Speaker Recognition*

With the massive amounts of audio and video streams we discussed earlier in this chapter, there is a growing need to build an analysis of those streams for more information, known as **metadata**, which is data about the details of the media being captured. In audio formats, we might capture the language being spoken and information about the rate of speech, create an audio footprint of the speaker, and more such detail. This type of metadata can then be added to the details of a file in order to help catalog those details and improve the process of searching for relevant audio without having to listen to the whole thing or categorize the type of audio it is.

The **Speaker Recognition** service allows for an audio "fingerprint" to be created that captures the unique features of a person's speaking voice, which in turn helps to more easily identify that person and catalog that detail. In order to deploy the service, you must first train an ML model with some sample audio of the person you are looking to identify and build a profile for that person. The profile is then used in the future for speaker verification purposes. This verification process can be done in two distinct ways, as follows:

- The service uses a **text-dependent** verification process where the subject reads specific text in their normal speaking voice when their voice is captured for the profile being built around that person.

- The service can also use a **text-independent** capture process whereby a sample audio file is submitted for building a profile and uses the service features to capture relevant aspects about the voice to build the profile.

Once a profile for a speaker is built, the Speaker Recognition service can be used to identify audio where the person is speaking, and at which points in time.

We will elaborate further on how this service is used to improve the customer service experience when reviewing call logs from a call center example later in the book, in our chapter focusing on speech service implementations.

## Language

Continuing with the theme of enabling accessibility and efficiencies with AI where it has been beneficial with speech services, **language** services offer similar enhancements. In order to extract key details, offer insights, and augment processes where language is critical, the services developed can help with language understanding, analytics about your text, translation services, and Q&A-type dialog. A common use case for language services is using several of the services in conjunction with a chatbot for customer interaction in a website or application. Chatbots have grown significantly in popularity in recent years for this type of use case, and a lot of that growth is due to having more capabilities around language understanding and processing. Alleviating the challenges of needing interpreters for various language translations at two ends of a conversation or reducing the need for human-to-human interaction with an intelligent bot leads to significant cost reductions. Without needing to have a staffing overhead, or greatly reducing that overhead, this has been a cornerstone argument for deploying and further developing these types of services because of those cost implications. Granted—the human disconnect from normal interaction when chatting with a bot, or even an automated answering service, can certainly reduce the customer service experience. Because of the potential for that disconnect, using a service such as text analytics or sentiment analysis, necessary individuals can be notified of these types of challenges early in the process, hopefully lessening the negative implications.

With that, we will jump in and discuss each of the services in greater detail in the next section.

### Language Understanding (LUIS)

A key differentiator between interacting with a human versus the experience of interacting with a computer is that a computer doesn't understand context and may not handle synonyms to words unless otherwise programmed to do so. With the **Language Understanding** (**LUIS**) cognitive service, a developer is handed an already-developed ML model with some of those capabilities already accounted for and the ability to customize further to handle other situations. Most commonly, the service is used with an application such as a chatbot for extracting details of a conversation and being able to interpret a request or the nature of the conversation. The purpose of this is to better understand what the proper response to a question should be by inferring what the conversation is about and giving an appropriate response. This is where the service differs from a traditional chatbot that could only respond to a question or phrase with a canned response or without an understanding of the nature of the conversation at all. When visiting `https://www.luis.ai`, you are presented with several examples where this type of service can be deployed. The following samples are provided on the landing page:

- *Book me a flight to Cairo*
- *Order me two pizzas*
- *Remind me to call my dad tomorrow*
- *Where is the nearest club?*

As you can see from these examples, the intent is to present a common question or phrase that would have an associated action related to it, then confirm that is the action you want to take, and execute that action. This is probably executed in the application with some sort of trigger that responds to the scenario request. For instance, "Order me two pizzas" could suggest to the user "I have 10 locations within 2 miles of you," or "Sure, where would you like to order from?" and take a user down the path of choosing which establishment to order their pizzas from.

As mentioned in the opening of the *Language* section, the goal of services of this type is to make an action easier for the consumer to execute—or assist, in the case of accessibility services being required. Ultimately, the goal of language understanding is to capture the intent of the individual using the service, understand the intent to be able to offer a solution, and take an action based on that determined solution.

The `LUIS.ai` service website also helps you build customized models and enhance model training for capturing some of the uniqueness of your use case. The service also integrates with a suite of developer tools that have enhanced integrations with other common applications such as calendars, music apps, and device support to more quickly deploy solutions, with less coding required.

We will discuss the LUIS service in greater detail later in the book with our full example, but for now, we will discuss the next service, QnA Maker.

## QnA Maker

Many organizations today have websites for their customers to find information, interface with teams, purchase goods and services, and many other purposes. These websites will often contain a **Frequently Asked Questions (FAQ)** page, containing common questions that customers have about a product or service, and so on. There are challenges with this approach, however, as the information is infrequently updated and very static in nature, commonly requiring the customer to have to contact someone after all and wasting their valuable time. Because of the drawbacks of the FAQ approach, **QnA Maker** and similar technologies have been developed over time. This gives the customer the ability to ask questions in more of a natural way rather than a rigid format or syntax, improving the customer experience as a result.

The QnA Maker service sits atop the data that a developer provides to the service in order to extract key information, ignoring unnecessary filler words such as "and", "is", "at", "of", and so on to help build a more dynamic knowledge base of information. The service can be applied in several ways, such as the following:

- Chatbots provided by many vendors
- Social media applications
- Productivity suites such as Microsoft Teams and Slack
- Speech-enabled digital assistants, such as those in the list mentioned previously in this book

Whatever the application, QnA Maker provides a better overall solution for getting a customer an answer to a question they may have quicker.

The service is commonly used with other language and speech cognitive services where language understanding and translation services might be required among other needs. However, it should be noted that at the time of this writing, multiple languages in a single knowledge base are not supported. Instead, only a single language at a time is supported and determined by the underlying dataset that is provided to build the knowledge base, such as **Portable Document Format (PDF)** documents and **Uniform Resource Locators (URLs)** and whichever language they are in. In order to satisfy multiple language requirements, services such as the Translator cognitive service must be used to translate the question into the language being used for the knowledge base.

So, with that, it only makes sense to talk about the Translator cognitive service next.

## *Translator*

As global economic markets have exploded in recent years with improvements in internet performance around the world and increasing capabilities of communication, so has the requirement to communicate with those who speak other languages. Translation services have been a part of common productivity suites such as Microsoft Word and internet services such as **Google Translate** for several years. Spoken word translation services, however, have only become a reality in the past couple of years with improved performance and the shrinking footprints of **central processing units** (CPUs), **graphics processing units** (GPUs), and **field-programmable gate arrays** (FPGAs). Being able to use better-performing processors inside of mobile devices and significantly faster internet service have greatly accelerated the process by which audio can be translated from one language to another in near real time. Essentially, it has got to the point that real-time translation is only dependent on how fast the internet service connection to it is.

One such service that is helping with that real-time translation service is the **Translator** cognitive service. Translator is a **neural machine translation** (NMT) service that allows a developer to integrate translation capabilities into an application, website, or as part of a larger AI deployment where translation services are required as part of the workflow. At the time of writing, the service is able to support over 80 languages and dialects, proving to be a very robust option for global implementation. The service has support for translation on the fly as already described, but can also be used to translate documents with a batch process while maintaining the grammatical structure and intent of the document upon translation. The service also gives the ability to build a domain-based ML model where there could be a specific language that accompanies the industry related to the documents and languages being translated.

Rounding out the *Language* category of Cognitive Services, we will next discuss Text Analytics for deriving more detail and intent around the text that is being processed.

## *Text Analytics*

Maintaining our theme of wanting to do more with various language components, we are now going to discuss a set of services that help us dig deeper into what is happening within the text we are extracting for the various challenges we're looking to solve. The **Text Analytics** service analyzes the text presented to capture four main themes of the text, as follows:

- **Sentiment analysis**—The ability to extract the sentiment or tone of a text and map it to human emotion, being positive or negative. A common example of this is understanding the tone of something such as a review of a product or service and can be collected to give an overall sentiment score of a posting.

- **Key phrase extraction**—Analysis of text to determine the key point of the sentence being analyzed. The Microsoft product website `https://docs.microsoft.com/en-us/azure/cognitive-services/text-analytics/overview#key-phrase-extraction` uses the sentence "*The food was delicious and there were wonderful staff.*", extracting the main talking points of the sentence focusing around "*food*" and "*wonderful staff.*" With a full analysis of a block of text, you can define tags related to a document for better searching and use these with a knowledge mining solution, which we will cover in *Part 2: Deploying Next-Generation Knowledge Mining Solutions with Azure Cognitive Search*.

- **Language detection**—The Language Detection service is used to detect the language of a document that is to be analyzed. After analysis, the document is assigned a score between 0 and 1 based on the confidence that the document is in the language assessed, with 1 being the most confident. This score is then aligned to the input document alongside scores for all other documents analyzed with the identified languages and the language **identifiers** (**IDs**) that helped the service select the assigned language.

- **Named Entity Recognition** (**NER**)—The NER feature allows for documents to be analyzed, then to extract and disambiguate entities found in the analyzed text. In order to disambiguate that text, the service uses a knowledge base to help categorize the entity using the context found within the complete text. A complete list of these categories can be found at `https://docs.`
  `microsoft.com/en-us/azure/cognitive-services/text-analytics/`
  `named-entity-types?tabs=general`; they are generally focused on a person, place, event in time, or personal details. As such, the service can be used to help identify **personally identifiable information** (**PII**), or **personal health information** (**PHI**) within documents and redact that information if the developer so chooses.

Finally, we will complete our overview of Azure Cognitive Services with the Vision category, where we will discuss how to use AI to take action based on what is being captured by a camera.

## Vision

As we have discussed somewhat in this book, the advancement of AI over the past several years has exploded in capabilities due to faster and smaller processors and cloud-scale capabilities. Another significant advancement along those lines, however, is the dramatic improvement of digital cameras, digital video cameras, and digital cameras embedded in mobile devices. Because of the dramatic improvements in image-capture capabilities, cameras can more quickly and more accurately capture events that could be missed by the human eye because they occur too quickly or are smaller than the eye can detect. This improved accuracy has also created more opportunities to use AI to detect anomalies and build workflows on how to react to anomalous activity. The **Vision** category of Cognitive Services is able to take advantage of these enhanced image-capture techniques and detail in a plethora of ways where the following applies:

- Images can be loaded into a repository or pointed to a URL for analysis, identification, matching, **optical character recognition** (**OCR**), spatial analysis, and categorization.

- An organization can build its own custom image classification service for use within its process to capture key details or compare images of products being produced for **quality control** (**QC**) purposes.

- Human faces can be detected, recognized, and analyzed, then cataloged for later use in the case of facial detection for security needs, speaker identification, and other applications of this type.

With this list of capabilities, we commonly see situations where the technology can be used for unintended purposes. The nature of many of the consumer-grade devices being mass-produced is that they are of a very low cost to buy but are inherently poorly designed and insecure. There are countless stories of these devices being hacked because of poor security and consumers being unaware. These concerns should be considered when deploying devices of any type inside your corporate network as it is advisable to ensure reasonable measures are taken to secure the devices themselves and any images that are captured. More recently, certified hardware has been produced that is designed to work with AI solutions on the market and is likely a better choice of hardware for your use case.

Let's dive deeper into how these services are being used by organizations.

## Computer Vision

When thinking about **computer vision** (CV), for whatever reason, I cannot help but think of images of spy agencies during the Cold War using a magnifying glass on an old black and white photograph of a satellite image. Clearly, photography and satellite equipment has been enhanced greatly since then, but, for many, the need still prevails. Organizations of all types want to be able to get a closer view of an image at the best possible resolution, and equipment today is becoming able to support it more and more. This is true of consumer-grade and professional-grade equipment where 10-plus **megapixel** (MP) cameras are embedded in our smartphones, and we're able to zoom in on the picture to see far more than the human eye can at a quick glance.

The three core areas that are covered with the pre-built examples and capabilities in Computer Vision are listed here:

- **OCR**—This tried-and-true capability is certainly nothing new in concept. The goal of using this technology is to be able to extract text that is printed or handwritten within an image or document. As of late 2021, the OCR capabilities in Azure can extract printed text from over 122 languages, support mixed languages within a document, and catalog the results into an Azure storage location or database with ease. These capabilities are constantly increasing, and the latest standards can be found here: `https://docs.microsoft.com/en-us/azure/cognitive-services/computer-vision/overview-ocr`.

- **Image Analysis**—The Image Analysis capability can recognize thousands of objects from a pre-trained ML model while building a collection of tags about the image for easier searchability later. Not only does the analyzer capture the object in the foreground of the image, but it can also describe the image in completeness. Imagine a picture of a person who is being photographed with scenery behind that person, for instance. The Image Analyzer service will describe the image in totality, including all aspects of the person: approximate age, gender, facial expression, or mood, and other possibilities using the face detection feature. Other features that can be determined based on ML models within images are listed here:

    - Describing an image in human-readable form

    - Detecting an image type such as a drawing or clip art

- Domain-specific content such as celebrities or famous landmarks

- Detecting the color scheme of an image; black and white or colors used

- Generating a high-quality thumbnail of an image focusing on a key object within the image

- Determining an area of interest in an image for a focus point

- Detecting adult content in images for moderation

- **Spatial Analysis**—The Spatial Analysis capability is one of the newer cognitive services that allows organizations to analyze video captured to track movements of people on video. This is helpful for organizations to understand what is happening in public spaces without needing a human to physically watch this activity. A good example of where this type of technology could be used is to analyze how frequently a piece of equipment is being used at a health club. If used frequently and in demand, perhaps a second piece of equipment is purchased; if it is not used frequently, another piece of equipment could be purchased to replace it with something that might get more use. This type of situation is only a simple example but can be applied to hotel lobbies, banks, museums, and many other situations where understanding this information can help improve a customer experience, and so on.

This overview should provide a pretty good understanding of how the Computer Vision cognitive service can add value to organizations of many types, and this creates a good segue into Custom Vision for use cases that cannot be satisfied by Computer Vision.

### Custom Vision

There are thousands of classifiers to help describe images and objects within those images, but Microsoft also recognizes situations where even the most robust of ML models for classification can't satisfy certain nuanced use cases. The **Custom Vision** cognitive service was specifically built for those edge use cases where an organization has something so nuanced that it requires a custom-built ML model to analyze and extract details to align with industry needs. Later in this book, we will give a detailed example of how to put this service to work by analyzing lobster tails to determine the level of quality as they are being processed. Custom build requirements for finely tuned manufacturing examples are another great example of how the service can be used in this case. Not only does the service give us the ability to reduce the number of individuals on the manufacturing floor, but QC also gains a significant advantage in the ability to "zoom in" on objects that might be too small for the human eye. It also helps to lessen the need to handle and inspect each product individually.

In order to build a custom ML model that will check good versus bad products, a collection of sample images needs to be loaded into the model. However, there needs to be a consideration as to whether good, bad, or both product samples should be loaded into the model for processing comparisons. Those images you load are used by the service to train the model, then the model is run against the same set of images to test its accuracy. The more samples loaded into the system for training, the more accurate the testing will be against production examples. There is also an accompanying website that Microsoft provides for uploading images (`https://customvision.ai/`), as well as using the **software development kit** (**SDK**) provided for pointing to a storage account in Azure and other locations.

Finally, we are going to look at the last subcategory of the Vision category with one of the most controversial cognitive services—the Face cognitive service.

### *Face*

For many years, facial recognition services were found only in spy movies in super-secret locations where the highest security was needed. More recently, we have seen them adopted for uses as simple as unlocking our computer or smartphone by mapping unique elements of a person's face, loading them into an ML model, and then testing against that model with each login. We might ask "*Why would this seemingly innocuous capability be labeled as controversial?*" It's certainly not the intent, but how it has been used causes alarm in some.

When visiting the Azure **Face** service website (`https://docs.microsoft.com/en-us/azure/cognitive-services/face/overview`), you are immediately greeted with the following statement from Microsoft:

> *On June 11, 2020, Microsoft announced that it will not sell facial recognition technology to police departments in the United States until strong regulation, grounded in human rights, has been enacted. As such, customers may not use facial recognition features or functionality included in Azure Services, such as Face or Video Indexer, if a customer is, or is allowing use of such services by or for, a police department in the United States. When you create a new Face resource, you must acknowledge and agree in Azure Portal that you will not use the service by or for a police department in the United States and that you have reviewed the Responsible AI (RAI) documentation and will use this service in accordance with it.*

> **Important Note**
>
> The use of the Face service API from many vendors has led to much controversy at all levels of government and politics because of perceived and potential misuse of the technology. This book does not take a position on whether the service has been misused or not, but intends to guide the reader in the capabilities of the service.

The Face service gives implementors the ability to detect, recognize, and analyze human faces from images presented to the API. The service helps with areas of identity verification, access control, and face redaction, or blurring of a face when needed to keep anonymity and comply with privacy requirements. The way it works is to capture an image, and then create a map of the face by placing the face into a rectangle, then capture coordinates of various features of the face to then assign a unique ID that will later be used for verification and identification purposes.

## Reviewing past and future investments

With the explosion of AI among enterprises, Microsoft's investment in their Cognitive Services suite started back in 2015 with Project Oxford. At the *Microsoft Build* conference (typically targeted at developers) that year, it was announced that this new set of ML-based **REpresentational State Transfer** (**REST**) API and SDK tools were being built. There have been many directional changes and iterations of deployments, but the majority of the services released back then are still being used today. The only major difference is the approach to Face APIs, as discussed briefly in the last section.

> **Updates**
>
> Microsoft maintains a blog for notable changes to Azure and tags articles based on technology. Cognitive Services-specific articles are tagged and can be found here in their complete form: `https://azure.microsoft.com/en-us/blog/topics/cognitive-services`.

Later on, the *Azure updates* blog was announced and articles about new services and features started to be added to `https://azure.microsoft.com/en-us/updates/?category=ai-machine-learning`.

This section of the chapter is designed to give an overview of investments that have been made since the initial release and show where heavier investment has been made recently. The first four APIs, listed here, were tested heavily with other Microsoft products, such as Office and Windows:

- **Vision APIs**—Analyze Image, OCR, and Generate Thumbnail

- **Face APIs**—Face Detection, Face Grouping, and Face Identification

- **Speech APIs**—Speech Recognition, Text to Speech, and Speech Intent Recognition (later named Sentiment)

- **LUIS**—Detect Intent, Determine Entities, and Improve Models

Through the years, as services have been added, Microsoft had three core categories: language, speech, and vision-related services. A few years later, the fourth, Decision, was added with services that include several skills rolled into one cognitive service. As you read through the releases of features and services over the years, you will notice a strong commitment to enhancing the services and ensuring global support for many.

There are also several other initiatives Microsoft has been driving forward by adding services that help with accessibility, sustainability, open source contribution, and—of course—operational efficiencies.

## Accessibility

Microsoft's mission statement is "*To empower every person and every organization on the planet to achieve more.*" Part of delivering on that mission statement is to ensure all people from all walks of life are treated equally, and AI use for accessibility purposes is a big part of delivering on that. With significant enhancements in Computer Vision, Language Translation, and even the Emotion API, there have been notable advancements in these services. Many of the services were applied to the free "Seeing AI" iOS app that was developed along the way. This app is able to perform tasks in near real time that can help augment natural senses if they are missing or impacted. Some of the capabilities the app can help augment in the way of vision is to be able to read short snippets on a page aloud or recognize products by scanning a barcode. The app also has the ability to "read" the age and facial expressions of a person before you, describe a scene for a person who may be sitting on a park bench, and read currency to identify dollar values. All of these features are based on the same technology and ML models used to power the APIs provided for Cognitive Services. Further, the Kinect service uses the Bing Entity Search API for gesture recognition within applications, helping to use hand gestures to control functions in applications.

With this technology, we see an opportunity to use this service to read a person's lips when speaking or recognize hand movements to read sign language. It is strongly believed by the authors that there will continue to be significant investment in these services to help with accessibility initiatives. This also includes many accessibilities in the Microsoft Office suite of productivity tools by adding closed captions to PowerPoint, the Immersive Reader capability, and continuing to add similar features powered by Azure Cognitive Services.

## Sustainability

Another key area Microsoft has focused on and is applying AI techniques to is sustainability for the planet. Microsoft has made a commitment to becoming **carbon negative** by 2030. As part of that commitment, they are endorsing the use of cognitive services in organizational quests to follow suit with technology. Services such as Sentiment Analysis are able to parse documents and web logs to see the sentiment score of certain keywords over time. As the term *sustainability* has gained support over the years, more and more positive positions are documented and momentum continues. Microsoft has also developed a sustainability calculator for customers to understand the impact made by moving from a datacenter to the Azure cloud. Although it doesn't use any Azure cognitive services at this time, there could be an opportunity to use the ML models behind Anomaly Detector to predict what impact could be made by comparing alternate solutions to the environment. We will focus on the Anomaly Detector service in *Chapter 9, Identifying Problems with Anomaly Detector*, to demonstrate how it can benefit Ocean Smart. Organizations such as Ombori use Cognitive Services as part of their "Smart Recycling" services that translate how the recycling of different goods positively impacts the environment. As more and more organizations adopt sustainability initiatives, it is fully expected that more creative solutions will be developed with the use of AI and Azure Cognitive Services.

## Operational efficiencies

A key driver for many organizations that want to implement AI using Cognitive Services is to attain operational efficiency on mundane and cumbersome tasks that can be repeated with the use of technology. Automating key functions in organizations such as receiving, processing, and paying invoices using Form Recognizer or using Computer Vision for alerting to anomalies in quality are just two examples. We will cover Form Recognizer in *Chapter 8, Decluttering Paperwork with Forms Recognizer,* to give examples of how Ocean Smart is able to automate processing invoices. In *Chapter 10, Streamlining the Quality Control Process with Custom Vision*, we will cover Custom Vision for detecting quality issues early in the process and avoiding costly quality issues. Personal digital assistants such as Cortana use many of the cognitive services to satisfy requests that would otherwise require more cycles of effort from a user by automating simple tasks such as *"Remind me to turn over the laundry in 30 minutes"* or *"What does my schedule look like today?"* while a user is moving from one meeting to another. Chatbots are becoming more mainstream every day to help improve the customer experience on a website or other deployments such as helpdesks or **human resources** (**HR**) within an organization. These services use Language Understanding, Translator, Speech to Text, Text to Speech, and many other cognitive services that are creeping ever closer to human parity for accuracy with the services. Microsoft is a leader in many categories for vision, speech, and other transcription services where human senses may be diluted. They have also centralized many academic resources with the Academic Knowledge API and the Recommendations API. Although not commonly used in enterprise, the Academic Knowledge API still exists today and can be found at `https://www.microsoft.com/en-us/research/project/academic-knowledge`. This project allows you to tap into academic content featured in the Microsoft Academic Graph API. Lastly, Microsoft has opened up Cognitive Services development to the community, announcing Cognitive Research Technologies: `https://www.microsoft.com/en-us/research/group/cognitive-research`.

> **Effect of the Pandemic**
>
> It is important to note that the coronavirus pandemic of 2020 and 2021 has caused many disruptions across the technology sector. With changes in process, employee impact, illness, family challenges, and many other areas of everyday life affected, we saw significant impacts on technology advancements. This should be considered when looking at the low number of new cognitive services released in these years as it should not be considered representative of normal development life cycles.

Microsoft continues to invest heavily in its AI services, supporting both the Cognitive Services and ML suites of tools. As with many software providers, products are developed based on market demand and market gaps. Very few services that have been released have been retired, and are mostly brought into other services as features as they get more mature. As previously covered, many of the services at their core are not new concepts, but the accompanying services and features help Microsoft stand apart from other market leaders, and they are some of the fastest-growing services in Azure.

# Summary

In this chapter, we discussed the current offerings of Cognitive Services from Azure, with an explanation of how each of the services can be used. We explored many examples from various industries and practical applications of the services that hopefully set a foundation for ways the services can be used. Although not all services are covered, later chapters in this book will give a deep dive into actual implementation steps for deploying the services and building use cases. The complete examples will help provide context for the use case that you want to build and help provide the best possible value for your organization.

These services change frequently. Many will have features added and dropped or enhanced and deprecated. This is the nature of technology and, largely, those decisions are made based on the value of the offering. Commonly, the services will be looked at based on the adoption rate compared to other services and how expensive it is to maintain. Be mindful, however, that even if a service is deprecated, there is a significant amount of notice before it is shut down or a migration path is provided to adopt a new service or related feature.

In general, Microsoft supports its products for significantly longer than competitors. There are many examples of support being offered 10 to 12 years after the initial release of enterprise operating system and server products, with plenty of notice given ahead of time. This is less true of competitive offerings, where there are many cases of a product being developed and deprecated in just a couple of years or even less.

In the next chapter, we are going to explore architectural considerations for associated services that Azure Cognitive Services will use to build a complete solution. We are also going to look at optimizing the costs that are associated with these services for the **proof of concept** (**PoC**), initial production, and full production deployments of the solutions you develop.

# 3

# Architectural and Cost Optimization Considerations

In this chapter, we are going to focus on some of the other services you will likely need in most, if not all, deployments of **Cognitive Services** within **Azure**. We will discuss *Ocean Smart* evaluated options and demonstrate how they fit into an overall architecture to build a full solution. After describing these services, we will discuss how Ocean Smart was able to optimize its costs while building the complete solution. We will also cover what considerations should be made as you progress from PoC to Pilot, to user testing, and finally to production. This can be very complicated as it requires significant attention to detail and constantly keeping an eye on deployments to minimize costs and follow best practices.

This chapter will cover the following topics:

- Exploring core Azure services and costs
- Estimating the costs for a proof-of-concept solution, including all services
- Understanding data orchestration for loading data into Azure

Let's start by looking at the services you will likely become very familiar with when building your cognitive services solutions.

## Exploring core Azure services and costs

In this section, we are going to look at what services Ocean Smart used when building solutions in Azure. When examining some of the architectures provided by the Azure documentation, it is generally assumed that the data that is being used for the solution has already been uploaded into Azure, except for streaming data examples. Later in this chapter, we will look at some of the options you have for getting your data into Azure for batch loading and streaming.

When considering costs, as described in each of this chapter's sections, we will always provide a balance of costs and services for optimal configurations. As it goes, the better the service, the higher the cost. Only you can determine what your business requirements are, with help from other stakeholders, to ensure an optimal mix of services and costs. It is important to note that **service-level agreements (SLAs)** do not guarantee service – they simply provide a mechanism to recover costs that are incurred while a service is down. If a service goes down for longer than the stated SLA over a month, you can get service credit back from Microsoft for that lost time. To ensure guaranteed uptime of your services, it is advisable to work with Microsoft directly or request Microsoft-certified experts to review your proposed architecture. By working with these experts, you can deliver a relatively accurate cost versus risk analysis for key stakeholders in your organization for evaluation. It is also advisable to have a written plan and evaluate the risks of the deployment for documentation and accountability purposes.

For now, we will look at the most common services you will use when you start your cognitive services deployments with a storage account.

## Storage accounts

When you're building an **artificial intelligence (AI)** solution, one of the most critical components is clean, trusted data that will be used as a basis for all the predictions or observations that will be made as part of your solution. For Ocean Smart to build solutions, that clean dataset is required to understand what the use case is to make decisions on what will happen next. This is based on what data was captured in the past from internal systems, such as ERP data and so on. Typically, the data that's being used is stored in a **storage account** and used for downstream activities that are performed to build the complete solution.

When deploying a storage account, you will be presented with a series of options, both required and optional. Let's outline the services that we consider to be important when deploying a storage account based on experience:

- **Subscription** (*Required*): This is the level where all the resources are created and rolled up to for billing purposes. Different organizations have different policies as to how subscriptions are set up, and if you do not have one yet, consider working with finance and accounting to ensure the structure of your subscriptions adheres to common payment processes. For instance, Ocean Smart charges departments directly for the services they consume; other organizations may charge based on a per-project basis.

- **Resource group** (*Required*): This is your logical container and it will be used to contain all the Azure services you will use for the workload. It is suggested that you use a consistent naming convention when creating resource groups to quickly decipher the project or contents the resource group is for.

- **Storage account name** (*Required*): This will be the name of your storage account and it cannot be changed, so choose carefully. Again, there is likely to be some standardization within your organization on how this is named, though I recommend an identifier for your services as a prefix when deploying services. Ocean Smart used the *sa* prefix for all its storage accounts they deployed because it makes them easier to find when searching through a bunch of Azure services that have been deployed to resource groups.

- **Region** (*Required*): A region is selected to determine where the services will be hosted. At the time of writing, there are over 60 Azure regions around the world, and it is recommended to deploy this service to the region that is nearest to the consumers who will be using the workload. It is also noteworthy to understand that each region has a **region pair**, which is a secondary Azure region that has been designated for disaster recovery purposes. These regions are physically connected through Azure-owned fiber connections and are a logical failover when an Azure datacenter has an outage. It is important to note, however, that this is not automatic unless your solution is built in a certain way. Just because a region pair is available and considered the closest datacenter, in the case of an outage, does not mean you are deployed for redundancy unless you've specifically designed it to do so. It is advisable to place all your related resources for a solution in the same region if possible, or if there is a requirement otherwise:

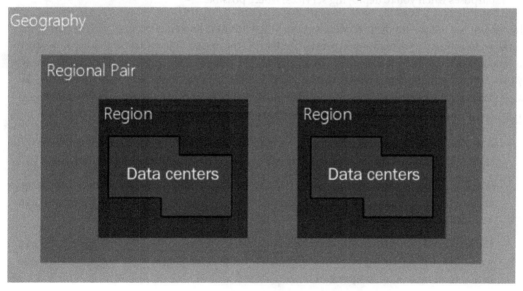

Figure 3.1 – Sample region pair visualization

- **Performance** (*Required*): When you're creating a storage account, you must understand why you're deploying it to determine whether you will need the low latency performance of the premium tier. Most workloads will be satisfied with the standard v2 tier, especially in the case of batch data loads, but it is not recommended to use the generation 1 option as it will be deprecated soon.

- **Redundancy** (*Required*): The redundancy you choose while deploying your storage account depends on the environment you are deploying it for. To keep costs down, it is recommended that pilot and proof-of-concept deployments use **locally redundant storage (LRS)** or, at most, **zone-redundant storage (ZRS)**. When building production workloads, **geo-redundant storage (GRS)** or **read-access geo-redundant storage (RA-GRS)** can determine whether it is necessary to have access to the data in multiple regions for read purposes.

- **Enable hierarchical namespace** (*Optional*): This setting falls under the **Advanced** tab and should be considered based on how you plan to set up your data lake. In **Azure Data Lake Storage Gen 2 (ADLS Gen 2)**, the ability to have **role-based access control (RBAC)** and **access control lists (ACLs)** was developed down to the file level. This gives us the ability to finely control access to files and folders and helps us structure our data lake to maximize security and performance. If the storage account you plan to use will simply be a file repository where no additional security is required, save some costs and use blob storage. If the planned deployment will require multiple types of security access, use ADLS Gen 2.

- **Tags** (*Optional*): Tags help organizations search for resources and build reports around services that can help with billing segmentation. It is highly recommended that you use tags for these purposes when you're deploying services, where possible.

The choices you make with the preceding options will determine how the service is used as part of the overall architecture. As we mentioned previously, there is the option to have a basic storage repository for landing data and using it as needed. Then, logical folder hierarchies can be applied. Alternatively, by turning on the hierarchical namespace, you will be able to build in physical folder structures. By using the latter, the developer can build *zones* for moving the data through the workflow. It is common to provide at least three zones for data orchestration and transformation purposes:

- **Raw Zone**: Also known as a *landing zone*, the **Raw Zone** is where the data will land into the storage account in Azure, where it is intended to stay in its raw form and archived over time.

- **Staging Zone**: In the **Staging Zone**, data can be manipulated for aggregation, cleansing, enhancement, and more. This zone is designated to be transient in that redundancy and high availability are not necessary.

- **Curated Zone**: Sometimes known as the *finished or trusted zone*, the **Curated Zone** is the area where data will be trusted as clean and complete for the final phase before being used in a data model training or similar operation.

The following is a sample overview of how the *zones* of ADLS Gen 2 can be laid out with folder and file hierarchies within each zone:

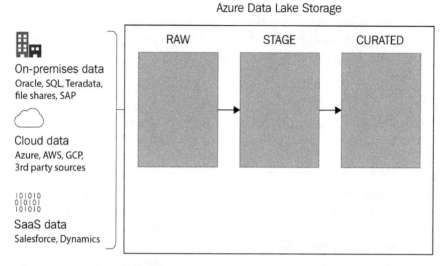

Figure 3.2 – Sample ADLS Gen 2 structure

By deploying these zones, you have a logical and physical strategy for data movement and security.

Azure Storage costs are determined by numerous factors, as outlined here:

- **Region**: Azure regions are spread throughout the world, and different regions have different costs associated with them. The best way to get started with pricing is to visit the Azure pricing calculator to build an estimate: `https://azure.microsoft.com/en-us/pricing/calculator/`.

- **Type**: With this option, you can select the type of storage you need for your use case. You have many options for the type, and each has specific costs associated with them. The available options are as follows:

  - **Block Blob Storage**
  - **File Store**
  - **Table Storage**
  - **Queue Storage**
  - **Data Lake Storage Gen 2**
  - **Page Blobs**
  - **Managed Disks**

- **Performance tier**: Currently, Azure Storage allows for two performance tiers: Standard and Premium. Since performance limits, costs, and SLAs frequently change, you will want to evaluate these options when building your solution.

- **Storage account type**: As services evolve in Azure, they are frequently added to the offerings rather than being replaced or renamed, although that is not always the case. In the case of storage accounts, Azure combined the capabilities of ADLS Gen 1 and Azure Blob Storage to create ADLS

- Gen 2. All three services are still listed as current options.

- **Access tier**: This helps the creator specify how the data will be stored concerning how frequently it will need to be accessed. The three current tiers are as follows:

  - **Hot**: Data that can be accessed regularly and updated frequently. This is the most expensive tier.

  - **Cool**: Data that will take longer to access as it needs to be retrieved from a semi-hibernated state. Charges could be applied to the retrieval, depending on how long it was stored there. This data is less expensive to store on a per-GB basis, though it could cost more if it's accessed within a specified amount of time – currently, 30 days.

  - **Archive**: Data that will take significantly longer to restore (up to 24 hours) but the lowest in cost to store. To pay the minimal penalties for retrieving this data, it must remain in the Archive tier for at least 180 days.

- **Redundancy**: The redundancy options that are available determine the resiliency of the data that has been stored. Data storage in Azure is always stored across three locations for redundancy purposes, but depending on your regional requirements, storage can be replicated in one of several ways, as follows:

  - **LRS**: LRS ensures that there are three copies of the data within the same physical location in the Azure region the data resides in. This is typically best for scenarios where the data can easily be reconstructed in the case of an outage or if your data must stay within a region or datacenter for regulatory reasons.

  - **ZRS**: ZRS ensures that the data is replicated across three Azure availability zones within a region, which is a separate physical datacenter with independent power, cooling, and networking. ZRS is typically a great solution for high performance, low latency, and resiliency requirements, though it poses some risk if the entire region were to have an outage.

  - **Geo-Zone-Redundant Storage (GZRS)**: GZRS has the same capabilities as ZRS and then replicates all the data to a different Azure region with ZRS in both regions. This lets you ensure your data is available and protected, even if a complete Azure region and all the datacenter in that region go down.

- **GRS**: GRS allows LRS data to be replicated to another Azure Region, but only to one physical datacenter.

- **RA-GRS**: RA-GRS provides the same capabilities as GRS but with the added benefit of allowing read access to the data that's available in the secondary region the data has been replicated to. The data is replicated to the secondary region asynchronously and can be failed over to, which lets it become the primary region once complete.

  - **Read-Access Geo-Zone-Redundant Storage** (**RA-GZRS**): RA-GZRS has the same capabilities as GZRS but provides read access to the secondary region.

- **Capacity options**: When you're purchasing Azure storage services, as well as other compute services, you have the option to choose pay as you go, 1-year reservation, or 3-year reservation. The pay-as-you-go option allows the service to be used without any commitment, but at the full price of the service monthly. The reservation options offer significant discounts regarding the monthly cost of the service but at a discounted rate, depending on your willingness to commit to using the service for longer periods. One advantage Azure has over competitive public clouds is its flexibility with reservations as they can be adjusted or canceled for a fee.

- **Other costs**: These are the costs associated with helping build the structure in terms of how the storage account will perform and they are relatively static once chosen. The majority of the remaining costs associated with the storage account are dynamic, depending on how much data is persisted in the storage and read/write operations. Each has a price associated with how many transactions are made per month, and are charged in the order of thousands or tens of thousands. Because of the options we discussed previously, these charges will change, depending on the configuration you choose for your monthly variable costs.

Next, let's look at Azure Virtual Network.

## Azure Virtual Network (VNet)

In traditional office settings, networks are deployed within an office for a variety of reasons, including communication between computers and servers, network security, logical segmentation, and performance acceleration where needed. As more of these networks were moved to datacenters, the need for managing network racks and cabinets gave rise to a proliferation of software networks that have become common necessities. This allowed for the simple segmentation of networks without the need to physically move hardware and provided the segmentation needed for the reasons listed in the previous section.

As cloud services evolved and requirements for scalability, availability, and better-defined isolation grew, physical hardware networks became less prevalent. **Azure Virtual Network (VNet)** is the second most critical component that's required for deploying resources in Azure and building your AI solutions. Azure VNet offers several capabilities that are required for workloads to be deployed successfully, many of which align with the same core requirements of networking in the past. To connect to Azure assets, other networks, on-premises environments, filter and route network traffic, and the internet, configurations need to be made to Azure VNet to support that communication. As with storage accounts, the following is an overview of the more critical decisions that you will need to make when deploying a VNet:

- **Subscription** (*Required*): Select the subscription being used for the workload being deployed using the same guidance that was provided for Azure storage accounts.

- **Resource group** (*Required*): Select or create the resource group being used for the workload being deployed using the same guidance that was provided for Azure storage accounts.

- **Name** (*Required*): Create a name for the VNet being deployed using the same guidance that was provided for Azure storage accounts.

- **Region** (*Required*): Select the region where the workload you are deploying will reside using the same guidance that was provided for Azure storage accounts.

- **IPv4 address space** (*Required*): This is where things begin to become more strategic. Depending on the level of sophistication the developer has with IP addressing schemes, some direction may be required for following the standards. IP address ranges can be assigned based on how many private IPs are required by the complete workload. Some room for growth may be considered, depending on how many IPs are needed now and into the future. For proof-of-concept building, consider deploying all the addressable addresses in that subnet. Then, as you gain a better understanding of the full number of required addresses for the full deployment, assign the appropriate subnet.

VNets are considered free services in Azure (up to 50) as they are a base service requirement for networking. If you need to peer a VNet to another VNet for communication between them, charges will be associated based on the region and how much data will pass between the peered networks.

## Network Security Groups

Security is of utmost importance when you're building your Azure solution. To secure network components and other Azure assets, you can deploy **Network Security Groups (NSGs)**. NSGs are used to filter network traffic between the Azure resources you will deploy in your resource group and other assets in Azure. This filtering is done by applying security rules that can allow and deny connectivity to be configured for source and destination IP addresses and TCP and UDP ports:

| Priority ↑ | Name ↑↓ | Port ↑↓ | Protocol ↑↓ | Source ↑↓ | Destination ↑↓ | Action ↑↓ | |
|---|---|---|---|---|---|---|---|
| ∨ **Inbound Security Rules** | | | | | | | |
| 100 | databricks-control-plane-ssh | 22 | Any | 23.101.152.95/32 | Any | ✅ Allow | 🗑 |
| 110 | databricks-control-plane-wor… | 5557 | Any | 23.101.152.95/32 | Any | ✅ Allow | 🗑 |
| 200 | databricks-worker-to-worker | Any | Any | VirtualNetwork | Any | ✅ Allow | 🗑 |
| 65000 | AllowVnetInBound | Any | Any | VirtualNetwork | VirtualNetwork | ✅ Allow | 🗑 |
| 65001 | AllowAzureLoadBalancerInBo… | Any | Any | AzureLoadBalancer | Any | ✅ Allow | 🗑 |
| 65500 | DenyAllInBound | Any | Any | Any | Any | ❌ Deny | 🗑 |
| ∨ **Outbound Security Rules** | | | | | | | |
| 65000 | AllowVnetOutBound | Any | Any | VirtualNetwork | VirtualNetwork | ✅ Allow | 🗑 |
| 65001 | AllowInternetOutBound | Any | Any | Any | Internet | ✅ Allow | 🗑 |
| 65500 | DenyAllOutBound | Any | Any | Any | Any | ❌ Deny | 🗑 |

Figure 3.3 – Sample NSG rule definition list

An example of how the NSG rules and the relevant details are defined is as follows:

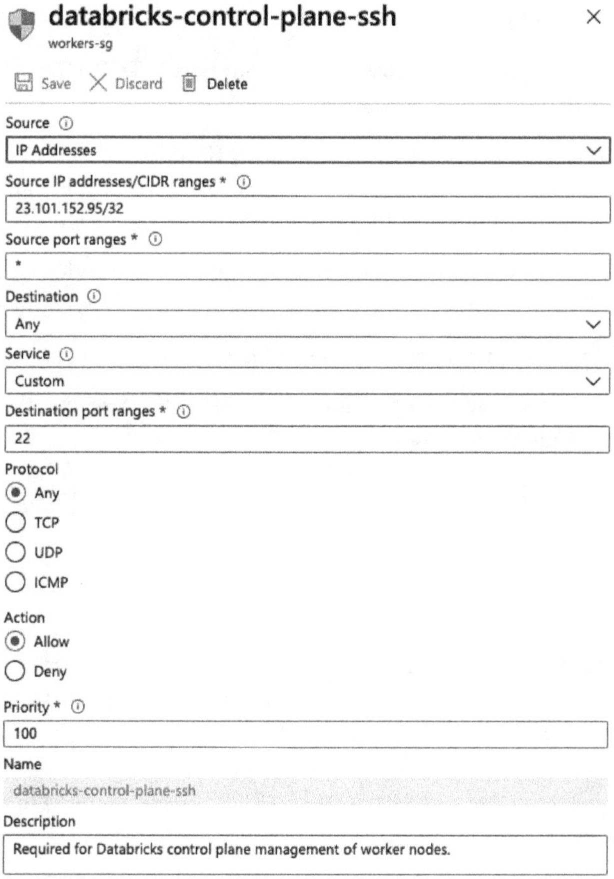

**databricks-control-plane-ssh**
workers-sg

💾 Save    ✕ Discard    🗑 Delete

Source ⓘ
```
IP Addresses                                                    ∨
```
Source IP addresses/CIDR ranges * ⓘ
```
23.101.152.95/32
```
Source port ranges * ⓘ
```
*
```
Destination ⓘ
```
Any                                                            ∨
```
Service ⓘ
```
Custom                                                         ∨
```
Destination port ranges * ⓘ
```
22
```
Protocol
◉ Any
○ TCP
○ UDP
○ ICMP

Action
◉ Allow
○ Deny

Priority * ⓘ
```
100
```
Name
```
databricks-control-plane-ssh
```
Description
```
Required for Databricks control plane management of worker nodes.
```

Figure 3.4 – Rule definition menu for NSG rule configuration

Let's take a quick look at each of the settings listed in *Figure 3.3*:

- **Priority**: This setting is required to help define the priority of the rule. In certain instances, a rule must supersede another rule or all the other rules in the list, so the lowest-priority number defines the most important rules.

- **Name**: A reference name that's used to specify what the defined rule refers to. It is typically advisable to create logical names for rules with standard nomenclature to ensure you understand them for troubleshooting purposes down the road. In the previous definition, the rule was created automatically when the Databricks asset was deployed in this VNet, so it cannot be changed.

- **Port**: The port is specified based on the service traffic that is being filtered. Port **22** with a priority of **100** refers to the TCP port for SSH, a common service that's used for remotely accessing systems. There is a commonly defined list of ports that are assumed for various services (**SSH, SMTP, HTTP, HTTPS,** and so on) that can be defined for easily selecting filters, but they are not absolute. If two different services use the same port, one would have to be disabled on the destination to avoid conflicts.

- **Protocol**: This is where you can specify whether your port is **TCP, UDP, ICMP,** or, if there is no differentiation for your application, **ANY**.

- **Source**: Here, you specify the source of your traffic by IP address or one of the services you are using that is named. For **Inbound Security Rules**, your source will be outside your network the NSG is protecting. For **Outbound Security Rules**, your source will be inside.

- **Destination**: Here, you specify the destination IP address or service name of your traffic. Inbound and outbound security rules are the opposite of the source configurations.

- **Action**: The NSG rules require explicit **Allow** or **Deny** options for your security rules.

- **Description**: This is where you can provide full details of the rule, mostly to document why the rule was created and what it does.

Since NSGs are part of VNet configurations, there is no charge for them, though there is a limit of 5,000 rules for an NSG, as per Azure's limits.

## Databases

Typically, after Cognitive Service is run, the results would be put in a database of your choosing. For example, with Ocean Smart's Form Recognizer use case, details are captured and then stored from the document that is being processed. The details about that document and other documents that are being processed are stored in a SQL database for later reference. There is a multitude of options for databases in Azure to give developers a choice, but it is highly recommended to choose a hosted or PaaS database option. Ocean Smart has a small number of IT staff and by selecting the PaaS option for databases, they can limit the required maintenance and management of those databases. Each of the database flavors that's offered has various performance, scalability, redundancy, and auto-tuning options for performance, so make sure that you determine your requirements before deciding. Here is a quick overview of the current PaaS database options in Azure that you can choose from:

- **Azure SQL Database**: This is a fully managed Microsoft SQL Server on Azure that doesn't have the full feature set that it would on-premises. However, it's typically a good choice for simple database requirements. The Azure SQL Database option offers **serverless** compute for customers who want to build applications that do not require a database to be on all the time, such as something that's only used sporadically.

- **Azure Database for PostgreSQL**: PostgreSQL is a popular open source option for developers, so Microsoft developed this fully managed offering that offers high availability, scaling, and intelligent performance support for customers. Azure PostgreSQL also lets you turn off compute – the highest cost component – and persist data to keep costs low when it's not in use.

- **Azure Database for MySQL**: Another popular open source option for developers, MySQL has a fully managed option in the Azure platform. This version offers intelligent performance recommendations, direct integrations with other Azure services, and enhanced security capabilities.

- **Azure Database for MariaDB**: The MariaDB database is a variant of the MySQL database that was created when MySQL was acquired by Oracle. It has gained in popularity as an option for open source developers that is hosted in Azure. Some of the features that are boasted by the service include built-in high availability, languages, frameworks of the developer's choice, fast and flexible scaling, and pricing with more security options.

- **Azure CosmosDB**: This unique database service offering by Microsoft is the first of its type, allowing for multi-modal and multi-master support. This database can be used for relational, non-relational, and graph data, among other options. It also provides sub-10 millisecond replication to Azure datacenters globally.

Database costs vary widely based on the type of database, the SLA, the redundancy, the resiliency, how much data needs to be stored, and the compute requirements. The best way to determine the service levels depends on several factors, all of which we will describe briefly. However, ultimately, these will be unique to each solution. Also, it is important to realize that the database costs are going to be among the highest of the overall solution because they require heavy compute resources, since this is a significant cost for any public cloud. Here are some of the considerations you will want to make when choosing the best database offering:

- **Current skillset**: One of the first decisions that will need to be made is what database the team who will support the solution has experience with. A key strength of the Azure platform is the freedom to choose, though you want to be sure that a major skilling effort won't be required to use the database of choice.

- **Modality**: Depending on your workload type, you will need to choose whether the solution will use a **relational database**, **non-relational database** (sometimes referred to as a **document database** or **NoSQL database**), or an **in-memory database**. Various offerings can support different modalities, and CosmosDB can support several.

- **Data volume**: Some applications require massive amounts of data to be stored, in which case you may need to consider a solution that supports Hyperscale. **Hyperscale** is available on several relational database offerings and supports data sizes of 100 TB+. Database platforms that don't offer Hyperscale have much lower database maximum data sizes.

- **High Availability (HA) and Data Replication (DR)**: Another consideration you will want to evaluate is how resilient the database system is that you are using. Many of the offerings have some form of HA and DR available, but all at varying SLAs.

- **Serverless compute**: If you are developing a system that is not being built to run 100% of the time, you will need to evaluate your serverless compute database options. These databases or tiers have been developed to support solutions that aren't intended to run constantly, therefore saving money on the overall monthly cost. Be mindful when evaluating this option and the costs that are associated with it. The serverless compute databases are more expensive to run per minute, hour, or month than the persisted database options. By comparing the serverless and persisted database costs for the same service levels, you can quickly evaluate the less-expensive option. Consider how many hours per month the application needs to run and compare those costs to determine which will cost less. Also, it is not safe to assume that the serverless and persisted options have the same features. Often, the serverless option is deployed long after the persisted version is offered, and it is important to double-check which features are available for which. After a while of staring at the features side by side, it can be quite easy to confuse the features.

- **Hybrid Transaction and Analytical Processing (HTAP)**: The last major decision category is whether the database you are using would perform ideally by being able to deploy both analytical and transactional databases. The purpose of these types of operations is to be able to report directly from transactional data. This is beneficial to organizations because they don't need to replicate or move data from their transactional systems. This also gives them the benefit of not requiring significant hardware investments to support both operating modes without causing performance bottlenecks. Currently, several sources are supported, and the data is processed by Azure Synapse using the Synapse Link capability. Several other options are also being developed.

The database is a critical component for ensuring a structured data repository. However, you need a place to run the services, from a compute perspective, so you will likely need to deploy Azure App Service.

## Azure App Service

**Azure App Service** was developed for hosting web applications, REST APIs, and other services that require HTTP or HTTPS services. Commonly, developers use a web app for building proof of concepts and minimum viable products when creating a use case. As the complete solution is built, the services would be redirected to the existing web application for production deployments, whether they are built in the service or not. Azure App Service has the flexibility to offer developers the most popular languages and frameworks for building applications, as well as full DevOps capabilities using GitHub, Azure DevOps, and other source control tools. The real benefit to Ocean Smart is its ability to deploy another infrastructure service with little or no maintenance required to have the services available. The following are the most important options when deploying a web app:

- **Subscription** (*Required*): Select the subscription being used for the workload being deployed using the same guidance that was provided for Azure storage accounts.

- **Resource group** (*Required*): Select or create the resource group being used for the workload being deployed using the same guidance that was provided for Azure storage accounts.

- **Name** (*Required*): Create a name for the app being deployed using the same guidance that was provided for Azure storage accounts.

- **Publish** (*Required*): Here, you have the option to deploy your web app as code or using a Docker container. The decision you must make here is based on the normal operating procedures in your organization. The majority of containers run the Linux operating system, so if you're not comfortable working with Linux or have experience with containers, it is recommended to deploy your web app as code.

- **Runtime stack** (*Required*): In the runtime stack, you will determine the framework and language you want to build your application on, as well as what version of that language.

- **Operating system**: Here, you have the option to choose your operating system for deployment, which may be determined by your organization's policy or needs.

- **Region** (*Required*): Select the region where the workload you are deploying will reside using the same guidance that was provided for Azure storage accounts.

- **Windows or Linux plan**: The resources you will require for your service plan are going to largely depend on whether you are building a proof of concept, pilot, or production application. You will also determine what type of resiliency will be included with the deployment of your application. Each of the plan types addresses how much compute and storage will be allocated and how protected your web application will be in the event of an outage.

- **Deployment settings** (*Optional*): With this setting, you can configure your GitHub environment for the **Continuous Integration and Continuous Deployment (CI/CD)** of your application.

- **Application Insights** (*Required*): Application Insights is a service that allows you to monitor the web application you've deployed in more depth. It helps you watch for service outages and provides analytics tools for building custom reports so that you can monitor performance requirements.

App Service helps you provide an *internet presence* for Ocean Smart without having to purchase and deploy hardware. However, it has many complexities when it comes to understanding complete workloads. For the sake of brevity, we will not discuss all the features and options that are available when understanding costs, but let's cover the basics so that you can deploy your first solution:

- **Region**: You will choose your region based on the requirements for your application. Bear in mind that you will need to evaluate the requirements for high availability and likely need more than one region for support. Costs and features vary based on region, so make sure that you have the complete picture of your workload before finalizing the region to ensure you have supportability and optimal costs.

- **Operating system**: As we discussed previously, will your application run on Windows or Linux?

- **Service tier**: Currently, there are five service tiers: Free, Shared, Basic, Standard, and Premium. Each of these tiers provides features and SLAs that are reasonably representative of the price point for that tier. As an example, the following are descriptions for the Free tier and the Premium tier:

  - The Free tier is described as follows: "*Use the Free plan to quickly evaluate App Service and convert the app at any time into one of the paid plans without delays or downtime.*" So, this could be a good tier if you need to understand the service, features, and options better.

  - On the other hand, the Premium tier is "*Designed for production apps. Supports larger numbers of scale instances, additional connectors, and BizTalk capabilities, while including all the advanced capabilities found in the Standard plan.*"

Once you have deployed your App Service for your requirements, you may come across situations where a full deployment may not be required. In this case, you will want to look at Azure Functions.

## Azure Functions

**Azure Functions** gives Ocean Smart the ability to augment solutions with a small bit of code to fill in where a native service isn't able to complete a task. Another important characteristic of Azure Functions is its ability to use a small bit of code for a simple operation that would otherwise require a more robust, costly service. Some common uses of Functions would be for simple data movement operations, to trigger an action or API, to react to some activity with an action, and to build a message queueing system. Azure Functions provides a development interface for building blocks of code called functions with native support for Java, JavaScript, C#, Python, PowerShell, or a choice of your own with a custom handler. This ability is served to developers instead of them having to build and maintain servers for a development environment.

When setting up an Azure function (called a function app in the Azure portal), you will have several options for deploying the app infrastructure that's required to build your code. You are offered the standard options by default, which are **Subscription, Resource Group, App Name, and Region**. As always, align these options with what your overall workload requires. One point to note is that the app name must be unique as it is a publicly available name with an FQDN of `<function app name>.azurewebsites.net`. The specific requirements for a function are as follows:

- **Publish**: Here, you have the option to publish your function as code or in a Docker container. If you choose code, you will need to select your runtime environment and the version of that runtime. The Docker container will allow you to configure your environment, so those options will disappear from the configuration.

- **Storage**: On the **Hosting** tab, you will need to specify a storage account for storing the files that are required by the function as **Blob**, **File**, or **Table** storage.

- **Operating system**: The operating system's configuration is determined by what your developers want to use for their environment.

- **Plan type**: The plan type will provide you with options based on your use case. For a PoC or small project, it is recommended to use the **Consumption** option as it allows for serverless compute and helps minimize costs. You also have the **Premium** and **App Service** options, again, depending on your required SLA, HA, and the other resiliency options that are required for your deployment.

- **Application Insights**: Application Insights is a monitoring and logging system for your functions that helps ensure you are notified of anomalous behavior in your environment, such as malicious attacks. The service also provides analytics about your deployment for understanding traffic patterns and user behavior when users are visiting your site.

The pricing calculator will help you build rough estimates for the services based on what is known to give you a ballpark of what your monthly spending will encompass. However, until the workload is fully in production and the amount of traffic is fully known, it will be difficult to have an exact cost. Next, we are going to look at what it took for Ocean Smart to build a semi-accurate estimate for a PoC.

# Estimating the costs for a proof-of-concept solution, including all services

To build relatively accurate costing models, Ocean Smart needed certain estimates to be made based on logic and some guesswork. When you're building your costing models, be mindful that it is very difficult to get exact costs initially. As Ocean Smart was able to bring the solution that was developed into a production state, they started to see how long it took to move data, how much data was being stored to maintain the model, how much compute was required, and how long it would take to execute model training and retraining. In turn, they began to build a basis to add more compute that was required to meet internal SLAs for processing time. The remainder of this section will go through the decisions they needed to make when it came to building an estimate for a Form Recognizer proof of concept solution in Azure. The prices and tiers of each of the components are built in the *East US 2* region of Azure in US dollars and will be based on *pay-as-you-go* pricing. These prices should be used for estimation purposes only and will likely change over time.

When you're considering a reference architecture for a Form Recognizer solution, you will need the following technologies:

- **Storage account**: Used to land documents initially and store them long-term for further use or reference

- **Azure Functions**: Used to process pieces of code and invoke the Form Recognizer API

- **Form Recognizer API**: Used to capture details of the forms being processed, match key-value pairs, and output the data to a structured database for further use

- **Azure SQL Database**: Used to store the results of the forms that are being processed for consumption by reports and other needs

To help you visualize how this example is built, let's look at some of the components that have been placed into a pricing estimate using the Azure blob storage pricing calculator.

Beginning with the storage account, we are going to use simple block blob storage. In general, storage in Azure is relatively inexpensive. The following screenshot shows some of the basic options you will find when deploying a storage account:

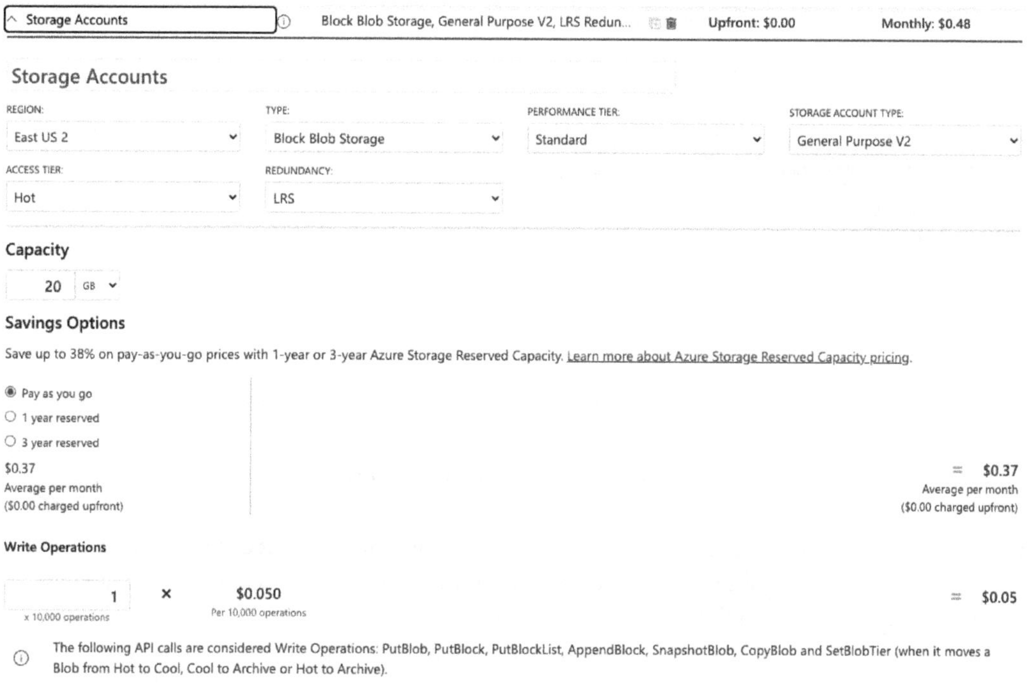

| Storage Accounts | | Block Blob Storage, General Purpose V2, LRS Redun... | Upfront: $0.00 | Monthly: $0.48 |

**Storage Accounts**

| REGION: | TYPE: | PERFORMANCE TIER: | STORAGE ACCOUNT TYPE: |
|---|---|---|---|
| East US 2 | Block Blob Storage | Standard | General Purpose V2 |

| ACCESS TIER: | REDUNDANCY: |
|---|---|
| Hot | LRS |

**Capacity**

| 20 | GB |

**Savings Options**

Save up to 38% on pay-as-you-go prices with 1-year or 3-year Azure Storage Reserved Capacity. Learn more about Azure Storage Reserved Capacity pricing.

- Pay as you go
- 1 year reserved
- 3 year reserved

$0.37
Average per month
($0.00 charged upfront)

= $0.37
Average per month
($0.00 charged upfront)

**Write Operations**

| 1 | × | $0.050 | = $0.05 |
| x 10,000 operations | | Per 10,000 operations | |

The following API calls are considered Write Operations: PutBlob, PutBlock, PutBlockList, AppendBlock, SnapshotBlob, CopyBlob and SetBlobTier (when it moves a Blob from Hot to Cool, Cool to Archive or Hot to Archive).

Figure 3.5 – Basic storage account deployment options

We will use the free tier of the Form Recognizer service because this is for PoC purposes only and we can process up to 500 document pages per month using this tier:

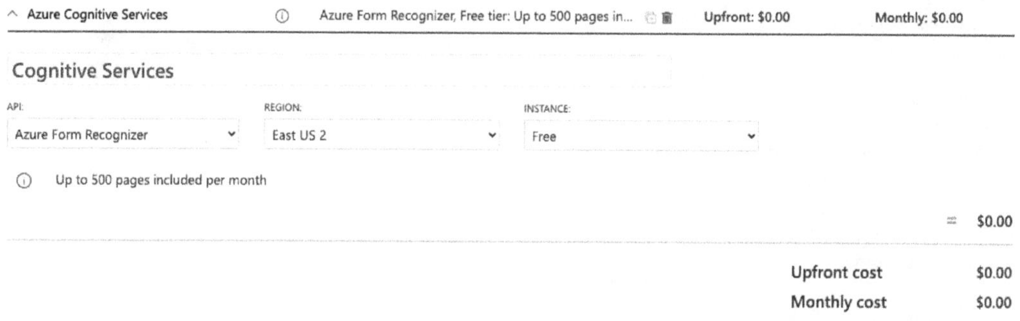

| Azure Cognitive Services | | Azure Form Recognizer, Free tier: Up to 500 pages in... | Upfront: $0.00 | Monthly: $0.00 |

**Cognitive Services**

| API: | REGION: | INSTANCE: |
|---|---|---|
| Azure Form Recognizer | East US 2 | Free |

Up to 500 pages included per month

= $0.00

| Upfront cost | $0.00 |
| Monthly cost | $0.00 |

Figure 3.6 – Azure Cognitive Services – Form Recognizer option pricing example

For the Azure Functions service, we can get additional free services at the lower consumption tier. Here, let's assume we are going to process 50 documents, with 10 pages per document, and have 100 Azure Functions executions per month:

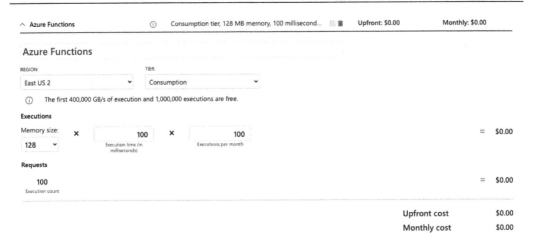

Figure 3.7 – Azure Functions option pricing example

The bulk of the cost for our proof of concept is going to be the database charges as our requirements grow. In this case, we can take advantage of the *Basic* tier, which is minimal in cost and will not select any long-term retention for backups or resiliency options:

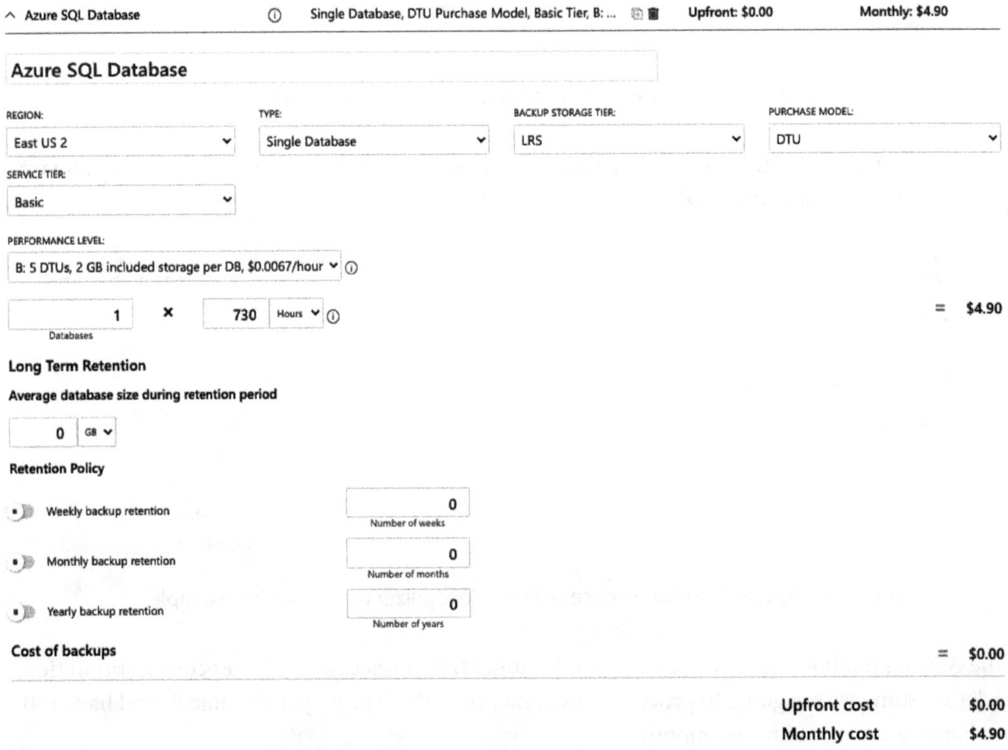

Figure 3.8 – Azure SQL Database options pricing example

The pricing calculator allows us to save our estimates and output them to an Excel spreadsheet for sharing or other activities. In this case, the total cost of building our solution is $5.37 per month:

**Microsoft Azure Estimate**

**Your Estimate**

| Service type | Custom name | Region | Description | Estimated monthly cost | Estimated upfront cost |
|---|---|---|---|---|---|
| Storage Accounts | | East US 2 | Block Blob Storage, General Purpose V2, LRS Redundancy, Hot Access Tier, 20 GB Capacity - Pay as you go, 1 x 10,000 Write operations, 1 x 10,000 List and Create Container Operations, 1 x 10,000 Read operations, 100,000 Archive High Priority Read, 1 x 10,000 Other operations. 20 GB Data Retrieval, 1,000 GB Archive High Priority Retrieval, 20 GB Data Write | $0.48 | $0.00 |
| Azure Cognitive Services | | East US 2 | Azure Form Recognizer, Free tier: Up to 500 pages included per month | $0.00 | $0.00 |
| Azure Functions | | East US 2 | Consumption tier, 128 MB memory, 100 milliseconds execution time, 100 executions/mo | $0.00 | $0.00 |
| Azure SQL Database | | East US 2 | Single Database, DTU Purchase Model, Basic Tier, B: 5 DTUs, 2 GB included storage per DB, 1 Database(s) x 730 Hours, 0 GB Retention | $4.90 | $0.00 |
| Support | | | Support | $0.00 | $0.00 |
| | | | Licensing Program | Microsoft Online Services Agreement | |
| | | | Total | $5.37 | $0.00 |

**Disclaimer**

All prices shown are in US Dollar ($). This is a summary estimate, not a quote. For up to date pricing information please visit https://azure.microsoft.com/pricing/calculator/

Figure 3.9 – Azure pricing calculator exported pricing example

Keep in mind that this example is for instructional and reference purposes only. As we begin to use more detailed examples later in this book, we will start to see higher costs associated with the workloads.

In the last section of this chapter, we are going to look at how to move data into, throughout, and out of Azure with various tools.

# Understanding data orchestration for loading data into Azure

To get data into Azure, Ocean Smart had a multitude of choices for orchestration, with a variety of suggested uses. These tools can use either a **command-line interface** (CLI) or **graphical user interface** (GUI) and have various capabilities for automating, scheduling, and triggering actions. These tools can also be local to a user's workstation for moving the data or purely reside in the Azure portal. First, we will start with the workstation-based tools:

- **AzCopy:** AzCopy is a command-line tool that is installed on a user workstation or server within an organization. It is intended to be used to send files into an Azure storage account from the local computer. Using this tool requires secure connectivity using TLS to connect and send files to the storage account in the desired folder. The account that's being used can be authenticated using Azure Active Directory or using a **Shared Access Signature** (SAS) key. A SAS key is a randomly generated key that allows delegated access to resources in a storage account. The tool can be run on a Windows, Mac, or Linux computer in both x32 and x64 formats. An example command using a SAS key is as follows:

```
azcopy copy "C:\local\path" "https://account.blob.core.
windows.net/mycontainer1/?sv=2018-03-28&ss=bjqt&srt=sco&sp=r
wddgcup&se=2019-05-01T05:01:17Z&st=2019-04-30T21:01:17Z&spr=
https&sig=MGCXiyEzbtttkr3ewJIh2AR8KrghSy1DGM9ovN734bQF4%3D"
--recursive=true
```

- **Azure Storage Explorer**: This is another tool that is installed on a user workstation for connecting to Azure storage accounts. When you install this tool on the workstation, as opposed to using AzCopy, which is just a self-contained executable, you can traverse your storage accounts in a familiar window-exploring fashion. The tool supports Windows, Mac, and Linux and has most of the functionality that the command-line tool does. You can also create SAS keys for securely sharing access to storage accounts within applications, as well as for users.

The workstation options are good for sending small batches or single files and managing the physical and virtual structure of the storage accounts. Ocean Smart was able to take advantage of those tools when it was initially loading data for the PoC. When it comes to larger data movement activities, however, some tools are better suited for larger files and batch loading operations, as described here:

- **Azure Data Factory Gen 2 (ADF)**: ADF is a unique cloud data orchestration and transformation tool that is cloud-only and the first of its kind. Born of the same foundation as Microsoft's **SQL Server Integration Services (SSIS)**, which was introduced in SQL Server 2005, many of the foundational elements are similar in ADF. One major difference is that it can only be developed in the cloud, whereas SSIS was only built in the Visual Studio IDE. ADF is the primary tool for data orchestration and transformation in Azure, with the ability to trigger data movement using a scheduled, manual, data landing, and API-based activity. The most common uses for ADF are pulling data from on-premises data sources or other public cloud sources, such as Amazon's S3 storage, and being able to directly connect to other cloud SaaS providers, such as Salesforce and Quicken.

- **Azure Data Box**: This is a purpose-built device designed to help customers move large amounts of data from on-premises into an Azure storage account. When a customer orders a Data Box device, they can quickly move data to Azure without needing to rely on the speed of the internet and have four formats to choose from:

  - **Azure Data Box Disk**: This is similar to a network-attached storage device, about the size of a small toaster oven, that can be physically deployed in your network and be connected to via SMB or NFS shares on your network. Upon receipt, customers simply add the files they would like to move to Azure, which can be up to 40 TB in size. Once the data has been loaded, the device is encrypted with 256-bit encryption and is drop- and spill-proof. It is shipped back to the Azure datacenter of choice and then loaded into the storage account specified.

  - **Azure Data Box**: The first data box that was developed has a format more similar to a large workstation appliance that is loaded into a network rack in a server cabinet. It can store up to 80 TB of data and has the same capabilities and protections as Data Box Disk.

- **Azure Data Box Heavy**: The largest and most recent addition to the Data Box family, the Data Box Heavy can handle up to 1 PB of data. Typically, this format is used for moving entire datacenters and sits on a pallet that must use equipment to move around.

- **Azure Data Box Gateway**: In a different application with a similar purpose, Azure Data Box Gateway is a virtual gateway to Azure from your local environment. The virtual appliance is loaded into your hypervisor environment and offers a direct connection to your Azure storage account, allowing for a continual stream of the data in your environment. This allows you to easily use Azure for archiving data or loading massive amounts of data while managing the flow to not saturate bandwidth during key operating hours.

The following diagram serves as a handy infographic that can help you understand where and when to use each of the data ingestion methods mentioned in this section:

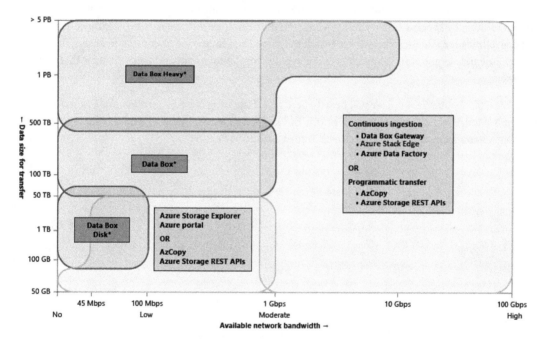

Figure 3.10 – Data transfer options for Azure

In this section, we covered the more popular and common data movement tools that are offered by Microsoft as part of the Azure platform. There are many third-party options available for data ingestion and streaming as well. As with many other suggested solutions in this book, your experience will vary, so it is best to evaluate what the best solution for your data movement needs is.

## Summary

This chapter covered the essential information that Ocean Smart used to understand the common Azure services that are used with cognitive services deployments. We also explored the most important things we must consider when deploying the services successfully at optimal costs, as well as their corresponding SLAs. We also went through a simple pricing exercise by comparing service tiers, looking at the services that are required to build a Form Recognizer PoC, and exporting the pricing calculator. These estimates will help you build the ROI and TCO models that we discussed in *Chapter 2, Why Azure Cognitive Services?*. As we diver deeper into this book and the build solutions for the specified use cases, we will look closer at the modeling costs for the solutions. Finally, we wrapped up this chapter by providing an overview of some data movement tools that can help you get your data moved to Azure efficiently for your requirements.

As we discussed earlier in this book, SLA, HA, DR, and other resiliency options are determined based on Ocean Smart's specific deployment needs. Furthermore, as the services evolve, more features and capabilities are added, so be sure to watch the public roadmaps for upcoming features. This can also include new generations of products, new regions for deployment, and price changes that affect these services.

From the next chapter onward, we will head to *Section 2, Deploying Next-Generation Knowledge Mining Solutions with Azure Cognitive Search*, of this book, where we will begin to explore the benefits of building a knowledge mining solution with Azure Cognitive Search.

# Part 2:
# Deploying Next-Generation Knowledge Mining Solutions with Azure Cognitive Search

In this part, we will describe how Ocean Smart took its legacy document management repository and built a **knowledge mining (KM)** solution to hold a vast library of valuable information.

This section has the following chapters:

# 4

# Deriving Value from Knowledge Mining Solutions in Azure

Giving your organization the ability to collect all relevant documents and media in one location with intelligence about those documents provides tremendous value. The level of intelligence that can be provided sets apart a knowledge mining solution with **artificial intelligence** (**AI**) compared to traditional document storage in a significant way. The next generation of enterprise search provides the ability to do the following:

- Score sentiment in documents.
- Correlate object images with text from documents.
- Identify personalities in audio, images, and video.
- Detect anomalous behavior in activities.

The preceding abilities, with little or no configuration of the services, and pre-built **machine learning** (**ML**) models to support base examples are readily available by coupling Azure Cognitive Services.

By injecting AI into its knowledge mining solution, *Ocean Smart* is able to take advantage of the skills highlighted in the preceding list and greatly enhance its asset management experience. This section of the book is dedicated to all the opportunities available by using Azure Cognitive Search and other accompanying services to build a next-generation knowledge mining solution.

Starting in this chapter, we are going to spend some time unpacking the following areas:

- Reviewing a brief history of document collection solutions
- Understanding the drawbacks of traditional data collection systems
- Exploring the purpose and benefits of knowledge mining solutions
- Using cognitive services to develop knowledge mining solutions

So, next, we will explore why knowledge mining solutions were originally developed and implemented many years ago.

# Reviewing a brief history of document collection solutions

The term *knowledge mining* is much newer than the concept, with a 21st-century enhancement that includes the cloud and AI. In fact, organizations around the world have sought after a centralized management system of their documents and other assets containing company-specific information for decades now. When we consider that **document management systems (DMSees)** have been around for decades, due to a proliferation of documents and data, it is no surprise that the opportunity has surfaced to align with AI for enhancements. These systems were developed to have a central repository of documents for archival and reference. DMSees align context with the documents themselves by providing tags and hierarchical structure for simpler retrieval and searching. tagging and describing documents is manual in process, as each document needs to be described and tagged individually. As the volume and variety of documents increase dramatically, this becomes an arduous process—it's basically not worth the time and effort to add those details. In the case of Ocean Smart, an investment in a DMS would have been sizeable and it would have been difficult to justify the **total cost of ownership (TCO)** for that investment; after some consideration, the company decided a DMS was not the right solution.

The next step in the next step in the evolution, in a way, from DMSees was **enterprise search**. Enterprise search added more capability to run **optical character recognition (OCR)** technology on documents for faster searching of a collection of documents. As storage space increased and indexing technology improved, along with some of the DMS capabilities of tags and descriptions, more detail about each document could be stored as metadata. This made it possible to capture more details in a central search and allowed for faster information return to an end user. As a complete solution for digitized documents, plus the fast search option, *Ocean Smart* considered this technology until it looked at what was stored in files. This is when the realization came that even with its strengths, the enterprise search capabilities were incomplete as they had asset details that could not be captured due to their format. Enterprise search has no capabilities to capture what is happening in video, audio, or image files, requiring manual processes for cataloging. As with DMSees, *Ocean Smart* was unable to justify the significant TCO required and lack of completeness in the solution, deciding to look at other solutions.

Knowledge mining solutions encompass the capabilities of DMSees and enterprise search and augment those capabilities with AI, reducing the solution to minimal human intervention. This, of course, adds significant value on top of the former systems as a more complete solution. Applying Azure Cognitive Services to Azure Cognitive Search and developing workstreams for new documents added to the system, a knowledge mining solution allows for nearly instantaneous business value. Throughout this chapter, we will explore where the business value is gained and how *Ocean Smart* can take advantage of it.

Before we dive into the value extracted, it is good to explore challenges faced in the past with extracting key insights as data volumes exploded.

# Understanding the drawbacks of traditional data collection systems

As previously described, the proliferation of data began in the early 1980s due to the rapid adoption of computer workstations within organizations. **Material requirements planning (MRP)** and **enterprise resource planning (ERP)** systems came onto the scene and provided significant business value to organizations needing to centrally manage day-to-day operations. These systems used a database developed to house data flowing through the systems and then archived this when no longer relevant. Word processing and spreadsheet applications also helped organizations to create documents outlining planning, budgeting, financial, and other types of details about the company.

If we examine these systems more closely, we can see that they were severely limited by the compute resources available to run efficiently on the hardware they were deployed to. Also, the limitations of the software compilers and languages these systems were developed on required many inefficient practices for development to fit specific business objectives.

This caused limitations on how the data could be surfaced, both within the applications and when collected. Operational reporting from these systems was required to ensure information was surfaced regarding what was happening throughout the day. Analytical systems might follow rudimentary statistic models, helping with projections for the coming months and years but not providing significant insight. These operational systems could be searched for relevant details, but only in the existing database systems and with very slow results due to limited hardware. Even today, try using these older systems that run on legacy programming languages such as **Common Business Oriented Language (COBOL)** and C for reporting and information gathering; options are limited and lagging.

In order to load a DMS with the data, adding the required context for each document or source database system was a painfully manual process. Assigning tags to documents and outputted data from these source systems limited organizations' ability to effectively search those resources. A description that was tied to the base document or system would only give an overview of the topic of the document or system, providing very little else of value. Plus, the manual nature of this process for a company such as Ocean Smart, with a smaller staff, would likely have created more work for the organization than—potentially—the value received.

The next evolution of data processing gave us the ability to scan the details, index those details, and load all that metadata into a single search engine for our corporate data. This increased the usefulness of the data as it allowed us to describe and catalog the data more completely. It also provided indicators for businesses to use to improve operations. The proliferation of data extended far beyond structured databases and text-based documents, rendering the effectiveness of these systems lower than optimal. So many systems deployed within organizations were outputting data that went beyond these structured and semi-structured data types, but users were unable to extract key insights from the data due to these limitations.

Regardless of the legacy system chosen for comparison, a significant amount of human intervention is required for tagging and describing documents. This is the major challenge when adopting a system of this type, as the output and information are based only on the manual processes taken and the assets that are chosen. Unless all the assets can be tagged, cataloged, indexed, and searched using the same means, it is unknown what other insights and correlations can be derived from all this data. This scenario commonly refers to that data as *dark* as it lies latent and unbeneficial, further expressing concerns about the completeness of one of these legacy systems.

Now, we are going to dive into why these document storage systems evolved and the value attained by organizations as they did.

## Exploring the purpose and benefits of knowledge mining solutions

*Ocean Smart* is constantly acquiring new digital assets and physical paperwork from customers, partners, suppliers, and internal employees. This proliferation of data has developed a tremendous opportunity for organizations to extract critical information from all those data sources. Documents are delivered via email containing details of products being procured, inventory levels, financial documents, sales-related documents, and much more. Customer call centers are capturing audio details of calls in a digital format used to improve training systems and customer experience. Cameras are capturing video of production-floor processes, the movement of products and employees around different areas in buildings, the exteriors of facilities for security tracking, and other relevant details about business operations. They also gather images of finished goods, raw materials, products being delivered to customers, and other opportunities to have visual evidence available for future use. The ability to unlock key insights provides tremendous value to *Ocean Smart* and helps it operate more efficiently while providing excellent customer service.

These are just some examples of unstructured data flowing into organizations that goes largely unused and holds significant value when details can be extracted and cataloged. With the legacy systems described in the previous sections, these types of files could be captured in a central repository, but without significant manual intervention as the files are cataloged, they are rendered virtually useless. Data is classified in three ways, as outlined here:

- **Structured**—Data that lives in a database of some sort that is commonly referred to as **tabular** as it takes the form of a table of data constructed of rows and columns containing data that is related. This data will conform to a pre-defined schematic structure.
- **Semi-structured**—Data that is contained in documents that have text and that can be scanned to digitize that text using OCR technology and cataloged with those details for other use. This data is schemaless and is commonly brought into NoSQL- or DocumentDB-style databases, relying heavily on tagging and descriptions.

- **Unstructured**—Data that has no structure to it at all. Audio, video, and image files, as well as data that doesn't adhere to a data structure, are all considered to be unstructured and difficult to extract and relevant information from.

The following table represents each of the data types and systems that align well in a *Good, Better, Best* description:

| | Document management systems | Enterprise search solutions | Knowledge mining solutions |
|---|---|---|---|
| Structured data | Original intended purpose | Enhanced capabilities with indexing and fast search | Enhanced further with AI capabilities |
| Semi-structured data | Adds value when able to provide OCR | Adds value when able to provide OCR plus added to an index and searched | Adds value by inherently providing OCR data, and additional AI capabilities |
| Unstructured data | Unable to add value | Unable to add value | Adds significant value by aligning AI capabilities and extracting relevant details |
| | Good | Better | Best |

Figure 4.1 – Description of data types and solutions aligned

As described, structured data has been able to accommodate the "deeper insight" capability that organizations search for going back decades; however, when we consider semi- and unstructured data, that changes dramatically.

When we process the data in a knowledge mining solution, we generally follow these five steps:

1. **Ingest**—We begin pulling the data into our storage location, most likely Azure Blob storage.

2. **Prepare**—When we prepare the data, we are using the AI capabilities listed in the next section to extract key information from all the data in our storage location.

3. **Analyze**—At this stage, we build an index of the data for fast searching and return of information.

4. **Publish**—Next, we will publish the data using some frontend service—typically, a chatbot, a web application, or a mobile device.

5. **Visualize**—Finally, we have the ability to visualize the results and correlated information that have been derived from the data repository.

We will dig deeper into each of these steps as the book continues and with the examples published in later chapters.

Using AI, knowledge mining solutions were developed to unlock key insights in latent data—that is, what largely makes up data stores across organizations. In fact, a 2019 survey (*KNOWLEDGE MINING: The Next Wave of Artificial Intelligence-Led Transformation*; see the *Further reading* section at the end of this chapter) found that the following was the case:

> *82% of executives say that exploring, understanding, and using unstructured information contained in such things as PDFs, Images, and Audio files in a timely way is a significant challenge for their organization.*

Knowledge mining solutions were developed to explore, understand, and use the data contained in business assets. The capability to explore, understand, and use that data was created with the alignment of AI solutions to help with and minimize the manual processes required to capture the details without AI. Microsoft developed its cognitive services aligned with categories around text, vision, and language to help augment these manual processes, making them more efficient.

Next, we are going to look at other **cognitive services** that are being used to unlock insights in your data as part of a knowledge mining solution.

## Using cognitive services to develop knowledge mining solutions

When considering which cognitive services to use to enhance your knowledge mining solution, you can assume certain options will be used by default. These are the services that are most commonly used for text-based operations where you may have handwritten documents or notes, and further details can be extrapolated from that text. Let's go through the services that will enhance your document stores and help build a more complete knowledge mining solution in Azure, as follows:

- **OCR**—OCR capabilities provide organizations with the ability to capture text within documents and surface that text for searching and indexing. These capabilities are extended beyond what can be extracted from digitized text to handwritten and other forms of text to be captured.

- **Sentiment analysis**—This gives us the ability to gain insight into the tone of the resource being analyzed and helps with determining whether there is a positive, negative, or neutral tone. This is especially useful when working with unstructured data sources such as social media and customer opinion blogs.

- **Entity recognition (ER)**—Using ER, we can leverage pre-built classifiers to determine entities within unstructured data. By being able to capture which objects are within images, we can classify said image and apply tags automatically as relevant details of that data.

- **Language translation and detection**—In the legacy systems we discussed earlier in this chapter, many assumptions were made around having data sources available for indexing and searching. If one language is being used throughout an organization, those systems are sufficient; however, in this ever-global world, that is less likely the case. Using the Azure translation services, we can extract key insights from documents in many languages and then surface those insights into our supported language of choice.

- **Key-phrase extraction**—With key-phrase extraction, we can go beyond the ability to index singular words, but now have the ability to clump together words to provide a different level of context. By using key-phrase extraction, we can now search our document stores for more specific details, allowing for a more targeted search and fewer unrelated documents as a result.

- **Form processing**—We have previously discussed the **Form Recognizer** service and how it enables companies to process forms more quickly without human intervention. We can also align this service as part of a knowledge mining solution to be able to not only automatically process these forms, but also add them to the index for other enhancements.

By calling these and other various cognitive services, we are beginning the process of structuring our unstructured data, which is the ultimate goal of a knowledge mining solution. By structuring the data, we gain an ability to delve deeper into the various topics in the preceding list, and this can all be done while saving the countless man-hours it would take to add these details. By highlighting the details, we are now adding significant value to the data and our organization as a result. Of course, each of the technologies has a process for handling miscategorized data or false positives in order to improve the data models serving the **application programming interfaces** (**APIs**). As we go deeper into the technologies in later chapters, we will further describe each of these processes for providing feedback to the service. We will also dive deeper into the base ML model, what it consists of, and how to develop the most optimal model for your application.

As we go deeper into the book, we will demonstrate how *Ocean Smart*—and your own organization—can take advantage of these capabilities by doing the following:

- Extracting key insights from various forms of media

- Automating the process of receiving an invoice, processing it, and paying without human intervention

- Detecting anomalous behavior in data collection and production workflows

- Enhancing call center activities, recommending products, and other related capabilities to enhance the customer experience

These capabilities and more will be discussed, including complete solution deployment examples you can consider implementing in your own organization.

## Summary

In this chapter, we discussed some brief histories of DMSees, enterprise search solutions, and the foundation for knowledge mining solutions. We wanted to establish how much value is added to your data when enhancing a standard search index with AI for automation and better insights. So many of these processes were manual for so long and continue to be because companies are frequently unwilling to release their technical debt. When a company invests significant amounts of money into a product, it is extremely difficult for those who decided to invest in it to take a step back and say: "*This isn't the right solution going forward.*" Having been that guy a few times, it was really painful to walk into my boss's office and say: "*We need to change direction.*" However, when you can get back on the right track, things improve much quicker.

We discussed the limitations of DMSs, which are great with structured data and data that can be easily digitized for searching but require manual intervention for tagging and describing information. Likewise, enterprise search had a lot of promise, as it was able to build a complete index of all data, present a fast search experience, and give quick results. This search, however, was very flat in nature, so it couldn't decipher the intent of text within a page or even be sure of which meaning to use for the word you used to search. This also requires tagging and description building for completeness of search results and is very manual in nature.

Finally, we discussed the advantages of having a knowledge mining solution with all the accompanying AI capabilities for the automatic enhancement of our data. This should hopefully set the stage for the next chapter, which is centered on Azure Search, and the base capabilities your knowledge mining solution is built on before any additional AI enhancements. With that, why don't we move on to the next chapter and learn all about Azure Search?

## Further reading

- *KNOWLEDGE MINING: The Next Wave of Artificial Intelligence-Led Transformation* (https://azure.microsoft.com/mediahandler/files/resourcefiles/knowledge-mining-the-next-wave-of-artificial-intelligence-led-transformation/HBR-analytic-services.pdf)

# 5

# Azure Cognitive Search Overview and Implementation

As we discussed in *Chapter 4, Deriving Value from Knowledge Mining Solutions in Azure*, the proliferation of data, documents, and other corporate digital assets has perpetuated a need to extract insights from latent data that's left behind. There have been several iterations and attempts at building solutions that can consistently unlock those insights, but all have fallen short and require significant manual intervention. Having the ability to align AI with award-winning accuracy, the flexibility to deploy solutions on-premises, in Azure or other clouds, and a robust and mature search index helps propel Azure Cognitive Search to a category all by itself for your enterprise.

Since you have stayed with us this far in the book and read a fair amount of the overview, history, and operations, it will be a relief to hear that we are going to start building. In this chapter, we will begin the more technical phase of the book, where we will build solutions for examples and give guidance on the critical technical questions you will face when deploying the solutions. That all starts with Azure Cognitive Search and building your first deployment. As part of that, we will explore the following areas for a better understanding of the solution overall:

- Understanding how Cognitive Search is built
- Exploring what services will be used as part of a Cognitive Search solution
- Pairing common services with Cognitive Search for your KM solution

With that, let's get to building solutions after a quick overview of the underlying technology.

## Technical requirements

To build your Azure Cognitive Search solution, you will need to have an Azure subscription with at least Contributor rights to the subscription for deploying services. You will need an Azure Storage account for storing your documents pre- and post-processing. You will need to have Visual Studio Code installed for working with the search indexer. (Download Visual Studio Code for Mac, Linux, and Windows an, https://code.visualstudio.com/Download)

# Understanding how Azure Cognitive Search is built

Azure Cognitive Search is a robust and mature service with roots in the Azure Search service that was created back in 2014 originally. The Search service was developed by using the same technology that powered Microsoft Office and Bing Search. Azure Search was retired in 2019 and the capabilities were folded into Azure Cognitive Search with newer, enhanced AI features. The service was originally developed to provide a flexible API-based search solution for developer applications without requiring infrastructure deployments. This freed developers' time up by reducing the number of hours needed to build and maintain an in-house, full-text search solution for their applications.

At its core, Cognitive Search offers two main functions, indexing and querying:

- **Indexing** – As with other search service providers, indexing is simply the process of loading data and documents into a repository or pointing an indexer to the data you are using. Then, the service gives us the ability to process that data for fast searching. It does this by assigning a schema to the data that is processed, creating a JSON document with associated fields extracted from the document. The **index** and **indexing** should not be confused with an **indexer**, which we will discuss shortly.

- **Querying** – After an index has been built, the application that you deploy uses the querying service to call an API, query against the search index, and return results. The way a query is structured includes parameters, details about the query, and what is expected in return in the form of results. A query is structured in the following REST API format:

```
Post <URL>
{
"queryType": "<simple|Lucene>",
"searchMode": "<all|any>",
"search": "<search term(s)>",
"searchFields": "<field(s)>",
"select": "<field(s)>",
"top": "<number>",
"count": "<true>|<false>",
"orderby": "<field>|<relevance score> <asc|desc>"
}
```

The following descriptions provide context for each parameter:

- `"queryType": "<simple|Lucene>",` – This specifies a full-text search or something more advanced, such as expressions, proximity, fuzzy, and wildcard search types.

- `"searchMode": "<all|any>",` – This specifies whether you get search results on any of the terms or all the terms in the search.

- `"search": "<search term(s)>",` – This parameter allows you to specify which terms or phrases you want results on and allows for operators.

- `"searchFields": "<field(s)>",` – Here you can specify which fields from the index you want search results from.

- `"select": "<field(s)>",` – This parameter lets you specify which fields are returned in the query response.

- `"top": "<number>",` – This lets you specify how many search results you want to return with the query response.

- `"count": "<true>|<false>",` – This returns the total number of documents in the index that have matched your search terms.

- `"orderby": "<field>|<relevance score> <asc|desc>"` – This allows you to order your results by a field or relevance score in ascending or descending order.

A complete list of parameters and options can be found in the Microsoft documentation here: `https://docs.microsoft.com/en-us/rest/api/searchservice/search-documents`.

So, now that you understand the main components of the Cognitive Search solution for querying and returning results, let's dig a little deeper into the different search capabilities provided.

## Search types

As you build your solution, you will have varying types of documents, media, images, and other types of data loaded into your index. Because of the varying data types loaded and what they contain, you may find that different types of searches will be better suited to return the most relevant results. When deploying a search solution, you are given the default full-text search, and more recently added is the ability to align your results with semantic search. The following is an overview of each of the search types and relevant uses.

### Full-text search

The full-text search engine in Azure Cognitive Search is based on the open source **Apache Lucene** (`https://lucene.apache.org/`) search engine with some added features and enhancements. This is the default search engine provided when your documents are loaded into the index and returns results based on keywords that match your search. The full-text process, in general, is as follows:

1. **Query parsing** – This step looks at the search terms provided in the request and parses the details of the terms. The parsing engine evaluates the terms provided and makes accommodations for special characters such as "+" or "*" for how to process the search. Using these symbols and others helps the parser to determine which terms are required in the results returned in the search.

2. **Lexical analysis** – The lexical analysis helps to better structure the search with several activities to simplify what is being searched for. Breaking words to use the core of the word, removing unnecessary stopwords ("*the*", "*of*", and "*and*", for example), and removing the case of the words for consistency.

3. **Document retrieval** – At this point in the search, you have the terms and phrases you want to match on, so those are compared against what is in the index. When that is complete, the documents are to return as results of the search as a list of documents where there is a match either in the title or description fields.

4. **Scoring** – Each of the documents returned is assigned a score based on the relevance of the results to the original search request. Each document is ranked based on the score and assigned a weight as it compares to the underlying machine learning model and the prediction that the document will match best. The basis for that scoring is from the **term frequency-inverse document frequency (TF/IDF)**. Find more information about TF/IDF here: `https://en.wikipedia.org/wiki/Tf%E2%80%93idf`.

Let's cover semantic search next.

### Semantic search

The semantic search capability is the newest feature added to Azure Cognitive Search. This feature is a premium capability that can provide more accurate search results by providing an enhanced relevance score and language understanding elements. Semantic search essentially uses the inverted indexing process that happens with a full-text search as described before, and then enhances the search with a few activities given as follows:

- **Spell correction** – The first thing the semantic search does is ensure that search terms are spelled correctly, and fixes any spelling errors prior to processing.

- **Full-text search** – Next, the standard search process takes place.

- **Enhanced scoring** – After the standard search is complete and provides the documents as they are scored, they are re-scored with semantic search. This process uses the default similarity scoring algorithm (`https://docs.microsoft.com/en-us/azure/search/index-similarity-and-scoring#similarity-ranking-algorithms`) and calculates the score based on the similarity of terms and the results from the index. Then it re-ranks the documents based on the enhanced score provided.

- **Captions and answers** – Finally, the document is analyzed further to extract key sentences and paragraphs that describe the broader context of the document. This can be surfaced for review by a user to gain a quicker understanding of what the full document consists of. This also provides a basis for an *answer* if a question is asked with the initial search request.

Because of the premium nature of the semantic search service, it does incur additional costs and should be evaluated if required for your search requirements.

Now, let's take a closer look at what the rest of Cognitive Search is doing for us with indexing and AI enhancements.

## Underlying index and search activities

As we dig deeper into what is happening within your search application, there are several components and concepts that add significant value to what is provided with a traditional search. The following is not intended to be an exhaustive list of all capabilities and concepts; however, it should provide a good overview of the areas you will need to focus your efforts on when deploying a Cognitive Search solution:

- **Indexer** – Not to be confused with an index, the indexer gives you the ability to create a workflow that allows for documents and other assets from an external data source to be loaded and helps to build the index. The indexer takes the curated content and builds a serialized JSON document that will be included in the index to be searched. In general, this is how a typical search solution would be developed and they vary in capability and search engine algorithm. With Azure Cognitive Search, an indexer for AI was introduced for further enrichment of data extracted from the source.

- **AI enrichment** – The ability to run additional cognitive capabilities against files and documents stored in data repositories is a key differentiator for Azure Cognitive Search as compared with a traditional search. By using the AI enrichment indexer, you can go beyond traditional text-based operations, such as OCR, by detecting entities in images and text, understanding the tone of the document, and more capabilities. This is created by attaching a skillset to an indexer.

- **Skillset** – The skillsets available within Azure Cognitive Search are provided from the machine learning models that were developed for the Computer Vision and Text Analytics Cognitive Services resources. The capabilities have been ported to Cognitive Search for this data enrichment and essentially add to the newly created enriched document that has the added substance provided by the skillset(s) used.

- **Custom skills** – If there is another machine learning model available that may further enhance the processing and enrichment of data, you can align additional skills by building a custom skill. With a custom skill, for example, you could integrate the processing of forms by using the Form Recognizer service as part of the enrichment. The following diagram provided by Microsoft is a good representation of the flow of the enrichment process.

This diagram represents the process of using an indexer and related services:

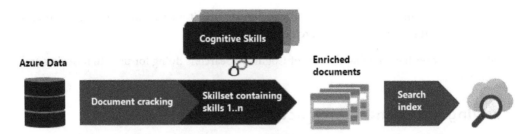

Figure 5.1 – Document enrichment process using skillsets

The end-to-end process of using an indexer is as follows:

1. Connect to your data source in Azure, typically a database or storage account.

2. **Document cracking** allows you to open the file (programmatically) and analyze what information can be extracted from the documents loaded. Examples would be capturing pages, text, and images in the documents that will be analyzed further.

3. Indexing and applying skillsets to your documents will enrich the overall information related to the document you have. These skillsets are built with the capabilities you want to include, in the order you want to include them. You define which skillsets you want to be applied to your document; they are applied with the skills available, native or custom.

4. The output of the skillsets applied is a new document that contains the original document with all the detail added through the enrichment process.

5. This document is then added to the search index for user-searching from an application.

6. Two optional outputs that are highly recommended through this process are as follows:

   I. **Knowledge store** – An optional output that can be used as you begin to build a complete KM solution or to be reported from.

   II. **Enriched document caching** – By default, the enriched documents are only added to the search index and are only used for that purpose. There may be other use cases you have for these documents and the enrichment content where the information is used elsewhere. The caching also allows us to enable the ability to allow for incremental enrichment. You can enable the cache capability by including the `cache` property in your indexer definition call.

So, now you have an idea of what is entailed when deploying an Azure Cognitive Search workload, and some of the work that is happening behind the scenes. Let's now look at the other components Ocean Smart used in their solution.

# Exploring what services will be used as part of a Cognitive Search solution

Cognitive Search solutions are an amazing way to quickly enrich documents in just about any workload in Azure, on-premises, or in another cloud. You will need to understand, however, the common components required beyond Cognitive Search to deploy a complete solution. In this section, we are going to explore those additional services as Ocean Smart deployed them for the Cognitive Search portion of their KM solution.

For simplicity's sake, all that's really required to deploy the service is a storage account and the Cognitive Search service to have a working solution. After deploying the asset and loading your files into the storage account, you can point your indexer at that storage account and begin an indexing process. This is a fine process for testing the service and understanding how it works, but as you'll see in *Chapter 7, Pulling It All Together for a Complete KM Solution*, more services are required to build a full solution. When logging in to the Azure portal and finding the deployment page for Azure Cognitive Search, you will see something similar to the following:

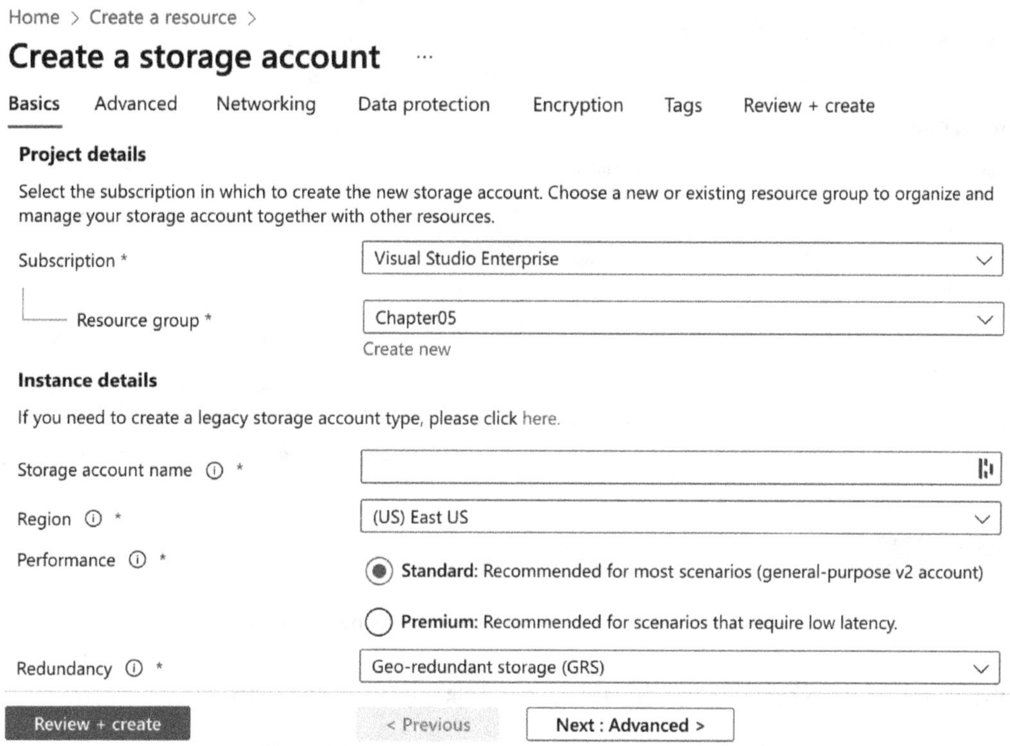

Home > Create a resource >

## Create a storage account    ...

**Basics**    Advanced    Networking    Data protection    Encryption    Tags    Review + create

### Project details

Select the subscription in which to create the new storage account. Choose a new or existing resource group to organize and manage your storage account together with other resources.

| Subscription * | Visual Studio Enterprise ∨ |
| --- | --- |
| Resource group * | Chapter05 ∨ |
| | Create new |

### Instance details

If you need to create a legacy storage account type, please click here.

| Storage account name ⓘ * | |
| --- | --- |
| Region ⓘ * | (US) East US ∨ |
| Performance ⓘ * | ⦿ Standard: Recommended for most scenarios (general-purpose v2 account) |
| | ◯ Premium: Recommended for scenarios that require low latency. |
| Redundancy ⓘ * | Geo-redundant storage (GRS) ∨ |

| Review + create | < Previous | Next : Advanced > |
| --- | --- | --- |

Figure 5.2 – Azure storage account creation screen

The following gives an overview of how to deploy the services for a simple solution.

To deploy your Azure storage account service, perform the following steps:

1.  Search for `Storage Account` in the **Create a resource** window.

2.  Choose your basic configurations for **Subscription**, **Resource group**, **Storage account name**, and **Region**.

3.  It is recommended to choose **Standard** for **Performance** for this proof of concept.

4.  It is also recommended to choose **Local redundant storage** for the proof of concept. Note that when you build a full production solution, these settings will vary based on your needs.

5.  The rest of the settings are fine if you choose the defaults, and as long as all validation checks are passed, choose **Review + create**.

Next, we will look at the process for deploying the Azure Cognitive Search service. The wizard within the Azure portal will look something like the following:

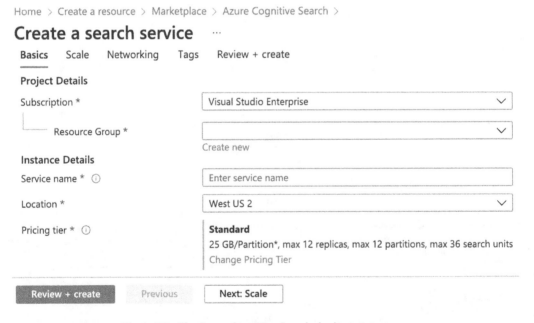

Figure 5.3 – The Azure Cognitive Search deployment screen

To deploy your Azure Cognitive Search service, go through the following steps:

1.  Search for `Azure Cognitive Search` in the **Create a resource** window.

2.  Choose your basic configurations for **Subscription**, **Resource group**, **Service name**, and **Location**.

3. For **Pricing tier**, be sure to change from the default of **Standard** to the **Free** tier for proof-of-concept purposes.

4. **Scale** and **Partition** are not able to be modified in the Free tier, and you may add **Tags** if necessary, but otherwise, you can select **Review + create** to finish deploying the service.

Next, you'll need to create a container and load your files into your storage account for later indexing. For the purposes of this demonstration, we are only going to use the browser-based data exploration tool, **Storage browser**; however, you could also use the installable **Azure Storage Explorer** tool from your desktop for loading the files after you've created your storage account:

1. Navigate to your newly created storage account in the Azure portal.

2. On the **Overview** screen of the storage account, you will get a glimpse of some of the settings you configured, and some advanced features you will use later for optimization purposes and connectivity.

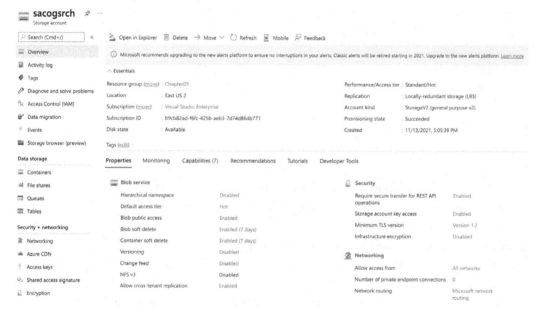

Figure 5.4 – The Azure storage account overview screen

3.  To create the Blob container, complete the following steps:

  I.    Select **Storage browser (preview)** from the left-hand menu.

> **Note**
>
> This may be titled **Storage Explorer** in your options as that is the legacy name of the feature.

  II.   Select **Blob containers** on the right:

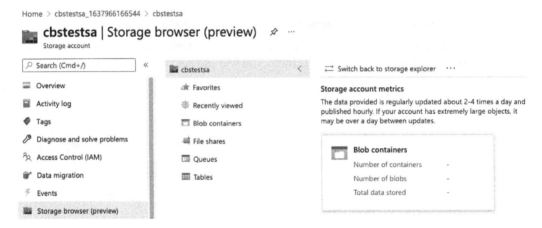

Figure 5.5 – An example of the Storage browser service in the Azure portal

4.  You will now see any containers that already exist, as well as the **$logs** container created by default. It is not expected that you'll have any containers at this point unless you decided to use an existing storage account.

5.  Click **Add Container** and the **New container** dialog box will be brought up. Give your container a name and accept the remaining default settings. Click **Create** to complete the container creation process.

6.  Next, you will see the new container created within the **Blob containers** dialog still using the **Storage browser** tool.

7.  Browse into the container and in the top ribbon of the window you'll see the **Upload** button. Select the button to open the file upload dialog.

8.  Browse on your local source to where you want to add the files to the index and search on into Azure Blob storage.

Okay, so now you have the files you want to create an index on in Azure. Next, we are going to configure the Cognitive Search service to connect to use the indexer service:

1.  Connect to the deployed Cognitive Search service from earlier in this process, where you'll land on the overview screen:

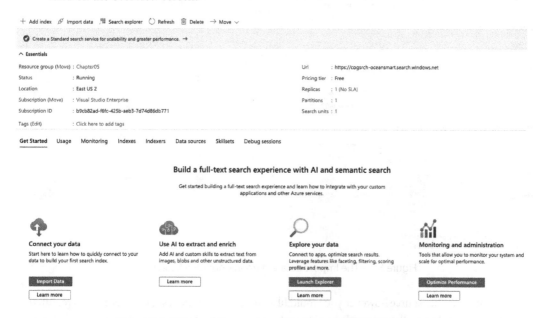

Figure 5.6 – The overview screen of the Cognitive Search service

From here, you'll see that you have many options on how to work with the Cognitive Search service, including importing and exploring your data.

2.  Click **Import data** from the menu at the top, or **Import Data** in the quick links at the bottom. The wizard that is launched will allow you to connect to data sources that already exist, sample data for exploration, several other Azure storage and database resources, as well as SharePoint Online.

3.  You will need to add access to the storage account you created in the previous steps; in our case, it was Azure Blob storage, or whatever you set up your storage account as. You will then see the following dialog box for input:

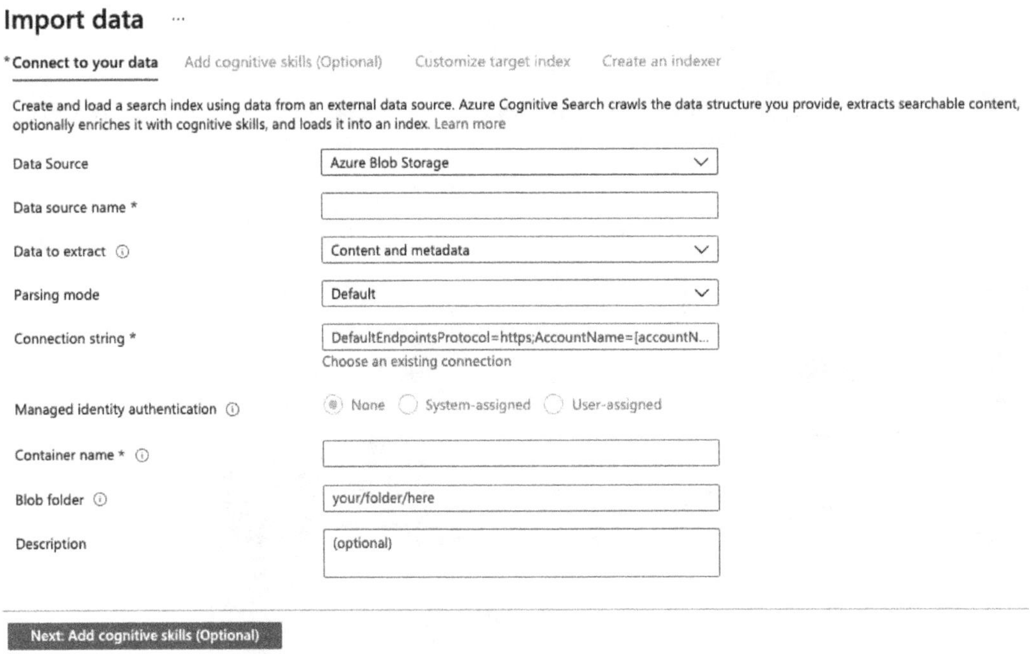

## Import data   ...

**\*Connect to your data**    Add cognitive skills (Optional)    Customize target index    Create an indexer

Create and load a search index using data from an external data source. Azure Cognitive Search crawls the data structure you provide, extracts searchable content, optionally enriches it with cognitive skills, and loads it into an index. Learn more

| | |
|---|---|
| Data Source | Azure Blob Storage ⌄ |
| Data source name \* | |
| Data to extract ⓘ | Content and metadata ⌄ |
| Parsing mode | Default ⌄ |
| Connection string \* | DefaultEndpointsProtocol=https;AccountName=[accountN... |
| | Choose an existing connection |
| Managed identity authentication ⓘ | ⦿ None  ○ System-assigned  ○ User-assigned |
| Container name \* ⓘ | |
| Blob folder ⓘ | your/folder/here |
| Description | (optional) |

**Next: Add cognitive skills (Optional)**

Figure 5.7 – The Import data wizard in Cognitive Search

4.  Name your data source however you would like and configure the rest of the settings as required. You will need to get the connection string and container name from your storage account settings.

    Part of this step will require you to create a shared access token for the storage account. More details on how to generate this key and other guidance can be found here: `https://msdn.microsoft.com/library/azure/mt584140.aspx`.

5.  After you have added your storage account, click **Next: Add cognitive skills (Optional)**, and the defined index schema will be detected. This process can take a while depending on how much data you have in the storage account.

6.  Our next step is to determine which of the cognitive skills we want to include in the indexing process if we want to add enrichments. To use a Cognitive Services resource that is not included as a skill in Cognitive Search, we can create that service here in the dialog. We can also include some of the built-in enhancements from the dialog using the following reference to understand all of the capabilities: `https://go.microsoft.com/fwlink/?linkid=872709`.

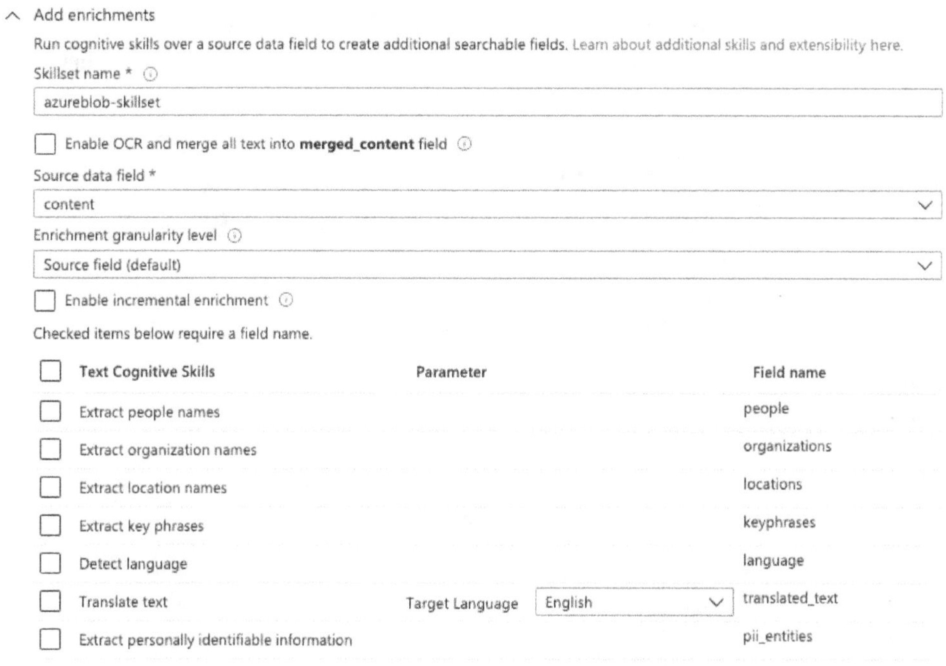

**Add enrichments**

Run cognitive skills over a source data field to create additional searchable fields. Learn about additional skills and extensibility here.

Skillset name * ⓘ

> azureblob-skillset

☐ Enable OCR and merge all text into **merged_content** field ⓘ

Source data field *

> content    ⌄

Enrichment granularity level ⓘ

> Source field (default)    ⌄

☐ Enable incremental enrichment ⓘ

Checked items below require a field name.

| ☐ | Text Cognitive Skills | Parameter | | Field name |
|---|---|---|---|---|
| ☐ | Extract people names | | | people |
| ☐ | Extract organization names | | | organizations |
| ☐ | Extract location names | | | locations |
| ☐ | Extract key phrases | | | keyphrases |
| ☐ | Detect language | | | language |
| ☐ | Translate text | Target Language | English ⌄ | translated_text |
| ☐ | Extract personally identifiable information | | | pii_entities |

Figure 5.8 – AI enrichments natively available in the Cognitive Search service

7. After determining which of the skills you'd like to include, the final portion of the wizard to **Save enrichments to a knowledge store** allows you to project your enriched documents in a table to Blob storage for further consumption. More details can be found here: https://go.microsoft.com/fwlink/?linkid=2088416. The following is a sample of what it will look like if you select all options:

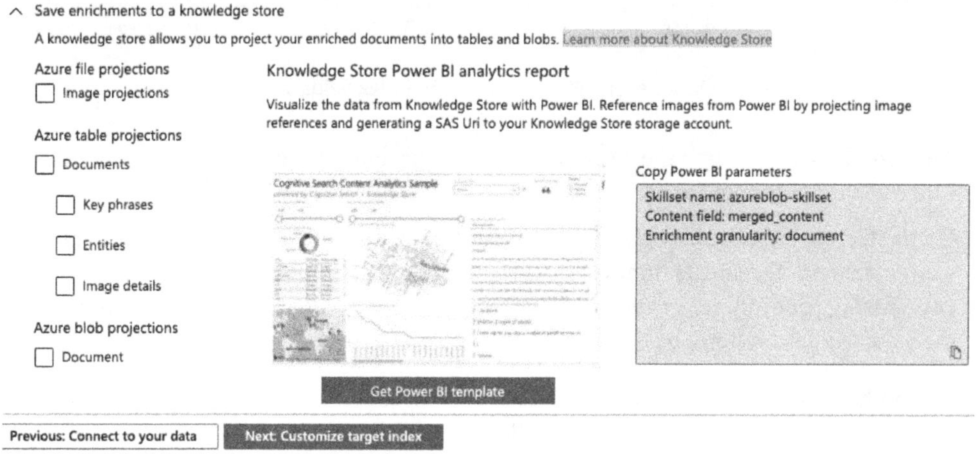

**Save enrichments to a knowledge store**

A knowledge store allows you to project your enriched documents into tables and blobs. Learn more about Knowledge Store

Azure file projections
☐ Image projections

Azure table projections
☐ Documents
  ☐ Key phrases
  ☐ Entities
  ☐ Image details

Azure blob projections
☐ Document

Knowledge Store Power BI analytics report

Visualize the data from Knowledge Store with Power BI. Reference images from Power BI by projecting image references and generating a SAS Uri to your Knowledge Store storage account.

Copy Power BI parameters

Skillset name: azureblob-skillset
Content field: merged_content
Enrichment granularity: document

Get Power BI template

Previous: Connect to your data      Next: Customize target index

Figure 5.9 – Options for where to save enrichments and other features

8.  Next, select **Next: Customize target index**, where you will be able to modify the names of the fields that are extracted from your documents, or add and remove any additional fields that apply, as seen in the following screenshot:

| Field name | Type | Retrievable | Filterable | Sortable | Facetable | Searchable | Analyzer | Suggester | |
|---|---|---|---|---|---|---|---|---|---|
| content | Edm.Stri... ⌄ | ☑ | ☐ | ☐ | ☐ | ☑ | Standard - Luce... ⌄ | | ⋯ |
| metadata_storage_content_type | Edm.String | ☐ | ☐ | ☐ | ☐ | ☐ | | | ⋯ |
| metadata_storage_size | Edm.Int64 | ☐ | ☐ | ☐ | ☐ | | | | ⋯ |
| metadata_storage_last_modified | Edm.DateTi... | ☐ | ☐ | ☐ | ☐ | | | | ⋯ |
| metadata_storage_content_md5 | Edm.String | ☐ | ☐ | ☐ | ☐ | ☐ | | | ⋯ |
| metadata_storage_name | Edm.String | ☐ | ☐ | ☐ | ☐ | ☐ | | | ⋯ |
| 🔑 metadata_storage_path | Edm.Stri... ⌄ | ☑ | ☐ | ☐ | ☐ | ☐ | | | ⋯ |
| metadata_storage_file_extension | Edm.String | ☐ | ☐ | ☐ | ☐ | ☐ | | | ⋯ |
| metadata_content_type | Edm.String | ☐ | ☐ | ☐ | ☐ | ☐ | | | ⋯ |
| metadata_language | Edm.String | ☐ | ☐ | ☐ | ☐ | ☐ | | | ⋯ |
| people | Collection(E... | ☑ | ☐ | | ☐ | ☑ | Standard - Luce... ⌄ | | ⋯ |
| organizations | Collection(E... | ☑ | ☐ | | ☐ | ☑ | Standard - Luce... ⌄ | | ⋯ |
| locations | Collection(E... | ☑ | ☐ | | ☐ | ☑ | Standard - Luce... ⌄ | | ⋯ |
| keyphrases | Collection(E... | ☑ | ☐ | | ☐ | ☑ | Standard - Luce... ⌄ | | ⋯ |
| language | Edm.String | ☑ | ☐ | ☐ | ☐ | ☑ | Standard - Luce... ⌄ | | ⋯ |
| translated_text | Edm.String | ☑ | ☐ | ☐ | ☐ | ☑ | English - Lucene ⌄ | | ⋯ |
| ▶ pii_entities | Collection(E... | | | | | | | | ⋯ |
| masked_text | Edm.String | ☑ | ☐ | ☐ | ☐ | ☑ | Standard - Luce... ⌄ | | ⋯ |
| merged_content | Edm.String | ☑ | ☐ | ☐ | ☐ | ☑ | Standard - Luce... ⌄ | | ⋯ |
| text | Collection(E... | ☑ | ☐ | | ☐ | ☑ | Standard - Luce... ⌄ | | ⋯ |
| layoutText | Collection(E... | ☑ | ☐ | | ☐ | ☑ | Standard - Luce... ⌄ | | ⋯ |
| imageTags | Collection(E... | ☑ | ☐ | | ☐ | ☑ | Standard - Luce... ⌄ | | ⋯ |
| imageCaption | Collection(E... | ☑ | ☐ | | ☐ | ☑ | Standard - Luce... ⌄ | | ⋯ |
| imageCelebrities | Collection(E... | ☑ | ☐ | | ☐ | ☑ | Standard - Luce... ⌄ | | ⋯ |

Figure 5.10 – Options for customizing target index fields and names

9.  After you have finished up the customization of your index, click **Next: Create an indexer**, where you can finish up the deployment.

10. On the **Create an indexer** screen, you can configure a schedule for the indexer to pick up new or changed documents from your storage account, and some other advanced settings for customizing your indexer processing. This will start the indexing process, and if you stay in the same window, you will be notified of the indexer's completion.

Now that you have created your indexer, you are ready to explore your data to see what type of intelligence the enrichments have extracted and added to your documents. You will do this using the **Explore your data** tool that is on the **Overview** tab of the Cognitive Search service screen:

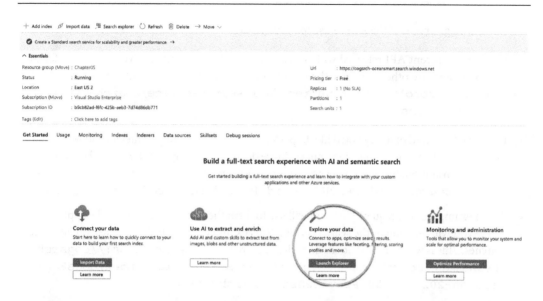

Figure 5.11 – The overview screen for Cognitive Search highlighting the Explore your data tool

With this tool, we are given the ability to do some test searching on the data that has been indexed and the enrichments that have been applied to the documents we loaded in our storage account. This tool is designed for ad hoc exploration of the data and testing some of the searches to see what is being returned as a result of a query. The following is an example of the interface for this ad hoc experience:

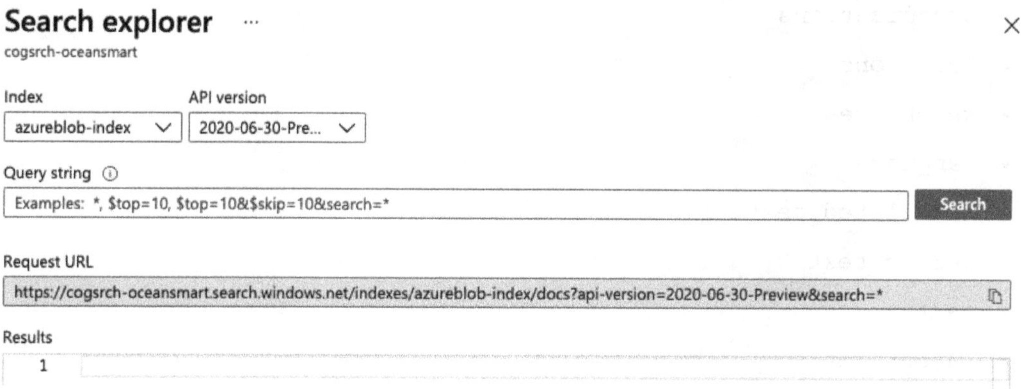

# Search explorer   ...                                                                    ✕

cogsrch-oceansmart

| Index | API version |
| --- | --- |
| azureblob-index  ⌄ | 2020-06-30-Pre...  ⌄ |

Query string ⓘ

| Examples: *, $top=10, $top=10&$skip=10&search=* | **Search** |
| --- | --- |

Request URL

https://cogsrch-oceansmart.search.windows.net/indexes/azureblob-index/docs?api-version=2020-06-30-Preview&search=*

Results

1

Figure 5.12 – The default options for a basic Cognitive Search service in the data explorer tool

From the screenshot provided, you can see that the options presented are limited but can, however, be used for some rudimentary testing. A quick overview of what you can do is as follows:

- Choose which index to search in.

- Select which version of the API to use for your testing:

  - The most recent API released will be selected by default; however, if you would prefer to explore and use other versions, the version history notes can be found here: `https://docs.microsoft.com/en-us/rest/api/searchservice/search-service-api-versions`.

- Choose which kind of query you'd like to perform with the types of parameters you would like to include to shape the results of the query. More details around options beyond what is shown in the screenshot can be found here: `https://docs.microsoft.com/en-us/azure/search/search-explorer?WT.mc_id=Portal-Microsoft_Azure_Search`.

- See an example of the request URL you will use to form the code you use inside the application where you will implement the search service. This example dynamically updates as you make searches. This is what the URL looks like when I search for `lobster`: `https://cogsrch-oceansmart.search.windows.net/indexes/azureblob-index/docs?api-version=2020-06-30-Preview&search=lobster`.

Finally, after you complete your search, the tool will return results formatted in JSON that will include the enrichments nested in arrays as part of the output. Using the same example of searching for `lobster`, I get returned results for the following:

- `@search.score`
- `people`
- `organizations`
- `locations`
- `keyphrases`
- `language`
- `translated_text`
- `merged_text`
- `text`
- `layoutText`
- `imageTags`
- `imageCaption`
- `imageCelebrities`
- `pii_entities`

All of these areas have associated text that has been identified and extracted by the enrichments. Each of the categories that are returned can be surfaced in your application based on requirements and how it is being used by pointing to the associated element.

Using the same process when we apply the semantic search component to our search, the results come back quite differently. With this feature turned on, by navigating to the **Semantic Search** link in the menu on the left and choosing a tier of service, we have the option within the **Query options** menu now available:

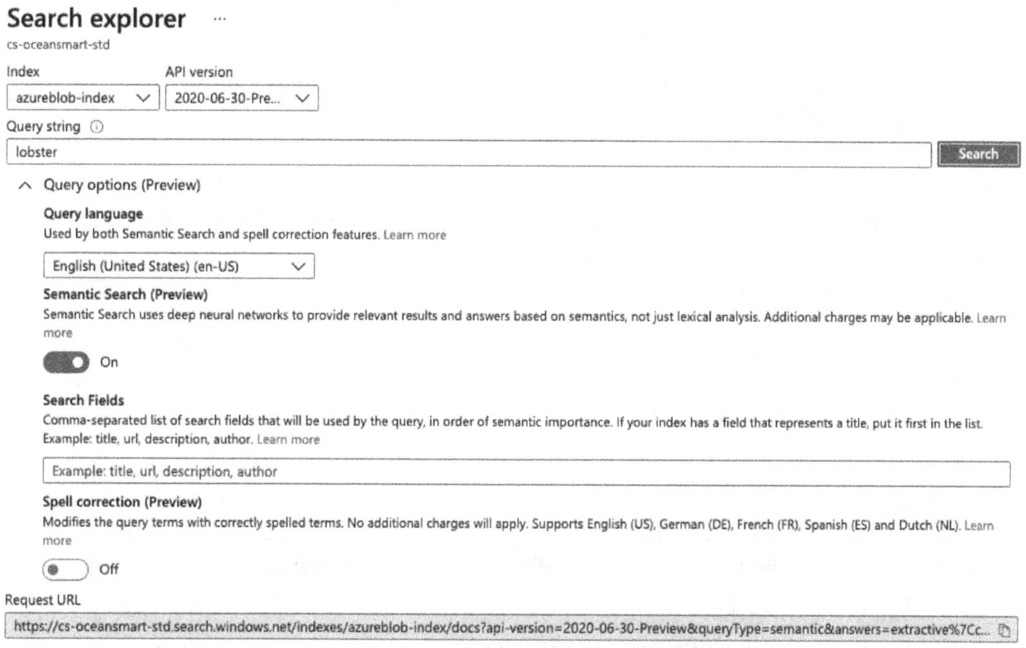

Figure 5.13 – The Search explorer dialog box including the Semantic Search and Search Fields options

As a result of turning this feature on, still using my `lobster` example, I now have the returned search results of all the same fields listed previously, but also `@search.rerankerScore` and `@search.captions`. With these two additional results, we now have the ability to highlight our secondary ranking score for more accurate results and a summarizing statement of what the document entails.

It should be noted that, even though many results were returned from my search example, there are certainly some imperfections in what the index did return. For the production deployment, you will need to take this into account and consider significant testing on the searches anticipated to be performed on the source data. By analyzing the results, you should be able to determine which elements will be beneficial for the consumers of your applications to meet their needs.

So, now that we have given you a brief overview of the basics of the Cognitive Search service, let's look at some of the additional services you will deploy as part of a complete solution.

# Pairing common services with Cognitive Search for your KM solution

So, now we know the Cognitive Search service has quite a few capabilities to not only do traditional search activities, but also enrich what we load into the index for extracting additional details that can only be built by reading the documents themselves. We have also looked at what the enhancements can return regarding augmenting the documents and interpreting their contents. However, we have also shown that simply deploying the service does not really help our users search for what they need in a user-friendly interface, which we will need to have for effective use.

This interface may also vary depending on the content of the search index. Because we can use additional Cognitive Services resources to build our complete KM solution, we could potentially load video and use the video indexing service as part of the complete solution, for instance. For these reasons, we are now going to look at the additional services that will be considered when building the complete solution. The following items discussed aren't intended to be an exhaustive list of services and have been discussed in more detail elsewhere in the book, mostly in *Chapter 3, Architectural and Cost Optimization Considerations*:

- **Azure Functions** – The Azure Functions service is one you will likely use frequently. With the ability to trigger actions and perform other code-related activities, Azure Functions seemingly finds its way into many deployments.

- **Azure App Service** – As we will display in the following, and many examples within this book, Azure App Service will allow you to host a web portal or container with ease and limit the hands-on nature of managing that infrastructure. This service is really where many of your applications will be built, and will potentially serve as the user interface for your deployment.

- **Azure Bot Service** – In the case where you've added an index to your web application or another interface where Azure Bot Service can be directly integrated, this service will be invaluable. You will also be able to use additional Cognitive Services resources with Bot Service for interacting with customers in an enhanced way, such as using natural language processing, translation services, and many more features.

- **Azure Event Grid** – Azure Event Grid is a service that monitors other services in Azure and can route the information about an event to another service for some action to be taken. An example of this is if you were monitoring Azure Data Lake Storage for when a new file is added. When the event happens, you can send a notification about the event, or trigger another event. For instance, if you wanted to trigger a re-index of your Azure Cognitive Search container because a new file is added, Event Grid would be an option.

So, now we have all the required information to build a basic search solution. Let's go and look at how Ocean Smart was able to take advantage of the service and uncover their latent data.

# Summary

With all the documents related to transactions, purchases, sales, quality, and many more aspects of day-to-day operations at Ocean Smart, many details surrounding these documents can be easily overlooked. Employees are frequently looking for documentation for the purposes of audit retrieval, paperwork related to purchases, and many other uses. Without the ability to extract the additional insights from the documents loaded into the index, it can prove difficult to find these documents if not well organized. Because Ocean Smart is now able to have these additional details in an easy-to-use search interface, finding related paperwork is easier than ever.

This details just one of the many use cases that can be deployed with Cognitive Search. Whether processing incoming payment documents, transcribing and translating recorded audio files to enhance the customer service experience, or indexing video files for speaker and content extraction, **Cognitive Search** is the foundation for these and many other applications.

Expanding on the basic search functionality and AI enrichments that we've covered in this chapter, the next chapter looks at adding additional functionality with other Cognitive Services resources. Allowing for the flexibility of using existing Cognitive Services resources, custom-developed AI capabilities, and building conditional workflows of these services will help to even further enhance the value of Cognitive Search. We will cover the details of how to deploy these types of enhancements in the next chapter. Won't you join us?

# 6
# Exploring Further Azure Cognitive Services for Successful KM Solutions

So far in this book, we have explored quite a few ways that AI is enhancing our everyday lives by making us more productive and helping us to predict what could be coming in the near future. As discussed, we are aligning AI enrichments to our formerly inadequate document management systems to uncover our latent data and gaining additional value from that data as a result. That value just covers the standard enrichments included in **Cognitive Search**, but as with so many other AI capabilities available in Cognitive Services, this chapter will explore the additional enhancements that can be achieved. With the ability to build customized skills using the non-standard AI enrichments available with other cognitive services, we are able to layer in significantly enhanced capabilities as a result. This chapter will look at some of those services where it makes sense to add them to a standard Cognitive Search deployment and provide some example solution deployments, including those services, in the next chapter.

We will then go through the deployment steps required for aligning one of these additional services. In this chapter, we will discuss the following topics:

- Exploring native AI enrichments in Azure Cognitive Search
- Reviewing advancements in OCR and image recognition
- Considering other cognitive services commonly used in knowledge mining
- Adding additional skills to your Cognitive Search indexer

With the perspective of adding these services to your knowledge mining solution, you should have a baseline for areas of your organization where you might be able to add value with the AI enrichments we cover.

Now that you have an overview of what we will cover, let's look at the standard AI enrichments already included with Azure Cognitive Search.

# Technical requirements

To build your complete **Knowledge Mining** (**KM**) solution with additional cognitive services, you will need to have an Azure subscription with at least Contributor rights to the subscription for deploying services. You will need an Azure Storage account for storing your documents pre- and postprocessing. Depending on whether you plan to deploy the solution to a Docker container or an Azure web app, you should have experience with those technologies to ensure proper deployment. You will need to have Visual Studio Code (download Visual Studio Code for Mac, Linux, or Windows at `https://code.visualstudio.com/Download`) with the `node.js` extension installed (`https://nodejs.org/en/download/package-manager`). Some other services you may use for your deployment are as follows:

- **Azure Functions**: For building functions and executing code

- **Azure Data Factory or similar**: For data orchestration and transformation

- **Azure Logic Apps**: For workflow and triggering mechanisms

- **Azure Database**: For storing output data postprocessing

Of course, the more complex and automated your solution is, the more tools you will likely need to know how to use and manage. As with everything, start with the basics, build your **proof of concept** (**PoC**), and add new features. This will help you to reduce precious time wasted troubleshooting and so on.

# Exploring native AI enrichments in Azure Cognitive Search

In *Chapter 5, Azure Cognitive Search Overview and Implementation*, we did a deep dive into the world of search and indexing, and then queried from what we built within that index, but we only lightly touched on the AI enhancements included natively with Cognitive Search. This section will give a more thorough look at what those additional enrichments are, how they are applied, and some best practices for using them.

The enhancements included in Cognitive Search come from the **Computer Vision** and **Text Analytics** cognitive services to better extract key information using the most common use cases in a KM solution. The features of those services included are listed in the output of the queries completed in *Chapter 5, Azure Cognitive Search Overview and Implementation*, and also include the following:

- **Entity recognition**
- **Language detection**
- **Key phrase extraction**
- **Text manipulation**
- **Sentiment detection**
- **PII detection**

- **Optical character recognition**

- **Facial detection**

- **Image interpretation**

- **Image recognition** (celebrities and landmarks)

Each of these services can be selected as options when building the search index for Cognitive Search and are applied as data is ingested into the index. They use the base Microsoft models that have been deployed as part of the cognitive services mentioned in the preceding paragraph but have limited capabilities. When building your solution, be sure to compare the full capabilities of the available cognitive services as they compare to the built-in options in Cognitive Search to check that they are not identical. This is especially important when you need to compare the base ML model that the skill uses, compared to the ability to build a custom model for a cognitive service. After developing the parameters required for this added skill, it can be inserted into the process and with any other custom skills developed, which we will outline in the following section.

Determining which of the services you would find beneficial to your document enrichment is an exercise you should consider before deploying the indexer. It certainly is a simple solution to just have all the enrichments available; however, this will slow down your indexing process, as well as cycling more compute, leading to more cost. This decision process, of course, requires an analysis of your data and what documents are being loaded for processing. If you know there will be certain categories of enrichment unused due to the type of media, skip it, and save yourself the time and cost.

Part of the reason for the inclusion of the **Optical Character Recognition** (**OCR**) and image recognition enhancements in the AI enrichment steps is because of the significant advancements in the services in recent years. We will explore these enhancements in the following section.

# Reviewing advancements in OCR and image recognition

As we discussed in *Chapter 4, Deriving Value from Knowledge Mining Solutions in Azure*, OCR is not exactly a new technology. However, some enhancements in recent years along with the ability to couple OCR with other text-related capabilities have helped many customers expand what they are now able to do with OCR. We have also seen similar increases in image processing capabilities as well as significant improvements in digital photography technology. As a result of these enhancements, we have much more ability to leverage the insights pulled using these technologies. Let's start with understanding what enhancements we gain by using OCR technology in Cognitive Search.

## Understanding OCR enhancements

The OCR enhancement skill included with the Cognitive Search service allows us to extract text from images that are processed. The text extracted can come from  handwritten or printed text as well as digits and currency symbols from PDF documents and images, with support for 122+ printed languages and 7+ handwritten languages. The service also has the capability to extract text from mixed-language documents.

After documents are digitized, the text is extracted from the images and documents, including handwritten text, and it is then structured using the JSON format for better accessibility. This extraction can autodetect the orientation of the text being extracted from the images, the language being used, where a line or sentence ends, and give an output of the location in the document where the text can be found. The location is specified using traditional $x$ and $y$ coordinates and allows us to jump to the text when accessing the API with our application to bring us directly to the text. We also have the ability to treat handwritten text and printed text as one and the same and extracted inline for reference. Furthermore, by leveraging the Entity Recognition skill alongside the OCR skill, extracted text can lead to entities in the text being called out and leveraged for further enhancement on how the information within documents can be used.

These capabilities and more available with the service help us to better extract key information from documents, no matter how the details appear within the documents that are within the text. It is important to note that this service is being provided by the Computer Vision API. Next, we will explore enhancements afforded by the same service when it comes to image processing.

## Exploring image recognition enhancements

The Image Analysis capabilities within Computer Vision allow us to analyze and provide a description of what is happening within an image. This ability allows us to describe a scene in a photo with text and add captions to photos. As the analysis is complete, the description is added to the other extracted elements from documents and allows for inclusion when searching using our deployed Cognitive Search application. This component alone is another outstanding feature of Cognitive Search AI enrichments, as without a manual description being added previously, it would have been impossible to ascertain from document management or an enterprise search tool previously. The underlying ML model used is loaded with famous landmarks, such as the Eiffel Tower, and celebrities, such as past US presidents, for recognition with Image Analysis. Also, part of this process allows us to map entities to objects within the images processed, which is another AI enrichment available in the service.

As we begin to look deeper at the service and define parameters, the first thing we can do is dictate what language our results are returned in. Currently, there are five options for languages, with the default being English. The next parameter we can specify relates to the type of content that is being analyzed. The following provides a high-level list of capabilities currently available categorizing the content:

- **Tags**: When the images are analyzed, they are assigned tags for the visual features of the images. As part of the tagging, each element in the image is tagged and assigned a confidence score for each item identified.

- **Object detection**: The detect object functionality makes a list of all items detected in an image with the coordinates of the object within the image itself.

- **Brand detection**: With the brand detection component, you can identify popular brands within videos and images that are included in the underlying model.

- **Categories**: Categories are similar to tags; however, tags create a hierarchical system whereas a category has a parent/child relationship with several items within it – for example, if an animal is detected and that animal is a dog, the category assigned would be `animal_dog`. The complete list of categories can be found here: `https://docs.microsoft.com/en-us/azure/cognitive-services/computer-vision/concept-categorizing-images`.

- **Describing an image**: By describing an image, we are creating a text description of what is happening in a photo along with the other detection features being used. Think of a farmhouse in Vermont set in a green pasture with a blue sky and a windmill in the background. This type of feature is very useful for developing accessibility features in modern software.

- **Detecting faces**: With the facial detection features, we are able to scan faces in photos, take measurements for identification purposes, use those details in future matching or security implications, and collect other features of the person in the image.

- **Adult content**: The service also detects images that may contain nudity, other sexual content, and images depicting violence. This capability is helpful to ensure content is not displayed to an inappropriate audience unintentionally.

The previous list gives an overview and idea of some of the highly advanced features within the Computer Vision service. There are also new services being rolled out frequently when common scenarios are presented as popular requests. Now that you have a better understanding of the services that are coupled with Cognitive Search, let's look at some other customer skills you may want to add to your KM solution.

# Considering other cognitive services commonly used in KM

In *Chapter 5, Azure Cognitive Search Overview and Implementation*, we gave a good overview of the capabilities available in the cognitive search tool when deploying the next-generation search solution using AI enrichments. Although Microsoft provides an extensive list of capabilities when building your KM solution natively to Cognitive Search, we recognize there are situations when other features are required to build your most effective solution. In this section, we are going to explore some other scenarios where we may want to process documents and other media further to add even more enrichment. This is done so by adding a **custom skill** to an enrichment pipeline within the **Cognitive Search indexing** process. Beyond adding other cognitive services as custom skills, you can also choose to use your own ML model that you have developed for one of the skills already included within the AI enrichments. There were frequently such cases where custom models were required for a business language and other situations where the Microsoft-managed and developed model was not sufficient.

In order to add a custom skill to your pipeline, you need to create a skillset that is executed when the text and Computer Vision enrichments are run. To create a skillset, you first need to decide whether you are using a cognitive service as it has been developed, your own custom skills that you have developed, or skills that involve logic for linking skills to be used together. You will define a name and description for your skillset, and then you must determine what type of skill you require from the former list. If using a cognitive service, you will need to use the `cognitiveServices` property as part of your JSON code. This ensures that you have ample compute for running the skillset, as it requires a billable plan you must set up to run. If you are using the native skills as available, you can specify them with the `skill` property, and it is billed by using the Cognitive Search compute already designated for running the pipeline. These are the skills we have previously discussed related to text and vision skills. The complete list of built-in skills can be referenced here with more details: `https://docs.microsoft.com/en-us/azure/search/cognitive-search-predefined-skills`.

Another option you can specify as part of the properties is whether you will extract the information to your knowledge store with the `knowledgeStore` property. We discussed this capability in *Chapter 5, Azure Cognitive Search Overview and Implementation*, but as a refresher, a knowledge store is where you can store your documents after they have been enriched with AI capabilities. This is in case you have downstream uses for the enriched documents, with metadata available for other uses as well. Finally, the last property is for connecting your enrichment skill to **Azure Key Vault**, for storing keys and secrets of **customer-managed keys**. By specifying the `encryptionKey` property in your skill, you can point to the Azure Key Vault where these keys are stored, assuming they are not **Microsoft-managed keys**. If you aren't specifying customer-managed keys for encrypting the skills you are deploying, this property isn't required. It is, however, always advisable to use encryption for any resource deployments when possible, but it is left to the discretion of each workload.

## Skills arrays

After you have determined which of the skills you would like to incorporate into your enrichment pipeline, you can include them in a **skills array**. This allows you to enter the parameters for each skill you would like to run, whether built-in or custom. When creating your JSON structure for running your pipeline, each of the skills will be defined separately with their **type**, **context**, **input**, and **output**. Each of the parameters is described in a bit more detail in the following list:

- **Type**: The type tag defines which of the built-in or custom skills you plan to use. Types use the following structure, beginning with the `"@odata.type"`: tag:

  - `"#Microsoft.Skills.<Category>.<Version>.<Skill Name>"` in the case of a built-in skill.

  - `"#Microsoft.Skills.Custom.WebAPISkill"` for using custom skills. If you would like to use Azure Machine Learning as a type, you would use `AmlSkill` in place of `WebAPISkill`.

  - `"#Microsoft.Skills.Util.ConditionalSkill"` for including the Conditional cognitive skill. The alternative options for `ConditionalSkill` would be `DocumentExtractionSkill`, allowing us to extract specific areas within a document using the Azure Cognitive Search service, or `ShaperSkill` for building custom datatype outputs such as concatenating fields.

- **Context**: The context tag defines the level where the skill is applied. The default level is the entire document; however, sub-nodes can be defined for more targeted operations. It is defined with the `"context"`: tag.

- **Inputs**: The inputs tag defines what the skill should expect for a source when processing. Examples of this are image, text, or video, depending on the skill that is being used.

- **Outputs**: The outputs tag allows us to define where the output of the process will go. This definition varies, based on what is available for each skill. As an example, the skill output for the OCR cognitive skill can be text or layout text. It should be noted that in order to use any of the details of the output operation, further considerations must be made. You can choose to send the output to a future skills input in your pipeline, send the details to the indexer by mapping to a field created, or create a projection and send the details to your knowledge store. Otherwise, the details of the output will not persist and cannot be used downstream.

By including these parameters, you can chain events together for running enrichments against your documents. The following code block gives an example of a skillset with a skills array chaining the skills together. The first section covers `name`, `description`, and built-in `skills` that can be added to the pipeline:

```
{
    "name":"skillset-template",
    "description":"A description makes the skillset self-documenting
```

```
(comments aren't allowed in JSON itself)",
    "skills":[
  {
    "@odata.type": "#Microsoft.Skills.Text.V3.EntityRecognitionSkill",
    "context": "/document",
    "categories": [ "Organization" ],
    "defaultLanguageCode": "en",
    "inputs": [
      {
        "name": "text",
        "source": "/document/content"
      }
    ],
    "outputs": [
      {
        "name": "organizations",
        "targetName": "orgs"
      }
    ]
  },
  {
    "@odata.type":
```

The section in the following code block displays the input and output for the Sentiment Analysis scoring enrichment:

```
"#Microsoft.Skills.Text.SentimentSkill",
    "context": "/document",
    "inputs": [
      {
        "name": "text",
        "source": "/document/content"
      }
    ],
    "outputs": [
      {
        "name": "score",
        "targetName": "mySentiment"
      }
    ]
  }
  ],
```

Finally, in the following section, we connect to a Cognitive Search instance using its key, as well as defining the location of our knowledge store and encryption key:

```
"cognitiveServices":{
    "@odata.type":"#Microsoft.Azure.Search.CognitiveServicesByKey",
    "description":"A Cognitive Services resource in the same region
as Azure Cognitive Search",
    "key":"<Your-Cognitive-Services-Multiservice-Key>"
},
"knowledgeStore":{
    "storageConnectionString":"<Your-Azure-Storage-Connection-
String>",
    "projections":[
        {
            "tables":[ ],
            "objects":[ ],
            "files":[ ]
        }
    ]
},
"encryptionKey":{ }
}
```

As the previous example is structured, you can see that we provide a name and description for the skillset we are developing. Next, we will define our skills to be performed – in this case, Entity Recognition and Sentiment. Then, we will align the cognitive service skills being used with Cognitive Search by ensuring it is in the same region. Optionally, we can define a knowledge store for our output documents with metadata to be used later in the process. Finally, we can define our encryption key as recommended, but it is not required.

Now that we have explored what a skills array looks like with some of the built-in skills and the structure of the document, let's look at what it takes to build a **custom skill** that can also be used as part of a skills array or by itself.

## Custom skills

Although the list of built-in skills is extensive for the text and Computer Vision services available, there are going to be situations where you need to use other cognitive services. The custom skill capability gives us the opportunity to tap into other services available and is deployed in largely the same way as a built-in skill. The following code is an example of how a custom skill is structured for deployment:

```
{
    "@odata.type": "#Microsoft.Skills.Custom.WebApiSkill",
    "description": "This skill calls an Azure function, which in turn
calls custom code",
    "uri": "https://<your function>.azurewebsites.net/api/
```

```
InvokeCode?code=foo",
  "httpHeaders": {
      "Ocp-Apim-Subscription-Key": "foobar"
  },
  "context": "/document/orgs/*",
  "inputs": [
    {
      "name": "query",
      "source": "/document/orgs/*"
    }
  ],
  "outputs": [
    {
      "name": "description",
      "targetName": "companyDescription"
    }
  ]
}
```

As you can see from the previous block of code, the structure of a custom skill is mostly the same as a built-in skill, with a few minor differences and the following parameters that are available with custom skills:

- `uri`: In our custom skill, we now have the ability to point where the service is that we want to run our custom code from in the form of a custom web API URL that we can connect to.

- `httpMethod`: Used to differentiate between a `Put` or `Post` operation when sending the payload to a web API.

- `httpHeaders`: Used to send header information with a payload for telling a web API how to handle an incoming data stream. An example would be to send configuration settings for handling the payload.

You also have the following optional parameters that can be used for the described purposes:

- `timeout`: When we specify the `timeout` parameter, it allows us to set how long to wait before timing out of an operation. The default is 30 seconds and can currently be set in a range of 1 to 230 seconds.

- `batchSize`: The `batchSize` parameter allows us to specify how many records will be sent in each web API call. There is a trade-off between the size of a payload as data is indexed coming in and how large the overall payload is to be considered for performance reasons.

- `degreeOfParallelism`: This parameter helps to tell the indexer service how many attempts should be made in parallel to your web API service. The default value is 5 and can range between 1 and 10, and is determined by the amount of incoming traffic the web API can handle.

After you have made the web API call with appropriate parameters for the complete payload sent by the indexer, the custom skill will then return a JSON payload with the results from running the skill. The returned results will be a set of **records** that are grouped into **values**. These can be used downstream in the application or returned as a result when used for a specific function.

There is a considerable amount of capability that can be offered by coupling built-in skills with custom skills, running them in a skills array, and using conditional logic to make determinations of how the indexer will use the skills. There is a public GitHub repository of common custom skills using other Azure cognitive services available here: `https://github.com/Azure-Samples/azure-search-power-skills`. When looking at the current list available in this repository, solutions have been developed utilizing many of the other cognitive services that aren't included in the Cognitive Search enrichments. Other OCR, text, vision, and Form Recognizer capabilities have been leveraged to give even more capabilities to your indexers for returning more accurate or pointed results.

Now that we have given some background on a few of the options available for AI enrichment in Azure Cognitive Search, let's take a look at getting started and including a custom skill into the indexer service you are using.

# Adding additional skills to your Cognitive Search indexer

It is once again time to build our solution for testing out the capabilities offered by Azure Cognitive Services – in this case, by deploying custom skills to our Cognitive Search indexer. The examples available are wide-ranging but help customers to gain the maximum value from their investment in their Cognitive Search solutions. Solutions for building the next-generation call centers where voice recordings are transcribed, indexed, flagged, and sent to the appropriate person for action have been developed using Cognitive Search with multiple custom skills. This type of deployment helps organizations to enhance their customer service experience, identifies individuals on the calls, translates various languages, makes text searchable from transactions, and so on.

The Form Recognizer service is commonly used as a custom skill within an enrichment pipeline. The service can be leveraged for identifying document types, building a chronology of events from documents, contract handling and detail captures, and many examples of processing payable and receivable documents, as they can be extracted and then sent to an **Enterprise Resource Planning (ERP)** system, as covered in *Chapter 8, Decluttering Paperwork with Form Recognizer*. If we wanted to use this example as a custom skill in our indexer pipeline, we would point our Cognitive Search enrichment service to the location of the web API where the service has already been deployed.

Using the Cognitive Search environment that we built in *Chapter 5, Azure Cognitive Search Overview and Implementation*, we can easily add a built-in or custom skill to our indexer by selecting **+ New Skillset** in our Cognitive Search overview environment on the **Skillsets** tab, selected in the lower pane:

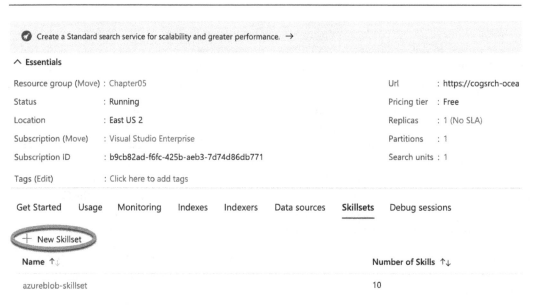

Figure 6.1 – The Overview screen of Cognitive Search where we create a new skillset in the Azure portal

The feature allows us to select or add a custom skill, a built-in Text skill, or a Util skill, including Conditional and built-in Vision skills. All the while, it helps to structure your JSON code for the necessary definitions of skills, input, and output required to build a full solution. We also have the ability to spin up new cognitive services as required for our deployment and to connect to the knowledge store, which we will use for downstream operations, if necessary, as shown in the following screenshot:

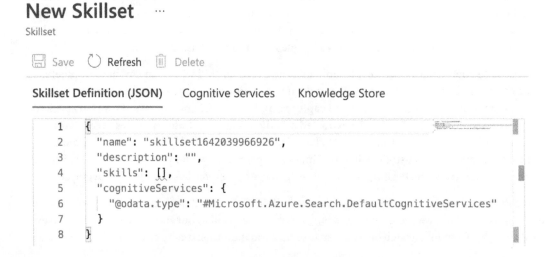

Figure 6.2 – The New Skillset dialog box with Cognitive Services and Knowledge Store connection options

As we choose the various types of skills we want to add, whether a custom skill, a custom skill with an Azure function, or many other options, our JSON template is built with the required structure, as shown in the following screenshot:

Figure 6.3 – Skill definition JSON templates for adding built-in and custom skills

By connecting to an existing service, or adding new services, you have many options for adding AI enrichments to your Cognitive Search indexer to fully experience your next-generation KM solution.

# Summary

As we finish up the overview of bringing custom enrichments to your KM solution, you should now have some ideas as to how you can enhance the solution for your environment. As popularity grows for certain enrichments, they may be added into the Cognitive Search service along with some of the already included options we covered in the previous chapter.

Alongside what we covered in *Chapter 5, Azure Cognitive Search Overview and Implementation,* you should be able to pull the details together and fully deploy your own solution from what you learned in this chapter. If you are still not quite sure what that entails, fear not, because in the next chapter, we are going to show you what it takes to deploy a complete KM solution with custom AI enrichments. We will also cover how using these services together can assist with improving productivity and operations inside your organization.

# 7

# Pulling It All Together for a Complete KM Solution

In the previous three chapters, we have provided a business case for why a **knowledge mining (KM)** solution will help your organization leverage troves of dark data – or data that sits in the shadows and is unavailable without manual searching by humans. We also discussed the process, in *Chapter 5*, of building your initial Azure Cognitive Search environment with associated built-in enrichments and indexers for building a metadata repository to enhance the search experience beyond traditional solutions. Finally, in *Chapter 6*, we provided the process for attaching other Azure Cognitive Services and custom solutions to your Cognitive Search environment to extract maximum detail from your latent data.

In this chapter, we are going to pull it all together to help you understand what a complete KM solution can provide to your organization, with further examples of ways to leverage the services available. To provide these examples, we will walk you through the following activities:

- Getting your Azure environment set up to support your KM solution
- Deploying the Azure Cognitive Search service
- Ingesting your data for indexing and related activities
- Connecting to and deploying related services
- Deploying the KM solution with monitoring and notification considerations

These examples will take you through how Ocean Smart was able to leverage the Cognitive Search service to index documents, connect to Form Recognizer to process documents, and extract key information from recorded customer service audio files to enhance the customer experience. All of these activities will be demonstrated in our Ocean Smart demo portal to test the solutions and provide code for your own deployment.

So, let's get started with the considerations you will need to make when approaching the full project and architecture for this solution and setting up your required Azure environment after quickly reviewing the technical requirements.

# Technical requirements

To build your complete KM solution with additional Cognitive Services, you will need to have an Azure subscription with at least *Contributor* rights to the subscription for deploying services. You will need an Azure storage account to store your documents pre- and post-processing. Depending on whether you plan to deploy the solution to a Docker container or an Azure web app, you should have experience with those technologies to ensure proper deployment. You will need to have Visual Studio Code (download Visual Studio Code for macOS, Linux, or Windows at `https://code.visualstudio.com/Download`) with the `node.js` extension installed (`https://nodejs.org/en/download/package-manager`).

Some other services you may use for your deployment are as follows:

- **Azure Functions** – for building functions and executing code
- **Azure Data Factory** or similar – for data orchestration and transformation
- **Azure Logic Apps** – for workflow and triggering mechanisms
- **Azure CosmosDB** – for storing output data post-processing
- **Azure Key Vault** – for the storage of secrets and certificates
- **Azure Storage Explorer** – for file movement from local storage to Azure Storage

Of course, the more complex and automated your solution is, the more tools you will likely need to know how to use and manage. As with everything, start with the basics, build your PoC, and add new features. This will help you to save precious time wasted with troubleshooting, and so on.

# Getting your Azure environment set up to support your KM solution

As with any deployment to Azure, you should determine what type of project you are building and what type of availability and redundancy you will need to support the project type. This is true even when looking at various production deployments of workloads. Is your application expected to be running all the time such as an e-commerce website, or are you deploying services to perform a once-a-month activity that has some flexibility, such as a movement of on-premises data to archive storage in the cloud? Depending on the business requirements, you will take into consideration how many additional services and capabilities will be required to meet those requirements.

To build your Azure Search solution with custom Cognitive Services and AI enrichments, you will need to understand the business requirements for developing the appropriate solution. In the case of Ocean Smart, our KM solution helps with processing invoice files, leveraging the Form Recognizer service, and transcribing recorded audio messages and conversations. This helps Ocean Smart improve the customer experience by analyzing the sentiment of the conversations, and to ensure that call center staff are properly trained. For Ocean Smart, the files are analyzed on a weekly basis with the output being reviewed by the customer service team. This data is also cross-referenced with details about when the audio was received via voice message or when the customer service call was recorded. Using that information together, Ocean Smart has a general idea of when the call took place, who the customer is, which support representative worked with the customer, and the overall sentiment score for the conversation. These details allow for further analysis to determine the best way to handle a negative interaction with a caller or message. The audio files captured can be listened to individually using the Ocean Smart portal. This allows for the actual tone and details of the call, as well as an opportunity to train the machine learning model used to score sentiment more acutely. Other key details can be pulled from the transcript of the call as well in the case where key data is captured by the call, such as the following:

- A service case number

- Product or sale details

- Caller details such as name, phone number, address, and more

These details are extracted when using the Speech Cognitive Service to capture a transcript of the audio contained in the files, then the transcript is indexed and enriched as part of the Cognitive Search process. Additional features of the Cognitive Search service will be used for the following capabilities:

- **Sentiment analysis** – The **Sentiment** skill contained within Text Analytics can be leveraged as part of the Cognitive Search service using the AI enrichment capability, as discussed in *Chapter 5*. This gives us the ability to analyze the text contained within a document and extract words and phrases that are aggregated to create a sentiment score. Using the API, a score is calculated from zero to one, which will help Ocean Smart get an overall sentiment score for a conversation or message.

- **Key-phrase extraction** – The Text Analytics Cognitive Service also gives us the ability to analyze our documents and extract key phrases for better context about the document. This skill is one of the more challenging capabilities to accurately derive results from, as overall insight is subjective. However, a finely trained and retrained model with feedback for continual improvement and a general sense of what is occurring in the text can be extracted.

- **Personally Identifiable Information (PII) extraction** – PII extraction can be critical for obtaining details about who the caller is and how they can be reached by phone or email, among other details. Depending on the nature of the business, securing these details can be critical to ensuring compliance with handling PII for regulations such as **Global Data Protection Regulation (GDPR)** for European customers and the **California Consumer Privacy Act (CCPA)**. Even if these standards aren't relevant to your use case, it would be beneficial to have a broad understanding of these regulations to ensure any possible present or future compliance concerns when handling customer data.

- **Silence detection** – Knowing when a customer is on hold or waiting idly for a customer service representative can be a factor in overall customer sentiment and service. We can determine the time in which a call is silent, and the proportion of the overall call time where this is the case, then correlate it to the sentiment of a call. With this information, we may be able to better understand the point at which a customer begins to lose patience and use this data as another area to assist with training or proper staffing requirements.

- **Translation services** – Where Ocean Smart has global distributors and customers they directly sell to, we can take advantage of Speech Translation services to gain a better understanding of what concerns a foreign customer has. This can also be used as a mechanism for enumerating locales where calls are coming from that are non-English speaking to consider what types of languages are most common among customers. Also, identifying and documenting what language is being spoken can assist with finding a person within the company who speaks the language and more quickly serve the customer's needs.

- **Historical detail capture** – After the key details of the calls are captured, we can then take the documented information and associate it with a customer service case. As we capture these details historically, it can help with customer churn and retention details. If we see that a customer has had similar concerns that are founded, we can ensure to provide even better customer service to hopefully retain a customer who has had repeated negative experiences. Retaining good customers is always less costly than acquiring new customers, so Ocean Smart wants to ensure all measures are taken to retain them.

Using all the services and analyses just listed, we will be able to have significant data about what Ocean Smart customers experience when calling customer service for support. To obtain all this data, we will have to deploy the following Azure services as part of our project:

- Azure Storage

- Azure Functions

- Azure Cognitive Search with built-in and custom skills, including the following:

  - Speech-to-Text

  - Sentiment

  - PII extraction

  - Text translation

  - Language detection

  - Key-phrase extraction

  - Custom **Named Entity Recognition (NER)**

- Azure CosmosDB

We will also use these services to extract key details from contracts with customers, partners, and suppliers, along with Form Recognizer for documents with a consistent structure. These details will allow us to have all the content available for additional details related to each customer when examining relationships and necessary activities to ensure superior customer service.

As discussed in the *Technical requirements* section earlier in the chapter, ensure you have the appropriate permissions to deploy these services, as well as the development tools you'll use for deploying the solution. Now that you have a good idea of the services you will use, let's start with deploying our foundation services with Azure Cognitive Search and related configurations needed to use service enhancements.

# Deploying the Azure Cognitive Search service

To support your complete KM solution, you will use Azure Cognitive Search as the foundation for all the additional capabilities you will deploy for maximizing the value of your KM, and many of the features that set apart a KM from traditional data management solutions. For detailed instructions on deploying your Cognitive Search service, refer to *Chapter 5*. Here, we will focus on specific configurations that will be required when going beyond your proof of concept and looking to deploy a production solution. First, let's take a look at deploying your storage account.

## Azure storage account deployment

As you get started deploying your storage account, keep in mind the application of the solution and the business requirements you need to consider as part of the configuration. If you intend to have multiple search service deployments – for instance, access from multiple geographies – storage redundancy and speed will be paramount to performance. An example of this is evaluating the two performance tiers for the storage account:

- **Standard Tier:** The Standard tier for Azure Storage is used to deploy hierarchical data lakes, block blob, and other storage types where service level agreements for speed and availability meet the requirements specified.

- **Premium Tier:** The Premium tier for Azure Storage provides higher throughput for workloads that require more volume of smaller data files. Because this tier leverages **solid state drives** (**SSDs**), as opposed to **hard disk drives** (**HDDs**) on the Standard tier, you can expect faster performance but also a higher cost. For more details on SLAs for Azure storage accounts, refer to the Microsoft documentation found here: `https://azure.microsoft.com/en-us/support/legal/sla/storage/v1_5/`.

So, as you evaluate which tier of service you will want to use, be sure to consider the availability options, covered in more detail in *Chapter 2*, and the cost ramifications of the chosen tier. As with many other topics we have covered thus far in the book, there will always be a cost versus benefit analysis in deciding which levels of service, and the business requirements that have been defined. You can also consider having a more diversified architecture, where only the most important and highest-demand documents are stored in the Premium tier and everything else is in the Standard tier, to help save some cost. A practical application for this would be to store documents and files that need processing quickly in a Premium storage account, then move them to a different location after being processed, and then the enriched documents for post-processing can be stored in a Standard storage account. There are many ways to build your architecture for a Cognitive Search solution, so evaluate options of complexity, availability, features, and costs for best results. Next, we will look at the deployment considerations you should make when creating your Cognitive Search service in a more detailed exercise.

## Deploying Cognitive Search for your KM solution

In *Chapter 5*, we went through the details of what configurations you will need for deploying the Cognitive Search service, but that was mostly focused on building a proof of concept. For a production workload, you must take into consideration the performance requirements and the volume of data needed to support your KM solution. To best evaluate which tier will be required for deploying your solution, there are several variables that must be determined to ensure proper performance, features, and storage thresholds. Requirements are challenging to ascertain without implementing the service directly with so many variables to consider, so our recommendation is to get started with the guidance in *Chapter 5* and build from there. The list of variables is described here briefly, but as limits, tiers, and offerings frequently change, always check with the most recent Microsoft documentation for evaluation:

- **Storage requirements** – It is important to realize that when we talk about storage in a Cognitive Search solution, we are not just referring to the base documents we will use for extraction. Storage requirements will certainly include the source documents, but you will also need to consider imported data, text analysis, and index configuration, such as whether you enable suggesters, filtering, and sorting. One thing to keep in mind is that you should only load documents that can actually be searched. You don't want to load binary documents, as they will just take up space and cost you more to store.

- **Number of indexes** – Depending on the complexity of operations, you could need any number of indexes for your Cognitive Search deployment. You will also need to evaluate the number of indexes required against your storage requirements to determine whether you will use Standard or Storage-Optimized tiers. For the latter, it is assumed you have large volumes of data but simple on the indexing side as they only allow for a max of 10 indexes.

- **Scale out units** – When talking about cloud workloads, there are two concepts it would be good to understand: horizontal scaling and vertical scaling. Horizontal scaling means that we are adding compute nodes to our workload, essentially deploying the compute resources side-by-side to double, triple, and so on, the compute resources. Vertical scaling means we add compute to the existing nodes in the form of processor speed and memory added to the node. If we want to minimize the amount of time required to process our search workloads, we can run operations in parallel by scaling out our compute resources in the form of partitions and replicas. Depending on your requirements for partitions and replicas, your tier will be determined based on the limitations per tier:

  - **Partitions** – Partition sizes are assigned to various tiers and levels available based on Microsoft's analysis of combinations of compute and storage pairings. If your indexes require more available storage and perhaps less querying compute, you will want larger partition sizes as opposed to the number of partitions assigned. This is another analysis that will likely take some fine-tuning over time to run optimally for your operations. You can refer to the following link for more detail on making estimates: `https://learn.microsoft.com/en-us/azure/search/search-sku-tier`.

  - **Replicas** – Replicas are copies of your indices running on independent hardware for each copy. The amount and configuration of your replicas will also determine the SLA you receive from Microsoft. To achieve 99.9% availability, you will require two replicas for querying, and three replicas for workloads that will be queried and indexed.

- **Document cracking and custom entity lookup skills** – As we get further down the list of capabilities for our Cognitive Search deployment, we start to see services that rely on the Azure Cognitive Services suite and App Services for running more custom enrichments. These are priced based on a per thousand counts of documents, images, and so on, and then based on the size of each of the documents. Use the pricing calculator to review the latest costs associated with each activity.

- **Private endpoints** – To provide enhanced security for your Cognitive Search environment, you can deploy private endpoints at a cost per endpoint. Private endpoints further secure your environment by allowing access to your private IP assigned to your resources from other Azure assets deployed, and only those assets. This prevents the need to expose these resources to the public internet and is recommended wherever possible to be used.

- **Semantic Search** – We covered Semantic Search in more detail in *Chapter 5*, but it is important to note that the minimum tier it can be deployed to is the Standard tier. Semantic Search gives you the ability to match a document more closely to your query by using AI to summarize the document and add a secondary ranking system for results. Currently, the Standard tier starts at $249 per compute month, but 0-1,000 semantic queries in a month are included in that tier. Anything above that threshold is a flat fee per month for up to 250,000 queries and a minimal charge per query thereafter. As demonstrated, this service adds quite a bit of value to your service – however, at a hefty cost – so be sure to evaluate your needs to maximize value.

- **Customer Managed Keys (CMKs)** – CMKs or **Bring Your Own Key (BYOK)** concepts are handled universally across Azure in that if you have a requirement to use your own key in Azure, they are available with certain services. In the case of Azure Cognitive Search, as long as you are using a paid tier, they are included within the service and are at no extra charge. If using CMKs, you will also need to use Azure Key Vault to store secrets, certificates, and so on. For more details on implementing CMKs in Cognitive Search, refer to this document: `https://docs.microsoft.com/en-us/azure/search/search-security-manage-encryption-keys`.

- **Managed Identities** – Another feature frequently used within production-level deployments in Azure is Managed Identities. Managed Identities allow you to use a system-assigned or service account for authentication to resources to avoid needing traditional username and password authentications. This is useful when services are used in sequence, and you would be required to pass the authentication through a connection string or similar mechanism. Managed Identities are supported in a subset of use cases, so it is advisable to review those situations listed within the documentation here: `https://docs.microsoft.com/en-us/azure/search/search-howto-managed-identities-data-sources?tabs=portal-sys%2Cportal-user`.

To reiterate, you will want to start with a smaller deployment and add resources and compute as you add enrichments. Because of all the configurations and ways the service costs can begin to add up, try to maintain the focus on providing quick wins and building value over time – the recurring theme of this book. Next, we are going to look at the various ways we will acquire our data, the most important piece of our KM solution.

## Ingesting your data for indexing and related activities

Ok, so we have discussed how we are going to store the data we will use, but there are many considerations about how we want to attain initial data for indexing and how we will continue to add data to our KM solution to enhance the value of our data.

In common data acquisition scenarios, we can extract the data from a myriad of locations through various **Application Programming Interfaces (APIs)**, databases, document storage locations, and so on. In the case of acquiring and transcribing your audio files, there are a few ways this could be handled, and as the writers of this book, we struggled to determine the best option. The reason for this is somewhat of the positive, yet negative, mailability of the Azure platform. I will spare you some cheesy colloquialism about having many ways of doing the same thing, but know each solution is unique to the organization it is being built for, so oftentimes, it will come down to what is the most cost-effective for you. Ultimately, we want to grab our audio files, either left in voice mail or an audio file that was from a recorded phone conversation, and whatever phone system you use will help determine the best way to do this. We can pick up those files from a stored location using a data orchestration tool such as Azure Data Factory, or similar, and land them in our storage account.

Alternatively, we could have a mechanism for sending the files and data from the location they are stored, such as a small service or application running locally, to our storage account. In the example we will provide for the Ocean Smart portal, we use a traditional web form for uploading the file. When it lands in our storage account, we will trigger an action to begin extracting text from the file to build our transcript. This extraction will be done using the Azure Speech-to-Text Cognitive Service, which is covered in full in *Chapter 13*.

## Azure Speech-to-Text for audio transcription

The Azure Speech-to-Text Cognitive Service (try saying that five times fast!) is one of the more mature Cognitive Services, which achieved human parity in 2016, as described in the following blog: `https://blogs.microsoft.com/ai/historic-achievement-microsoft-researchers-reach-human-parity-conversational-speech-recognition/`. Over 100 languages are supported for converting recorded or streaming audio to text, and the service has been embedded in other popular Microsoft applications, such as PowerPoint, for real-time captions while delivering presentations. In our case, we will call the Speech-to-Text service prior to our indexing activity with the Cognitive Search pipeline when the audio file lands in our storage account using **batch transcription**. The option to provide transcription services in real time is available but we would require a different method of acquiring our data, including capturing the audio at the time of it being recorded and redirecting it to the service. While this is certainly a viable option, it doesn't have a practical application in the case of Ocean Smart's requirements, so batching will be sufficient.

The Speech-to-Text service offers the ability to use the standard Microsoft machine learning model to transcribe the audio or build a domain-specific model for transcribing business-related terminology. For the initial application, we deployed the standard model as, with our customer service enhancement workload, it is far less technical than if we were transcribing audio from production operations or similar. We cover the differences and specifications for employing the two models in greater detail in *Chapter 13*. As we process our files and produce the transcript, we will then land that transcript in our storage account for processing with the additional activities performed by the Cognitive Search service.

## Loading files in Form Recognizer for processing

As with the audio files required for transcription, Ocean Smart needs a location to upload contracts for extracting details of agreements established with vendors, partners, and customers using Form Recognizer. We give a complete example of Form Recognizer in *Chapter 8*, where we elaborate on the full details of the service and considerations when deploying it for a PoC or production workload. We also give an example of how the files are uploaded for processing using the Ocean Smart portal. In that example, we describe how to process an invoice provided by a vendor and various downstream activities and options you have for the invoices. For the KM, although there is value in capturing this detail as part of the overall document indexing, the invoices have a transactional purpose. In our KM solution, however, we felt there was more value in recognizing and cataloging our agreements for capturing details of terms, dates, and details of who each agreement is with. As part of our complete KM solution, we will provide complete details of how to call the Form Recognizer service from Cognitive Search and add the custom skills to capture and catalog these details.

There are numerous ways to load our contract documents into the storage account for processing, so we can have two options:

- The first is by using Cognitive Search to recognize a document as an "agreement" or "contract" in our KM pipeline

- The second is to directly load a document as a contract in a specific storage container to be directly processed by Form Recognizer

Our example later in the chapter will elaborate on this process more completely. Next, we will look at what we are going to do with the rest of the data to load it into our KM solution.

## Bulk loading of everything else

The previous two sections focus on our data related to a specific purpose, extracting text from audio files, and details from contractual documents. In this section, we are going to discuss strategies for the rest of the content we want to load into our KM. Again, the flexibility of the Azure platform allows us many ways to accomplish the task of loading gigabytes, terabytes, and even petabytes of data in some cases initially, as well as how we will load new documents and files as we acquire them.

So, you have a ton of latent historical data that you want to extract value from, and you want to build a strategy to get that data into a KM solution but are unsure where to start. Does this sound familiar? There are seemingly endless options for getting the data there, from command-line tools to streaming and bulk-loading of data. The first place to start building this strategy is to evaluate costs and time requirements. You are also going to want to have a good understanding of where all your data is being sourced from, and if all your documents have been digitized as well. Oftentimes, organizations have troves of paper files they need to hang onto for regulatory and other purposes, so you'll want to determine whether that should also be considered as part of your KM solution, as you'll need to make arrangements to get that data digitized.

With these considerations in mind, the following provides a brief overview of some tools Microsoft provides to get your data into Azure, but only really highlights some of the most popular options:

- **AZ Copy** – AZ Copy is Microsoft's command-line file copy tool, which provides a secure connection to your storage account from where you want to load files. Generally, you will use this tool for one-off or scripted operations in the form of a "push" of data. Really ambitious folks could script the entire file-based data push from a location to their storage account, and the service will eventually get the data there; however, connection interruptions and large file sizes could cause challenges with this approach.

- **Azure File Explorer** – Azure File Explorer is a graphical user tool for moving files from a local system to a storage account in a familiar Microsoft Windows interface. In a similar fashion to the AZ Copy tool, File Explorer is good for one-time operations for files, but it cannot be batched with scripting, so it is not advisable to be used for large movements of data.

- **Azure Data Factory (ADF)** – ADF is a common tool for batch data movement operations running on a schedule or triggered by an API call or some other action. ADF has additional features for transforming data and is frequently used for data warehousing activities, but could be used for massive data loads if desired. General recommendations for ADF would put the data amounts in the tens of gigabytes at a maximum size but could be used for recurring loads of data after the initial data load is complete. ADF can also be used to extract data from on-premises databases and put the data into file formats such as `.parquet`, which are ideal for distributed systems such as Azure Storage. This may be a good use case if you have legacy database systems where there may be valuable data stored, and will add more value to your KM solution.

- **Azure Data Box** – Azure Data Box was designed for the bulk loading of data into a storage account. There are various sizes and iterations of Data Box devices, ranging from approximately 40 TB of storage to 1 PB of storage. The device is connected to the local network, has files loaded onto it, and is then shipped to the Azure Region where your storage account resides, and the data is loaded. Each appliance is hardened to protect against physical issues such as drops and wet conditions and includes data encryption for the files that are loaded. Another option in the Data Box family is the Azure Data Box Gateway. The Gateway is a virtual appliance that is deployed to a hypervisor at the local facility with network access and has a synchronization feature that will continually send data to the chosen storage account. Features are available to limit when and how much data is sent to avoid network and internet congestion during normal working hours.

- **Third-party tools** – Beyond the native Azure options and features listed previously, several third-party options are available in the Azure Marketplace that offer the ability to stream data into Azure storage and other destinations such as a data lake or Blob Storage. There are also third-party storage options within Azure for working with existing products, such as NetApp and other leading vendors of file storage and replication. These options may be cost-effective means of moving your data into Azure if you are already licensed for the products and services these vendors provide.

Although not exhaustive, the preceding list was intended to give some suggestions on how you might want to load your data into your storage account to then be processed by Cognitive Search with AI enrichments. With that, you should now have a basis for how to load all your data types initially and repeatedly for new data created. Next, we will discuss how to use various connectors within Cognitive Search and how the flow of data will be completed.

## Connecting to and deploying related services

Okay, one more overview until we deploy our full solution, where we will cover the process of connecting to services that reside outside of the core functionality of Cognitive Search. In *Chapter 6*, we covered the ability to deploy custom enrichments from the Cognitive Search service for when you want to have skills that are not native in detail. Here, we will look at the flow of the various enrichments we will use, and how the entire operation will be stitched together as we build out our full solution.

As we discuss the full solution in this context, we are referring specifically to the various operations that the Ocean Smart portal will handle for processing audio and data files that will add to the overall intelligence the KM solution provides to the company. For this purpose, there are three main operations:

- Processing audio files with Cognitive Speech-to-Text and outputting the transcript from those audio files for downstream details to be extracted

- Extracting key details from contract and agreement documents with customers, vendors, and other business partners, such as dates, terms, organizations, individuals, and other relevant information

- All the processing of the remainder of data and documents that are enhanced with AI skills, and the insights that can be extracted in totality, adding to the overall value of the KM solution

Although the three operations handle the files differently as they are ingested, they all eventually add to the KM solution and provide additional intelligence assets to the details about a specific customer, vendor, or partner. For instance, we can capture details from an audio recording with a customer and have that detail available to us as part of the KM solution when looking for details about that specific customer with a search. This would also be true of a contract and other related documents when searching for a particular customer name. Depending on whether the Semantic Search feature is enabled, and understanding there are added costs for this service, each of the files could be summarized in paragraph form using the AI enrichment and displayed as part of the results of a search.

In the following subsections, we will show the flow of files as they are added for each of the scenarios listed previously, then finally, we will show the details of the solution as it is built in Azure. We will start with the flow of information for processing audio files using Speech-to-Text and outputting a transcript of the call.

## Batch processing audio files with Cognitive Speech

As we begin looking at the transcription operations, I want to make sure that I remind you that handling streaming audio is a very different process than batch transcription. Our example is for taking calls that have been recorded previously and then transcribed with the transcription being sent to Cognitive Search for further enrichment. For streaming audio workloads, we are transcribing in near real time and then sending that transcription to an application or something similar. This feature is the same as is used in applications such as PowerPoint for live captions of what is being spoken as an accessibility feature.

Our examples will be of two types:

- A voicemail recording that a customer left for customer service or a similar department
- A recorded customer service call that has been recorded between a customer service representative and a customer

We could choose to handle these types of calls separately and more accurately specify the features used for handling the different call types, but that adds complexity to the architecture and, ultimately, more likely additional costs. The most obvious feature where this applies is **diarization**, otherwise known as **speaker recognition**. This feature can recognize two different speakers within a conversation that is being transcribed and labels them as a "1" or "2" within the transcription output document. This is an optional feature, but we will leave it on for simplicity of deployment overall. Another feature that we will use in our example is sending the transcribed document to a location where it will be processed by the Cognitive Search service. This feature is called the **destination container URL**. If this isn't specified, the files will instead be stored in a Microsoft-managed container, and we have no control over how long that document would persist. Because we are looping Cognitive Services together, Speech then Search, we want to have control over where the document resides pre- and post-processing. We also want to ensure we can reference back to the source audio file after processing in case we need to listen to the audio at a future date. To make sure the audio is available and referenceable, we will need to move it to a storage blob and have it referenced from some interface – in our case, the Ocean Smart portal.

The following represents the flow of data as it moves from ingestion to processing and onto Cognitive Search for further processing:

1. The audio file lands in the blob storage landing zone.
2. An action is triggered using an Azure Functions app to start audio processing with the Speech-to-Text service.
3. The text is extracted into a document and saved to a storage blob for pick up later by the Cognitive Search service using the `destinationContainerUrl` parameter and specifying the storage container.
4. The audio file is copied to the storage container where it will be permanently stored and referenced later by the Ocean Smart portal.
5. The source audio file is deleted to ensure unnecessary files are not taking up unnecessary space, resulting in unnecessary costs, and eliminating the risk of double processing.
6. Downstream operations will commence on files sent to the Cognitive Search pickup container.

Now that the text has been extracted from our audio file, it will be processed by Cognitive Search to apply our AI enrichments and capture critical details about the call or message. Next, we will discuss the process for extracting key information from contracts we want to track as they relate to customers, crucial dates, and other details we want to keep track of.

## *Extracting key details from contracts with Form Recognizer*

In *Chapter 8*, we provide full details of a Form Recognizer example where we can extract key elements of an invoice from a vendor and use those elements in downstream operations. If you are looking for the full deployment steps for the service, that is the best place to start. Here, we will discuss the process at a higher level, for loading our contracts using the Ocean Smart portal and using the Form Recognizer service to capture the critical details of those contracts and agreements. The Form Recognizer can be used for many types of examples of documents where standard rules apply to the document and we can extract the required details. This process can use a layout that is defined by the service for various types of documents, ranging from invoices to receipts and more. For more custom or proprietary documents, such as our case of a contract or agreement, we will likely use a custom layout and define the details where they exist and can be extracted. This works great when we are using a standard Ocean Smart contract that we provide to a partner, customer, or vendor after we build our custom model using the **Layout** tool with five examples of a contract. However, it gets a bit more challenging when we want to use a contract that is provided to us alternatively. For this purpose, we will cover the details of extracting the contents using a custom layout we create for our contract, and lightly address the process for using one-off or custom documents provided to us.

The following is an overview of the process for landing the contract files in our storage container using the portal and processing the document, which will ultimately land in our KM solution for further processing:

1.  To get started, as with our audio files, we will have a storage blob that our Ocean Smart portal will send the files to when they are uploaded.

2.  As these files land in the blob, an action will be triggered to use an Azure Functions function to start the Form Recognizer service API.

3.  As we will do in *Chapter 8*, our Form Recognizer service has been containerized to allow for the portability of the service and will use the trained custom model to process the document and extract the defined insights.

4.  From there, we will complete the processing of the enriched document and add it to our KM solution for additional detail extraction.

5.  We will also take the key details from the contract, such as organization details, start and end dates, and specific contract terms.

6.  These details are then written to a database for tracking purposes and can be displayed using the Ocean Smart portal.

7.  After processing by the Form Recognizer service is complete, we will then remove the document from the landing blob and choose to archive or delete it at the discretion of key stakeholders.

Our example in the next section of this chapter will elaborate further on some of the settings and configurations we make to support the data extraction described previously.

Finally, we will next look at the rest of the processing of data that we will do with Cognitive Search as we finish the deployment of our KM solution.

### Collecting other documents for completing our KM solution

As previously described, our KM solution is composed of a collection of documents and data from a variety of sources. These could be electronic documents from a file server, details extracted from a database or data warehouse, or in our previous two examples, the output of processing audio files with the Speech-to-Text Cognitive service and contract details using Form Recognizer. Mind you, this is just the beginning of the list of sources that can be used for building the complete solution. The real value is when we have all the documents and source data in a single location so that when an associate goes through a search for a customer or some other type of query, all related documents and information are centralized and returned. This value comes from the significant time and complexity saved when performing our search and being able to quickly sort through all assets available as they relate to that specific query. Whether we capture the overall sentiment analysis of customer-related documents or use Semantic Search to be able to quickly digest what a complete document is about with a quick summarizing paragraph, it helps our teams be more efficient when looking for key information.

In *Chapter 5*, we covered the considerations you should make when designing and building your Cognitive Search solution. Reference that detail to understand what is required for the solution you intend to build and the steps for doing so. Here, we will pull the complete solution together, including the previous two sections of this chapter, and display the flow of data as we work through our indexer to build the completed index. As described in the previous sections, we are performing several steps to satisfy any of the preliminary data collection steps needed to centralize our data for pickup and processing by our indexer, somehow landing that data into a storage container. From there, we will follow the process described in the next list, eventually populating our index to search and using the Ocean Smart portal to display those results and relevant details:

1.  Initially, we must define how frequently we want to index our storage container. We have options to trigger a new indexing based on files landing in our starting storage container or running on a schedule based on a time of day, week, and so on. If we decide we'd like to trigger an action based on a file landing in storage, this could become quite expensive and may require a slightly more sophisticated architecture to support the on-demand nature of the triggering.

2.  Next, we will bring the source data into our temporary storage, where the documents are indexed and metadata added.

3.  After the documents are loaded into the temporary storage, we will begin to apply our AI enrichments for all related services we choose to use, from NER to sentiment score to PII detection. These are all defined by your pipelines and the enrichments you choose. Remember though, in *Chapter 5*, the more enrichments you add, the more costs you incur, and the longer the indexing process takes to complete. All these considerations are necessary for defining SLAs for the consumers of your KM solution.

4.  At this point, you will decide whether you want to send those enriched documents with metadata applied to another storage location for further use downstream. If so, those documents would be stored in another storage container and used elsewhere later.

5.  When our index is built, we decide what interface we will use to query our data and return the results of that query – in our case, using the Ocean Smart portal, a web interface, but it could just as easily be a Microsoft Power App or an other similar option. In the portal, we give users the ability to perform a search, with defined parameters such as specific types of results to return and so on based on the enrichments we have applied. Initially, this returns a list of results and allows the user to preview the document, data, audio file, and so on for closer inspection, as well as allowing them to download the file if required.

Hopefully, this provides some thoughts on how you might want to approach your own KM solution, and now we'll show you what it looks like in an all-in-one interface by walking you through a full solution deployed to the Ocean Smart portal.

## Deploying the KM solution with monitoring and notification considerations

The capabilities of the Cognitive Search service discussed in the past few chapters along with the enhanced skills available make it clear how powerful this solution can be. Now, let's look at a practical deployment of the service for a KM tool within Ocean Smart. We wanted the common user to be able to search for data within the repository of captured files, including documents, images, audio, and video. Using our Django portal that we use throughout the book, we have a simple interface allowing the common user to search and decide which file types they would want to be returned. In the following screenshot, you see an example of a simple search for `lobster` with the resulting files within a document and image search:

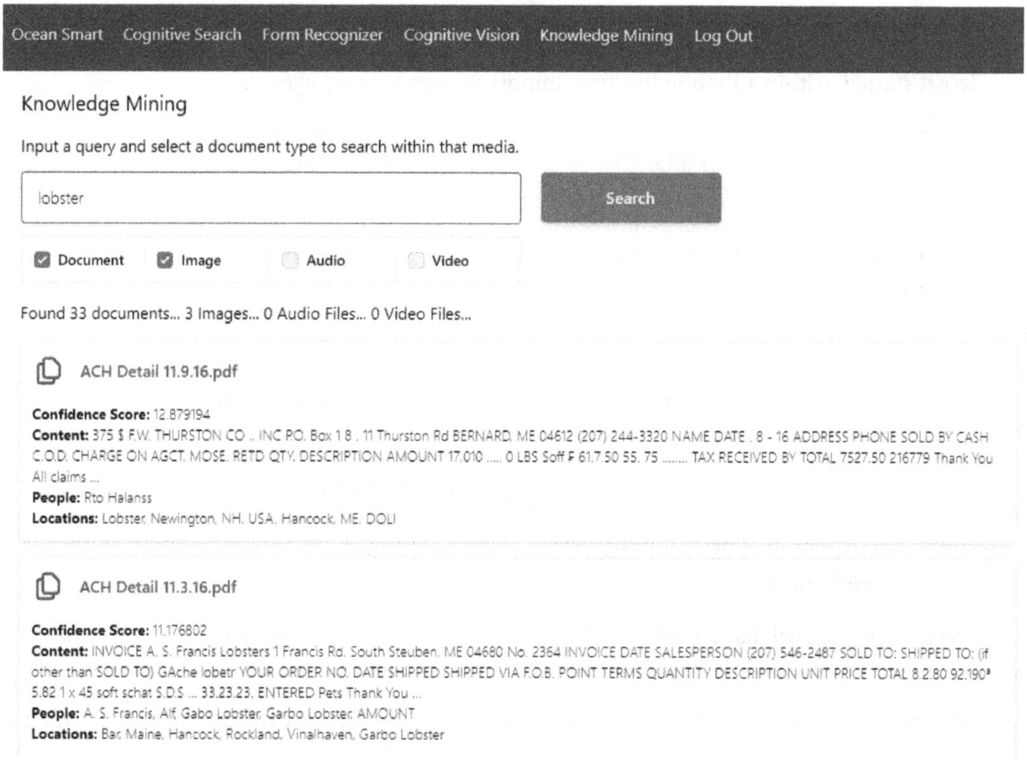

Figure 7.1 – Ocean Smart search interface for identifying files
containing information related to our search term

Because of how we have configured the portal, we have selection criteria that will provide instructions as to what types of media to return in a search. When the list of files is returned, we can opt to have the user download and review the file, or configure our portal to display the file, show a picture, or play a video in a preview tool. This will be left up to how you want to deploy your solution, but all aspects of search and display can be configured through the portal or via your REST API call.

In the next subsection, we will take you through how we develop the code to deploy this solution.

## Showing the code

Searching the indexers is the same process as any other search within the Cognitive Services Search service. The differences are which skillsets we specify within the indexer and how we want to ingest data into the search service to be mined.

Let's look at building our input and expected output from running the code:

1. To get started, within a Python file, first, import the needed packages:

```
import os
from azure.core.credentials import AzureKeyCredential
from azure.search.documents import SearchClient
```

2. Now create a function to use a query and an indexer ID to return a list of results from the search service:

```
def search_index(query: str, indexer: str = None) -> list:
    endpoint = str(os.getenv('AZURE_COG_SEARCH_ENDPOINT'))
    credential = AzureKeyCredential(str(os.getenv('AZURE_COG_
SEARCH_CREDENTIAL')))
    client = SearchClient(endpoint=endpoint,
                          index_name=indexer,
                          credential=credential)
    results = client.search(search_text=query)
    return results
```

The resulting list will have a JSON blob of data for each item returned. Depending on what is specified in your index in Cognitive Search, you will render out each item as you see fit.

3. An example of a JSON returned result from an Image Analyzer skill will look similar to this output:

```
{
    «id»: «aabbccddeeffgg",
    «metadata_storage_name": "cooked-lobster.jpg",
    «description»: [
        {
            «tags»: [
                «animal»,
                «arthropod»,
                «invertebrate»,
                «red»,
                «lobster»
            ],
```

Here, we see a list of captions applied to the image:

```
"captions": [
    {
        «text»: «a red hand with a white background»,
        «confidence»: 0.3059108853340149
    }
]
}
],
```

4.    Now, we list the categories identified, if any:

```
"categories": [
  {
    «name»: «others_»,
    «score»: 0.00390625,
    «detail»: null
  }
],
```

5.    The tags can help to identify characteristics of the contents of the image:

```
"tags": [
  {
    «name»: «invertebrate»,
    «hint»: null,
    «confidence»: 0.9990673065185547
  },
],
«objects»: [],
«content»: «\n»,
«metadata_storage_path": "images/cooked-lobster.jpg",
«@search.score": 0.8871527,
«@search.highlights": null
}
```

Using the Image Analysis skill allows you to take an image document such as a JPG or PNG and Azure will process this image and return data on it. An example of using Image Analysis can be created with a JSON definition with a new skillset within Cognitive Search.

An example of an image analysis skillset is in the following code:

```
{
  «@odata.context»: «https://<cog_search_name>.search.windows.
net/$metadata#skillsets/$entity",
  «@odata.etag": "\"0x8DB0E59927A5F42\"",
  «name»: «<custom_name>",
  «description»: «»,
  «skills»: [
    {
```

6.    Here, we specify which skill we will use with a name, description, context, and default language:

```
      «@odata.type»: «#Microsoft.Skills.Vision.
ImageAnalysisSkill»,
      «name»: «#1»,
      «description»: «Extract image analysis.»,
      «context»: «/document/normalized_images/*",
      «defaultLanguageCode": "en",
```

In this snippet of code, we call out which of the features we want to identify from the following list:

```
«visualFeatures": [
  «adult»,
  «brands»,
  «categories»,
  «description»,
  «faces»,
  «objects»,
  «tags»
],
«details»: [],
```

7. Next, we define our input:

```
«inputs»: [
  {
    «name»: «image»,
    «source»: «/document/normalized_images/*"
  }
],
```

8. We will also define the output we want returned to us. In this case, we want categories, description faces, and tags returned, as seen in the following code:

```
«outputs»: [
  {
    «name»: «categories»,
    «targetName": "categories"
  },
  {
    «name»: «description»,
    «targetName": "description"
  },
  {
    «name»: «faces»,
    «targetName": "faces"
  },
  {
    «name»: «tags»,
    «targetName": "tags"
  }
  ]
}
],
```

9.   Finally, we identify aspects of the Cognitive Services we are leveraging and information about where they are hosted:

```
"cognitiveServices": {
    "@odata.type": "#Microsoft.Azure.Search.
CognitiveServicesByKey",
    "description": "/subscriptions/<subscription_id> /
resourceGroups/<resource_group> /providers/Microsoft.
CognitiveServices/accounts/<cognitive_account> ",
    "key": "<cognitive_services_key>"
  },
  "knowledgeStore": null,
  "encryptionKey": null
}
```

After this, an index must be created to hold the data returned from the Image Analyzer indexer. A full list of fields can be found within the Microsoft documentation: `https://learn.microsoft.com/en-us/azure/search/cognitive-search-skill-image-analysis?WT.mc_id=Portal-Microsoft_Azure_Search#sample-index`.

We can also fetch statistics for getting the last indexed result from the indexer. Here, we are using it to show the last indexed timestamp:

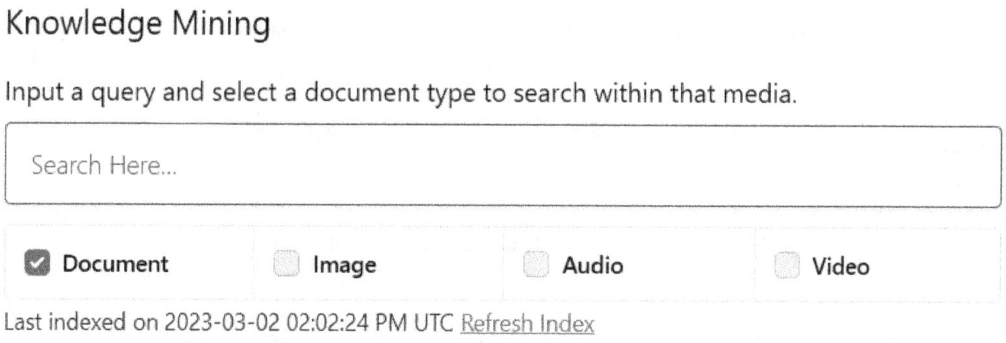

## Knowledge Mining

Input a query and select a document type to search within that media.

```
Search Here...
```

☑ Document        ☐ Image        ☐ Audio        ☐ Video

Last indexed on 2023-03-02 02:02:24 PM UTC Refresh Index

Figure 7.2 – The portal interface for searching our data repositories

To fetch the indexer statistics, you can create a `SearchIndexerClient` instance to pull all the related information from the indexer, like so:

```
def search_index_stats(indexer: str = None) -> dict:
    endpoint = str(os.getenv('AZURE_COG_SEARCH_ENDPOINT'))
    credential = AzureKeyCredential(str(os.getenv('AZURE_COG_SEARCH_
CREDENTIAL')))
    indexer_name = os.getenv('AZURE_COG_SEARCH_INDEX')
    client = SearchIndexerClient(endpoint=endpoint,
credential=credential)
```

```
    results = client.get_indexer_status(name=str(os.getenv('AZURE_COG_
SEARCH_INDEXER')))
    last_run = results.last_result.end_time.astimezone(timezone.utc).
strftime("%Y-%m-%d %I:%M:%S %p %Z")
    return results.last_result
```

Also, we can request that the indexer do a manual index at any time using this snippet of code:

```
def reindex(indexer: str = None) -> bool:
    endpoint = str(os.getenv('AZURE_COG_SEARCH_ENDPOINT'))
    credential = AzureKeyCredential(str(os.getenv('AZURE_COG_SEARCH_
CREDENTIAL')))
    indexer_name = os.getenv('AZURE_COG_SEARCH_INDEX')
    client = SearchIndexerClient(endpoint=endpoint,
credential=credential)
    client.run_indexer(name= str(os.getenv('AZURE_COG_SEARCH_
INDEXER')))
    return True
```

To choose which index to search, on the page, we have a simple HTML form with checkboxes to determine which document type to check against. Here is a snippet of the HTML form with checkboxes; more of this example can be seen in the accompanying GitHub repository:

```
<form>
  <input type="search" placeholder="Search Here..." name="query">
  <ul>
    <li>
      <input name="document_type" id="document" type="checkbox"
value="1" checked>
    </li>
    <li>
      <input name="image_type" id="image" type="checkbox" value="1">
    </li>
    <li>
      <input name="audio_type" id="audio" type="checkbox" value="1">
    </li>
    <li>
      <input name="video_type" id="video" type="checkbox" value="1">
    </li>
  </ul>
  <div>
    <button type="submit">
      Search
    </button>
  </div>
</form>
```

The same search code earlier will read this form request and search each document type as requested. Use these and whatever other ideas you can come up with to enhance your KM solution and bring all that dark data into the light!

## Summary

Here, and in the previous few chapters, we have helped to provide you with a broad overview and real solutions to apply the capabilities by combining Azure Cognitive Services technologies. Many organizations struggle with leveraging the significant volumes of data that lie in storage and file shares untapped for the significant value they hold. Beyond simply returning search results and bringing the data to the surface, we can also begin to analyze the data deeper and begin mining the data for other potential uses of AI by building machine learning models to predict future results.

A fully built KM solution is no small undertaking, but the value can greatly outweigh the costs of deployment and services. A small proof of concept to surface some of the details of latent data could be a great place to start, and relatively cost-effective. After making a case for a full implementation, you can harness all the power of the full solution we laid out in these chapters. Whether your goal is to identify objects, extract text and document details, analyze audio or video files, or so many other options, the combination of the various services built-in or extended will give you many options. Also, as we've seen even in the time of writing the chapter, by adding features such as the Semantic Search component, Microsoft continues to make significant investments in Cognitive Search and other Cognitive Services.

The next chapter begins the final section of the book, where we cover individual Cognitive Services in greater detail. As you begin reviewing these options, be mindful that many, if not all, of the services we will cover can be used as custom skills in a KM solution. We'll get started with Form Recognizer to extract details from standard forms in your organization.

# Part 3:
# Other Cognitive Services
# That Will Help Your Company
# Optimize Operations

In this part, we will cover some of the most popular Cognitive Services that can help you understand, justify, and build solutions to help your organizations observe the streamlined operations that AI solutions can offer.

This section has the following chapters:

# 8

# Decluttering Paperwork with Form Recognizer

When we strategize about opportunities for reducing wasted effort and time in businesses, we do not get very far before landing on the vaunted paper shuffle. Inefficient processes live and breathe within the paperwork shuffle at every organization around the world. Certainly, organizations work on ways to minimize these inefficiencies, but even when we think we've got them cleaned up and optimized, more inefficiencies pop up. I would not suggest that any department is better or worse than another, and countless workflow and approval systems have been developed over the years, but the challenge persists. This is certainly the case in the example of Ocean Smart, where, as with any organization, there are constant challenges with processing paperwork. With that in mind, in this chapter, we are going to use a couple of examples where we have come across some of the more common areas where these inefficiencies exist.

In legacy **Document Management Systems (DMSs)**, which we covered in more detail in *Chapter 4, Deriving Value from Knowledge Mining Solutions in Azure*, we discussed the ability to capture details from structured data or scanned and OCRed documents. Some DMSs are more sophisticated in that they allow you to specify a zone within a scanned document that might contain an invoice number, for example. Another scanned zone might be specified for capturing a company name and address, for another. These worked as a good solution for a decent portion of the documents that were scanned, let's say 80% for a ballpark figure. Some more advanced DMSs would even allow the data to be captured into a database, and/or a barcode system that allowed for a start and end to a related document batch. There have been many approaches to try to improve these processes, but in reality, there have always been nuances preventing consistency and accuracy. Ocean Smart evaluated these options for deployment and help with processing standard forms such as invoices, incoming payments, associated paperwork for quality, trucking, and other critical operational processes.

With all of this in mind, Microsoft developed the Form Recognizer Cognitive Services resource to enable the use of AI to augment and improve the processes for documents of many kinds. Using the rest of the Azure platform, you can automate the retrieval, enrichment, processing, indexing, and storage of forms, then use the data in downstream applications. All of this can be performed with a variety of tools and methods using templated form designs or fully customized form processing. In this chapter, we will review those tools, form templates, and customer form designs, as well as the following:

- Understanding Form Recognizer machine learning model options
- Using the Form Recognizer development studio
- Exploring the AP process at Ocean Smart
- Deploying Form Recognizer with related services for mostly automating the AP process
- Integrating the complete solution for production use

Along the way, we will describe decision points Ocean Smart came across and you are likely to encounter when deploying your Form Recognizer solution. This should help you to develop the best solution possible for your production use case. But first, we will cover the technical aspects you will need to understand prior to building your solution.

## Technical requirements

To build your Form Recognizer solution, you will need to have an Azure subscription with at least Contributor rights to the subscription for deploying services. You will need an Azure storage account for storing your documents pre- and post-processing. Depending on if you plan to deploy the solution to a Docker container or an Azure web app, you will need experience with those technologies to ensure proper deployment. You will need to have Visual Studio Code (*Download Visual Studio Code - Mac, Linux, Windows*) with the node.js extension installed (https://nodejs.org/en/download/package-manager). Some other services you may use for your deployment are as follows:

- **Azure Functions** – For building functions and executing code
- **Azure Data Factory or similar** – For data orchestration and transformation
- **Azure Logic Apps** – For workflow and triggering mechanisms
- **Azure Database** – For storing output data post-processing

Of course, the more complex and automated your solution is, the more tools you will likely need to know how to use and manage. As with everything, start with the basics, build your PoC and add new features. This will help you to save precious time that would otherwise be wasted on troubleshooting and so on.

# Understanding Form Recognizer machine learning model options

When deciding which model will work best for your solution, you will first have the choice of several models that are purpose-built for specific types of forms. The templated model types are self-explanatory based on their names:

- General document
- Layout
- Invoice
- Receipt
- ID document
- Business card
- Custom

These templated models were designed with a base set of fields to extract from the documents as they are processed. From the documents using the model type chosen, there are varying abilities for the extraction of text, key-value pairs, fields, selection marks (checkboxes, for example), tables, and entities. There are also variables around the processed documents, such as the document file type, number of pages, and dimensions of the pages being processed. For a more complete list of these variables to ensure your use case would be a good fit, refer to the following reference in the Microsoft documentation: https://docs.microsoft.com/en-us/azure/applied-ai-services/form-recognizer/concept-model-overview.

When the data is extracted from the forms, it is placed in the corresponding fields, as identified in a JSON file that can be used for downstream activities. By creating the JSON file, you are completing the process of taking unstructured data and structuring it, capturing many details about the document processed. As was the case with Ocean Smart, there is also the ability to build your own custom model using forms that you scan and identify key data in.

## Building custom models

Each industry and organization is going to have its own proprietary forms for use and for these cases, you can use the **Train Custom Model** tool. Later in the chapter, we will provide examples of a form provided by Microsoft for capturing the details of an invoice, and another sample of an invoice that wasn't able to be fully recognized by the invoice model. In our case, we were required to build our own custom model for recognizing the data in the form. The tool will have you train from a minimum of five filled-in forms of the same type having different values or being blank. In order to identify key areas in a form, you will use the sample labeling tool for supervised learning model development.

The sample labeling tool can be used locally on your computer as a small application running in a Docker container or using an Azure container instance for running the tool in Azure. Detailed instructions for deploying the tool can be found here: `https://docs.microsoft.com/en-us/azure/applied-ai-services/form-recognizer/label-tool`.

After getting the tool running, you can point it to your storage account for consuming the documents. Just be sure that all the documents are of the same form type and scanned in as the same document format type (JPEG, PNG, BMP, TIFF, and PDF are currently supported.) Later in the chapter, you will see how we were unable to capture all relevant information with the Invoice model for an invoice document for our example. Instead, we were required to use the custom model capability because the invoices used as samples did not adhere to the provided model.

In the case where you want to capture information that is structured in the form of a table and does not follow the standard key and value structure, you can train the model to use **table tags**. With Form Recognizer, tables are automatically found and extracted, and table tags are useful for selecting whether the table is dynamic or fixed-size. Fixed-size tables are just that, fixed, in the number of rows consistently across your documents. In the case of dynamic tables, you can define the columns, but the number of rows varies. After making this distinction, you can define the column name, data type, and format for each of the tables and the number of rows for fixed-data type tables.

Now let's look at the **Form Recognizer Development Studio** for building custom models and identifying key fields in documents.

## Using Form Recognizer Development Studio

In version 3.0 of Form Recognizer, Microsoft released Form Recognizer Studio as well as a general document model. The general document model was designed for generic forms to be processed and does not require a model to be trained by the user. It can extract key-value pairs, entities, text, tables, and structure from documents processed in the system. The underlying model being used is managed by Microsoft and retrained periodically to improve the model and improve the results of using the tool.

When using the tool, you will point to your storage account where your documents live, and each document in storage will be processed. It is important to note that the documents to be processed should be separate. In the case of a collection of documents, as they could be scanned into a single PDF, for example, they will all be processed as a single document. This is not a suggested practice if there are multiple documents or document types scanned into a single file to be processed, as they should be cracked and separated. By default, the tool will use **optical character recognition** (**OCR**) on the document, capturing all the text, and using deep learning models to extract key-value pairs and entities from the documents. Upon processing your documents, keys will be identified, whether they have an associated value or not. This allows for some variation in how documents are filled out and will still capture field details, even if left blank. At the same time, the entity recognition model is run in parallel and will identify objects regardless of whether they are key-value pairs.

# Exploring the AP process at Ocean Smart

When the team from Ocean Smart began exploring inefficient processes in their organization, they quickly determined that the **accounts payable (AP)** process could be improved with some automation. By streamlining and automating the AP process, Ocean Smart can reduce the number of errors made by AP staff. The reductions are made because they can eliminate the possibility of transposing or inaccurately entering information in their **enterprise resource planning (ERP)** system. The following provides a flowchart of the process for paying vendor invoices, then a written description of the process:

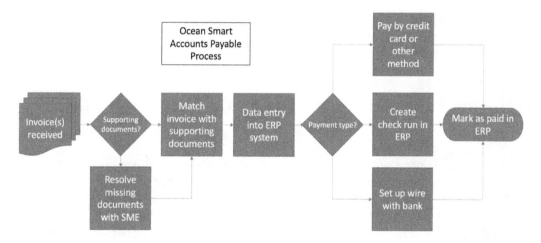

Figure 8.1 – AP process flowchart

1.  The invoice from the vendor is received by mail, fax, or email and submitted to the AP team for processing.

    There are no guarantees that an invoice makes it to the AP team, however, because there are no validation steps confirming receipt. Even if the invoice is submitted by email and a request for receipt is made, it is unlikely to be responded to. This creates a proverbial "black hole" for invoices.

2.  Invoices are ideally processed using **first in first out (FIFO)** processing; however, there are no guarantees the ordering is followed as the process can be circumvented by another employee asking about a particular invoice. To process an invoice, the AP clerk must have all supporting documents before entering the payable into the ERP. If supporting documents are not available, the AP clerk will work with internal team members or the vendor to collect those documents.

3.  When all supporting documents are available, the data is entered into the ERP with associated activities for adding to the payment queue based on the terms with the vendor for the appropriate timing of payment.

4.   At the appropriate time, the AP clerk then prepares the ERP for setting up payment by credit card, paper check, or wire transfer.

5.   After the payment has been completed, the ERP is updated with the information around payment status necessary to close out the payable.

The process described in the preceding list provides a general idea of what typically occurs. There are occasions where the process is different, but those represent a minimal percentage of the overall transactions.

With this process in mind, we set out to find the best way to use Form Recognizer at Ocean Smart to help automate the process and reduce human intervention, in turn reducing the chances of human error and simplifying the AP process. So now, let's jump in and discuss what it takes to implement Form Recognizer to automate the process.

## Deploying Form Recognizer for mostly automating the AP process

In an ideal world, I'd sit here and proudly claim "*We did it! We fully automated this process and saved Ocean Smart oodles of time and money!*", but that's just not the case. While developing the solution for this chapter, we found the Form Recognizer services to be incomplete as well as lacking in documentation and product flexibility. That being said, enhancements are being made all the time, and even though we were unable to use the Form Recognizer invoice model for our deployment, we were able to use the general document model released in *version 3.0* of the service.

As a result of the change from the invoice layout to the general layout, this section will focus on the activities required to deploy the services we will use as part of the overall solution. We will show you how to deploy the services with common settings that should provide a baseline to build your own solution with appropriate configurations. The following is a high-level architecture of the services required to be deployed to process the forms for extraction:

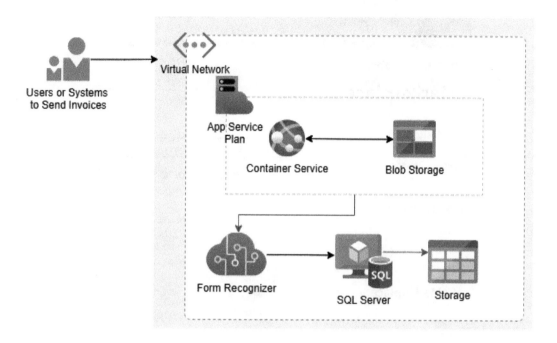

Figure 8.2 – Form Recognizer sample architecture

Using the previous diagram as a starting point, now let's take a look at what is required to deploy the resources to Azure.

## Creating Azure resources

When getting started with Form Recognizer, there are several components that need to be in place to take advantage of the API. We will cover those needs in this section, starting with deploying the services needed.

### Creating an Azure storage account

Our storage account is where we will store documents that are brought into the Form Recognizer service for processing. We will use the search tool in the Azure portal to find our storage account and start the deployment. After you complete your search, the following steps will help with the full deployment:

1.  You will receive many results from this search; however, look for the green icon with the table for creating any storage resources such as Blob Storage, file storage, Table Storage, and data lake storage:

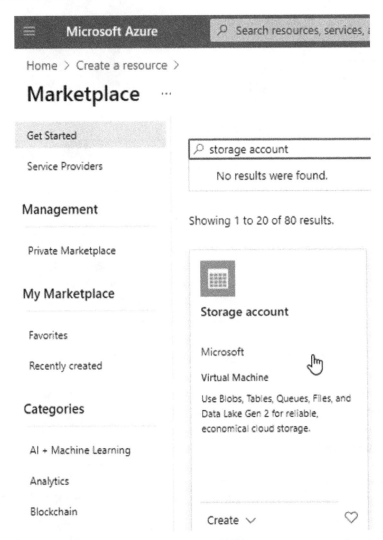

Figure 8.3 – Storage account search results in the Azure portal

2.   Click on **Create** as shown in the following screenshot:

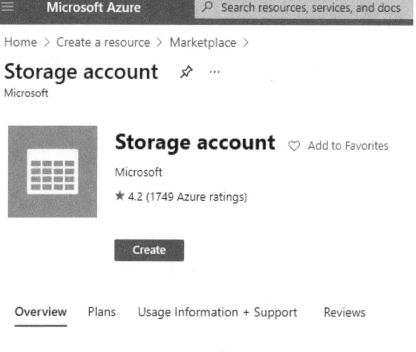

Figure 8.4 – Storage account marketplace option in the Azure portal

3.  The first section you will encounter in your deployment is **Basics**:

    I.   **Project details**: Select the subscription and resource group you used to create the Form
         Recognizer resource. However, if you decide to use this storage account for multiple projects
         or use cases, you may want to create a unique resource group for centralized storage.

    II.  **Instance details**: Choose a storage account name; this must be unique to the region and
         can *only* have lowercase letters and numbers. **Region** should be the same as the Form
         Recognizer service. **Performance** can be **Standard** since processing forms does not
         require low latency. For redundancy, in this example, **Locally-redundant storage (LRS)**
         is fine, but in production setup, you may want to use at least **Geo-redundant storage
         (GRS)** for additional protection. More details about recommendations can be found
         here: `https://docs.microsoft.com/en-us/azure/storage/blobs/`
         `data-lake-storage-best-practices`.

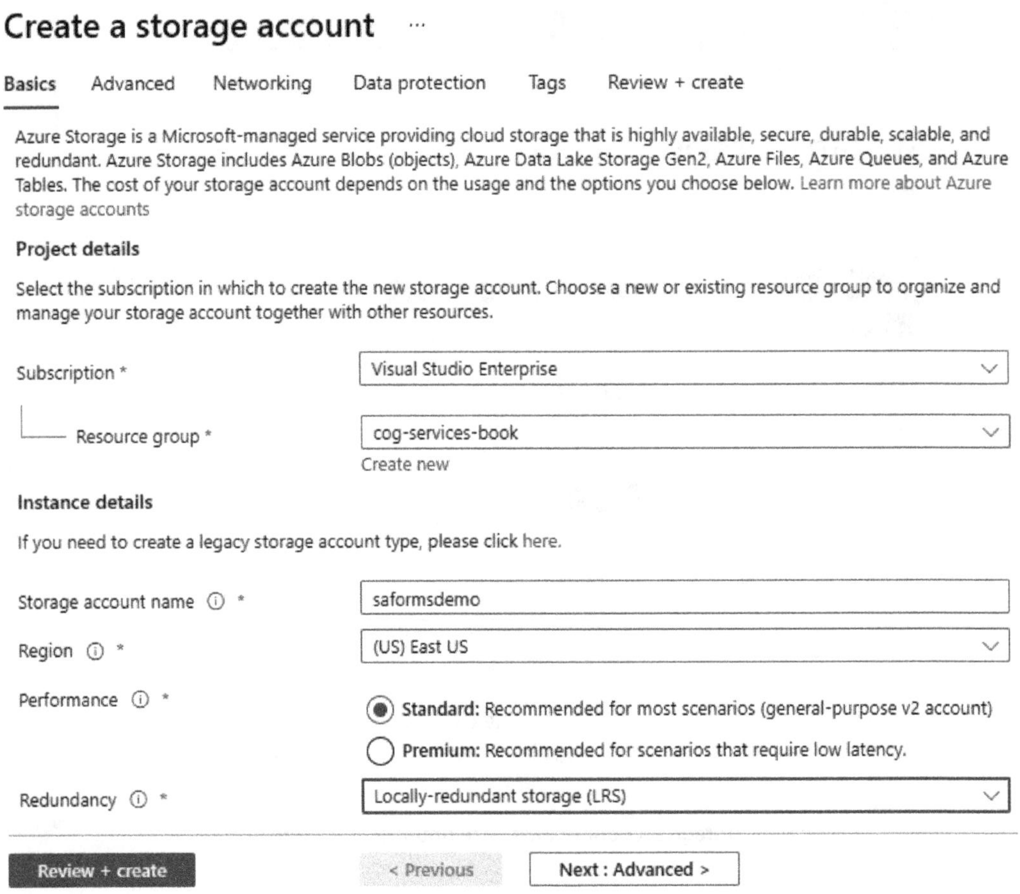

## Create a storage account   ...

Basics    Advanced    Networking    Data protection    Tags    Review + create

Azure Storage is a Microsoft-managed service providing cloud storage that is highly available, secure, durable, scalable, and redundant. Azure Storage includes Azure Blobs (objects), Azure Data Lake Storage Gen2, Azure Files, Azure Queues, and Azure Tables. The cost of your storage account depends on the usage and the options you choose below. Learn more about Azure storage accounts

**Project details**

Select the subscription in which to create the new storage account. Choose a new or existing resource group to organize and manage your storage account together with other resources.

| | |
|---|---|
| Subscription * | Visual Studio Enterprise ⌄ |
| └─ Resource group * | cog-services-book ⌄ |
| | Create new |

**Instance details**

If you need to create a legacy storage account type, please click here.

| | |
|---|---|
| Storage account name ⓘ * | saformsdemo |
| Region ⓘ * | (US) East US ⌄ |
| Performance ⓘ * | ⦿ **Standard:** Recommended for most scenarios (general-purpose v2 account) |
| | ◯ **Premium:** Recommended for scenarios that require low latency. |
| Redundancy ⓘ * | Locally-redundant storage (LRS) ⌄ |

Review + create          < Previous          Next : Advanced >

Figure 8.5 – Storage account Basics settings

4.  The next section of the wizard is titled **Advanced**:

I.   **Security**: The defaults here are fine, the only additional change was to set **Enable infrastructure encryption** to provide an encryption-at-rest compliance check.

II.  **Data Lake Storage Gen2**: For our purposes, it is not required to enable hierarchical namespaces. However, if you decide to use this storage account for multiple projects or use cases, you may want to enable them for security and access purposes.

III. **Blob storage**: Defaults are fine here; enable cross-tenant replication and set the access tier to **Hot**.

IV.    **Azure Files**: Large files are not needed to be selected for this example.

V.    **Tables and Queues**: Since we are not using tables or queues, we have opted to not enable support for customer-managed keys.

# Create a storage account  ...

Basics    **Advanced**    Networking    Data protection    Tags    Review + create

**Security**

Configure security settings that impact your storage account.

Require secure transfer for REST API operations  ⓘ    ☑

Enable infrastructure encryption  ⓘ    ☑

⚠ This option cannot be changed after this storage account is created.

Enable blob public access  ⓘ    ☑

Enable storage account key access  ⓘ    ☑

Default to Azure Active Directory authorization in the Azure portal  ⓘ    ☐

Minimum TLS version  ⓘ    | Version 1.2    ⌄ |

**Data Lake Storage Gen2**

The Data Lake Storage Gen2 hierarchical namespace accelerates big data analytics workloads and enables file-level access control lists (ACLs). Learn more

Enable hierarchical namespace    ☐

**Blob storage**

Enable network file system v3  ⓘ    ☐

ⓘ To enable NFS v3 'hierarchical namespace' must be enabled. Learn more about NFS v3

Allow cross-tenant replication  ⓘ    ☑

Access tier  ⓘ    ⦿ **Hot**: Frequently accessed data and day-to-day usage scenarios

◯ **Cool**: Infrequently accessed data and backup scenarios

**Azure Files**

Enable large file shares  ⓘ    ☐

**Tables and Queues**

Enable support for customer-managed keys  ⓘ    ☐

| Review + create |    | < Previous | Next : Networking > |

Figure 8.6 – Storage account Advanced settings

5.  The next section of the wizard you will encounter is **Networking**:

    I.    **Network connectivity**: For the purposes of this example, we have selected **Public endpoint (selected networks)**. This is to ensure that only the networks you give access to are allowed access to the storage. It is recommended that you never give full public access to your storage account resources to avoid any potential data leaks.

    II.   **Virtual networks**: Choose the virtual network and subnet that was created when the Form Recognizer service was created.

    III.  **Network routing**: Microsoft network routing is the preferred routing for this example.

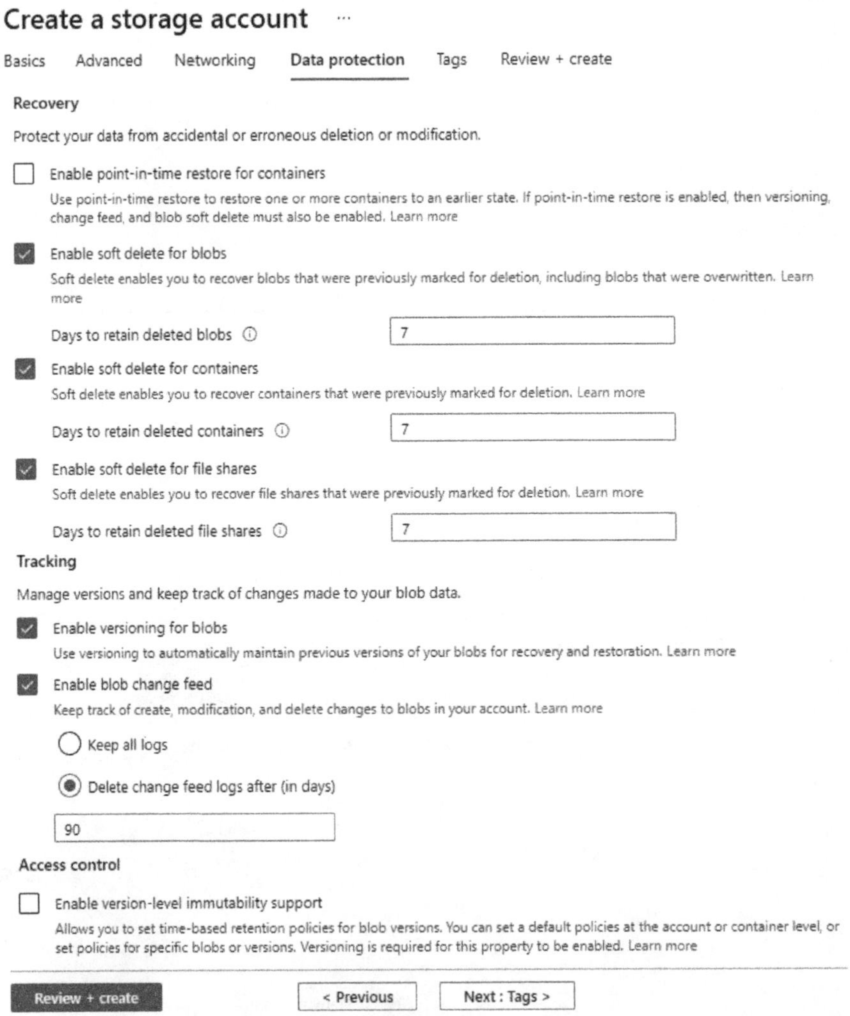

## Create a storage account    ···

Basics    Advanced    Networking    **Data protection**    Tags    Review + create

**Recovery**

Protect your data from accidental or erroneous deletion or modification.

☐ Enable point-in-time restore for containers

Use point-in-time restore to restore one or more containers to an earlier state. If point-in-time restore is enabled, then versioning, change feed, and blob soft delete must also be enabled. Learn more

☑ Enable soft delete for blobs

Soft delete enables you to recover blobs that were previously marked for deletion, including blobs that were overwritten. Learn more

Days to retain deleted blobs  ⓘ               | 7 |

☑ Enable soft delete for containers

Soft delete enables you to recover containers that were previously marked for deletion. Learn more

Days to retain deleted containers  ⓘ          | 7 |

☑ Enable soft delete for file shares

Soft delete enables you to recover file shares that were previously marked for deletion. Learn more

Days to retain deleted file shares  ⓘ         | 7 |

**Tracking**

Manage versions and keep track of changes made to your blob data.

☑ Enable versioning for blobs

Use versioning to automatically maintain previous versions of your blobs for recovery and restoration. Learn more

☑ Enable blob change feed

Keep track of create, modification, and delete changes to blobs in your account. Learn more

◯ Keep all logs

◉ Delete change feed logs after (in days)

| 90 |

**Access control**

☐ Enable version-level immutability support

Allows you to set time-based retention policies for blob versions. You can set a default policies at the account or container level, or set policies for specific blobs or versions. Versioning is required for this property to be enabled. Learn more

Review + create    < Previous    Next : Tags >

Figure 8.7 – Storage account Networking settings

6. The next tab you will encounter in the wizard is **Data protection**:

   I. **Recovery:** The defaults are acceptable for the purposes of this example. Enable soft deletes for blobs, containers, and file shares.

   II. **Tracking:** Enable versioning for blobs, and we enabled blob change feeds for a retention period of 90 days so that we can always go back and view changes within the blob storage.

   III. **Access control:** We do not want to set version-level immutability support.

## Create a storage account  ⋯

Basics    Advanced    Networking    **Data protection**    Tags    Review + create

**Recovery**

Protect your data from accidental or erroneous deletion or modification.

☐ Enable point-in-time restore for containers

Use point-in-time restore to restore one or more containers to an earlier state. If point-in-time restore is enabled, then versioning, change feed, and blob soft delete must also be enabled. Learn more

☑ Enable soft delete for blobs

Soft delete enables you to recover blobs that were previously marked for deletion, including blobs that were overwritten. Learn more

Days to retain deleted blobs  ⓘ            `7`

☑ Enable soft delete for containers

Soft delete enables you to recover containers that were previously marked for deletion. Learn more

Days to retain deleted containers  ⓘ         `7`

☑ Enable soft delete for file shares

Soft delete enables you to recover file shares that were previously marked for deletion. Learn more

Days to retain deleted file shares  ⓘ         `7`

**Tracking**

Manage versions and keep track of changes made to your blob data.

☑ Enable versioning for blobs

Use versioning to automatically maintain previous versions of your blobs for recovery and restoration. Learn more

☑ Enable blob change feed

Keep track of create, modification, and delete changes to blobs in your account. Learn more

◯ Keep all logs

◉ Delete change feed logs after (in days)

`90`

**Access control**

☐ Enable version-level immutability support

Allows you to set time-based retention policies for blob versions. You can set a default policies at the account or container level, or set policies for specific blobs or versions. Versioning is required for this property to be enabled. Learn more

[ Review + create ]          [ < Previous ]   [ Next : Tags > ]

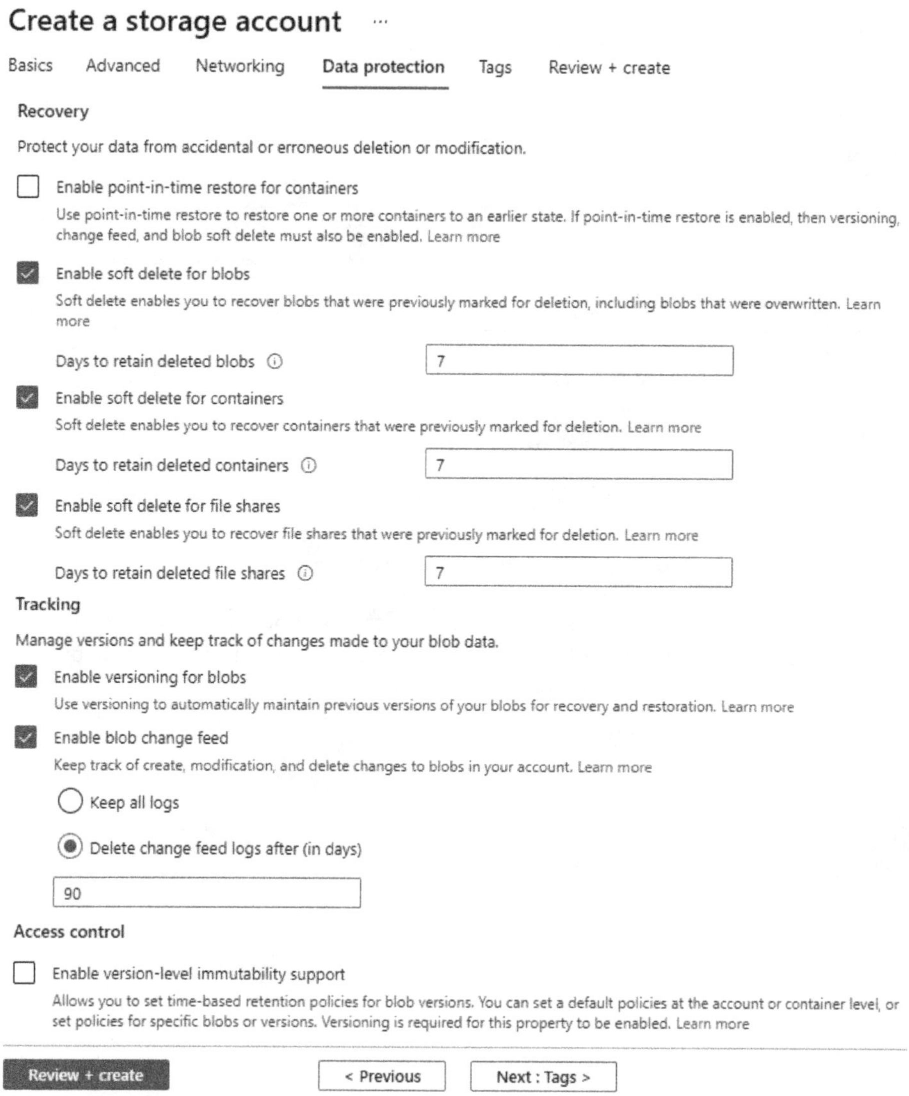

Figure 8.8 – Storage account Data protection settings

7.   The next item we will encounter in the wizard is **Tags**:

    I.    **Name/Value:** You can create any tags you would like to assign to the resource. This is generally a good practice to add any tags that would conform to your business logic or help with grouping resources based on projects, services, owners, or departments, for example. In this example, we added a couple of tags for use with reporting and other means.

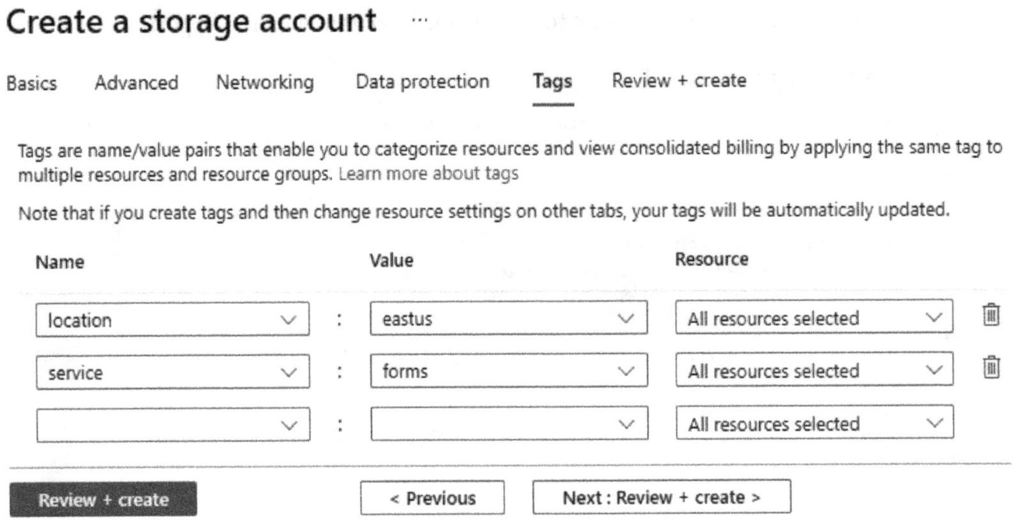

## Create a storage account ···

Basics   Advanced   Networking   Data protection   **Tags**   Review + create

Tags are name/value pairs that enable you to categorize resources and view consolidated billing by applying the same tag to multiple resources and resource groups. Learn more about tags

Note that if you create tags and then change resource settings on other tabs, your tags will be automatically updated.

| Name | | | Value | | Resource | |
|---|---|---|---|---|---|---|
| location | ⌄ | : | eastus | ⌄ | All resources selected | ⌄ | 🗑 |
| service | ⌄ | : | forms | ⌄ | All resources selected | ⌄ | 🗑 |
| | ⌄ | : | | ⌄ | All resources selected | ⌄ | |

[ Review + create ]          [ < Previous ]   [ Next : Review + create > ]

Figure 8.9 – Storage account Tags settings

8.   The final tab of the wizard that we will encounter is **Review + create**:

    I.    On this screen, if everything is configured correctly, you will see a green **Validation passed** section at the top of the page. With that, click on the blue **Create** button and Azure will begin the creation process.

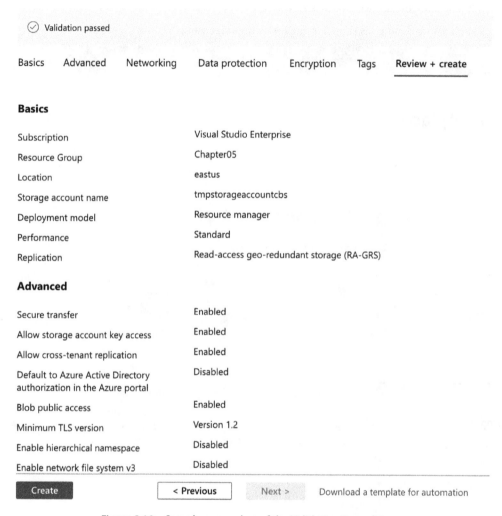

# Create a storage account    ···

✓ Validation passed

Basics    Advanced    Networking    Data protection    Encryption    Tags    **Review + create**

**Basics**

| | |
|---|---|
| Subscription | Visual Studio Enterprise |
| Resource Group | Chapter05 |
| Location | eastus |
| Storage account name | tmpstorageaccountcbs |
| Deployment model | Resource manager |
| Performance | Standard |
| Replication | Read-access geo-redundant storage (RA-GRS) |

**Advanced**

| | |
|---|---|
| Secure transfer | Enabled |
| Allow storage account key access | Enabled |
| Allow cross-tenant replication | Enabled |
| Default to Azure Active Directory authorization in the Azure portal | Disabled |
| Blob public access | Enabled |
| Minimum TLS version | Version 1.2 |
| Enable hierarchical namespace | Disabled |
| Enable network file system v3 | Disabled |

Create          < Previous          Next >          Download a template for automation

Figure 8.10 – Sample screenshot of the Validation Passed step

Next, we will show you how to deploy an Azure function for triggering the Form Recognizer service when a file is uploaded by a vendor.

## Deploying Azure App Service

Azure App Service provides us with the ability to host various services on the web that alleviates the need to deploy the infrastructure required to host these types of services. In our example, we are using App Service to host our Docker container that runs the Form Recognizer service.

The following provides steps for deploying the service:

1.  In the Azure portal, click **Create a resource**.
2.  Search for web app, as shown in the following screenshot:

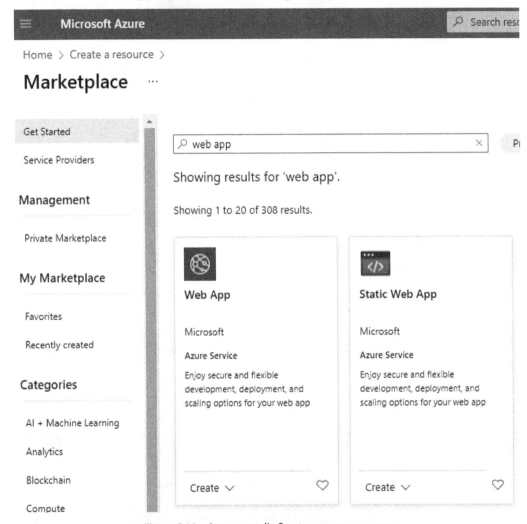

Figure 8.11 – Azure portal's Create a resource screen

3.  Click **Create**.

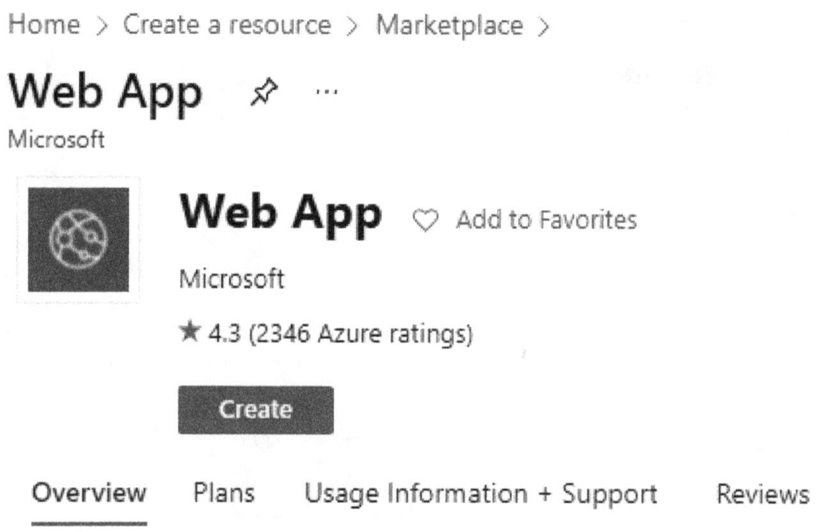

Home > Create a resource > Marketplace >

# Web App  ✄  ...

Microsoft

# Web App  ♡ Add to Favorites

Microsoft

★ 4.3 (2346 Azure ratings)

**Create**

Overview    Plans    Usage Information + Support    Reviews

Figure 8.12 – Web App marketplace option in the Azure portal

4.  Starting at the **Basics** tab in the wizard, you will need to do the following:

I.      Select the subscription.

II.     Select the correct resource group.

III.    Give a name you want to use for the instance:

*   The name should not match any special characters.

*   The name should be between 2 and 60 characters.

*   Make sure no web app with the same name exists in the location.

IV.     For **Publish**, choose **Docker Container**.

V.      Click **Linux**, as is this is the most typical container operating system, but if your container was built as a Windows container, choose **Windows**.

VI.     For **App Service Plan**, let the web app create a new plan for you, or if you already have a plan you wish to use, choose it here.

VII.    The default SKU and size are typically good for most scenarios but adjust it here if you need a larger or smaller instance. For testing, there is a **Free F1** instance you can select, but if you want to connect any Azure internal services, such as a storage account or a SQL database, you must select a production-based pricing tier, such as **P1V2** or **S1**. We selected **S1** for this purpose.

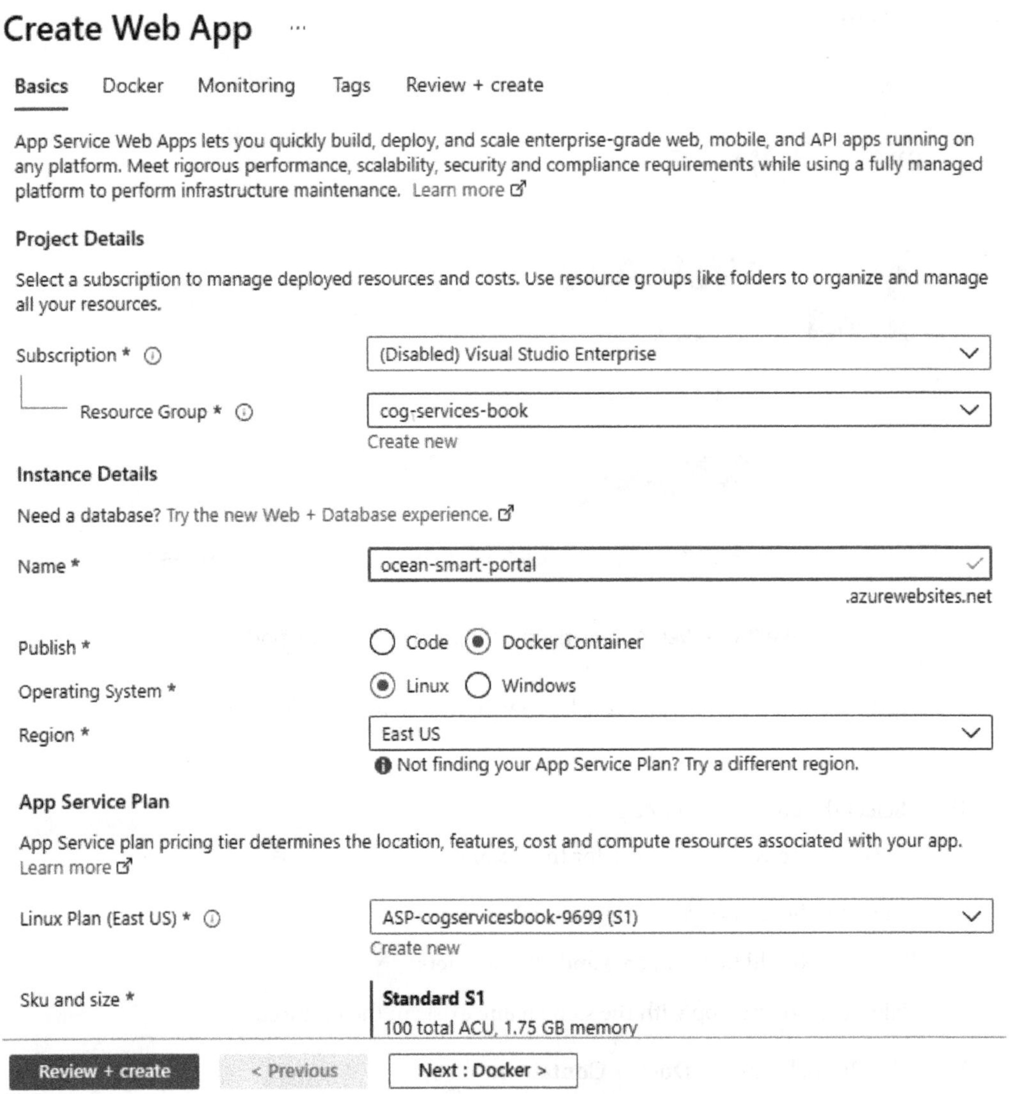

# Create Web App   ...

**Basics**   Docker   Monitoring   Tags   Review + create

App Service Web Apps lets you quickly build, deploy, and scale enterprise-grade web, mobile, and API apps running on any platform. Meet rigorous performance, scalability, security and compliance requirements while using a fully managed platform to perform infrastructure maintenance. Learn more ⬀

### Project Details

Select a subscription to manage deployed resources and costs. Use resource groups like folders to organize and manage all your resources.

| | |
|---|---|
| Subscription * ⓘ | (Disabled) Visual Studio Enterprise ⌄ |
| └── Resource Group * ⓘ | cog-services-book ⌄ |
| | Create new |

### Instance Details

Need a database? Try the new Web + Database experience. ⬀

| | |
|---|---|
| Name * | ocean-smart-portal ✓ |
| | .azurewebsites.net |
| Publish * | ◯ Code   ⦿ Docker Container |
| Operating System * | ⦿ Linux   ◯ Windows |
| Region * | East US ⌄ |
| | ❶ Not finding your App Service Plan? Try a different region. |

### App Service Plan

App Service plan pricing tier determines the location, features, cost and compute resources associated with your app. Learn more ⬀

| | |
|---|---|
| Linux Plan (East US) * ⓘ | ASP-cogservicesbook-9699 (S1) ⌄ |
| | Create new |
| Sku and size * | **Standard S1** |
| | 100 total ACU, 1.75 GB memory |

[ Review + create ]   [ < Previous ]   [ Next : Docker > ]

Figure 8.13 – Web App Basics screen

5.  Next is the **Docker** tab; complete it as in the following:

    I.   Select the **Single Container** option.

    II.  **Image Source** will be **Azure Container Registry**.

    III. The registry name will be the name of the Azure Registry you created earlier and will show as an option in the drop-down menu. Select it, and the image drop-down menu will auto-populate.

IV.    Select the relevant image; this would be the Docker container you pushed into Azure Registry from your computer.

V.    Select **latest** as the image tag.

VI.    **Startup Command** can be left blank.

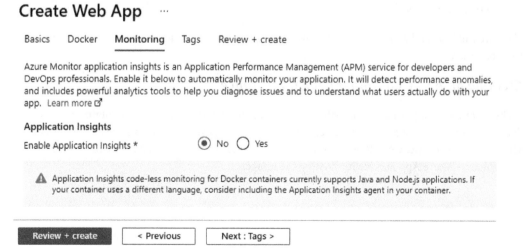

## Create Web App    ...

Basics    **Docker**    Monitoring    Tags    Review + create

Pull container images from Azure Container Registry, Docker Hub or a private Docker repository. App Service will deploy the containerized app with your preferred dependencies to production in seconds.

| Options | Single Container ⌄ |
| --- | --- |
| Image Source | Azure Container Registry ⌄ |

**Azure container registry options**

| Registry * | oceansmart ⌄ |
| --- | --- |
| Image * | oceansmart-portal ⌄ |
| Tag * | latest ⌄ |
| Startup Command ⓘ | |

[ Review + create ]    [ < Previous ]    [ Next : Monitoring > ]

Figure 8.14 – Web App Docker screen

6.    In the **Monitoring** tab, leave everything as default and click **Next: Tags >**.

## Create Web App    ...

Basics    Docker    **Monitoring**    Tags    Review + create

Azure Monitor application insights is an Application Performance Management (APM) service for developers and DevOps professionals. Enable it below to automatically monitor your application. It will detect performance anomalies, and includes powerful analytics tools to help you diagnose issues and to understand what users actually do with your app. Learn more ⬀

**Application Insights**

Enable Application Insights *        ⦿ No    ◯ Yes

⚠ Application Insights code-less monitoring for Docker containers currently supports Java and Node.js applications. If your container uses a different language, consider including the Application Insights agent in your container.

[ Review + create ]    [ < Previous ]    [ Next : Tags > ]

Figure 8.15 – Web App Monitoring screen

7.  In the **Tags** tab, you can create any tags you would like to assign to the resource. It is generally a good practice to add any tags that would conform to your business logic or help with grouping resources based on projects, services, owners, departments, for example. In this example, we added `location` and `service`, but you could leave all this blank.

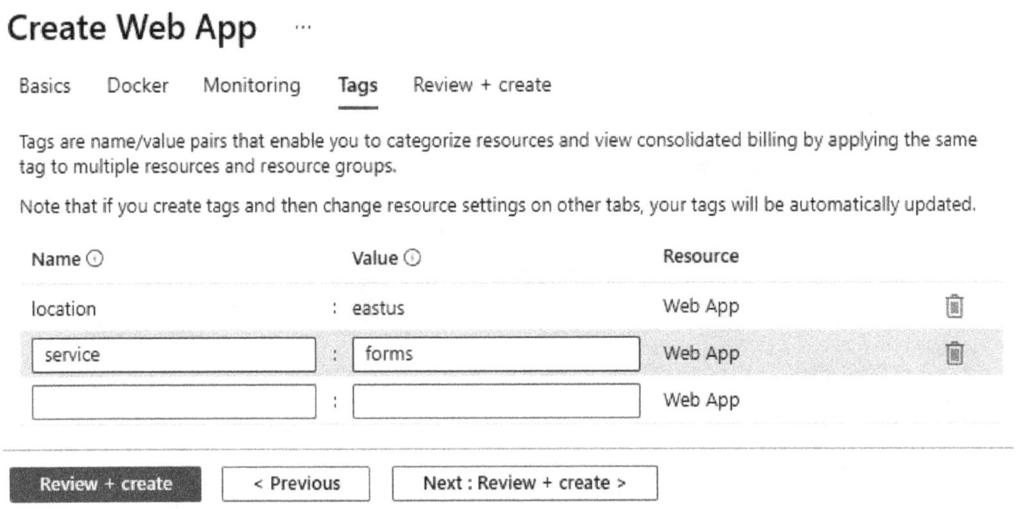

## Create Web App    ...

Basics    Docker    Monitoring    **Tags**    Review + create

Tags are name/value pairs that enable you to categorize resources and view consolidated billing by applying the same tag to multiple resources and resource groups.

Note that if you create tags and then change resource settings on other tabs, your tags will be automatically updated.

| Name ⓘ | | Value ⓘ | Resource | |
|---|---|---|---|---|
| location | : | eastus | Web App | 🗑 |
| service | : | forms | Web App | 🗑 |
| | : | | Web App | |

[ Review + create ]    [ < Previous ]    [ Next : Review + create > ]

Figure 8.16 – Web App Tags screen

8.  Finally, we come to the **Review + create** tab of the wizard.

9.  On this screen, if everything is configured correctly, you will see a green **Validation passed** section at the top of the page. With that, click on the blue **Create** button and Azure will begin the creation process.

Next, we will look at deploying Azure Container Registry for deploying the Form Recognizer service to a container.

### Creating an Azure Container Registry instance

To host your web application, you will need to create a registry to host your container. Azure App Service does not require Azure Container Registry, you could use your own private registry or Docker Hub. For this use case, we will build and store a container image within Azure Container Registry and link it to Azure App Service for hosting the image.

The following steps will lead you through the process of creating these resources using the Azure portal:

1.  In the Azure portal, click **Create a resource**.

2.  Search for container registry.

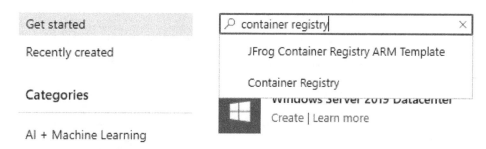

Figure 8.17 – Container registry search results in the Azure portal

3.  Click **Create**.

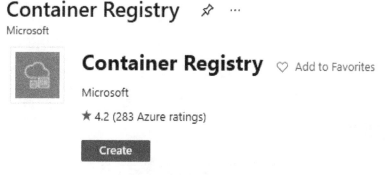

Figure 8.18 – Container Registry Create a resource screen

4.  Starting at the **Basics** tab in the wizard, you will need to do the following:

    I.    Select the subscription.

    II.   Select the correct resource group.

    III.  Give a name you want to use for the resource:

    •  The name should not match any special patterns.

    •  The name should be between 5 and 50 characters.

    •  The name may contain only alphanumeric characters.

IV.    Make sure no registry with the same name exists in the location.

V.    Choose **Standard** for the SKU.

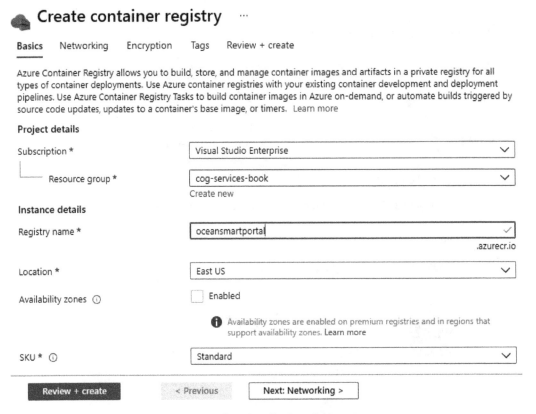

Figure 8.19 – Container Registry Basics screen

5.  Next, in the **Networking** tab, leave everything as the default, which should be grayed out due to selecting the **Standard** SKU from the **Basics** tab.

Figure 8.20 – Container Registry Networking screen

6.  On the **Encryption** tab, again leave it as it is and continue to the **Tags** settings by clicking **Next: Tags >**.

Figure 8.21 – Container Registry Encryption screen

7.  For the **Tags** tab, you can create any tags you would like to assign to the resource. It is generally a good practice to add any tags that would conform to your business logic or help with grouping resources based on projects, services, owners, departments, for example. In this example, we added `location` and `service`, but you could leave all this blank.

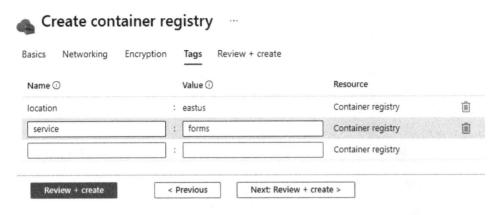

Figure 8.22 – Container Registry Tags screen

8.    Finally, we come to the **Review + create** tab of the wizard.

9.    On this screen, if everything is configured correctly, you will see a green **Validation passed** section at the top of the page. With that, click on the blue **Create** button and Azure will begin the creation process.

Next, we will look at the configuration of your Form Recognizer service.

### Creating a Form Recognizer service

The Form Recognizer service is what is going to extract the key information from the invoice we have received from our vendor and then send those details to a database, ERP, or another system for further processing. The following provides the steps required for deploying the Form Recognizer service using the Azure portal:

1.    In the Azure portal, click **Create a resource** and search for Form Recognizer:

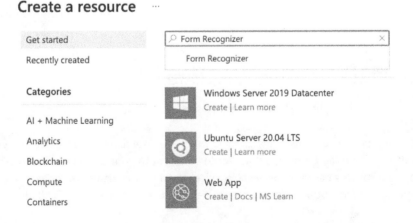

Figure 8.23 – Azure portal Create a resource screen

2.  You should receive this option from the Azure Marketplace:

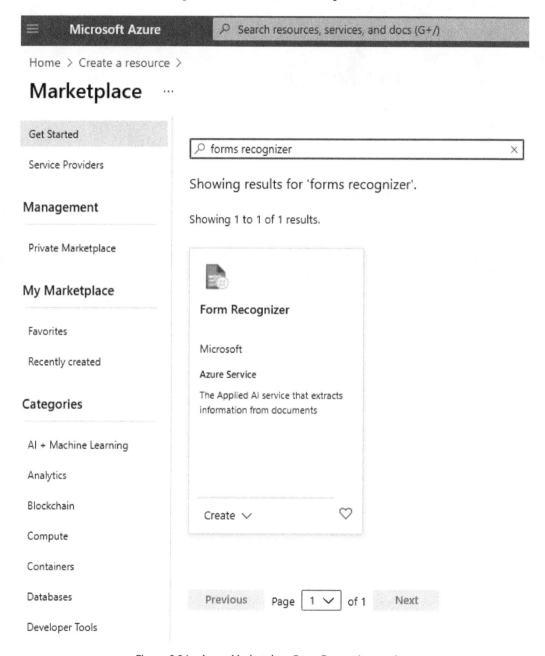

Figure 8.24 – Azure Marketplace Form Recognizer option

3.  Click on **Create**, as shown in the following screenshot:

# Form Recognizer 📌 ...

Microsoft

## Form Recognizer ♡ Add to Favorites

Microsoft

★ 4.0 (12 Azure ratings)

Create

**Overview**    Plans    Usage Information + Support    Reviews

Accelerate your business processes by automating information extraction. Form Recognize
tables from documents. With just a few samples, Form Recognizer tailors its understanding
data at a fraction of the time and cost, so you can focus more time acting on the information

Figure 8.25 – Azure portal Form Recognizer service screen

4. Some of the basic information you will need to enter is as follows:

    I.     Select the subscription you want to use.

    II.    Select the correct resource group you've created for your deployment.

    III.   Select the region you want to use.

    IV.   Give a name you want to use for the resource.

V.     Under the **Pricing tier** selection, you can select the free tier to get started, but be aware that there are limitations to using the free tier, such as the 20 calls per minute limit, which is not ideal for batch processing. For the purposes of building this PoC though, this tier will provide enough resources to test the solution.

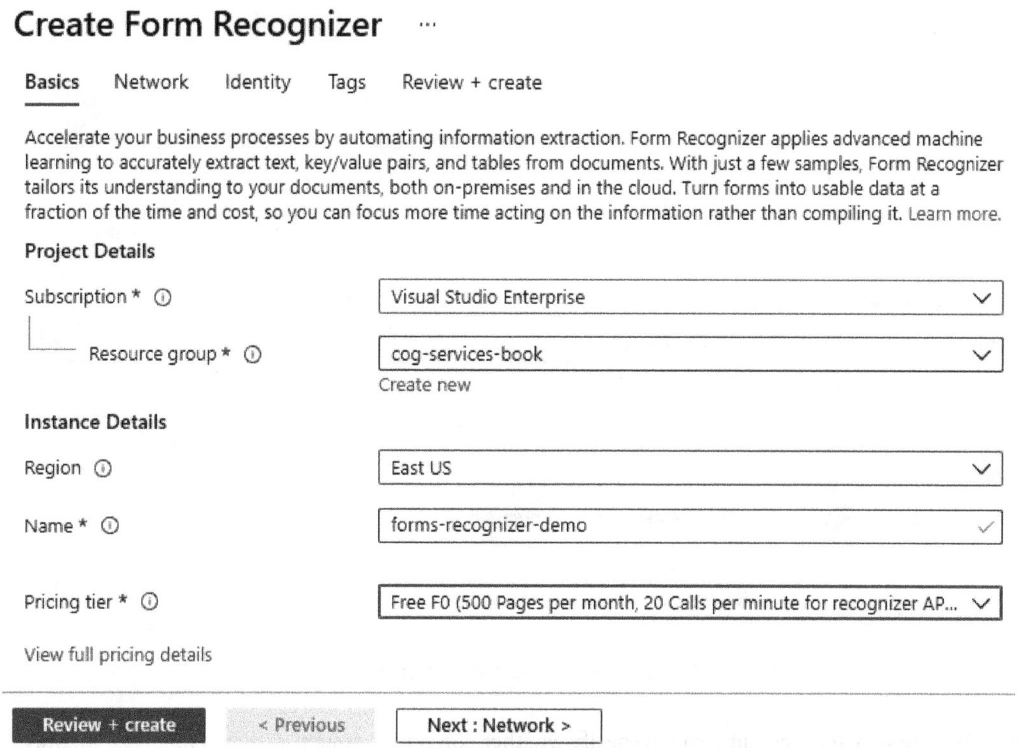

# Create Form Recognizer   ···

**Basics**   Network   Identity   Tags   Review + create

Accelerate your business processes by automating information extraction. Form Recognizer applies advanced machine learning to accurately extract text, key/value pairs, and tables from documents. With just a few samples, Form Recognizer tailors its understanding to your documents, both on-premises and in the cloud. Turn forms into usable data at a fraction of the time and cost, so you can focus more time acting on the information rather than compiling it. Learn more.

**Project Details**

Subscription * ⓘ

| Visual Studio Enterprise | ⌄ |

Resource group * ⓘ

| cog-services-book | ⌄ |
Create new

**Instance Details**

Region ⓘ

| East US | ⌄ |

Name * ⓘ

| forms-recognizer-demo | ✓ |

Pricing tier * ⓘ

| Free F0 (500 Pages per month, 20 Calls per minute for recognizer AP... | ⌄ |

View full pricing details

| Review + create |   | < Previous |   | Next : Network > |

Figure 8.26 – Form Recognizer service setup Basics screen

5.   Next, we will look at the networking configurations, so click **Next : Network >**:

I.     **Type:** For this demonstration purpose, we will choose **Selected networks**, which will lock down what networks have access to use the service. Only select **All networks** if you are aware of the security concerns and accept the risks.

II.    **Virtual network:** Create a new virtual network and a new subnet; using the recommended defaults here is acceptable unless you have special circumstances.

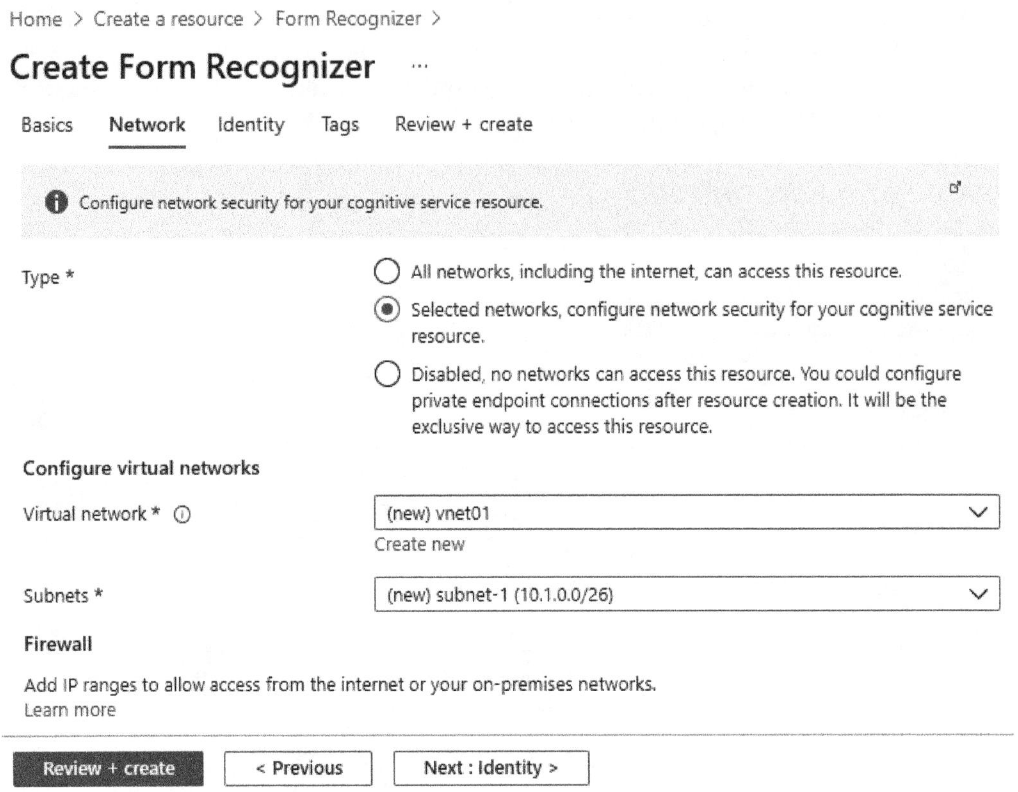

Home > Create a resource > Form Recognizer >

# Create Form Recognizer   ···

Basics    **Network**    Identity    Tags    Review + create

---

ⓘ Configure network security for your cognitive service resource.                                    ⬈

Type *                              ◯  All networks, including the internet, can access this resource.

                                    ◉  Selected networks, configure network security for your cognitive service
                                        resource.

                                    ◯  Disabled, no networks can access this resource. You could configure
                                        private endpoint connections after resource creation. It will be the
                                        exclusive way to access this resource.

**Configure virtual networks**

Virtual network *  ⓘ            | (new) vnet01                                               ⌄ |
                                  Create new

Subnets *                        | (new) subnet-1 (10.1.0.0/26)                               ⌄ |

**Firewall**

Add IP ranges to allow access from the internet or your on-premises networks.
Learn more

---

| Review + create |    | < Previous |    | Next : Identity > |

Figure 8.27 – Form Recognizer service setup Network screen

6.  The **Identity** settings allow you to specify whether you want a system-assigned managed identity
    or a user-assigned one:

    I.    **System assigned managed identity**: Since we want to use Forms Recognizer with other
          services in Azure, for simplification purposes, we are going to select **On**.

II.    **User assigned managed identity**: No users' identities are required at this time; you can leave this area blank.

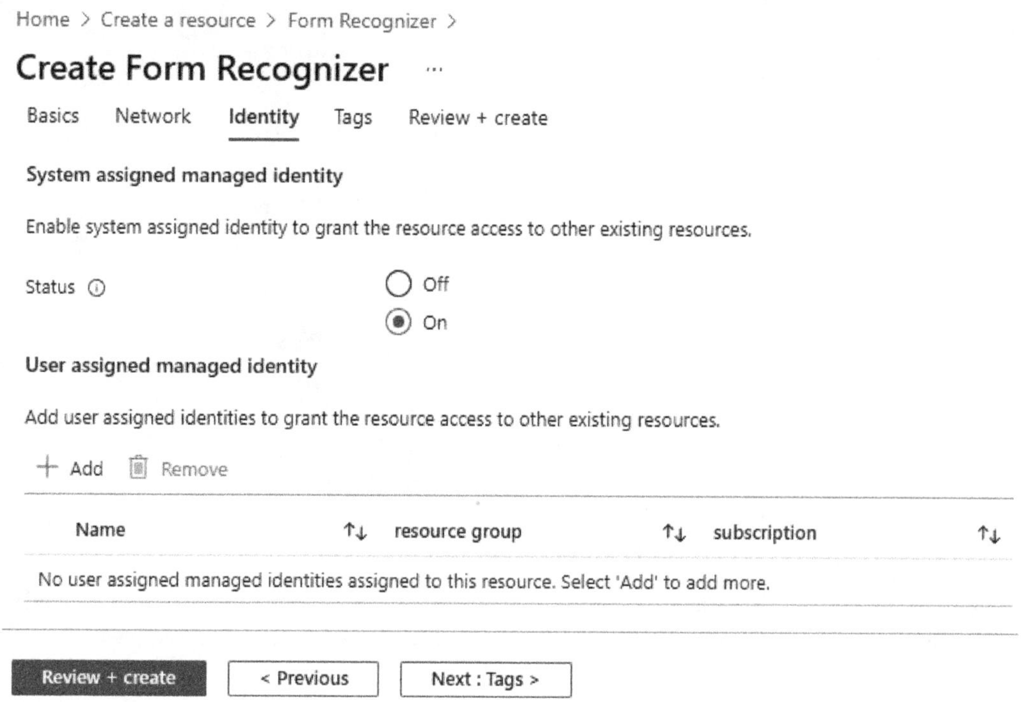

Home > Create a resource > Form Recognizer >

# Create Form Recognizer    ...

Basics    Network    **Identity**    Tags    Review + create

**System assigned managed identity**

Enable system assigned identity to grant the resource access to other existing resources.

Status ⓘ                    ○ Off
                           ◉ On

**User assigned managed identity**

Add user assigned identities to grant the resource access to other existing resources.

+ Add    🗑 Remove

| Name | ↑↓ | resource group | ↑↓ | subscription | ↑↓ |
|------|----|----------------|----|--------------|----|

No user assigned managed identities assigned to this resource. Select 'Add' to add more.

| Review + create | < Previous | Next : Tags > |

Figure 8.28 – Form Recognizer service setup Identity screen

7.    You can create any tags you would like to assign to the resource. It is generally a good practice to add any tags that would conform to your business logic or help with grouping resources based on projects, services, owners, departments, for example:

I.    **Name/Value**: In this example, we added `location` and `service`, but you could leave all this blank, as **Tags** are not required.

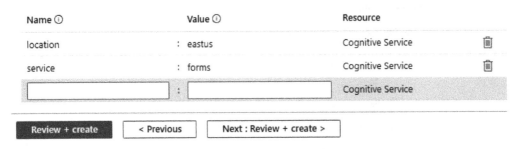

*Figure 8.29 – Form Recognizer service setup Tags screen*

8.   Finally, continue by clicking **Next : Review + create >**.

On this screen, if everything is configured correctly, you will see a green **Validation passed** section at the top of the page. With that, click on the blue **Create** button and Azure will begin the creation process.

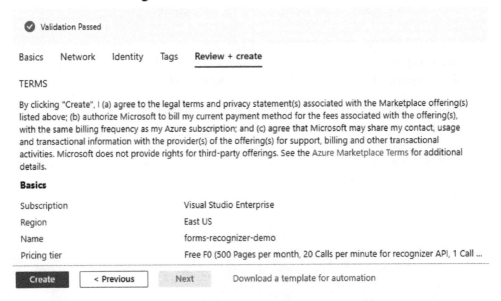

*Figure 8.30 – Form Recognizer service setup Review + create screen*

With that, you have deployed your Form Recognizer service that will be used for form processing. Finally, we will deploy our database service for the collection of data output from processing a form as an example of where the data can be sent.

### Creating your Azure SQL Database instance

In this section, we will deploy an Azure SQL Database instance. It should be noted, however, you can use whatever database you are comfortable working with. There is nothing proprietary in this example that would require you to use SQL. Our recommendation is to use a managed database, or PaaS, offering to minimize management and the ease of deployment, but that is up to your discretion as well.

In our example, the database is used to capture data that has been processed from the form that has been recognized with the service. This data can be used for reporting uses as well as further delivery of the data. An example of how it can be used would be if you were to capture the required details from the form and then send them to an ERP system. This would allow for the automation of adding details to the payables queue as we previously described in this chapter. With that, let's deploy our database:

1.  In the Azure portal, click **Create a resource**.

2.  Search for SQL Database.

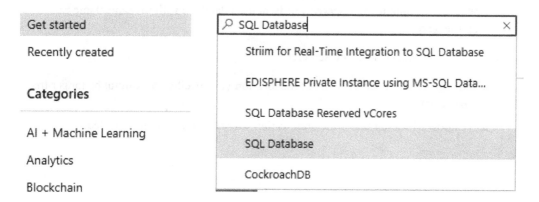

Figure 8.31 – SQL Database search results in the Azure portal

3.  Click **Create**.

Figure 8.32 – SQL Database Marketplace option in the Azure portal

4.   On the **Basics** tab from the wizard, you will need to do the following:

I.    Select the subscription for this deployment and the correct resource group.

II.   Give a name you want to use for the resource:

   •  The name should not match any special patterns, can be no longer than 128 characters, should not contain any reserved words, and no database with the same name can exist on the server.

III.  Next, you will create a new server:

   i.   Create a unique server name in the location you specify. This cannot be longer than 63 characters.

   ii.  Choose a location that is the same as the other resources you have created.

iii.  For the **Authentication** settings, it is recommended to use the following; however, be sure to work with security experts to ensure compliance with corporate policies that may exist:

- Choose **Use both SQL and Azure AD authentication** as this will allow you the flexibility to change how users and services access your database.

- Create a username and password that you will remember.

iv.  Choose **No** for using a SQL elastic pool since we will not be doing anything that requires multiple databases to share pool resources. However, if you plan to use such a feature, please check out the documentation about SQL elastic pools here: `https://docs.microsoft.com/en-us/azure/azure-sql/database/elastic-pool-overview`.

IV.  Under **Compute + Storage:**

- Using the default Gen 5 vCore is more than enough for any case but you can also switch to a DTU pricing tier, which is cheaper but has some limitations. In this example, we will leave it at the default, but if you want to change between vCore or DTU, please read this documentation before making a decision: `https://docs.microsoft.com/en-us/azure/azure-sql/database/purchasing-models`.

V.  Under **Backup storage redundancy:**

- The default is selected as **Geo-redundant backup storage**, which allows for the recovery of backups in any region that is needed. This is convenient in case of a failure and recovery must be done within a different location. If that is not required, **Zone-redundant backup storage** is the next best option. We do not recommend **Locally-redundant backup storage** as it provides very little benefit for recovery and no flexibility.

VI.  Next, we will move on to the networking settings for our database by selecting **Next : Networking >**.

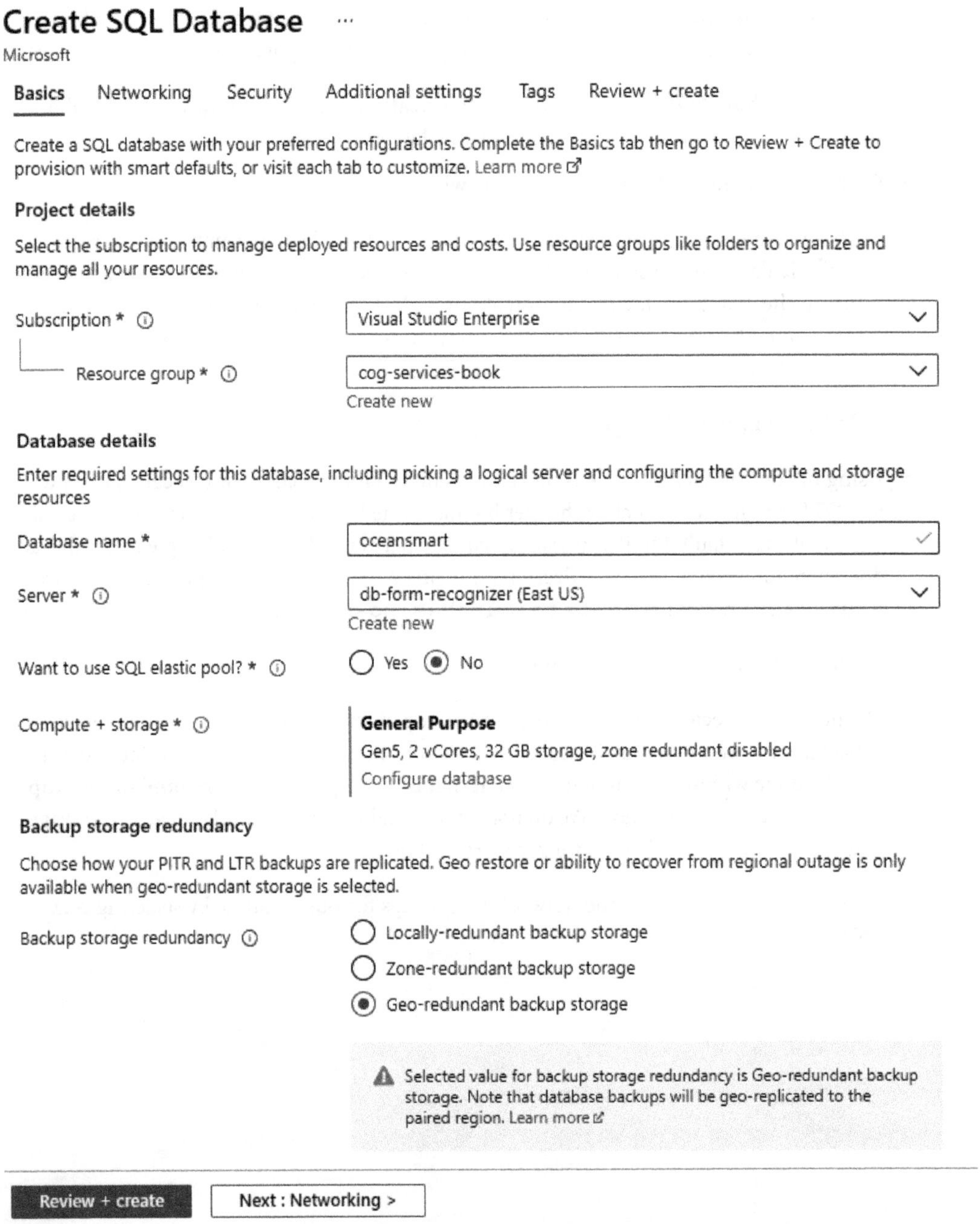

# Create SQL Database   ...

Microsoft

**Basics**    Networking    Security    Additional settings    Tags    Review + create

Create a SQL database with your preferred configurations. Complete the Basics tab then go to Review + Create to provision with smart defaults, or visit each tab to customize. Learn more ☐'

### Project details

Select the subscription to manage deployed resources and costs. Use resource groups like folders to organize and manage all your resources.

Subscription * ⓘ

| Visual Studio Enterprise | ⌄ |

└──── Resource group * ⓘ

| cog-services-book | ⌄ |

Create new

### Database details

Enter required settings for this database, including picking a logical server and configuring the compute and storage resources

Database name *

| oceansmart | ✓ |

Server * ⓘ

| db-form-recognizer (East US) | ⌄ |

Create new

Want to use SQL elastic pool? * ⓘ    ◯ Yes   ⦿ No

Compute + storage * ⓘ

**General Purpose**
Gen5, 2 vCores, 32 GB storage, zone redundant disabled
Configure database

### Backup storage redundancy

Choose how your PITR and LTR backups are replicated. Geo restore or ability to recover from regional outage is only available when geo-redundant storage is selected.

Backup storage redundancy ⓘ

◯ Locally-redundant backup storage

◯ Zone-redundant backup storage

⦿ Geo-redundant backup storage

> ⚠ Selected value for backup storage redundancy is Geo-redundant backup storage. Note that database backups will be geo-replicated to the paired region. Learn more ☑

---

[ Review + create ]    [ Next : Networking > ]

Figure 8.33 – SQL Database Basics screen

5.  Next, we will configure settings within the **Networking** tab. Within the **Firewall** heading, the default is **No access**, however, we know that in this example, we will need a private endpoint to be used to allow a connection to our application. Because of this, we will create a private endpoint by selecting the + **Add private endpoint**, which will open a new dialog box as follows:

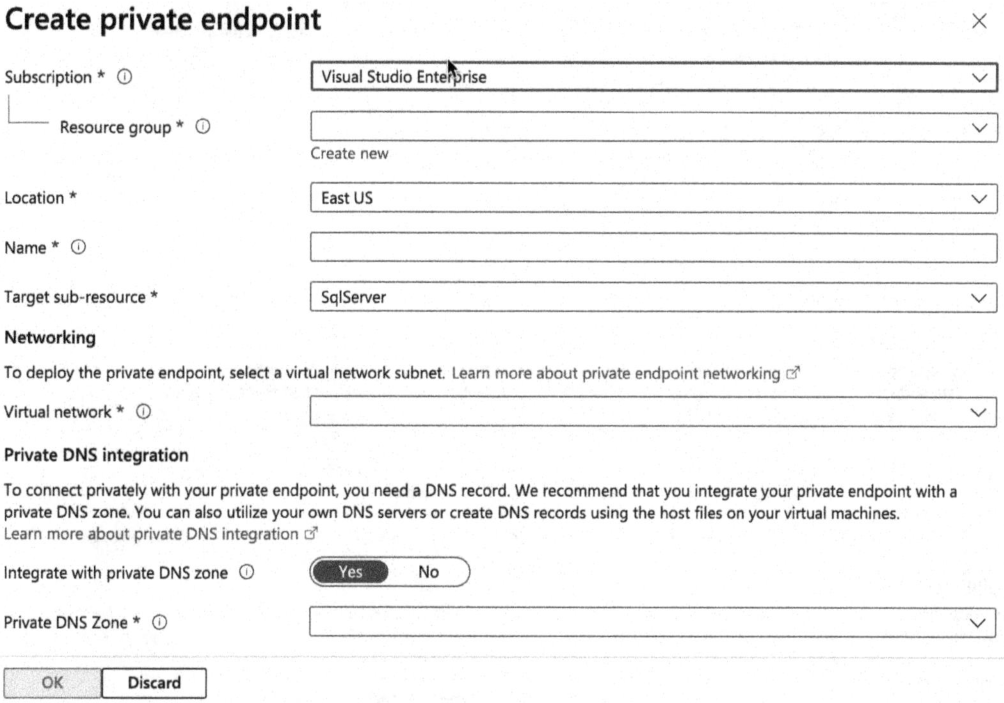

## Create private endpoint                                              ✕

| | |
|---|---|
| Subscription * ⓘ | Visual Studio Enterprise          ⌄ |
| └── Resource group * ⓘ | ⌄ |
| | Create new |
| Location * | East US                            ⌄ |
| Name * ⓘ | |
| Target sub-resource * | SqlServer                         ⌄ |

**Networking**

To deploy the private endpoint, select a virtual network subnet. Learn more about private endpoint networking ↗

| | |
|---|---|
| Virtual network * ⓘ | ⌄ |

**Private DNS integration**

To connect privately with your private endpoint, you need a DNS record. We recommend that you integrate your private endpoint with a private DNS zone. You can also utilize your own DNS servers or create DNS records using the host files on your virtual machines. Learn more about private DNS integration ↗

| | |
|---|---|
| Integrate with private DNS zone ⓘ | ( Yes    No ) |
| Private DNS Zone * ⓘ | ⌄ |

| OK | Discard |
|---|---|

Figure 8.34 – The Create private endpoint dialog box

6.  Use the same resource group, subscription, and location that you've been using for this example and choose a name.

7.  **Target sub-resource** will be defined as **SqlServer**.

8.  **Virtual network** and subnet can be the same virtual network you used when you created a Form Recognizer resource earlier.

9.  Under **Private DNS integration**, choose **Yes** and create a new private DNS zone:

    • Under **Connection policy**, choose **Default**, as this will allow you to use both a redirect and a proxy connection if needed.

    • Under **Encrypted connections**, the minimum TLS version default is **TLS 1.2**, and this is fine for our use case.

10.  Your completed **Networking** tab should look similar to the following screenshot:

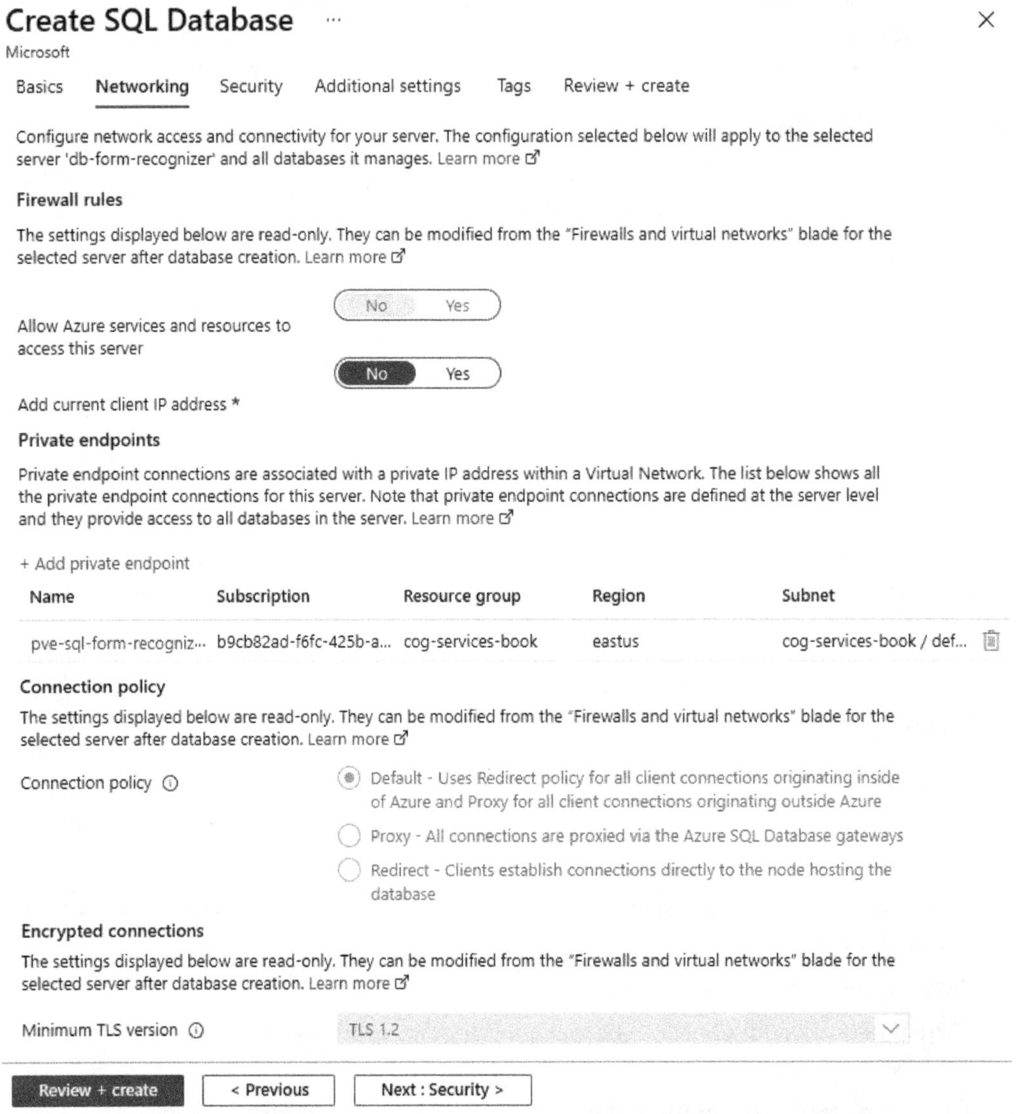

# Create SQL Database    ⋯                                                              ✕
Microsoft

Basics    **Networking**    Security    Additional settings    Tags    Review + create

Configure network access and connectivity for your server. The configuration selected below will apply to the selected
server 'db-form-recognizer' and all databases it manages. Learn more ⬀

**Firewall rules**

The settings displayed below are read-only. They can be modified from the "Firewalls and virtual networks" blade for the
selected server after database creation. Learn more ⬀

Allow Azure services and resources to               ( No    Yes )
access this server

                                                    ( No    Yes )
Add current client IP address *

**Private endpoints**

Private endpoint connections are associated with a private IP address within a Virtual Network. The list below shows all
the private endpoint connections for this server. Note that private endpoint connections are defined at the server level
and they provide access to all databases in the server. Learn more ⬀

+ Add private endpoint

| Name | Subscription | Resource group | Region | Subnet | |
|---|---|---|---|---|---|
| pve-sql-form-recogniz… | b9cb82ad-f6fc-425b-a… | cog-services-book | eastus | cog-services-book / def… | 🗑 |

**Connection policy**

The settings displayed below are read-only. They can be modified from the "Firewalls and virtual networks" blade for the
selected server after database creation. Learn more ⬀

Connection policy ⓘ          ◉ Default - Uses Redirect policy for all client connections originating inside
                               of Azure and Proxy for all client connections originating outside Azure

                             ○ Proxy - All connections are proxied via the Azure SQL Database gateways

                             ○ Redirect - Clients establish connections directly to the node hosting the
                               database

**Encrypted connections**

The settings displayed below are read-only. They can be modified from the "Firewalls and virtual networks" blade for the
selected server after database creation. Learn more ⬀

Minimum TLS version ⓘ          TLS 1.2                                                    ⌄

[ Review + create ]    [ < Previous ]    [ Next : Security > ]

Figure 8.35 – SQL Database Networking screen

11. For the **Security** tab, we will not be configuring anything in this panel and will leave everything as the default.

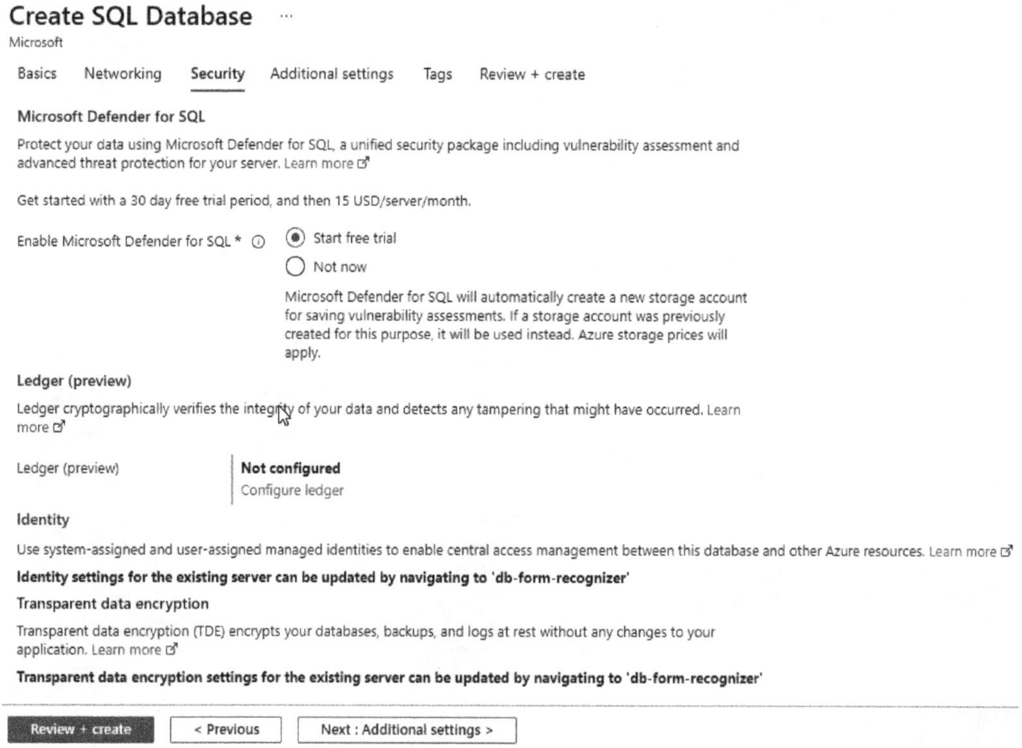

## Create SQL Database ...

Microsoft

Basics   Networking   **Security**   Additional settings   Tags   Review + create

**Microsoft Defender for SQL**

Protect your data using Microsoft Defender for SQL, a unified security package including vulnerability assessment and advanced threat protection for your server. Learn more ☐

Get started with a 30 day free trial period, and then 15 USD/server/month.

Enable Microsoft Defender for SQL * ⓘ   ⦿ Start free trial

◯ Not now

Microsoft Defender for SQL will automatically create a new storage account for saving vulnerability assessments. If a storage account was previously created for this purpose, it will be used instead. Azure storage prices will apply.

**Ledger (preview)**

Ledger cryptographically verifies the integrity of your data and detects any tampering that might have occurred. Learn more ☐

Ledger (preview)                    **Not configured**
                                    Configure ledger

**Identity**

Use system-assigned and user-assigned managed identities to enable central access management between this database and other Azure resources. Learn more ☐

**Identity settings for the existing server can be updated by navigating to 'db-form-recognizer'**

**Transparent data encryption**

Transparent data encryption (TDE) encrypts your databases, backups, and logs at rest without any changes to your application. Learn more ☐

**Transparent data encryption settings for the existing server can be updated by navigating to 'db-form-recognizer'**

Review + create        < Previous        Next : Additional settings >

Figure 8.36 – SQL Database Security screen

12. Next, we have the **Additional settings** tab:

A. **Data source** is **None** since we do not have any existing data to import.

B. **Collation** can be kept as the default unless you know ahead of time what collation you would need.

C.    **Maintenance window** can be kept as **System default (5pm to 8am)**.

# Create SQL Database    ···

Microsoft

Basics    Networking    Security    **Additional settings**    Tags    Review + create

Customize additional configuration parameters including collation & sample data.

**Data source**

Start with a blank database, restore from a backup or select sample data to populate your new database.

Use existing data *                    ( **None**    Backup    Sample )

**Database collation**

Database collation defines the rules that sort and compare data, and cannot be changed after database creation. The default database collation is SQL_Latin1_General_CP1_CI_AS. Learn more ⟁

Collation * ⓘ                        | SQL_Latin1_General_CP1_CI_AS                                    |
                                     Find a collation

**Maintenance window**

Select a preferred maintenance window from the drop down. Please note, during a maintenance event, Azure SQL Database are fully available and accessible but some of the maintenance updates require a failover as Azure takes SQL DB instances offline for a short time to apply the maintenance updates. If the database is part of elastic pool, the maintenance configuration of elastic pool will be applied. Learn more

Maintenance window                   | System default (5pm to 8am)                                ⌄ |

Review + create        < Previous        Next : Tags >

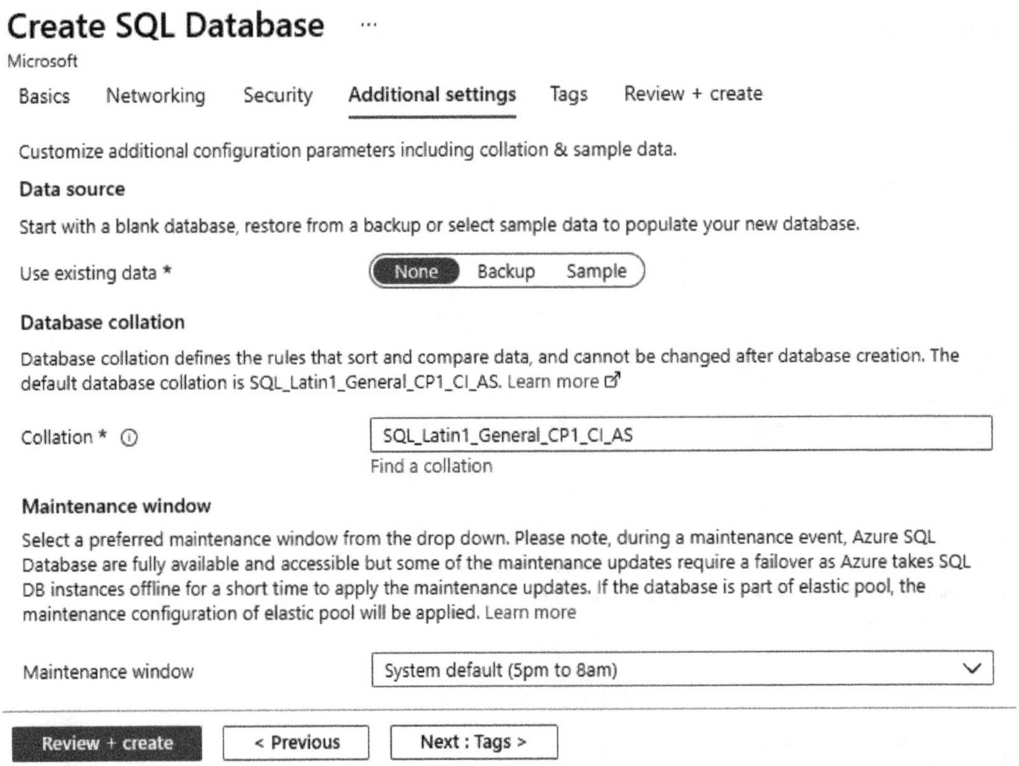

Figure 8.37 – SQL Database Additional settings screen

13. For the **Tags** tab, you can create any tags you would like to assign to the resource. It is generally a good practice to add any tags that would conform to your business logic or help with grouping resources based on projects, services, owners, departments, for example. In this example, we added `location` and `service`, but you could leave all this blank.

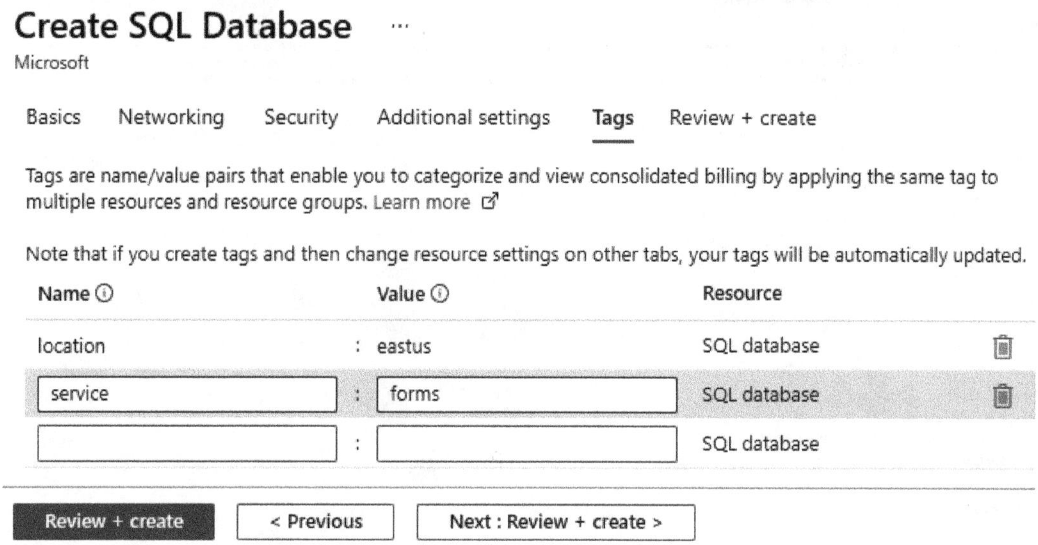

# Create SQL Database  ···

Microsoft

| Basics | Networking | Security | Additional settings | **Tags** | Review + create |

Tags are name/value pairs that enable you to categorize and view consolidated billing by applying the same tag to multiple resources and resource groups. Learn more ☑

Note that if you create tags and then change resource settings on other tabs, your tags will be automatically updated.

| Name ⓘ | | Value ⓘ | Resource | |
|---|---|---|---|---|
| location | : | eastus | SQL database | 🗑 |
| service | : | forms | SQL database | 🗑 |
| | : | | SQL database | |

| Review + create | | < Previous | | Next : Review + create > |

Figure 8.38 – SQL Database Tags screen

14. Finally, we come to the **Review + create** tab of the wizard.

On this screen, if everything is configured correctly, you will see a green **Validation passed** section at the top of the page. With that, click on the blue **Create** button and Azure will begin the creation process.

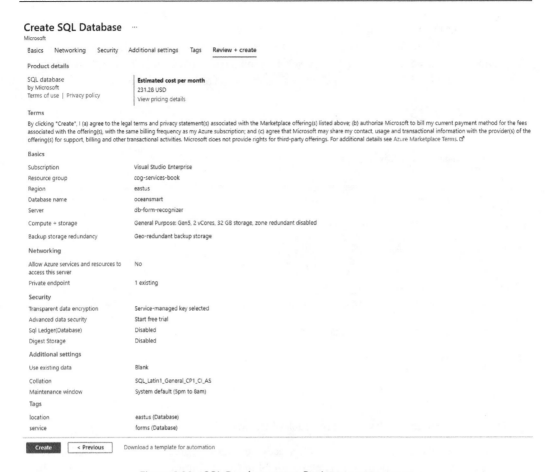

*Figure 8.39 – SQL Database setup Review + create screen*

You have now deployed your Azure SQL Database instance for storing your data from forms that are being processed, and with that, you have deployed all the required services to run your Form Recognizer example as displayed in our original diagram, as follows:

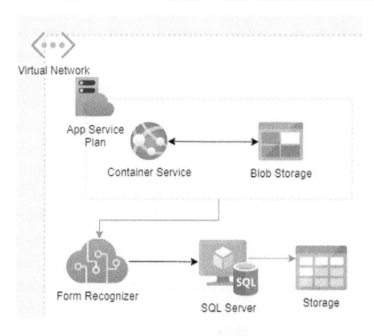

Figure 8.40 – Azure services deployed for our solution

Next, let's look at how the solution you've just built can be used in a production scenario.

# Integrating the complete solution for production use

So, now that you can see what the architectural components are that need to be deployed, it is time to look at how to deploy the services for production use and how it is used. We are also going to look at the Form Recognizer code that is running within the container for processing the forms, and what the sample output looks like. From there, we will present a sample of the code you will use for sending the data to an ERP for further use of the extracted data.

For the purposes of demonstration, we deployed a simple web application using the **Django** framework that vendors can log in to and upload their invoices for processing. After the form is uploaded into the vendor's portal, it is run through the architecture described in the previous section of this chapter to extract the key information. In our first attempts, using the invoice layout model, the Form Recognizer service was unable to extract the key details of our invoices due to not recognizing the format. As a result, we had to shift our focus to the general document layout model for document processing. Part of the reason for this is because, as a consumer of the invoice layout, you are not given the ability to help the invoice layout model "learn" and be enhanced along the way. It would certainly be beneficial if Microsoft were to give users the ability in the future to improve the model for other invoice layouts. The following shows a sample of an invoice used, the results of what was extracted from the invoice layout, and the results of what was extracted from the general layout:

Figure 8.41 – Ocean Smart portal Form Recognizer example

Using the portal, we can add documents to be processed with Form Recognizer, as displayed in the following screenshot:

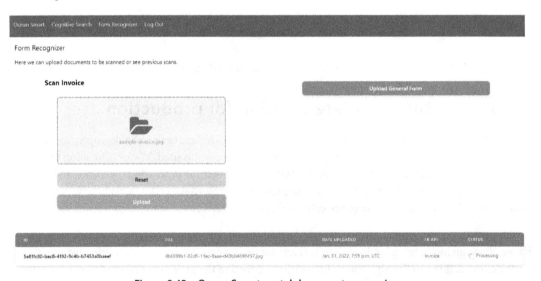

Figure 8.42 – Ocean Smart portal document processing

In the following screenshot, we can display the document that was processed using the Form Recognizer service:

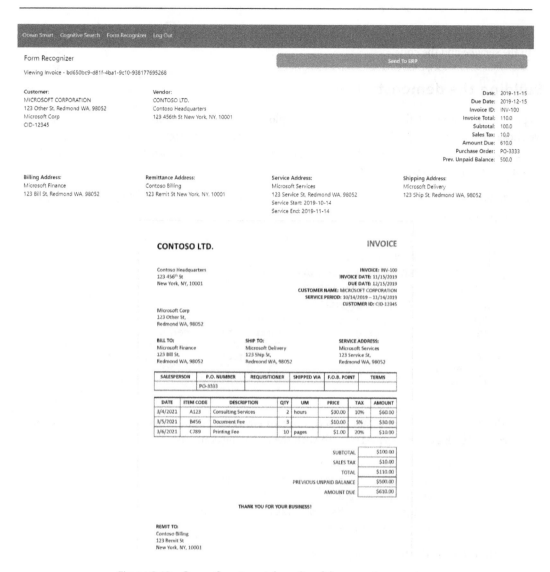

Figure 8.43 – Ocean Smart portal results of document processing

The next challenge we ran into was having multiple invoices in a batch being uploaded into the service. Form Recognizer does not have the ability to break up documents and process them separately. There are multiple ways this can be handled but we chose to remind vendors that the documents should only be uploaded one invoice at a time in the portal. Of course, an invoice can consist of multiple pages, and all that information will be processed for a single invoice that spans across multiple document pages. When uploading multiple invoices in a single batch, the service recognizes all the documents and will treat them as a single invoice and extract all those details into one stream of data. Another way to consider handling this issue is to crack the documents into multiple pages and process them separately; however, this runs the risk of not processing a multi-page invoice properly.

Now that you understand the process by which we developed the solution, let's look at what's happening with the service and the code.

## Building the demonstration

As previously mentioned, there are a few ways to deploy the Form Recognizer service. In our example, we chose to do so by using a **Docker container** and running it from App Service. Configuring and using Docker is beyond the scope of this chapter, but you can find more information here: https:// docs.docker.com/desktop/:

1. To begin with, a `Dockerfile` must be created to tell Docker how to build a container. Here is the example container manifest:

```
FROM python:3.9-slim-buster ENV PYTHONUNBUFFERED=1
ENV ENVIRONMENT=development
ENV DJANGO_SUPERUSER_USERNAME=admin
ENV DJANGO_SUPERUSER_PASSWORD=""
ENV DJANGO_SUPERUSER_EMAIL=admin@admin.com
WORKDIR /app RUN pip install pipenv COPY Pipfile* /tmp/ RUN
cd /tmp && \   pipenv lock --requirements > requirements.txt &&
\  pip install -r /tmp/requirements.txt COPY . /app RUN chmod
+x /app/docker-entrypoint.sh && \   groupadd -g 1024 django &&
\  useradd --no-log-init -u 1024 -g 1024 django && \   chown
django:django -R /app USER 1024 ENTRYPOINT [ "/app/docker-
entrypoint.sh" ]
```

2. The demo app will also require a script to run when the container is executed. Create a file called `docker-entrypoint.sh` with the following contents:

```
#!/bin/bash
python manage.py collectstatic --noinput
python manage.py migrate
python manage.py createsuperuser --noinput
python manage.py runserver 0.0.0.0:8000
```

This script will do the following actions:

- Bootstrap a database.

- Create an administrator login for the site.

- Run the server to accept all connections on port 8000.

3. Next, we will discuss how to build and run the container. To get started, build your container using the command in your favorite command prompt:

```
docker build -t oceansmart
```

4. Now, run the container; in this example, we will run it as a temporary container and make it interactive in the shell while also opening port `8000` to allow your browser to access it:

```
docker run --rm -it -p 8000:8000 oceansmart
```

That's it! Now open your web browser to `http://127.0.0.1:8000` and you can see the demo app!

Let's move on to the example code next.

## Example code

We have also included a snippet of code to test that your Form Recognizer service is configured correctly and returns results:

- In this example, Python 3.9 or higher is recommended, and using a Python virtual environment is also recommended, such as `virtualenv`, `anaconda`, and `pipenv`/`pyenv`. We will be using `pipenv`.

- The package required to run this example is as follows:

  - `azure-ai-formrecognizer`

- To install the package, just run the following command in a command prompt:

```
pipenv install azure-ai-formrecognizer
```

Now, you are ready to run your Python code for executing the service and processing a document:

1. Create a new file called `form_recognizer.py` and place the following code inside it, making sure to update the required details with your Azure environment.

2. To begin, add your required import statements; these are part of the Azure Form Recognizer SDK for Python (`https://github.com/Azure/azure-sdk-for-python`):

```
from azure.ai.formrecognizer import FormRecognizerClient
from azure.core.credentials import AzureKeyCredential
```

3. Next, let's create a client that will handle a session to Azure's Form Recognizer API. All that is required to make the connection is your Form Recognizer endpoint and an Azure key credential that is used to authenticate:

```
endpoint = "https://<your_endpoint_name>.cognitiveservices.
azure.com/"
credential = AzureKeyCredential("<your_key>")
form_recognizer_client = FormRecognizerClient(endpoint,
credential)
```

4.  The last part of the code will open an example invoice to be used for processing and will send the image to Form Recognizer. The result will be sent back to the program where it will iterate over all the recognized fields and print them out. The results will be the name of the field with their value and corresponding confidence score:

```
with open(f'sample-invoice.jpg', "rb") as invoice:
    poller = form_recognizer_client.begin_recognize_
invoices(invoice.read())
    for invoice in poller.result():
        for name, field in invoice.fields.items():
            if name == "Items":
                print("Invoice Items:")
                for idx, items in enumerate(field.value):
                    print("...Item #{}".format(idx+1))
                    for item_name, item in items.value.items():
                        print("......{}: {} has confidence {}".
format(
                            item_name, item.value, item.
confidence))
            else:
                print("{}: {} has confidence {}".format(
                    name, field.value, field.confidence))
```

You can find this example and a more advanced version that will save the results to a database in the accompanying GitHub code repository: https://github.com/PacktPublishing/Practical-Guide-to-Azure-Cognitive-Services.

5.  Now, you are ready to run the file in the Docker container. To execute this example, first place the files you want to analyze into the folder where your code is. Then run the Python command in a command prompt:

```
pipenv shell
python slim_example.py
```

6.  If successful, you will see the output of the Form Recognizer and the fields that were grabbed from the documents you submitted. This will also place them into a SQLite database that you can view and run SQL commands on:

```
......Date: 2021-03-06 has confidence 0.903
......Description: Printing Fee has confidence 0.899
......ProductCode: C789 has confidence 0.899
......Quantity: 10.0 has confidence 0.911
......Tax: None has confidence 0.802
......Unit: pages has confidence 0.893
......UnitPrice: 1.0 has confidence 0.829
PreviousUnpaidBalance: 500.0 has confidence 0.959
PurchaseOrder: PO-3333 has confidence 0.963
RemittanceAddress: 123 Remit St New York, NY, 10001 has confidence 0.95
RemittanceAddressRecipient: Contoso Billing has confidence 0.954
ServiceAddress: 123 Service St, Redmond WA, 98052 has confidence 0.949
AmountDue: 610.0 has confidence 0.971
BillingAddress: 123 Bill St, Redmond WA, 98052 has confidence 0.952
BillingAddressRecipient: Microsoft Finance has confidence 0.956
CustomerAddress: 123 Other St, Redmond WA, 98052 has confidence 0.952
CustomerAddressRecipient: Microsoft Corp has confidence 0.954
CustomerId: CID-12345 has confidence 0.962
CustomerName: MICROSOFT CORPORATION has confidence 0.946
DueDate: 2019-12-15 has confidence 0.971
InvoiceDate: 2019-11-15 has confidence 0.967
InvoiceId: INV-100 has confidence 0.971
InvoiceTotal: 110.0 has confidence 0.968
Invoice Items:
...Item #1
......Amount: 60.0 has confidence 0.916
......Date: 2021-03-04 has confidence 0.934
......Description: Consulting Services has confidence 0.9
......ProductCode: A123 has confidence 0.876
......Quantity: 2.0 has confidence 0.9
......Tax: None has confidence 0.8
......Unit: hours has confidence 0.895
......UnitPrice: 30.0 has confidence 0.831
...Item #2
......Amount: 30.0 has confidence 0.959
......Date: 2021-03-05 has confidence 0.902
......Description: Document Fee has confidence 0.901
......ProductCode: B456 has confidence 0.898
......Quantity: 3.0 has confidence 0.9
......Tax: None has confidence 0.787
......UnitPrice: 10.0 has confidence 0.832
...Item #3
......Amount: 10.0 has confidence 0.962
......Date: 2021-03-06 has confidence 0.903
......Description: Printing Fee has confidence 0.899
......ProductCode: C789 has confidence 0.899
......Quantity: 10.0 has confidence 0.911
......Tax: None has confidence 0.802
......Unit: pages has confidence 0.893
......UnitPrice: 1.0 has confidence 0.829
PreviousUnpaidBalance: 500.0 has confidence 0.959
PurchaseOrder: PO-3333 has confidence 0.963
RemittanceAddress: 123 Remit St New York, NY, 10001 has confidence 0.95
RemittanceAddressRecipient: Contoso Billing has confidence 0.954
ServiceAddress: 123 Service St, Redmond WA, 98052 has confidence 0.949
ServiceAddressRecipient: Microsoft Services has confidence 0.95
ServiceEndDate: 2019-11-14 has confidence 0.969
ServiceStartDate: 2019-10-14 has confidence 0.971
ShippingAddress: 123 Ship St, Redmond WA, 98052 has confidence 0.95
ShippingAddressRecipient: Microsoft Delivery has confidence 0.954
SubTotal: 100.0 has confidence 0.971
TotalTax: 10.0 has confidence 0.971
VendorAddress: 123 456th St New York, NY, 10001 has confidence 0.949
VendorAddressRecipient: Contoso Headquarters has confidence 0.954
VendorName: CONTOSO LTD. has confidence 0.954
```

Figure 8.44 – Slim example results of document processing

The details provided previously should give you everything to realize the requirements for deploying the Form Recognizer service.

The Form Recognizer service can certainly improve the process by which your company improves the flow of paperwork; however, it is highly recommended to evaluate the costs required to do so. Evaluating your costs will require an evaluation of many components you can ascertain by working with the department wanting to deploy this solution. When processing thousands of documents in a month, with the storage required for all the details of those documents combined with the services to host the solution, costs can certainly pile up. The Azure Pricing calculator can help with this cost evaluation, as well as several other tools available online for building costing models.

There should also be considerations for error checking and handling that we didn't cover in great detail with this example, such as establishing a list of the minimum required fields before sending to an ERP for automatic processing. In the case of Ocean Smart, the process of settling a purchase of seafood products from vendors became largely impossible due to the multitude of invoice formats and hand-written documents. For standard invoices from vendors, telecommunications companies, and similarly established vendors, the process could be automated with some success after building a consistent model.

## Summary

This chapter covered how the Form Recognizer service was deployed for Ocean Smart with details of the challenges encountered when building the solution. This includes deploying the storage used for document loading, storing, and processing. We also deployed a database for storing the details captured from the document processing with all the required settings for ensuring a secure deployment as well. For our example, we chose to use a Docker container with associated compute requirements to deploy our Form Recognizer example, so be sure to evaluate all options for your deployment. Finally, we provided an example of how Ocean Smart built an interface for the manual upload and processing of documents using the Django framework. There are many ways the service can be used in a production environment, while this chapter provided one option for building your own solution, so evaluate your options for your own deployments.

In the next chapter, we are going to explore how anomalies can be detected with manufacturing equipment on the shop floor of an Ocean Smart seafood production facility using the **Anomaly Detector** service.

# 9

# Identifying Problems with Anomaly Detector

As we've seen so far in this book, there are many opportunities where we can use **artificial intelligence (AI)** with the help of Cognitive Services for a variety of purposes to improve business operations and add value. When we look at the Anomaly Detector service, we will change our focus a bit and examine how Ocean Smart was able to reduce the risk of inventory and raw materials being spoiled. Through the years, millions of dollars worth of product has had to be written off due to spoilage that could potentially have been avoided. With better monitoring and notifications, these unfortunate and costly occurrences could be avoided.

The Anomaly Detector service allows us to monitor streams of data for unexpected or irregular events. We will examine how we can do this with single and multiple, univariate and multivariate, streams of data to recognize and alert about these events as part of daily operations. Our example will take us through the normal activity of chiller usage throughout the week and how to respond to events that occur outside of the normal activity. For example, we use the term chiller to mean a freezing or refrigeration unit where the product is stored within the manufacturing facilities Ocean Smart owns. These units are of critical importance for any perishable food services company, and strict monitoring of behavior and activity can ensure longer-lasting and better-tasting food products. If a chiller is left open too long, intentionally or otherwise, and temperatures increase, food quality can be affected, but it also causes the cooling units to run for longer periods of time, resulting in higher costs.

Traditionally, Ocean Smart did not deploy "smart" monitoring devices that could be monitored remotely, nor have they tracked usage over time. In this chapter, we will demonstrate how they were able to accomplish this, as well as look at seasonal trending information to be able to better anticipate whether an event was normal or anomalous. In this chapter, we will also cover the following areas of the service:

- Overview of the Anomaly Detector service
- Using the Anomaly Detector algorithms with your data
- Configuring and refining monitoring of data in your environment

- Define and detect anomalies in your organization
- Building the complete solution in Azure

This will provide a foundation for understanding how to best leverage the service for detecting your own anomalous activity and providing better visibility to your organization. First, let's look at the technical requirements for deploying the service.

## Technical requirements

To build your Anomaly Detector solution, you will need to have an Azure subscription with at least Contributor rights to the subscription for deploying services. You will need an Azure Storage Account for storing your documents pre- and post-processing. If you plan to deploy the solution to a Docker container or an Azure Web App, you will need experience with those technologies to ensure proper deployment. You will need to have **Visual Studio Code** (**VS Code**) (`https://code.visualstudio.com/Download`) with the `node.js` extension installed (`https://nodejs.org/en/download/package-manager`).

Some other services you may use for your deployment are as follows:

- **Azure Function**: This is for building functions and executing code.
- **Azure Data Factory or similar**: This is for data orchestration and transformation.
- **Azure Logic App**: This is for workflow and triggering mechanisms.
- **Azure Database**: This is for storing output data post-processing.
- **Azure Stream Analytics**: This is for receiving messages when anomalies are detected.

More details are included in the solution at the end of the chapter.

Of course, the more complex and automated your solution is, the more tools you will likely need to know how to use and manage. As with everything, start with the basics, build your **proof of concept** (**PoC**), and add new features. This will help you to save precious time wasted troubleshooting, and so on.

## Overview of the Anomaly Detector service

Anomaly detection is notably one of the most difficult activities presented to any data scientist or AI developer. Many will opt to not work on anomaly detection projects at all due to their inconsistent nature. This is the best way we can think to preface this chapter; it is daunting to get it right, and seemingly even when we get it right, it changes very quickly, as with all technology. As we navigate through the features of this Cognitive Service, try to keep this sentiment in the back of your head to ensure we are approaching the subject in a sobering fashion.

Merriam-Webster defines anomaly as something different, abnormal, peculiar, or not easily classified: `https://www.merriam-webster.com/dictionary/anomaly`.

So, when setting out to build the **Anomaly Detector Cognitive Service**, Microsoft determined its customers could leverage an API where any stream or collection of streams of data might occasionally contain anomalous behavior. The data they were targeting was that of time series, where events are logged over time and we can decipher something anomalous at a point in time, then provide some downstream reaction. This reaction could be a simple alert via SMS or email or a sophisticated cascade of events where we leverage **Internet of Things (IoT)** devices to terminate a physical piece of manufacturing equipment. As such, Ocean Smart looked to apply where the service could be useful in helping with operations or adding other value to the organization. For example, examining chiller operations where costs could be saved. There is a potential for unnecessary costs due to spoiled products or chiller motors constantly running to make up for a door left ajar or just open too long for loading and unloading of product.

The service can allow for single streams of data, called the Univariate Anomaly Detector service, and will look at a single variable, for instance, financial metrics. The second option is used for multiple streams of data, called the Multivariate Anomaly Detector, and looks at multiple data inputs defined by the developer and used to monitor things such as equipment on a manufacturing floor. In this case, we are looking for multiple events being generated simultaneously across several sensors on a machine, and there is a change across several of those streams of data at once because one change likely will not mean there is an issue, but multiple likely will. In the next couple of sections, we will discuss the services in more detail for each Univariate and Multivariate service.

## Univariate Anomaly Detector

As discussed, the Univariate Anomaly Detector service was created to detect anomalous behavior within a single stream of data over a period. After initially evaluating the data supplied to build a sample stream, an algorithm is chosen based on the best fit for the data, regardless of what the data represents. The example we will use later in the chapter displays chiller data for an Ocean Smart freezer unit. Many factors go into whether data is considered "normal" or "anomalous" for the freezer because of the way they are used. Some examples of this are products being pulled out of the freezer early in the morning to be thawed out or to finish a previous day's packing operations of frozen products. Throughout the day, a freezer would be opened to add or remove products for various stages of production, or potentially move products out of the facility altogether. Further, when production operations are finishing at the end of a shift or workday, products would be moved in for temporary or longer-term storage. All these events need to be factored in when evaluating the temperature data for the course of the day, week, month, and so on. There are also seasonality considerations that need to be made, as with the nature of the product being produced, there could potentially be more or fewer times a freezer would be used at different parts of the year. If, for instance, a certain product isn't produced and less freezer space is required in one year compared to the previous or next, we would have to consider this as we are look at the data we are using and providing to the service.

When considering use cases for the Univariate service, there are three features offered for the data you are providing:

- **Real-time detection**: For this feature, you will provide a base sample of data, and the service will pick which model to use with the dataset. Then you will feed a data stream into the service for monitoring as it is received from whatever service is sending the stream. Using the example described previously, that stream of data would be the recorded temperatures coming from the freezer unit on a given interval.

- **Batch anomaly detection**: In this feature scenario, a dataset containing a complete set of data for a given season or generally flat series of data. These two examples might have occasional dips or spikes in the flat series or known anomalies within a season and will have a single statistical model created against each data point in the sample.

- **Batch trending detection**: When the data that you are using has a dramatic change in the trend of the data, for instance using our previous example again, setting a freezer at a different temperature for a different season. In this case, we would have a trend of some negative number that the freezer would be set at in summer because lobster is being processed. For example, we might potentially set another temperature in the winter because another species is stored at a different temperature. The chosen statistical model would then reflect the changes in trends for the various seasons.

Now that we have a good understanding of the three feature types, you should be able to see that we will use the **real-time detection** option for monitoring our chillers during normal operations. It should also be clear that when we want to analyze data over a longer period of time or look for anomalous and change events, we can use a batch operation. So, on this basis, let's now look at how we provide the data stream or batch, the format, and other variables to ensure proper use of the service and the most accurate and performant anomaly detection.

As with many streaming data operations, we will be using the **JSON** format for sending data to the Anomaly Detector. As discussed, the service is expecting time-series data that is presented in a format ordered by time (JSON), such as the example that follows:

```
{
    "granularity": "daily",
    "series": [
        {
            "timestamp": "2018-03-01T00:00:00Z",
            "value": 32858923
        },
        {
            "timestamp": "2018-03-02T00:00:00Z",
            "value": 29615278
        },
    ]
}
```

You will note from the previous block of code that we have several parameters that are defined for sending to the service:

- `granularity`: `granularity` is a common term used in fields where we are visualizing data, such as **business intelligence** (**BI**) and similar practices. The granularity defines the rate at which your data is presented to the service, for example, every five minutes. One thing that is important to consider is that the service expects the granularity to be consistent through the data stream and will cause inconsistent results if it isn't.

- `series`: With the `series` parameter, we are stating that we will start providing the details of the data stream and events.

- `timestamp`: The `timestamp` parameter defines the date and time of the events as they occur in the data stream. This value is expressed in UTC.

- `Value`: The `value` parameter is whatever reading is pulled from what you are monitoring. In our previous example, this would be temperature.

The next group of parameters and details may be found useful for abnormal or well-known data streams from a configuration perspective:

- `CustomInterval` (optional): The `customInterval` parameter allows us to define whether there is a non-standard interval, periods other than a standard second, minute, hour, and so on, for when the data will be received. This parameter can be set with a minute value; for instance, `"customInterval" : 20` would represent a 20-minute span between data points.

- `Period` (optional): The `period` parameter allows you to set an expected number of data points over a certain period; for instance, if you expected 10 data points per hour, 24 hours a day, the period setting would be (10*24). By using this setting, the API knows what to expect over a given period and will lower the overhead on the compute and reduce latency by up to 50% for response time.

- `Boundaries` (optional): As your model is developed and refined over time, it will develop an `expectedValue` variable within the model. This is the value of a typical data point supplied. If you want to specify boundaries for your model which will trigger as anomalous data if outside those boundaries, you can do so by setting an upper and lower margin. This is specified by using the following parameters in your code using temperature as our expected value:

  - `upperBoundary` with a calculation of `expectedValue + (3 - marginScale) * upperMargin` will set our boundary to 3 degrees above the expected value.

  - `lowerBoundary` with a calculation of `expectedValue - (3 - marginScale) * lowerMargin` will set our boundary to 3 degrees below the expected value.

- Missing data points: It is a normal occurrence to lose up to 10% of data points, so the service takes that into account and tends not to record it as anomalous if data points are missing at expected intervals.

- There is a minimum of 12 and a maximum of 8,640 data points that can be sent in a batch to the API service, but note that the more data points, the longer it will take to detect anomalies.

When it is time to deploy the Anomaly Detector service, as with many Cognitive Services, you are essentially provisioning the compute required to train your model and other operations. For a real-time data stream to be sent to the Anomaly Detector, the devices you are working with will need to be able to send the data via some sort of stream. An option for this would be to use an **Azure Event Hub** to receive the data from the device, or chiller in this case, and pass the data to the service.

We will get into the deployment and development details for building a real-time solution with the example later in this chapter. However, now that you have a good overview of what the Univariate Anomaly Detector can do for your organization in the way of monitoring time-series data for anomalous activities in either batch or real-time form, let's look at what the Multivariate option brings us.

## Multivariate Anomaly Detector

As discussed, the Univariate Anomaly Detector gives us a good way to identify data that may be unexpected in a stream or batch, so let's discuss what the Multivariate option provides for a group of data streams. In this scenario, we look at multiple sources of data in batch or streaming format, how those data sources are correlated, and when one or more of the streams are abnormal. Standard uses for this service are typically centered around how the various streams of data are related on a macro level. For instance, monitoring an engine for various components, manufacturing equipment, and other examples where events may be dictated by different components.

The process for working with the Multivariate detector is somewhat different from the Univariate service, and given the varying use cases, it is important to determine which version to use for your case prior to deployment. Starting out, one of the biggest differences is that with Univariate detection, you aren't creating a machine learning model and instead using a standard statistical model to look for anomalies. With the Multivariate service, you develop your custom model related to the data you are providing to the service for later detection. As you prepare your data, you will have to split your datasets into two, one for training your model and the other for **data inferencing**. For training, the service requires the data to be loaded into **Azure Storage** and a **shared access signature key** (**SAS key**) to be passed via the API to pick up the dataset and choose a training API.

Now our data is where it needs to be, and we are ready to train our model. A couple of things to note about training your model:

- Your training dataset needs to be in a `.csv` format with only two columns, a timestamp, and a value in each row.

- The `.csv` file you are using needs to be compressed into a `.zip` file that will then be placed in your storage account. As of the time of writing, the column names must be `timestamp` and `value`, and the timestamp value has to conform to ISO 8601 standards in the format YYYY-MM-DDTHH:MM:SSZ.

- Your `.csv` file or files should be located in the root folder of the `.zip` file. If you place the files in a subfolder below the root, the files will not be processed properly.

- For the data inferencing portion, you have the option to use the same process as training, or you could send the data directly to an API formatted as JSON with either the **synchronous (Sync)** or **asynchronous (Async)** API.

When training your model, you will simply post a request to the API using the following format:

- There are only three required input parameters that are contained within your request header. A sample of the headers is as follows:

```
[POST] https://{endpoint-url}/multivariate/models
header ={"Content-Type": "application/json", "Ocp-Apim-
Subscription-Key": "azure_subscription_key"}
request=
{
"source": SOURCE_BLOB_SAS_KEY
"startTime": "2021-01-01T00:00:00Z",
"endTime": "2021-01-02T12:00:00Z"
}
```

Each of the parameters is described in the following:

- `Source`: The location of the source training file stored in the Azure Blob container specified with the SAS URL.

- `startTime`: The Zulu time of where the training data starts with the accompanying value of the reading.

- `endTime`: The Zulu time of where the training data ends, being later than `startTime`. If equal to `startTime`, the service will read this as a single data point that would be used in a streaming scenario.

- From this request, you will get a returned value of the location of the model resembling the following:

```
Location: {endpoint-url}/multivariate/models/{model id} # GUID
```

- The remaining available parameters are largely used to work with the data in the file, such as padding of data and alignment where needed. All available values can be found here: `https://docs.microsoft.com/en-us/azure/cognitive-services/anomaly-detector/tutorials/learn-multivariate-anomaly-detection`.

    To check the results of which models have been developed, we have to complete a request to show all available models and ensure our newly created model exists by using the following request:

    ```
    [GET] https://{endpoint-url}/anomalydetector/v1.1-preview/
    multivariate/models[?$skip] [&$top]
    ```

- The `$skip` parameter is optional and defines how many models you want to skip in your request, assuming you know the first set of models are already complete, and you're looking to see the results of a newer training only. This number is specified with an integer value.

- The `$top` parameter is optional and lists the number of models you want to list in your request by *display name* if defined and the model ID.

- Your request header should look like the following code block:

    ```
    header = {"Content-Type": "application/json", "Ocp-Apim-
    Subscription-Key": "azure_subscription_key"}
    ```

- If you get a 200 response, your request is successful, and the most current models trained will be displayed. The results will be returned with `modelID`, `createdTime`, `lastUpdatedTime`, `status`, `displayName`, and `variablesCount` in JSON format for each model detected.

- A 500, 403, or 405 from an error response means there is an error with your request or the model hasn't been trained yet.

Now that our model is trained and ready for detection, let's look at the difference between the Async and Sync APIs when identifying anomalies.

## Using the Anomaly Detector algorithms with your data

When looking at options for detecting anomalies using the Multivariate service, we can use the Async or Sync API. Your use case will dictate which one you choose, but typically the Async process is used for looking at a batch of data and pointing out the anomalous data points. The Sync process is typically used for real-time data monitoring for anomalies. This can be determined based on your particular need depending on the latency of the data and the number of data points. Let's start with the Async API first.

## Async API

To get the status of the detection activity with the Async API, you must request the status from the service by choosing the proper API. To do so, you must use the Request URL to display your Anomaly Detector service with models created earlier. After your model has been trained and you are ready for inferencing with another dataset, you can use the same process of sending your request through the API for detecting anomalies within a batch or single value being sent to the service using the Async API:

1. To get started, you must first identify which model you want to use for detection based on what you have already created.

2. After you know the model ID based on the results of the previous request, you will need to capture the ID for use with your detection request to specify the model you want to use, so copy and paste it somewhere, or if you must, write it down.

3. To start the detection process, send a POST activity to the API URL for your service specifying the model ID of the model you want to use, such as the following code. Your header request will look as follows:

```
[POST] https://{endpoint-url}/multivariate/models/{model_id}/
detect
header ={"Content-Type": "application/json", "Ocp-Apim-
Subscription-Key": "azure_subscription_key"}
request={
   "source": SOURCE_BLOB_SAS,
   "startTime": "2020-01-01T00:00:00Z",
   "endTime": "2020-02-01T00:00:00Z"
}
```

4. This request will return resultid that you will use to get the results of the detection request. Your header request will look something like this:

```
header ={"Content-Type": "application/json", "Ocp-Apim-
Subscription-Key": "azure_subscription_key"}
```

5. Finally, you can request the results of the detection operation with the following command:

```
[GET] https://{endpoint-url}/multivariate/results/{result_id}
```

6. For your headers, you're simply passing content type and Azure subscription key as shown in the following code block:

```
header ={"Content-Type": "application/json", "Ocp-Apim-
Subscription-Key": "azure_subscription_key"}
```

7.  What you will get back from this in the response is a list of any errors that occurred, the variables specified from the detection activity, and the results of the detection. A sample readout of the results would look something like the following:

```
Response={
        "resultId": "663884e6-b117-11ea-b3de-0242ac130004",
        "summary": {
          "status": "READY",
          "errors": [],
```

Here, we display the detection request variables, which are the time-series values and timestamps from the inferenced dataset:

```
"variableStates": [
    {
      "variable": "variable_1",
      "filledNARatio": 0,
      "effectiveCount": 30,
      "startTime": "2021-01-01T00:00:00Z",
      "endTime": "2021-01-01T00:29:00Z"
    },
    {
      "variable": "variable_2",
      "filledNARatio": 0,
      "effectiveCount": 30,
      "startTime": "2021-01-01T00:00:00Z",
      "endTime": "2021-01-01T00:29:00Z"
    },
    {
      "variable": "variable_3",
      "filledNARatio": 0,
      "effectiveCount": 30,
      "startTime": "2021-01-01T00:00:00Z",
      "endTime": "2021-01-01T00:29:00Z"
    }
  ]
```

- Here, we see the initial setup details for the location and start and end times of the input dataset:

```
"setupInfo": {
    "source": SOURCE_BLOB_SAS,
    "startTime": "2021-01-01T00:00:00Z",
    "endTime": "2021-01-01T00:29:00Z"
}
,
```

- Here, we display the results of the detection process. Note that we are provided with whether or not the value is an anomaly compared to the training data model, the severity of the anomaly, and its score:

```
"results": [
  {
    "timestamp": "2021-01-01T00:28:00Z",
    "value": {
      "isAnomaly": false,
      "severity": 0,
      "score": 0.6928471326828003
    },
    "errors": []
  },
```

This example in the following block shows an anomaly in the data with the associated severity and score, as well as its interpretation details:

```
  {
    "timestamp": "2021-01-01T00:29:00Z",
    "value": {
      "isAnomaly": true,
      "severity": 0.5337404608726501,
      "score": 0.9171165823936462,
```

This code block begins to provide the interpretation of the anomaly detected by a variable starting with `variable-2`:

```
"interpretation": [
    {
      "variable": "variable_2",
      "contributionScore": 0.5371576215,
      "correlationChanges": {
        "changedVariables": [
          "variable_1",
          "variable_3"
        ],
        "changedValues": [
          0.1741322,
          0.1093203
        ]
      }
    },
```

8.  Next, we look at the details from `variable_3`:

```
                     {
                       "variable": "variable_3",
                       "contributionScore": 0.3324159383,
                       "correlationChanges": {
                         "changedVariables": [
                           "variable_2"
                         ],
                         "changedValues": [
                           0.1229392
                         ]
                       }
                     },
```

9.  Finally, we look at the details for `variable_1`:

```
                     {
                       "variable":
    "variable_1",               "contributionScore": 0.1304264402,
                       "correlationChanges": {
                         "changedVariables": [],
                         "changedValues": []
                       }
                     }
                   ]
                 }
               }
             ]
           }
```

This completes the output for the async request of the results of our detection activity. Next, let's look at the sync API call in a simplified form.

## Sync API

To use the **Sync API**, typically for a stream of data points, you will make an API call and contain all the information in the previous section within a single request:

- This request requires a couple more parameters as well and will result in an initial post request looking like the following:

```
[POST] https://{endpoint-url}/multivariate/models/{modelId}/
last/detect
```

- As part of your header request, you will have to provide the `variables` parameter, containing the time-series and timestamp information and `detectingPoints`, providing instructions for how many timestamps to detect.

- This will return a similar result to what is displayed previously from the Async API call. In either case, that result can then be parsed, and further action can be taken, such as logging activity or notifying a user of the anomaly.

The results of those details can then be captured within a database or storage account for further use, such as displaying anomalous activity on a Power BI report or dashboard. The results can also be captured for re-training your model to eliminate false positives or looking at longer-term trend information. The service has a few other functions we didn't talk about in this section, but here is the list of the existing capabilities of the Multivariate Anomaly Detection service:

- List models: [GET]/`multivariate/models`

- Train a model: [POST] /`multivariate/models`

- Get a model: [GET] /`multivariate/models/{model_id}`

- Delete a model: [DELETE] /`multivariate/models/{model_id}`

- Detect anomalies: [POST] /`multivariate/models/{model_id}`/detect

- Detect anomalies with the Sync API: [POST] /`multivariate/models/{model_id}`/last/detect

- Get detection result: [GET] /`multivariate/results/{result_id}`

- Export model as a ZIP file: [POST] /`multivariate/models/{modelId}`/export

The developers of the service have deployed a GitHub repository where you can find reference information for all these capabilities, and that can be found here: `https://github.com/Azure-Samples/AnomalyDetector/blob/master/ipython-notebook/API%20Sample/Multivariate%20API%20Demo%20Notebook.ipynb`.

Next, we will give an overview of how to get the Anomaly Detector deployed in your environment that you can potentially take advantage of for solving your use case.

# Configuring and refining monitoring of data in your environment

Now that we have had a chance to look at what the Async and Sync APIs offer in the way of anomaly detection and the differences between the Univariate and Multivariate services, let's look at how to put this detailed understanding of the APIs into practice.

In the example we built for later in this chapter, you will find that we wanted to provide a simple example of how to send data from our freezer into Azure to leverage the service using an Event Hub. If we did not have the option to send the data to the cloud because of security reasons, or unavailability of internet connectivity, we could have used the Univariate service in a Docker container deployed to an IoT device. This could present other challenges for how to report on the anomalies and trend analysis but could be handled with other Microsoft products that can still be deployed on-premises, such as Power BI Report Server. Currently, only the Univariate service can be deployed to a container, so hopefully, Microsoft will follow suit and give us the ability to deploy the Multivariate service to a container in the future.

Our ultimate goal and purpose for using this service is to look for irregularities in one or more critical components of the business and to get started; we need to be able to get our data into Azure for monitoring. As mentioned previously, we can use something such as an Event Hub for receiving streaming data, then passing it to a database or storage account, or we can develop another method to stream the data directly to a storage account. As the following reference architecture from Microsoft shows, there are several methods by which we can take advantage of the service and use accompanying services to maximize its value:

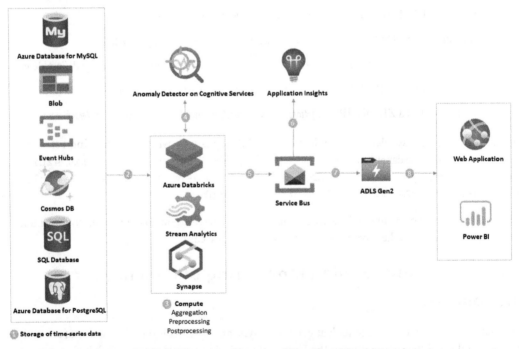

Figure 9.1 – Anomaly Detector reference architecture with additional services

If we dig a little deeper into the stages of this architecture in the previous diagram, we will discover there are many ways to utilize the service. Keep in mind, this is not an exhaustive list of services available and is only intended to give some ideas on how to use various components alongside Anomaly Detectors to satisfy use cases and provide value. The following provides an overview of how our data flows through the components and their purpose.

1.  Our data can be stored in several sources as our origination point where the data might be collected. The flexibility of Azure allows for various databases and other services where the data could persist.

2.  Other than the Blob service, we need an additional service to be able to send our data to the Anomaly Detector. Another decision point here is if you want real-time detection or batch processing to help decide which services you might use downstream.

3.  If our data requires any kind of processing, querying, cleansing, aggregation, or any other intervention, services such as **Azure Synapse**, **Azure Databricks**, and **Stream Analytics** can help with any of that data processing. Whichever specific service you will choose, it will largely depend on two things:

    *   You need to identify is the type of processing required to identify which service you will use. If it's a purely streaming workload that may need some querying or data consolidation, Stream Analytics will help push your data to Azure Blob post-processing.

    *   Azure Databricks or Synapse can help with processing large amounts of data by distributing the workload across many compute nodes, then sending the data to Azure Blob post-processing. Typically, this choice depends on your comfort level with the service you're using and the experience of the team. Azure Databricks requires the use of **Notebooks** and code for any processing needs, and Synapse can process data using a **graphic user interface** (GUI) for many activities.

4.  Now that our data has been processed and aggregated, we can send it to the Anomaly Detector directly and get our results back to determine what to do with our detected anomalies.

5.  We can use the **Service Bus** for message routing and performing downstream activity. So if we need to send a notification or want to do further analysis on the application, we can use **a Service Bus message queue** to do so.

6.  Application Insights is an Azure service that provides details about the usage of applications that are deployed. For instance, the service can provide details about the performance of the website (latency, connectivity, and so on) as well as monitor live websites, helping to ensure continuity. This step certainly shouldn't be considered a requirement but more just an example of how the service can be used to provide additional information about what's going on in the environment.

7.  We can send our data to **Azure Data Lake Storage** (ADLS) for additional information later. ADLS offers a great location for storing data hierarchically or raw at a very low cost.

8.  Finally, after we have collected all the information about our detected anomalies, you can report on it with Power BI. Alternatively, you could send the data to an application where it can be consumed by a customer or partner, for instance, or used in some other way.

A couple of other considerations for deploying your workload are given as follows:

- **Authentication**: For every request to an Azure Cognitive Service, an authentication header needs to be included. This header typically includes an **Azure subscription key** or an **authentication token**. Another option for authentication is to use **Azure Active Directory** (**Azure AD**), which is quickly becoming a standard authentication method for customers using Microsoft 365 and Azure services. Examples of these authentication types are as follows:

  - **Subscription key authentication**:

    ```
    curl -X GET 'https://api.cognitive.microsoft.com/bing/v7.0/
    search?q=Welsch%20Pembroke%20Corgis' \
    -H 'Ocp-Apim-Subscription-Key: YOUR_SUBSCRIPTION_KEY' | json_pp
    ```

  - **Access token authentication**:

    ```
    curl -v -X POST \
    "https://YOUR-REGION.api.cognitive.microsoft.com/sts/v1.0/
    issueToken" \
    -H "Content-type: application/x-www-form-urlencoded" \
    -H "Content-length: 0" \
    -H "Ocp-Apim-Subscription-Key: YOUR_SUBSCRIPTION_KEY"
    ```

  - Azure AD authentication requires several steps to create; however, it is more convenient once built. To complete this authentication, you will first need to create a custom subdomain for your Cognitive Service, then assign a service principal role to the subdomain with the **Cognitive services user** standard role and authenticate with your tenant. More detailed instructions can be found at https://docs.microsoft.com/en-us/azure/cognitive-services/authentication?context=%2Fazure%2Fcognitive-services%2Fanomaly-detector%2Fcontext%2Fcontext&tabs=powershell#authenticate-with-azure-active-directory.

- **Networking**: To secure any Cognitive Services resource, you should default to denying all requests and then specifying specific IP addresses, IP ranges, or a list of subnets that are allowed access. This can be done using various Firewall and Network Security Gateway resources depending on your vendor of choice or Azure-specific services. Many Azure services have the option to allow traffic from other Azure services in the *Networking* section of the deployment steps in the Azure Portal; however, be sure to understand the implications of allowing this traffic before you enable it. Furthermore, there are occasions when the service can only allow Azure traffic when it is deployed and can only be enabled or disabled afterward by destroying and re-deploying the service. Make sure to take every precaution when it comes to security considerations and validate your security procedures with qualified professionals before deployment.

This section should provide a good overview of how you might want to leverage one of the Anomaly Detector APIs and accompanying Azure services to build a production application. Next, we will discuss how to build a business case and determine areas where you might be able to take advantage of the services in your organization.

# Defining and detecting anomalies in your organization

Beyond giving examples of how the services can be deployed, this book intends to provide some insight on how to apply AI, hopefully helping to streamline operations and other related benefits. When you start to analyze activities where you might be able to use AI, it helps to look at where unexpected events can occur and how you can better predict the potential for failure. Even if the prediction is especially challenging, there is likely an opportunity to monitor equipment and other capital resources for unexpected events and develop predictability over time.

An area of interest where Ocean Smart could expand is to use the Multivariate detector to look at the overall freezer health, including some of the various elements of a freezer. Then taking that example, similar logic could be applied across locations for all freezers and chillers. This could potentially save significant electricity overhead costs and extend the life of the freezing and chilling units.

Continuing in the ilk of our freezer example from the previous section, we look at what events can be correlated from various components of the freezer unit. There are many elements that can be monitored from a single unit, including temperature, door status (open or closed), compressor state (on or off), electricity usage, vibration, fan speeds, and other features. If we monitor the states of all these streams of data or capture them in a file or database, we may be able to predict situations where the product isn't properly frozen, electrical costs increase, or other related events.

Even if a prediction is not an option because we are not monitoring the data in a real-time scenario, we can analyze where perhaps a failure is imminent or a freezer door is open too long. These types of detections can ensure that we minimize downtime for that freezing unit or be prepared by moving the product to a different freezer. This will allow us time to repair the faulty component before it causes a production interruption and, thus, additional cost. Furthermore, we could even consider employing other Cognitive Services such as Spatial Analysis, an option in the Vision category. This service could be used to monitor the capacity of the freezer and the percentage of fullness. If we aggregate this data with the other streams previously listed, we could correlate the effect of varying levels of fullness as it compares to the performance of the other components. More details of the Vision category can be found in *Chapter 10*.

Some other examples where the Univariate and Multivariate services have been deployed for real-world examples are as follows:

- **Medical device manufacturing**: Medical devices go through stringent testing procedures where massive amounts of data from several areas of the components being developed are captured and analyzed to ensure proper function, precision, and durability. An Anomaly Detector can analyze these massive batches of data to identify where there could be a quality issue or potential failure point.

- **Sales discount analysis**: Many market factors influence selling prices for products and how they are discounted for customers. With the Multivariate service, a company can analyze various factors impacting the appropriate discounting for maximizing profitability.

- **Aviation engine and autopilot monitoring**: The vast array of sensors that can be added to aircraft engines, as many as 150 or more, will send troves of data reported from each sensor. Also, the factors that need to be taken into account when autopilot is being used and when it shouldn't are growing as the sophistication of aircraft increases. With the Multivariate service, customers can easily monitor and analyze these streams of data for anomalous activity and notify the pilot of the aircraft and any ground operations to prepare for an incoming aircraft. This use case will help aircraft fly more efficiently and safely as the number of aircraft increases dramatically year over year.

Hopefully, these examples provide you some food for thought on how you might be able to take advantage of the Anomaly Detector services in your organization. Next, we will walk you through the full process of deploying the Univariate service in Azure step by step.

## Building the complete solution in Azure

Here, we will use the Anomaly Detector service to look for anomalies in refrigerator temperature readings. This example is a slice of what might exist in a real-world implementation; however, we have simplified the flow so we may concentrate on the Cognitive Service and not a full-blown IoT implementation. For our example, we will use the following diagram as our reference architecture:

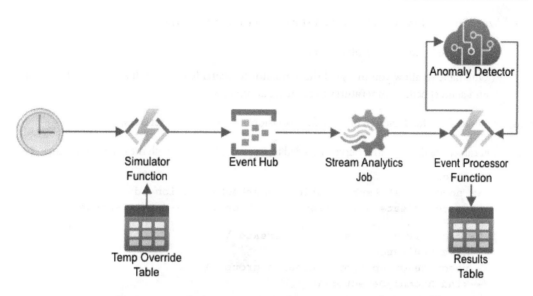

Figure 9.2 – Reference architecture for the example of building
an anomaly detector in an operational service

The basic building blocks of this solution include the following:

- An Azure function to simulate the refrigerator readings.

  - For ease of deployment and to keep things in one place, for this example, we have implemented the simulator as an Azure function. You could take the same basic code and implement it outside of Azure as well – as long as you have connectivity to the Azure Event Hub.

- An Azure Event Hub to receive these readings.

  - You would likely have a buffer, such as an IoT gateway between your refrigerator and Azure. An IoT gateway would broke the connection from your physical assets on-premises to Azure, so you only had one device directly connected to the internet. You would also be looking at Azure IoT Hub instead of Event Hubs. Again, for simplicity, we boiled this down to one Event Hub.

- **Azure Stream Analytics** will process events and send batches of them to a function that will call the Anomaly Detector API.

- An Azure function to receive the event batches from Azure Stream Analytics and detect anomalies using the Cognitive Service.

- For this example, we use the single-variable (univariate) method of Anomaly Detector, and we are only concerned with whether or not the latest reading is anomalous.

- Azure Storage Tables will be used for storing data as it is processed:

  - One table to hold the results of Anomaly Detector.

  - One table to allow you to signal the simulator to override the default simulation behavior and send specific temperatures to simulate anomalies.

Now, we will look at the deployment steps for provisioning the required services:

1.  You can create the Cognitive Services needed to support this process with the following commands:

```
az login
az account set -subscription <your-subscription-id>
az group create --location <your_location> --name <resouce_
group>
az cognitiveservices account create \
--name ch09-anomaly \
--resource-group <your-resource-group> \
--kind AnomalyDetector \
--sku F0 \
--location eastus2 \
```

2.  Next, we create the storage account and tables used by the solution:

```
az storage account create \
--name ch09storage \
--resource-group <resource_group> \
--location eastus2
az storage table create \
--name tempanomalyresults \
--account-name ch09storage
az storage table create \
--name temperatureoverride \
--account-name ch09storage
```

3.  Next, we will create the Event Hub. First, we create an Event Hub namespace. The namespace provides an endpoint for event publishers and consumers to connect to. Inside the namespace, you create the Event Hub to receive the event:

```
az eventhubs namespace create --name ch09-eventhub-ns \
--resource-group <resource_group> \
--location eastus
eventhubs eventhub create --name chillertemps \
 --resource-group <resource_group> \
--namespace-name ch09-eventhub-ns
```

Azure Stream Analytics will read events from the Event Hub and batch them to send to the Azure function responsible for detecting the anomalies:

```
az stream-analytics job create \
    --resource-group <resource_group>
    --name chapoter09asa \
    --location eastus2 \
```

Now we are set up to create our Azure functions. To follow this example, you will need:

- Python version 3.9.6

- Azure Functions Core Tools

- VS Code

- Python extension for VS Code

- Azure Functions extension for VS Code

If you open the \Chapter 09\Code Snippets\AnomalyDetectionFuncs folder in VS Code, you should see the following folder structure:

Figure 9.3 – Items found in the AnomalyDetectionFuncs folder

The following provides an overview of files and folders that are important to the function runtime:

- The `SimulateChillerEvents` and `ProcessChillerEvents` folders are the two functions in this function app. We will expand on them a bit later in the chapter.

- `local.settings-sample.json`: This contains the settings that the functions will need to execute properly. Notice that the key values are not specified.

- `local.settings.json`: This is not yet present in your repo. You will create this file shortly.

- `requirements.txt`: When you deploy your function app, the function app runtime pip installs any packages listed in `requirements.txt`.

Let's take a look at `local.settings-sample.json` and create a copy that is configured to your environment.

Make a copy of `local.settings-sample.json` and name it `local.settings.json`.

You should see the following:

```json
{
  "IsEncrypted": false,
  "Values": {
    "AzureWebJobsStorage" : "connection string to storage account",
    "chapter09_storage" : "connection string to storage account",
    "FUNCTIONS_WORKER_RUNTIME" : "python",
    "chillertemp_ connectionstring" : "connection string to event hub
with listen policy",
    "anomaly_detector_subscription_key" : "access key from anomaly
detector cognitive service",
    "anomaly_detector_endpoint" : "endpoint url from anomaly detector
cognitive service"
  }
}
```

`chapter09_storage` and `AzureWebJobStorage`: These values are the connection string to the storage account created previously. You can retrieve this connection string with the following command:

```
az storage account show-connection-string --name chapter09st
```

`chillertemp_connectionstring`: This is used to connect to our Event Hub namespace to send and receive event messages. You can retrieve this key with the following command:

```
az eventhubs namespace authorization-rule keys list --resource-
group <resource_group> --namespace-name <eventhub_name> --name
RootManageSharedAccessKey --query "primaryConnectionString"
```

anomaly_detector_subscription_key: This can be found with the following command:

```
az cognitiveservices account keys list \
--name oceansmart-anomaly-detector \
--resource-group <resource_group> \
--query "key1"
```

anomaly_detector_endpoint: This can be found with the following command:

```
az cognitiveservices account show \
--name oceansmart-anomaly-detector \
--resource-group <resource_group> \
--query "properties.endpoint"
```

At this point, we have the services deployed and the configuration set. We can look at the code in each of the functions and get ready to deploy the function app and code.

## The SimulateChillerEvents function

Each of the functions contains two main files:

- __init__.py: This contains the code for the function
- function.json: This contains the configuration and bindings for the function

Let's look at function.json first.

First, we see that "scriptfile" points to "__init__.py". This tells the runtime that the code to execute when this file is called is located in that file:

```
{
    "scriptFile": "__init__.py",
```

The bindings section lists input and output parameters that the function runtime will supply to the function. The first binding here is our trigger, a timer trigger that will run every 10 seconds:

```
"bindings": [
  {
    "name": "mytimer",
    "type": "timerTrigger",
    "direction": "in",
    "schedule": "10 * * * * *"
  },
```

We configure the `"tempoverride"` binding to connect to an Azure Storage Table. As you will see in the function code, when the function is called, it will look at the table and retrieve one entity from the `"temperatureoverride"` table and pass it to our function as an input parameter:

```
{
    "name": "tempoverride",
    "type": "table",
    "tableName": "temperatureoverride",
    "partitionKey": "temps",
    "take": "1",
    "connection": "chapter09_storage",
    "direction": "in"
},
```

Naming our binding `$return` indicates that the value returned from our function will be passed to this binding, in this case, our Azure Event Hub:

```
{
    "type": "eventHub",
    "name": "$return",
    "eventHubName": "chillertemps",
    "connection": "chillertemp_sender_connectionstring",
    "direction": "out"
}
]
```

In the `__init__.py` file, we find the code that will be executed when a new file lands in this storage container.

The entry point to the function is called `main`. Note that we have two parameters to this function that map to the bindings in `function.json`. The return type of the function is `str` and will hold the message that is sent to our Event Hub:

```
def main(mytimer: func.TimerRequest,
         tempoverride
    ) -> str:
```

Settings from our `local.settings` file are exposed to our function as **operating system (OS)** environment variables. With the following command, we read the connection string for our storage account:

```
STORAGE_CONNECTION_STRING = os.environ["chapter09_storage"]
```

As we will be simulating time series data, let's get the current date and time to send as part of our message with the following command:

```
now = datetime.datetime.utcnow()
date_string = now.strftime('%Y-%m-%d')
time_string = now.strftime('%H:%M:%S')
```

The parameter associated with the `temperatureoverride` storage table binding is of type string and, if there is an entity in the table, contains a JSON document with the first entity returned. The entity is wrapped in an array as the binding generally returns multiple entities – in our binding definition, we limit the query to return only one entity:

```
tempoverride_json = json.loads(tempoverride)
```

If an entity is found in the table, use the included value, and delete the entity. Unfortunately, we cannot delete an entity from the storage table binding, so we must use the Python **software development kit (SDK)** for Azure Storage Tables to delete the entity:

```
if len(tempoverride_json)>0:
    temperature = float(tempoverride_json[0]["set_temp"])
    table_client = \
        TableClient.from_connection_string( \
        STORAGE_CONNECTION_STRING, "temperatureoverride")
    table_client.delete_entity("temps", \
        tempoverride_json[0]["RowKey"])
```

If no entity is returned from the binding set the temperature to a random value close to the 43.2 degrees:

```
else:
    temperature = round(random.normalvariate(43.2, .3), 1)
```

We now have enough information to format the message that we send to the Event Hub. The model number and serial number are hard coded here, but you could experiment with sending temperature events for multiple refrigeration devices:

```
message = {
            'date_utc': f'{date_string}',
            'time_utc': f'{time_string}',
            'model': 'DWE',
            'chiller_serial': '16346834',
            'pod_serial': '19072218',
            'temp_f': temperature
        }
```

Finally, return the message from the function. Our output binding will send that message to the Event Hub:

```
return json.dumps(message)
```

Ok, so that wraps up the code on the simulate function, now let's look at the processing of events:

## The ProcessChillerEvents function

Each of the functions contains two main files:

- `__init__.py`: This contains the code for the function
- `function.json`: This contains the configuration and bindings for the function

Let's look at `function.json` first.

First, we see that the `scriptfile` points to `"__init__.py"`. This tells the runtime that the code to execute when this file is called is located in that file:

```
{
    "scriptFile": "__init__.py",
```

The bindings section lists input and output parameters that the function runtime will supply bindings to the function. The first binding here is our trigger. Our trigger here is an HTTP trigger. Our stream analytics job will execute this function via HTTP:

```
"bindings": [
  {
    "type": "httpTrigger",
    "direction": "in",
    "name": "req"
  },
```

We will output the results of our anomaly detection to an Azure Storage Table. In a real implementation, we would likely send this data to a dashboard or maybe trigger a notification via email or text message to create a maintenance ticket. For simplicity, in this example, we will leverage an Azure Storage Table to hold our results:

```
  {
    "name": "outputmessage",
    "type": "table",
    "tableName": "tempanomalyresults",
    "partitionKey": "results",
    "connection": " storage",
```

```
        "direction": "out"
     }
   ]
}
```

In the `__init__.py` file, we find the code that will be executed when a new file lands in this storage container.

The entry point to the function is called `main`. Note that we have two parameters to this function that map to the bindings in `function.json`. The data in the HTTP trigger is exposed through the parameter named `req`, and we will write data to the `outputmessage` parameter that is bound to our Azure Storage Table:

```
def main(req: func.HttpRequest,
            outputmessage: func.Out[str]):
```

Settings from our `local.settings` file are exposed to our function as OS environment variables. Here, we read the settings to connect to our Anomaly Detector Cognitive Service instance:

```
    ANOMALY_DETECTOR_SUBSCRIPTION_KEY = \
  os.environ["anomaly_detector_subscription_key"]
    ANOMALY_DETECTOR_ENDPOINT = \
  os.environ["anomaly_detector_endpoint"]
```

The body of the HTTP request should contain a `json` array of temperature readings. If it does not include a response or the array has no elements, we will just return without performing any work:

```
    req_body = req.get_json()

    if (len(req_body) == 0):
        logging.info("empty body")
        return
```

The Stream Analytics job returns an array of "windows" of data. Our job will only return one window. Here, we reference the first window with a `temperature_readings` variable:

```
    temperature_readings = req_body[0]
```

The Anomaly Detector service requires an array of the `TimeSeriesPoint` objects. We loop through the readings passed to us from the Stream Analytics job and build up the expected array. Our simulator passes date and time information as separate items. We need to put the date into the required ISO format for the Anomaly Detector service:

```
    series = []
    for reading in temperature_readings["details"]:
        time_parts = f'{reading["time_utc"]}'.split(":")
```

```
event_time= f'{reading["date_utc"]}' +
            'T{time_parts[0]}:{time_parts[1]}:00Z'
series.append(
    TimeSeriesPoint(
        timestamp=datetime.fromisoformat(event_time),
        value=reading['temp_f']))
```

We now have enough information to call the Anomaly Detector. First, we create an `Anomaly Detector request` object from our time series and tell the service to look at anomalies with a one-minute granularity. We create an instance of `AnomalyDetectorClient` with our endpoint and subscription key that we read from the settings and call the `detect_last_point` method. This will tell us whether the last point in our time series looks like an anomaly based on the other readings that we have:

```
request = DetectRequest(series=series,
    granularity=TimeGranularity.PER_MINUTE)
client = AnomalyDetectorClient(
    AzureKeyCredential(ANOMALY_DETECTOR_SUBSCRIPTION_KEY),
    ANOMALY_DETECTOR_ENDPOINT)
response = client.detect_last_point(request)
```

Finally, format the output message and store the data in the Azure Storage Table:

```
rowKey = str(uuid.uuid4())
data = {
    "PartitionKey": "result",
    "RowKey": rowKey,
    "is_anomaly": response.is_anomaly,
    "data": temperature_readings
}
outputmessage.set(json.dumps(data))
```

That concludes the code for the processing events function. Next, let's look at message receiving with Azure Stream Analytics.

## The Azure Stream Analytics job

The final piece we need to put in place for this solution is the Stream Analytics job that reads the events from the simulator and aggregates batches of events to send to our `ProcessChillerEvents` function.

A Stream Analytics job reads events from one or more sources, passes those event streams through a transformation query, and outputs windows of data to one or more outputs. In this case, our input is our Event Hub, and our output is the function:

1.  In the **Settings** section of the Stream Analytics job in the Azure portal, select **Inputs**:

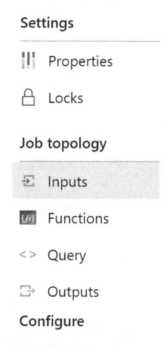

Figure 9.4 – Configuration options in the Azure portal for Stream Analytics

2.  Next, select **Add stream input**, then **Event Hub**:

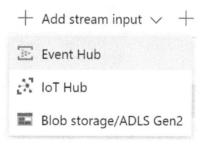

Figure 9.5 – Configuration of the Add stream input option in the Azure portal

3.  Select **Event Hub** from your subscription. The settings for the input should look something like the following screenshot:

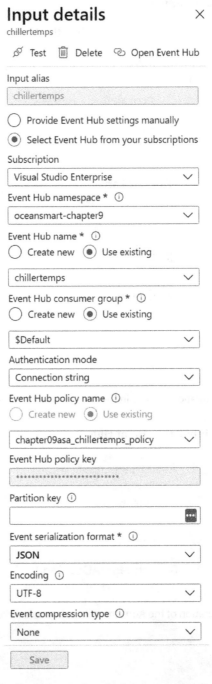

Figure 9.6 – Configuration options for input stream in the Azure portal

4.  Next, select **Outputs** and add an **Azure Function** output:

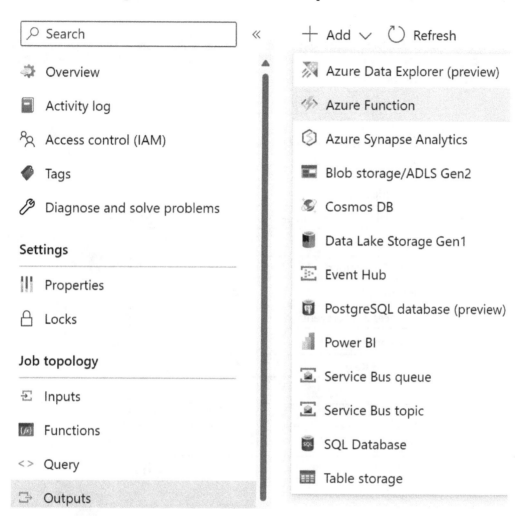

Figure 9.7 – Azure Stream Analytics output option screen

5.  Select the `ProcessChillerEvents` function from your subscription. The output should look similar to the following:

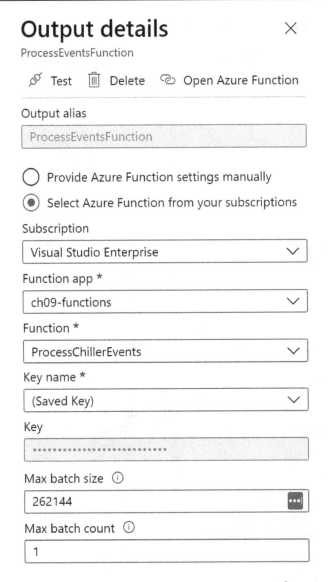

Figure 9.8 – Azure Stream Analytics output parameter configuration

6.  Notice that we set the **Max batch count** option to 1. That means that the query will return only one *window* of data at a time to our function. Our query will use two user-defined functions.

7.  From **Job topology**, select **Functions**, **Add**, and **Javascript UDF**:

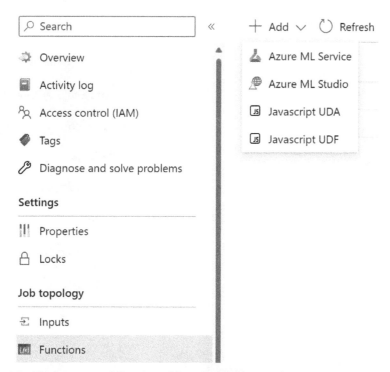

Figure 9.9 – The Azure portal showing adding a Javascript UDF from Functions Job topology

We will add two functions for getting the current time and details of the job. The first function is called `getCurrentTime` and has a datetime output type. The code for the function is as follows:

```
function main(s) {
    return new Date().toISOString();
}
```

The next function is called `getEventDetails` and has an output type of `any`, meaning it will return a `json` object. The text of this function is as follows:

```
function main(date_utc, time_utc, temp_f) {
  var event_details = {};
  event_details.date_utc = date_utc;
  event_details.time_utc = time_utc;
  event_details.temp_f = temp_f;
  return event_details;
}
```

The function is how we build complex objects to return as part of our stream analytics job.

Now that we have the inputs, outputs, and supporting functions defined, we can write the query.

From **Job topology**, select **Query**:

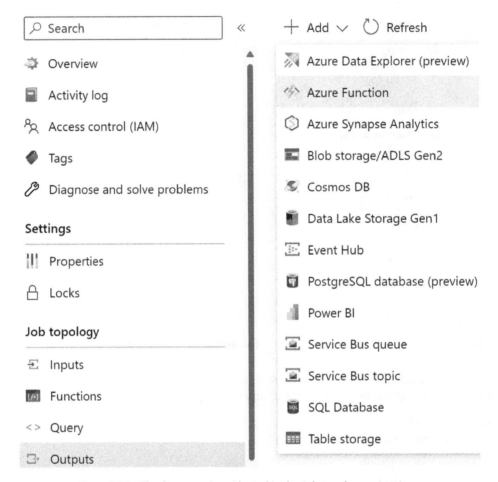

Figure 9.10 – The Query option selected in the Job topology menu item

In the first part of the query, we create a **common table expression** (**CTE**). This allows us to query the source once, and we could output the data to multiple outputs. For example, you may wish to output to a storage account for diagnostics as well as pass the data to your Azure function.

Most of the columns in our CTE are captured for diagnostics:

- `Window_size`: This is the number of events in our output.

- `window_start`: This is the time of the first event in our window.

- `window_end`: This is the time of the last event in our window.

These details will help to better identify when the anomaly took place. For looking at the specified time period, we use the following syntax for the `window_start` and `window_end` columns as you can see, it is similar for both:

- `topone()`: This returns the one row of data from the group specified in the group by clause of the query.

- The over/order by: This clause specifies how the data should be ordered when looking for that top one row.

- `EventEnqueuedUtcTime`: This is a column from the row returned by `topone()`:

```
with eventgroups as (
select window_size = count(*)
       , window_start = (topone()
                            over (order by EventEnqueuedUtcTime)
                        ).EventEnqueuedUtcTime
       , window_end = (topone()
                            over (order by EventEnqueuedUtcTime desc)
                    ).EventEnqueuedUtcTime
```

The details column of our CTE uses the `getEventDetails` function that we added earlier. The `collect` function creates an array of one item per row in the current group of the group by clause of our query. Each array item is an object created by the `getEventDetails` function:

```
, details = collect(UDF.getEventDetails(date_utc,
                                         time_utc,
                                         temp_f))
```

From `chillertemps` indicates that we are reading from the input named `chillertemps`:

```
from [chillertemps]
```

The group by clause indicates that we will be returning 15 minutes of data every time a new event arrives, and the `having` clause instructs the query to filter out groups of 12 rows or fewer – Anomaly Detector needs at least 13 data points to execute successfully:

```
group by slidingwindow(minute, 15)
having count(*) > 12
)
```

Finally, we take the output of our CTE and pass the data to our Azure function. Note that the `into` clause maps to the output that we created earlier:

```
select eventgroups.*
  into [ProcessEventsFunction]
  from eventgroups
```

Now we have built a complete solution that will log anomalies to an Azure Storage Table, and we can decide what to do with the data. We have the option to output the anomalies to a messaging event using various tools in Azure or a simple function. Alternatively, we can visualize the data in a Power BI report for looking at trending information or alerting through that platform. You have plenty of options for making these decisions, and it will depend on your business requirements to determine the best solution for your organization.

## Summary

As stated earlier in this chapter, anomaly detection can be a very challenging activity for any organization. As with the story of "The boy who cried wolf," when too many false positives occur, it can impact our decision-making. If we become complacent with our responses, it can cause tremendous issues in the way of costs and safety. With this in mind, it is recommended to ensure a deep analysis of pros and cons is performed for the example you want to test the service with. However, as we have displayed throughout this chapter, there are many of these considerations that have been taken into account for the service, and many options are available to hopefully avoid an abundance of false positives. Alternatively, there are certainly many advantages to having a finely tuned anomaly detection service in place that can help augment human monitoring of specified conditions. We have our typical **return on investment** (**ROI**) and **total cost of ownership** (**TCO**) analysis, as with any project, and these evaluations could be overwhelming in favor of taking on a project of this type. Just keep in mind that it is not always about the dollar amount required to justify a project, and other factors may weigh heavier in certain situations.

From the examples provided, hopefully, you have gained a better understanding of how to look for anomalous data captured from various places. We used a simple example here, but really, these techniques could be applied to a whole range of devices or data streams that could be pertinent to your organization. This also isn't limited to just equipment; we could certainly apply the same techniques to other sources of data streams throughout the company, internal or external.

In our next chapter, we will look at how using the Speech service can help improve your customer experience. Let's go!

# 10
# Streamlining the Quality Control Process with Custom Vision

A seafood company's reputation can rely heavily on many factors, and Ocean Smart built a reputation for quality by holding higher standards for its products. Customer service, perceived value, quality, and freshness of the product can all be differentiators in a heavily competitive segment of the food industry. The market in the restaurant, food distribution, and retail sectors for frozen lobster tails is quite lucrative. The quality of the products produced is determined by several factors, and when evaluating where AI could be used to help with improving this process, we determined a visual inspection of the product could be assisted by the **Custom Vision API**. Because the **quality control** process is so critical, a significant amount of inspection must take place to ensure a quality product is packaged and sent to customers. This inspection is visual – looking at lobster tails moving down the production lines for obvious defects. These defects could be a crack in the shell, a missing tail flipper, discoloration, or some type of shell disease, for instance.

In this chapter, we will explore how to train a model on what a good or bad lobster tail should look like before being packaged and sent to its next destination. We will use the **Custom Vision** Cognitive Service to help us with building this model and to identify when a tail is inspected and does not meet the quality standards specified. In order to do that, in this chapter, we will cover the following:

- Understanding the quality control process at Ocean Smart
- Evolving the quality control process with Custom Vision
- Training and improving the model
- Using smart labels for faster image labeling
- Sending notification of an irregular product
- Building the complete Custom Vision solution

So, to get started, we thought it would be helpful to define the existing quality control process for inspecting the tails to help identify where inefficiencies exist and display the opportunities for improvement. Let's make sure that you have all the tools and experience needed to successfully deploy your Custom Vision solution by looking at the technical requirements.

# Technical requirements

To build your Custom Vision solution, you will need to have an Azure subscription with at least Contributor rights to the subscription for deploying services. You will need an Azure storage account for storing your documents pre- and post-processing. Depending on it, if you plan to deploy the solution to a Docker container or an Azure Web App, you will need experience with those technologies to ensure proper deployment. You will also need to have **Visual Studio Code** (`https://code.visualstudio.com/Download`) if you intend to use the **Custom Vision SDK**. Some other services you may use for your deployment are as follows:

- **Azure Functions** – for building functions and executing code
- **Azure Data Factory** or similar – for data orchestration and transformation
- **Azure Logic Apps** – for workflow and triggering mechanisms

Of course, the more complex and automated your solution is, the more tools you will likely need to know how to use and manage. As with everything, start with the basics, build your **proof of concept (PoC)**, and add new features. This will help you to save precious time wasted troubleshooting, and so on.

# Understanding the quality control process at Ocean Smart

The frozen lobster tail market for Ocean Smart is a critical product from a revenue and profit standpoint, and that largely relates to how intricate they are with product inspections. Ensuring that products are inspected properly could mean the difference between a profitable week, month, or quarter, depending on the magnitude of the quality issue and volume of sales. For that reason, there are several areas of the product that are inspected visually and a sample is taken for more close inspection. The quality control team will take a sample of fluid from the product to check for any internal issues with the sample and will then capture and catalog details of the sample. The following is an expectation when an employee is handling the product:

1. It is the role of the employee who is first handling the product to quickly inspect for obvious defects, such as large cracks or obvious blemishes or disease.

2. Throughout the production process, the outside of the shell is inspected for shell disease, excessive cartilage, gills, broken shell, missing telsons (flippers), and meat discoloration (red or green tails).

   From there, quality control agents are inspecting as the tails are cleaned and prepared for freezing with the correct proportion of glaze adhered.

3.  A glaze is simply a thin layer of water applied before freezing that is helpful to ensure maintaining the quality of the meat and protect it from freezer burn.

4.  Finally, when the tails are aligned just right, they are packaged and palleted before heading to the freezer.

These checks can be performed at the time of production or can be sampled at various times after final production and packaging are complete. Additionally, certain strategic customers may require inspections to ensure quality standards are met prior to a shipment leaving the loading dock or at other intervals. In this process, the tails could be thawed to test for weight loss, visually inspected, have meat sampled, and split for even closer visual inspection, all to ensure quality standards are maintained.

The time required to carry out the additional inspections and quality samples takes even more time from the quality control inspectors, along with completing the corresponding paperwork for logging purposes. With the volume of tails that are produced daily, a severe bottleneck is created that slows down the production process, or an inspection isn't given as much attention as is required. We will get into some more of the inefficiencies and challenges that need to be balanced throughout the quality control process in the next section.

## Evolving the quality control process with Custom Vision

Computer vision as a discipline has made some amazing strides in recent years to help augment (or enable the augmentation of) human sight. Applications for facial recognition, description of images, and initial sensors being used for self-driving cars have become everyday technology, just to name a few common examples. In the case of self-driving vehicles, computer vision can be used to detect objects in the road, street signs, and the curvature of the road, which then sends signals to the appropriate action by the brakes, accelerator, and so on. However, the origins of computer vision date back to the early 1960s, when a key component of **AI** systems being developed at universities enabled robots to "see" what was in front of them and respond appropriately. Clearly, the original vision proved to be a bit more challenging than originally anticipated, as those original pioneers would be in their 80s and 90s at their youngest by now, but the seed was planted. The original process was derived from **digital image processing,** where a camera would scan an image and attempt to match it with a known image of some object. The evolution of that process instead worked to develop a three-dimensional image from the existing two-dimensional image. This translation of sorts would take into account shading surrounding objects, defining clear lines where objects are separated, how the objects were related in proximity, and other considerations. In truth, however, hardware limitations were a hindrance to significant progress right through the 1990s.

As we have seen an explosion in the 21st century of **Central Processing Units (CPUs)**, **Graphics Processing Units (GPUs)**, **Field Programmable Gate Arrays (FPGAs)**, and other specialized processors being developed with extremely fast computations, more capability has become possible quickly. Now, several cameras can work in unison to interpret more quickly what is being captured and used in downstream applications that are used daily. Also, as the speeds and capabilities of processors and cameras are increasing, these systems can identify objects in an image much more quickly and translate the image faster than the human eye processes an image and puts that description into words. From there, the application can take what is being described to complete whatever follow-on action is required. In the case of a self-driving car, there is a specific camera or set of cameras that are designed to evaluate street signs and tell the vehicle the actions it should be taking. When the camera detects a Stop sign, it registers the distance and tells the vehicle to decelerate until it is an appropriate distance from the sign or object in front of the vehicle (for instance, another car).

When we look at applications for computer vision that could assist with the manufacturing process of seafood products, several options come to mind almost immediately:

- Inspection of the product as it moves across an assembly line, including identifying foreign objects that should not be on the assembly line to avoid something improper landing in an outgoing package

- Monitoring of a manufacturing floor operation for potential security or safety risks, such as a person falling into a product cooling tank used for rapidly freezing or cooling products prior to packaging

- Various opportunities in quality checkpoints or overseeing the quality control process to help augment the quality control agents working for Ocean Smart to ensure quality standards are met

There are many opportunities for improvement well beyond what we have listed, and Ocean Smart had to determine what options would make the most impact and would fit within financial constraints. The final use case listed will be used as a basis for a demonstration of how computer vision technology can greatly improve the quality control process. We will also demonstrate how efficiency can be improved, as well as enhancing overall customer experiences when purchasing Ocean Smart products.

More specifically, Ocean Smart decided that an analysis of lobster tails being produced would serve as a good first use case to develop using the **Custom Vision** Cognitive service. The Custom Vision service gives us the ability to build your own image identifier service. This should not be confused with the **Computer Vision** Cognitive service, which does not allow for custom identification labels. The Computer Vision service was used in *Chapter 5*, *Azure Cognitive Search Overview and Implementation*, for identifying famous landmarks and celebrities, labeling and tagging entities, **Ocular Character**

**Recognition (OCR)**, and even being able to describe scenery contained in an image. The Custom Vision service allows us to build our own labels and build custom machine learning models that can be used to reference against. In our case, as lobster tails flow down a conveyor belt, cameras are capturing images of each tail. As the images are captured, they are checked against "good" lobster tails that we have trained our machine learning model on to identify tails that might look distorted, have cracks, or are missing a flipper. Any of these conditions would result in a tail being less valuable and set aside for use in a different way – likely to be cooked and packed as tail meat, assuming there was no spoilage or other quality issue.

When a quality issue is identified, the area on the belt where the tail is located is reported to a line supervisor for inspection. This location is captured using OCR to label grid location where the tail has been placed. The flow of this process is as follows:

1.  As the tails go through an initial inspection from a line worker, they are placed within a grid on a belt.

2.  The tails then flow down the conveyor belt with an overhead camera capturing images of the tails as they pass underneath.

3.  If there are no identifiable issues with the tail, it then flows to the "tail grading" line, where it is weighed and sorted for packing by weight.

4.  If an issue is discovered with Custom Vision against the trained machine learning model, an Azure function triggers the Computer Vision service to capture the grid identification as the photo of the suspect tail is sent along with the trigger.

5.  When the grid identifier is captured, another **Azure function** sends a notification to the appropriate notification mechanism. Ocean Smart uses a simple mechanism containing an LED display with a red light for notification purposes containing a Raspberry Pi device for input capabilities.

6.  The tail is then inspected by the supervisor for identified issues. To continually enhance and train the model developed, there are red and green buttons on the notification mechanism that allow the supervisor to identify whether there was a false positive by hitting the red button or a true positive by hitting the green button.

This input is then factored in, and the model is retrained with the image of the false positive to prevent future false positives for whatever issue was identified in the initial capture.

The following is a visual flow of the process that is described in the previous list:

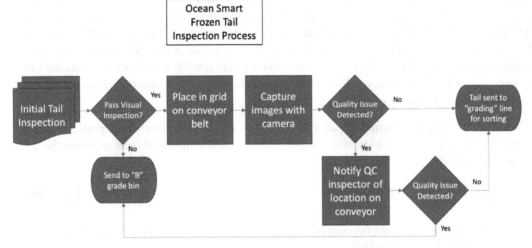

Figure 10.1 – Frozen tail inspection process flow diagram

The following figure provides an example of how the conveyor belt would appear from above:

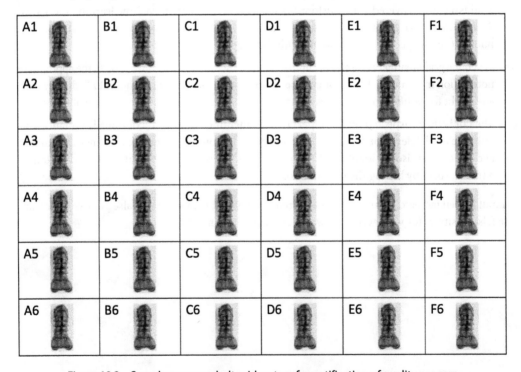

Figure 10.2 – Sample conveyor belt grid system for notification of quality concern

Of course, to have all the tails laid out perfectly parallel to each other and placed directly in the center of each grid location would be difficult to achieve, so the previous figure may be a bit misleading. The overarching point, however, is that we ensure two things:

- The tail should be placed within the grid so that it isn't covering any of the gridlines or the grid identifying number.

- The tails should be oriented in the same direction within the grid with at least an attempt to have the flippers fanned out.

These requirements can be challenging on the inspection line as the tails need to be processed as quickly as possible, and Ocean Smart wanted to ensure that no new bottlenecks were created within the production process. Because of these requirements, there could still be false positives we are notified about to make way for faster processing of the product due to improper placement or other errors. With all of that having been evaluated, greater efficiency of the quality process could still be gained, with fewer "bad" tails getting past inspectors by employing Custom Vision.

Now that we have provided a sense of some of the requirements for the development of a custom machine learning model and the associated manufacturing process, we will next look at how to get the initial model trained and how it can be improved over time.

## Training and improving the model

Many considerations should be taken into account when you are training your model based on the images you are using to build the model. Microsoft recommends at least 50 images for training purposes; however, other details need consideration too. These images should be representative of what a user will face when testing against the model that has been built. For instance, when building the model for frozen lobster tail testing, we had to ensure that tail images were representative of what would be captured by the cameras watching the conveyor belts for tail quality detection. For this reason, the images of the tails needed to capture what would be inspected for quality standards as well. We could not use a clump of lobster tails for our training process, as we couldn't easily identify the distinct characteristics of a typical tail as it was scanned on the production line.

In simple terms, we had to be very selective about which images to choose. Our cameras were capturing images of tails on a conveyor belt with minimal to no features, or objects were detected in the images outside of the tail itself. For this reason, we had to use images of tails with no other distractions in the images for the training process, as well as ensure the tails were configured in a way so that any issues could be detected. Simply laying a tail on the conveyor belt in any configuration would not allow proper scanning for defects, so tails have to be laid flat and, ideally, have the flippers fanned out for identification.

## Creating your first project

The training process begins with determining whether you would like to use the Custom Vision SDK (`https://docs.microsoft.com/en-us/azure/cognitive-services/custom-vision-service/quickstarts/image-classification`) to build your model programmatically, or use the Microsoft provided web interface (`https://www.customvision.ai/`). For this tutorial, we will use the provided interface for tagging and training. Because each project has its unique requirements, we will demonstrate the process for setting up a PoC of the service, but it should provide enough details required for a full deployment.

As laid out in the *Technical requirements* section, you need to ensure you have an Azure account with at least Contributor permissions to create your first project in the Custom Vision tool. When you navigate to the website (`https://www.customvision.ai/`) and log in with your Azure account, you are presented with a very simple interface:

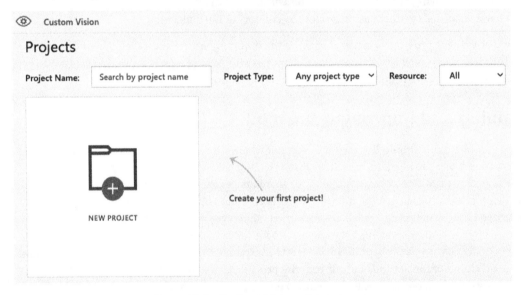

Figure 10.3 – Custom Vision portal start page

To begin with our first project, follow these steps:

1.  Simply click the **NEW PROJECT** button and you will be prompted with many options:

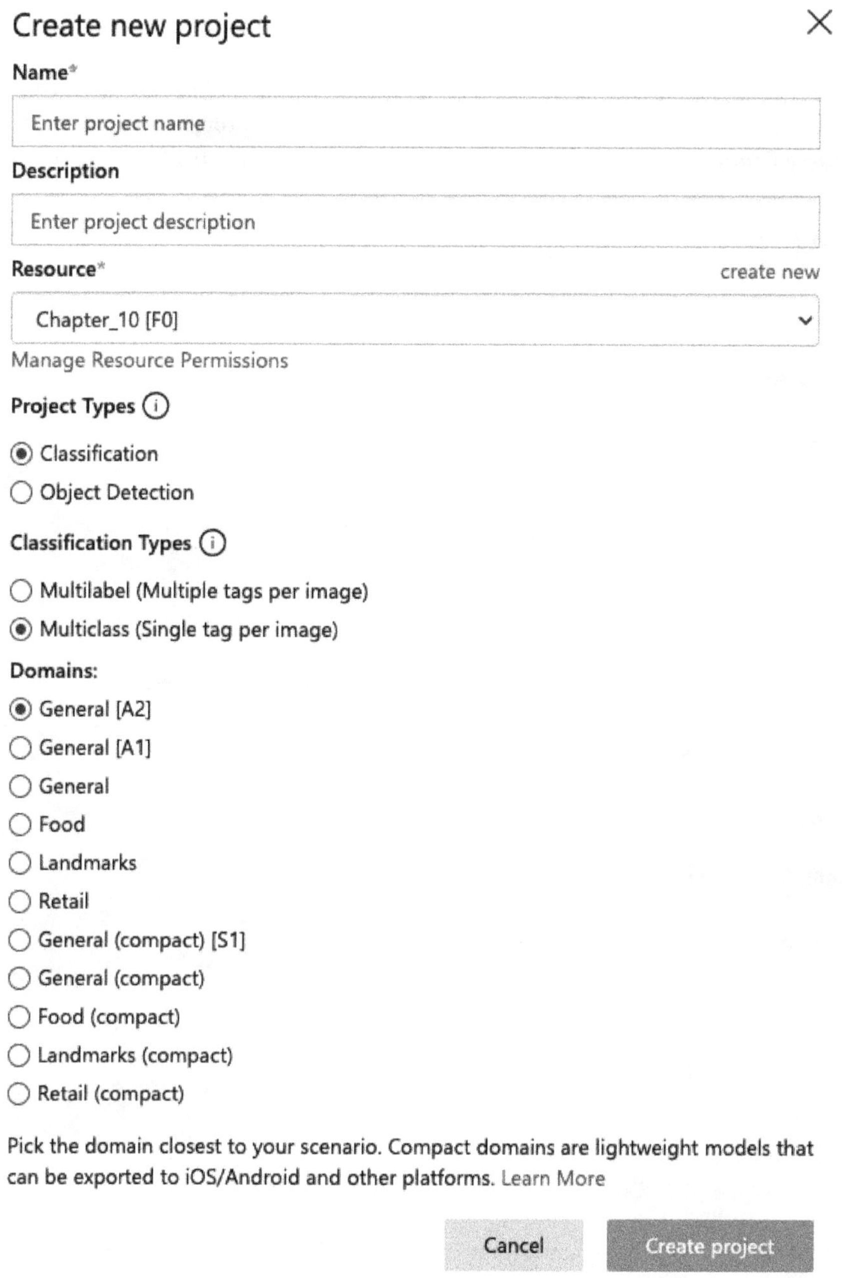

# Create new project                                        ✕

**Name***

> Enter project name

**Description**

> Enter project description

**Resource***                                            create new

> Chapter_10 [F0]                                              ⌄

Manage Resource Permissions

**Project Types** ⓘ

◉ Classification

◯ Object Detection

**Classification Types** ⓘ

◯ Multilabel (Multiple tags per image)

◉ Multiclass (Single tag per image)

**Domains:**

◉ General [A2]

◯ General [A1]

◯ General

◯ Food

◯ Landmarks

◯ Retail

◯ General (compact) [S1]

◯ General (compact)

◯ Food (compact)

◯ Landmarks (compact)

◯ Retail (compact)

Pick the domain closest to your scenario. Compact domains are lightweight models that
can be exported to iOS/Android and other platforms. Learn More

Cancel            Create project

Figure 10.4 – Create new project dialog box

Some options are self-explanatory, others may require a better understanding of what you are
looking to accomplish with the Custom Vision project model training requirements.

2.  You can name and describe your project as you determine best, and then you need to assign the compute mechanism. In the previous figure, you will see that my resource is named **Chapter_10[F0]**. I created this resource by clicking **create new** above the **Resource** box and following the prompts to create my service by entering the appropriate **Name**, **Subscription**, **Resource Group**, **Kind**, **Location**, and **Pricing Tier** details, as in the following figure:

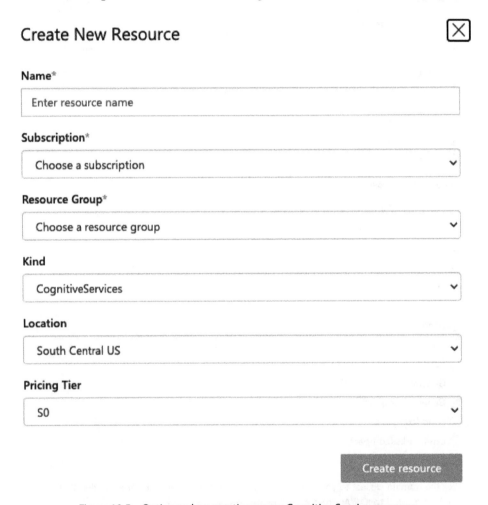

Figure 10.5 – Options when creating a new Cognitive Service resource

As with other examples throughout the book, these variables are to be designated at your discretion; however, it is logical to have all related services to a project in a single resource group and location whenever possible. In my case, I chose **Free Tier (F0)**, which has its limitations, but provides a good resource for building a PoC and is not recommended for production deployments.

3. Next, you will need to determine whether to use the **Classification** or **Object Detection** project type. Again, this will depend on your use case but, simply explained, you will use each as follows:

   • **Classification** – Treats the image as a single object that is tagged and used for training your model. In our case, we used this option as we used single tail images for training.

   • **Object Detection** – Extracts individual objects within an image, captures the location of each object, and allows you to tag that object to train the model.

4. The next decision you will need to make is what classification types you will use. This will determine how many tags you will have for each image. Your choice will come down to whether there are multiple items in each image that will need to be tagged, using **Multilabel**, or whether there will be one and only one tag per image, using **Multiclass**. For our example, we have chosen the **Multiclass** option as we are tagging images of lobster tails individually.

5. Finally, you will need to determine which domain will work best for your use case, where you are currently presented with 10+ options. These options will make the training process easier in the case where you can fit your example into one of the base domains of **Food**, **Landmarks**, or **Retail**, plus the ability to have more **General** examples that may not fit.

Because the Custom Vision service can be deployed to a mobile operating system such as **iOS** or **Android** or other locations outside of Azure, there are training domains labeled with the "(compact)" designation. More details can be found on each domain and its use cases here: `https://docs.microsoft.com/en-us/azure/cognitive-services/custom-vision-service/select-domain`. In our case, we chose the **General [A1]** domain, which is optimized for better accuracy with comparable inference used with larger datasets or more sophisticated scenarios. Because we are analyzing the images with more granular detail in mind, this is the best choice. The drawback to this choice is that it requires more time to complete the training of the model but, hopefully, allows us to get more details from the images as a result.

Next, we're going to look at uploading and tagging images.

## Uploading and tagging images

Now that your service is set up and you are ready to start training the model, as logic would dictate, you need to upload and tag some images for training. For simpler model training, due to a lack of quality examples of the various imperfections a tail can have, we are going to only use two tags for training: "good tails" and "Bad Tails." To train a more sophisticated model that allows for more specific reasons for a tail being bad, such as cracks or missing flippers, we would have to have more tags, and many samples of different tails that have these issues. Instead, for this use case, we are going to load about 50 images of "good tails" and 50 images of "Bad Tails" for training. In general, it is good practice to have a balanced sample of images for training your model, or else the results can be skewed. The website will also inform you of this when you train your model for the first time.

To add images to begin the training process, simply click the **Add images** button in the top-left corner of your newly created project:

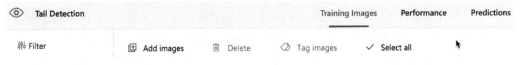

Figure 10.6 – Menu options inside the project portal

As your images are added, with the tag(s) you intend to use for the batch or individual images, this will also depend on which type of project and classification you selected when building your project. The following figure provides a visual for what you should expect when uploading and tagging your documents:

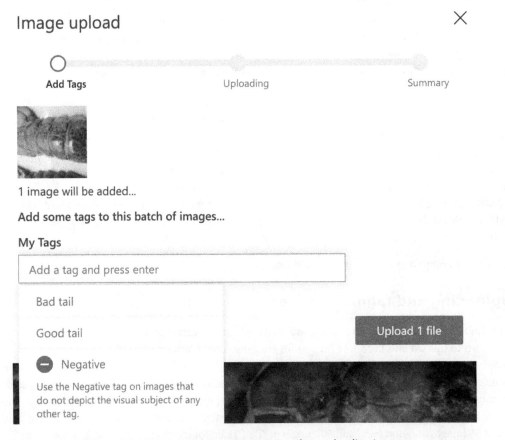

Figure 10.7 – Tagging and negative options when uploading images

Now that you have started the process of uploading and tagging your images, let's look at the training process next.

## Model training

When you have tagged and added all the photos you would like to use, it is time to train your model:

1.  Click the **Upload** button, and the computer vision service will do some initial analysis.

2.  If you have added all the images you want to use for the model, at least in this iteration of training, you will next click the **Train** button in the upper-right corner. If you want to add additional images to the model after, you can simply add them in the same interface and re-train, so don't be concerned about not having enough images when you get started.

3.  When you do so, you will have to choose between **Quick Training** and **Advanced Training**. Microsoft provides the following guidance:

> **Important note**
>
> Use advanced training for improved performance, especially on challenging and fine-trained training of datasets. With advanced training, you can specify a compute time budget for training and Custom Vision will experimentally identify the best training and augmentation settings. For quick iterations, you can use the quick training.

4.  You should be seeing something like the following figure:

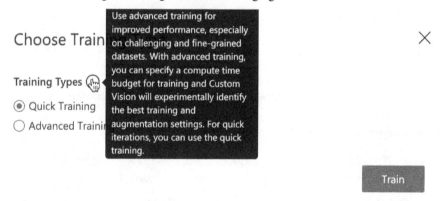

Figure 10.8 – Options presented when beginning the training process of your model

Because the **Advanced Training** option allows you to customize how deeply the images are analyzed, you are also given the ability to determine how long the training process will run. To reiterate an earlier point, this training process will be using compute, and compute is the costliest of operations in Azure, so be mindful of how this will affect your overall costs of training. For the purposes of this example, we will select **Quick Training**, and in just a few minutes, we will have a newly trained model using Good Tails and Bad Tails for our examples.

Next, we will look at the results of our model that was trained and the performance we can expect from the model.

## Model performance

So, now we have a nicely trained model with our two tags, we want to see what the performance of the training will look like so we know what to expect from the model as we begin to check images against it. Following the previously stated theme of building out a PoC, we will now look at how we can expect the trained model to perform. The statistics provided are based on the **probability threshold**, which is the minimum probability score for a prediction to be valid when calculating **precision and recall**. This is configurable, and as the threshold is raised, the precision and recall are affected as a result. We will use the following interface to evaluate the performance:

Figure 10.9 – Model performance evaluation interface in the Custom AI portal

The information we are provided from this interface is as follows:

- **Precision** – If a tag is predicted by your model, this is how likely it is to be correctly predicted. In our case, approximately 89% of the classifications were correct.

- **Recall** – Out of the tags that should be predicted correctly, this is the percentage that the model will correctly find. In our preceding example, 89% of our images uploaded (90 images) were accurately classified.

- **AP** – This stands for **average precision**, and is the measure of the model performance overall. Referring to statistical modeling, this is the area under the precision/recall curve that is represented.

- **Performance Per Tag** – This visual helps to present the preceding statistics for each of the specified tags.

As we move the **Probability Threshold** slider bar in the interface, our overall accuracy changes. The following shows the results when our probability is set at 75%:

Figure 10.10 – Results of changing our Probability Threshold to 75%

The higher the probability threshold, the higher the precision returned; however, that comes with a decrease in recall accuracy. This should be considered when you are determining what the best starting place is for your model, how you will test it, and how you will deploy it to production.

Now that we have reviewed the model performance and accuracy, the final step before moving the model to production is to perform a *quick test* of the model by using an image to test the model against. This can be uploaded via the portal, or by pointing to a URL that contains an image to test our model against. In our case, we will receive a percentage likelihood of the image being a "Good Tail" or a "Bad Tail." This function is designed to perform one-off tests of images that may be questionable or for quick demonstration purposes.

Hopefully, this section provides a clear picture of how Ocean Smart was able to train its model to identify when a frozen lobster tail may be below quality standards. Next, we will explore how Smart Labeler may be able to quicken the process of building your detection models.

## Using Smart Labeler for faster image labeling

So, now we have reached a point where we have built a model using our images of what a "good" or "bad" frozen lobster tail should look like. As we need to add more images to the model for training and accuracy improvement, we can use the Smart Labeler feature to quicken the process of tagging new images.

Getting started with the process is fairly straightforward now that we already have our model built and a sample set of images loaded. You will simply upload new images within the project using the previous steps, but don't tag them as you upload them. The images will upload and be labeled as **Untagged**, with the option to **Get suggested tags**, as shown in the following figure:

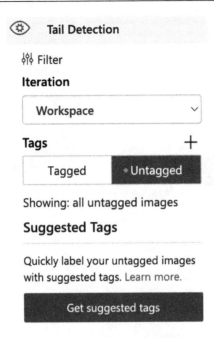

Figure 10.11 – Smart Labeler dialog box displaying Tagged and Untagged image options

When we select the **Get suggested tags** option, we then get the option to choose how many images we want to tag by default, with the warning that the more images are tagged, the more costs will be incurred for the Azure compute costs, as displayed in the following figure:

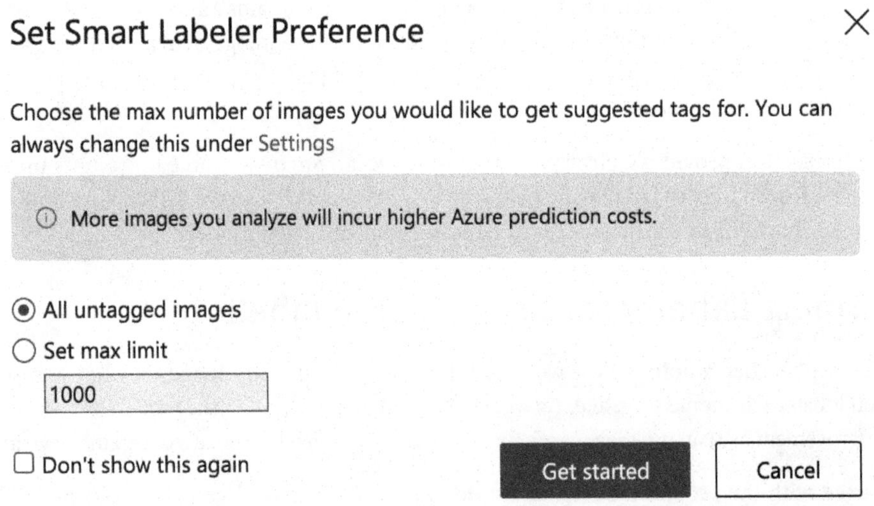

## Set Smart Labeler Preference                                    ✕

Choose the max number of images you would like to get suggested tags for. You can always change this under Settings

⊙ More images you analyze will incur higher Azure prediction costs.

◉ All untagged images
◯ Set max limit

1000

☐ Don't show this again          Get started          Cancel

Figure 10.12 – Set Smart Labeler Preference dialog box shown after asking for tag suggestions

As you load more images to be added to your model training set, you will need to determine whether to use this feature for automatic tagging based on what the model already contains or to manually tag the images. In this test, we loaded 35 new images of Bad Tails to our already existing 90 images but took no care to isolate what was in the images in order to see how the Smart Labeler would respond to images including occlusions and multiple tails. Overall, the performance was relatively accurate considering the smaller existing model sample, as well as some minor defects in the tails in the images. The following figure captures the results of the output:

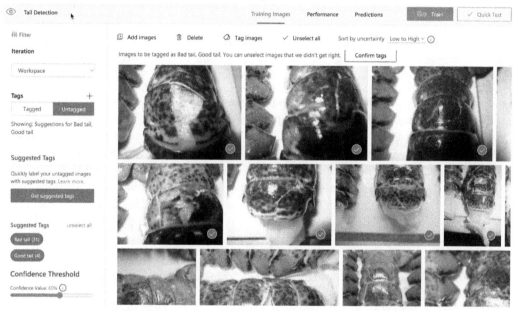

Figure 10.13 – Sample output from using the Smart Labeler displaying results and tag suggestions

We can now review the results of the Smart Labeler feature for accuracy, confirm that the tags are correct, or make changes as necessary. One thing to consider here is that because we knowingly loaded 35 Bad Tail images, if we were to confirm them as bad and fix the four that were incorrectly classified, we would then be unbalancing our model. In general model training best practices, as previously discussed, we want our tags to remain relatively balanced, otherwise, our model can suffer from what's known as **overfitting**. This can lead to accuracy problems as well as poor model training and prediction latency. Having a set of tags with minor percentage differences between them won't cause this problem, but in the example explained previously, a dramatic difference in the balance of tags would result. For this example, we chose to delete the images to prevent creating an unbalanced model.

Now that we have covered all the features required to build your own proof of concept, let's get back to the Ocean Smart use case and how the services used are put into production. First, we will cover the process for notifying quality inspectors of irregular products on the conveyor belt in the next section.

# Sending a notification of an irregular product

Our model is built, and we have established a system for capturing images of our tails to compare against our machine learning model. Now, we need to put the downstream processes in place to notify our quality inspector when a Bad Tail has been detected. As described previously, a system for sending notifications and providing feedback when a false positive has been detected was developed using a Raspberry Pi device for input and output of information. If you are unfamiliar with these devices, a Raspberry Pi computer is a lightweight computer commonly running the Linux operating system, which was originally designed for education and hobbyists. Its expansive nature and the add-on components that were designed due to the popularity of the devices led to significantly more adoption of Raspberry Pi devices than originally anticipated, and they have been commonly used in commercial applications as a result.

For our example, we connected an LED display to notify the quality inspector of an issue and what grid the suspect tail resides in. We also added two buttons, one green and one red, to allow us to provide feedback to the Custom Vision service to confirm Bad Tails or report a false positive and improve the model by adding that tail image to the "Bad Tail" category and periodically retraining the model with the newly identified tails. For demonstration purposes and to allow you to build your own solution without having to learn the ins and outs of working with a Raspberry Pi device, we will demonstrate a simulated environment in our Ocean Smart portal in the next section of this chapter.

To be able to identify the Bad Tails and display them on the LED, we need to iterate through the following process:

1. Capture images of each tail as they work their way down the conveyor belt and test those images against our Custom Vision model.

2. If a tail is classified as bad, we will then send the image through the OCR Cognitive Service to identify the grid where the Bad Tail lies.

3. We send the results of the OCR to an Azure function, which then sends the output to our LED display.

4. The quality inspector then further inspects the tail. If the tail is indeed bad, the inspector confirms it by hitting the green button. If the tail is good, meaning a false positive for our model, our inspector hits the red button.

5. This action will trigger another Azure function to pick up the image of the tail and place it in a storage blob, which will be used as part of a retraining dataset.

In the next section, we will build our full simulated solution, and review the architecture, services, and associated code for you to try at home.

# Building the complete Custom Vision solution

In this chapter, we use Cognitive Services to train a predictive model and deploy the model to a web endpoint to classify new images as they arrive. The following diagram provides an overview of how the tail images are processed and tested against our model to determine whether they are good or bad, as well as how we can frequently update the model to handle new examples:

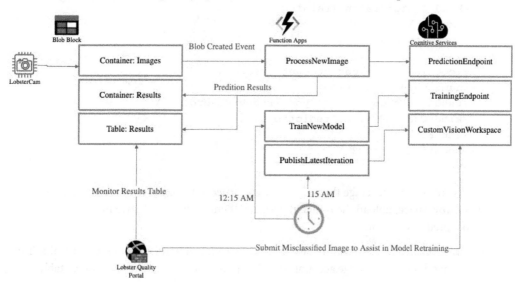

Figure 10.14 – Process flow of tail image classification testing against machine learning model

To support this process, we create the following:

- The cognitive services and custom vision workspace.

- A storage account where new images and results will be stored and a storage table will be used to communicate results to the frontend web application.

- A function app that contains functions to do the following:

  I.    Classify new images as they arrive. It is important to note that we were able to utilize the model trained for the PoC example described previously for the full deployment. After the model was trained, we published it and referenced connecting to it in the following code.

  II.   Train a new model each night if new images have been added to the Custom Vision workspace.

  III.  Publish the new model if one has been created.

You can create the cognitive services needed to support this process with the following commands:

```
az login
az account set --subscription <enter your-subscription-id>
az cognitiveservices account create \
--name ch10-training \
--resource-group <enter your-resource-group> \
--kind CustomVision.Training \
--sku F0 \
--location eastus2 \
--yes
az cognitiveservices account create \
--name ch10-prediction \
--resource-group <enter your-resource-group> \
--kind CustomVision.Prediction \
--sku F0 \
--location eastus2 \
--yes
```

From there, you can leverage the walk-through earlier in the chapter to create your **Custom Vision workspace**, upload the initial images, tag them, train a predictive model, and deploy it to the predictive service.

Our Azure functions make use of Azure Storage to receive images and communicate results. The following commands create a storage account with the appropriate containers and storage table:

```
az storage account create \
--name ch10storage \
--resource-group ch10-andy-tmp \
--location eastus2
az storage container create \
--name images \
--account-name ch10storage
az storage container create \
--name results \
--account-name ch10storage
az storage table create \
--name results \
--account-name ch10storage
```

Now we have the resources needed to create our Azure Functions. To follow this example, you will need the following:

- Python version 3.9.6
- Azure Functions Core Tools
- Visual Studio Code

- Python Extension for Visual Studio Code

- Azure Functions Extension for Visual Studio Code

If you open the \Chapter 10\Code Snippets\Process Image Function folder in Visual Studio Code, you should see the following folder structure:

Figure 10.15 – List of items found in the Process Image Function folder

A couple of files/folders that are important to the function runtime are as follows:

- The ProcessNewImage, PublushLatestIteration, and TrainNewModel folders are our three functions in this Function app. We will dig into the sections that follow.

- local.settings-sample.json contains the settings that the functions will need in order to execute properly. Notice that the key values are not specified.

- local.settings.json is not present in your repo. You will create this file shortly.

- requirements.txt: when you deploy your Function app, the Function app runtime pip installs any packages listed in requirements.txt.

Let's take a look at the local.settings-sample.json file and create a copy that is configured to your environment:

1.  Make a copy of local.settings-sample.json and name it local.settings.json. You should see the following:

    ```
    {
      "IsEncrypted": false,
      "Values": {
        "oceansmartst_STORAGE": "DefaultEndpointsProtocol=ht
    tps;AccountName=ch10oceansmart;AccountKey=<account-key>
    ```

```
EndpointSuffix=core.windows.net",
    "prediction_endpoint": "https://eastus2.api.cognitive.
microsoft.com/",
    "prediction_key": "<prediction_key>",
    "training_endpoint": "https://eastus2.api.cognitive.
microsoft.com/",
    "training_key": "<training_key>",
    "vision_project_id": "95de605d-bf06-42f9-8671-70d746650cdc",
    "vision_model_name": "CurrentModel",
    "prediction_resource": "/subscriptions/b9cb82ad-f6fc-425b-
aeb3-7d74d86db771/resourceGroups/Chapter10/providers/Microsoft.
CognitiveServices/accounts/Chapter-10-pred"
    }
}
```

2.  The `oceansmart_STORAGE` value is the connection string to the storage account created previously. You can retrieve this connection string with the following:

    ```
    az storage account show-connection-string --name ch10storage
    ```

    For the training endpoint and key, use the following:

    ```
    az cognitiveservices account show \
    --name ch10-training \
    --resource-group <enter resource-group-name> \
    --query "properties.endpoint"
    az cognitiveservices account keys list \
    --name ch10-training \
    --resource-group <enter resource-group-name> \
    --query "key1"
    ```

3.  For the prediction endpoint and key, use the same command as the preceding but replace the training service for the prediction service.

4.  `vision_project_id` can be found in the Custom Vision workspace.

5.  `prediction_resource` can be found with the following command:

    ```
    az cognitiveservices account show \
    --name ch10-prediction \
    --resource-group <enter resource-group-name> \
    --query "id"
    ```

When the function app is deployed, we publish this `local.settings.json` file to the function app. The function app creates environment variables for each of these settings for use by the function app code.

At this point, we have the services deployed and the configuration set. We can look at the code in each of the functions and get ready to deploy the function app and code.

# The processNewImage function

The processNewImage function is triggered when a new image is placed in the Images container of the specified storage account. The function reads the image and passes it to the prediction endpoint of our computer vision service to classify the image as a good or bad lobster tail. The function writes these results to a results container for long-term storage and to the results storage table, which is monitored by the frontend portal.

Each of the functions contains two main files:

- __init__.py contains the code for the function.
- function.json contains the configuration and bindings for the function.

Let's look at function.json first:

1. First, we see that "scriptFile" points to "__init__.py", which tells the runtime that the code to execute when this file is called is located in that file:

   ```
   {
       "scriptFile": "__init__.py",
   ```

2. The bindings section lists input and output parameters that the function runtime will supply to the function. The first binding here is our trigger. This binding tells the runtime to listen to events raised by the Blob Storage account located in the connection string in the oceansmartst_STORAGE configuration variable in the path images and execute when files are created or updated:

   ```
   "bindings": [
       {
           "name": "inBlob",
           "type": "blobTrigger",
           "direction": "in",
           "path": "images/{name}",
           "connection": "oceansmartst_STORAGE"
       },
   ```

3. Our next two bindings are output bindings. The function runtime will supply us with output parameters where we can write our results. The first is to a storage table:

   ```
       {
           "name": "outTable",
           "type": "table",
           "tableName": "results",
           "partitionKey": "result",
           "connection": "oceansmartst_STORAGE",
           "direction": "out"
   ```

4.   The next goes to an Azure Storage blob:

```
    },
    {
        "name": "outBlob",
        "type": "blob",
        "dataType": "binary",
        "path": "results/{name}-results.json",
        "connection": "oceansmartst_STORAGE",
        "direction": "out"
    }
  ]
}
```

5.   In the __init__.py file, we find the code that will be executed when a new file lands in this storage container.

6.   The entry point to the function is called main. Note that we have three parameters to this function that map to the bindings in function.json:

```
def main(inBlob: func.InputStream,
            outTable: func.Out[str],
            outBlob: func.Out[str]
            ):
```

7.   These settings are uploaded to the function configuration from local.settings.json when the function app is created. When the runtime starts, it pushes these values into environment variables accessible to the code:

```
prediction_endpoint = os.environ['prediction_endpoint']
prediction_key = os.environ['prediction_key']
vision_project_id = os.environ["vision_project_id"]
vision_iteration_name = os.environ["vision_model_name"]
```

8.   Create a client for the prediction service using the configured credentials and endpoint:

```
prediction_credentials = `
ApiKeyCredentials( `
  in_headers={"Prediction-key": prediction_key})
predictor = CustomVisionPredictionClient( `
  prediction_endpoint, prediction_credentials)
```

9.   Read the image data into a byte array and pass the data to the prediction service to classify the image:

```
results = predictor.classify_image(
    vision_project_id, vision_iteration_name, inBlob.read())
```

The prediction result will be a JSON document that contains a set of key-value pairs. Each key is a tag configured in the Custom Vision workspace, and the value is the probability that the image should be classified with that tag.

10. Here, we loop through the tags and add them to a dictionary along with the filename:

```
predictions_dict = {}
    predictions_dict["file_name"]=inBlob.name
    for p in results.predictions:
        predictions_dict[p.tag_name] = p.probability
    predictions_str = json.dumps(predictions_dict)
```

11. Write the resulting dictionary to the results container for longer-term records and analysis:

```
    outBlob.set(predictions_str)
```

12. Write the results in the results table that the frontend is monitoring. The format needs to be a little different than the file. Each entry in a storage table requires a unique key and must be stored in a partition. For this example, we are storing all results in the `"result"` partition and assigning a unique identifier to each table entry:

```
    rowKey = str(uuid.uuid4())
    data = {
        "rowKey" : rowKey
        , "partitionKey" : "result"
        , "result" : predictions_dict
    }
    outTable.set(json.dumps(data))
```

So, now the process is complete. When a new image lands in the blob container, the function app is triggered. The function reads the file, passes it to the model that we have trained, and writes the results to both a file in blob storage and a table that is monitored by the frontend application.

## The TrainNewModel function

The configuration of `TrainNewModel` only has one binding – the trigger. Throughout the day, users are monitoring the portal and if they detect that the computer vision model has misclassified an image, they direct the portal to submit the image to the computer vision workspace with the correct label. This function periodically checks the computer vision workspace to see whether new images were uploaded. If there are new images, we train a new model:

```
{
  "scriptFile": "__init__.py",
  "bindings": [
    {
```

```
    "name": "mytimer",
    "type": "timerTrigger",
    "direction": "in",
    "schedule": "0 15 0 * * *"
  }
 ]
}
```

This trigger specifies that the function will run based on a timer. The timer specified in the schedule says that the trigger will execute at 12:15 A.M. each day, when it is highly unlikely the existing model will be in use. Documentation for the time format can be found at https://docs.microsoft.com/en-us/azure/azure-functions/functions-bindings-timer?tabs=in-process&pivots=programming-language-python#ncrontab-expressions.

The entry point to the function in __init__.py accepts the timer as a parameter, but we are not using it in the code. The basic flow of this function is as follows:

1.  Find the currently published model.

2.  Determine how many images are in that model.

3.  Determine how many images are in the workspace.

4.  If there are more images in the workspace than the current model, train a new model:

    ```
    def main(mytimer: func.TimerRequest) -> None:
    ```

5.  These settings are uploaded to the function configuration from local.settings.json when the function app is created. When the runtime starts, it pushes these values into environment variables accessible to the code:

    ```
    training_endpoint = os.environ['training_endpoint']
    training_key = os.environ['prediction_key']
    project_id = os.environ['vision_project_id']
    ```

6.  Create a client for the prediction service using the configured credentials and endpoint:

    ```
    credentials = ApiKeyCredentials( `
      in_headers={"Training-key": training_key})
    trainer = CustomVisionTrainingClient( `
      training_endpoint, credentials)
    ```

7.  Loop through the iterations (trained models) and find the latest created iteration:

    ```
    iterations = trainer.get_iterations(project_id)
    latest_iteration = iterations[0]
    for iteration in iterations:
        if iteration.created > latest_iteration.created:
            latest_iteration = iteration
    ```

8.  If the workspace has more images than the latest model, train a new model:

```
workspace_image_count = trainer.get_image_count(project_id)
iteation_image_count = `
  trainer.get_image_count( `
    project_id=project_id, iteration_id=latest_iteration.id)
if workspace_image_count > iteation_image_count:
    project = trainer.get_project(project_id)
    iteration = trainer.train_project(project.id)
```

Training a new model may take longer than the 10 minutes maximum runtime of an Azure function, so instead of waiting for this asynchronous operation to complete, we will rely on the next function to publish the model after training has completed.

## The PublishLatestIteration function

Once the model training has completed, we need to tell our prediction service to use that new model. This function is triggered once per day and determines whether a new model has been trained. If the latest trained model is newer than the currently published model, then we publish the newest model.

The function.json for PublishLatestIteration looks very similar to TrainNewModel. The only difference is the timer is set to 1:15 A.M. instead of 12:15 A.M. You can see this in the schedule value of the function.json.

Looking at __init__.py, the basic flow of this model is as follows:

1.  Similar to TrainNewModel, start with the main function:

```
def main(mytimer: func.TimerRequest) -> None:
```

2.  Set up your environment variables:

```
training_endpoint = os.getenv("training_endpoint")
training_key = os.getenv("training_key")
project_id = os.getenv("vision_project_id")
model_name = os.getenv("vision_model_name")
prediction_resource = os.getenv("prediction_resource")
```

3.  Gather iterations to loop through:

```
credentials = ApiKeyCredentials(in_headers={"Training-key":
training_key})
trainer = CustomVisionTrainingClient(training_endpoint,
credentials)
project = trainer.get_project(project_id)
iterations = trainer.get_iterations(project_id)
latest_iteration = iterations[0]
```

4.   Loop through the trained models:

```
for iteration in iterations:
    if iteration.created > latest_iteration.created:
        latest_iteration = iteration
```

5.   Determine the latest model and, if completed, publish it to the prediction service:

```
if latest_iteration.status == "Completed" and latest_iteration.
publish_name != model_name:
    trainer.publish_iteration(
        project.id,
        latest_iteration.id,
        model_name,
        prediction_resource, overwrite=True
    )
    logging.info("iteration {latest_iteration.name} published")
else:
    logging.info("there was no new iteration to publish")
```

This concludes the functions created and their usage. Next, we'll look at deploying our functions to Azure.

## Deploying the functions

On the left-hand side of your Visual Studio Code window, you should see an Azure icon, which was placed there with the Azure Extension for Visual Studio Code (installed along with the Azure Functions Extension for Visual Studio Code).

Figure 10.16 – Azure extension from the menu bar in Visual Studio Code

When you select the Azure extension, you should see two sections in the navigation pane. The top section gives you access to Azure resources in your Azure subscription and the bottom section shows resources in Visual Studio Code related to Azure – in this case, your Azure Function project:

1.  In the **RESOURCES** section, you can navigate to your subscription and find the **Function App** section. Right-clicking on this section gives you the option to create a new function app in Azure.

Figure 10.17 – Create Function App menu item

2.  Click **Create Function App in Azure...** and follow the wizard:

    *   Name for the function app resource.

    *   Runtime stack – select **Python 3.9**.

    *   *Location For Resources* – this example uses *EastUS2*.

    *   *Select a Storage Account for the Function App* – It is a good idea to create a storage account to be used only for the function app. You can create the storage account right from the wizard.

    *   *Create an AppInsights instance for this app?* This is not needed for this example, so you can select **Skip**.

3.  If you hover your mouse over the top of the **WORKSPACE** section, you will see the icon to deploy the function project to Azure:

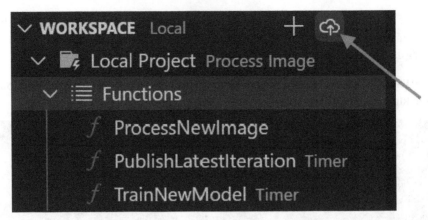

Figure 10.18 – Deploy Project function icon found when hovering over the screen

4.  Click the icon to *deploy to the function app*. This will prompt you to select a function app (you can use the one created in the previous step). At the end of the deployment, you will be prompted to upload the local.settings.json file to the Function App configuration.

Figure 1.19 – Function App configuration

5.  Upload the settings and you should have a function app deployed to Azure.

Next, we will demonstrate the options developed in the Ocean Smart portal to provide model feedback training.

## Using the Ocean Smart portal

Because we have a tangible application on the production floor for providing feedback as to whether a tail was classified correctly when flagged, we wanted to provide another option for providing feedback that didn't require the Raspberry Pi device. This gives us the ability to classify an image through the portal and add it to the repository of images that will be used when the model is retrained, as described in the previous section.

In the following figure, you will see the tails listed with pertinent details about when they were scanned and details about the results of the image tested against our current model:

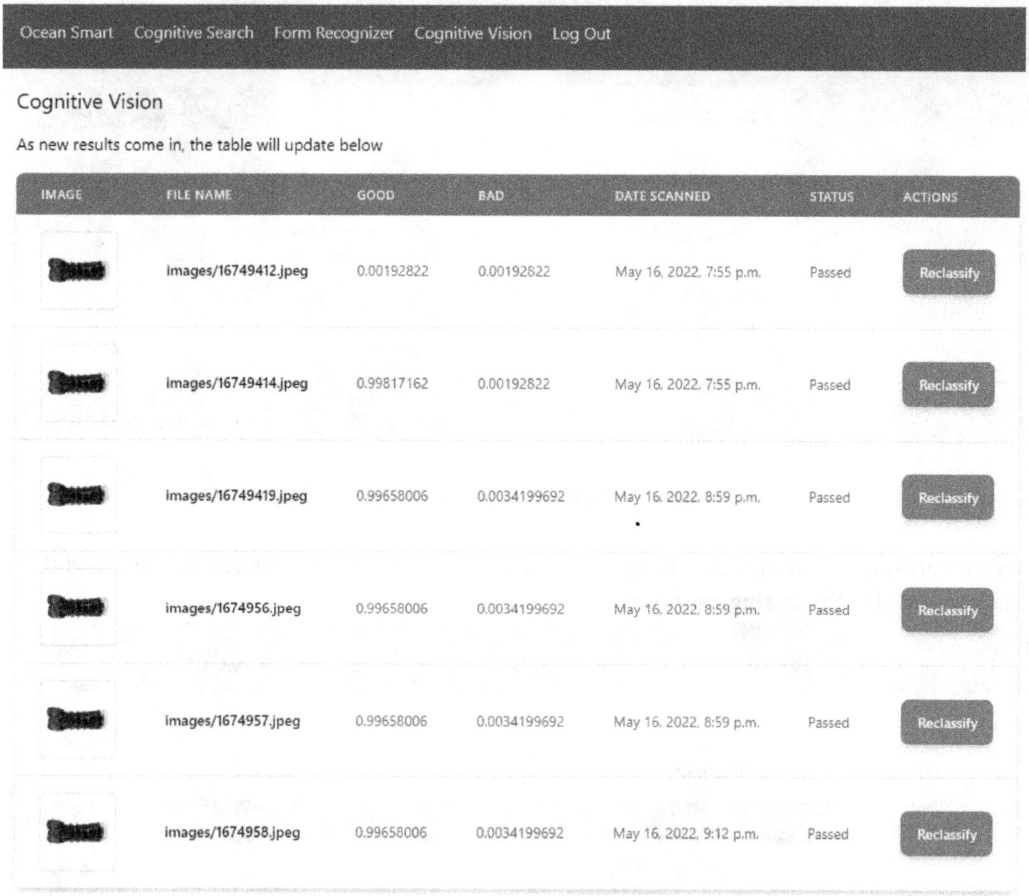
Ocean Smart
Cognitive Search
Form Recognizer
Cognitive Vision
Log Out
Cognitive Vision
As new results come in, the table will update below
IMAGE
FILE NAME
GOOD
BAD
DATE SCANNED
STATUS
ACTIONS
images/16749412.jpeg 0.00192822 0.00192822 May 16, 2022, 7:55 p.m. Passed Reclassify
images/16749414.jpeg 0.99817162 0.00192822 May 16, 2022, 7:55 p.m. Passed Reclassify
images/16749419.jpeg 0.99658006 0.0034199692 May 16, 2022, 8:59 p.m. Passed Reclassify
images/1674956.jpeg 0.99658006 0.0034199692 May 16, 2022, 8:59 p.m. Passed Reclassify
images/1674957.jpeg 0.99658006 0.0034199692 May 16, 2022, 8:59 p.m. Passed Reclassify
images/1674958.jpeg 0.99658006 0.0034199692 May 16, 2022, 9:12 p.m. Passed Reclassify

Figure 10.20 – Main page for viewing results of image scans

When we click on the **Reclassify** button on the right-hand side of an identified image, we are given the ability to report the image as a false positive – in this case, the tail was actually a good tail that was classified as bad.

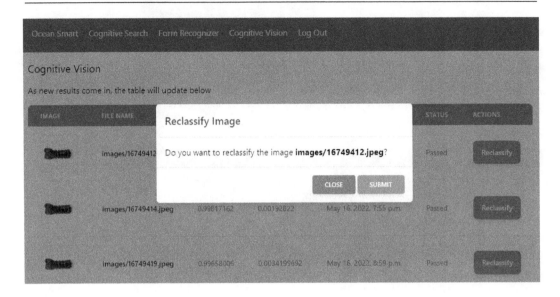

Figure 10.21 – Reclassifying an image

After we start the process of reclassifying, the code displayed in the previous section runs, and the status is changed to **Processing**, as shown here:

Figure 10.22 – Image reclassifying

When the process is complete, the status is changed to **Reclassified**, and when the next model training is run, this image will be used and labeled as a good tail, adding to our retraining of the model. This will then improve the model to better identify tails like this in the future.

Figure 10.23 – Reclassifying image completed

With that, we have provided the capability to manually reclassify images that are flagged in the production process and test the capabilities of the code provided in the previous sections without having to deploy all the hardware described. This provides a complete example for building your own Custom Vision solution. What will you use the service for to enhance operations in your business?

## Summary

The process for deploying the Custom Vision service itself for smaller examples and PoCs is relatively simple, as described earlier in the chapter. However, to bring the process to operation and establish a process for continual enhancement of the model with a feedback loop is quite a bit more involved, as described in the full deployment outlined in this chapter. As you can see, there are tools for the initial creation that make it easy to get started, but the complete example requires quite a bit of custom code and thought about the best way to provide the feedback necessary to maintain an evolving quality process. This is an important factor when evaluating projects using Cognitive Services as standalone APIs as compared to complete systems and services that can be purchased from vendors. Those vendors could, in fact, be using the APIs provided by Microsoft and training a custom model within the Azure services, but that would just be a part of their application and intellectual property.

In this chapter, we covered many of the elements for building a complete solution and maintaining an up-to-date machine learning model. We also discussed the deployment steps required for building a solution with Python code and deploying that code to an Azure function.

A full evaluation of required elements and development time should be part of the decision process as to whether you want to build or buy your solution.

Our next chapter will take us through the Content Moderator service, helping Ocean Smart to ensure that unwanted content doesn't make its way onto company websites, blogs, and other digital assets.

# 11
# Deploying a Content Moderator

Today, organizations can connect to customers, vendors, partners, and more with agility like never before. We commonly deploy applications that allow our customers to quickly contact us and research common challenges through the likes of chatbots, online forums, social media, company blogs, and numerous other outlets. The flexibility offered by these outlets certainly provides us with the opportunity to enhance the journey a customer takes with Ocean Smart, but also provides more surface for disgruntled customers and employees to express their dissatisfaction. That dissatisfaction can be expressed in the form of negative discussions and – worse – lewd or inappropriate content.

For these reasons and more, Ocean Smart has enabled the powerful Content Moderator Cognitive service to provide a screening mechanism to make the best attempt at avoiding any of that inappropriate material from ever being seen by its customers. In this chapter, we will discuss and provide examples of the following:

- Overview of the Content Moderator service
- Applying the service to text moderation
- Applying the service to image moderation
- Applying the service to video moderation
- Flagging and reviewing inappropriate content
- Building the complete solution

As we provide the details for deployment, we will also look at perspectives on how you might want to approach this challenge throughout your organization – whether the resources be external and customer-facing, or internal and helpful in promoting a positive and healthy workplace and customer experience. What's better is that this can mostly be done with little to no human intervention for many of the use cases based on Ocean Smart's custom lists of inappropriate content. We will also explore areas where Ocean Smart and other organizations can leverage the service at a later time, which goes beyond their traditional areas of use.

# Technical requirements

As with the other services we have discussed thus far in this book, the requirements for each service can vary a bit, depending on how you intend to use it, and which language you are most comfortable with. Whenever supported, we have attempted to standardize Python as our development language due to its popularity and flexibility. If you prefer to use another language, be sure to check the Microsoft documentation for supportability.

At a minimum, you will need Contributor rights to the Azure environment where you will be deploying services. The authors recommend Microsoft's Visual Studio Code for development with Python and related Azure extensions for managing your environment, storage accounts (if needed), and other services you may use to deploy your solution.

# Overview of the Content Moderator service

Filtering content is pervasive in many parts of our lives today. We have filters set up for incoming calls on our smartphones, social media settings for what content we want to see and content we don't, search results in our favorite browsers, and what we want our children to have access to on their tablets, computers, and phones. This is just a small list of where we see filters, which exist in a much larger sea of areas where we want to ensure we have not delivered content that's undesired. With the open nature by which the internet was developed, the creators wanted to provide as many opportunities for free speech, such as rhetoric, as possible, and with that unintentionally provide a playground for the malicious and immature. As a result, we have seen significant investment by organizations to either sell or provide filtering services to enable invisible barriers to unwanted content. On the other hand, we may run into filters we don't want to be in place, which can cause frustration when we're attempting to access content that may be improperly filtered.

When it comes to organizational content filters, many have been developed to reduce inappropriate content and distractions while in the workplace, so the techniques for these technologies are mature in their life cycle. Managing the existing systems can be cumbersome, they can be expensive to purchase, and they will often contain features that may not be desired. Many software companies now leverage a "bundling" sales methodology where it is frequently less expensive overall to purchase a complete package of solutions than to purchase just a feature or two for specific use cases. This can be less appetizing for organizations that have smaller use cases or don't have the staff and support to deploy such broad feature sets, but often, they find themselves struggling to find the right solution to fit their needs at a reasonable price.

The Azure Content Moderator API allows customers to use the service with associated machine learning models for image, text, and video content filtering. This gives customers the flexibility to leverage the API for as targeted or broad a use case as desired, allowing them to control the costs associated with the solution. Granted, the service is simply an API, so some associated development is required to enable its capabilities. However, for organizations that have deployed internal solutions, some rudimentary management tools can be developed relatively quickly. Some suggested options for these applications would be a simple web application, Microsoft Power Apps, the Django portal, which Ocean Smart uses. Each person would have to determine the best option for their organization's filtering needs, but Content Moderator provides three categories of content:

- **Text**: The Text API allows you to determine whether the content falls into one or more of the several categories that it scans material for, while also allowing you to provide a custom list of terms for the model. The main types of content the service will search for include offensive language, sexually explicit material, or **personally identifiable information** (**PII**), but by using a custom list, you can filter or allow specific content.

- **Image**: With the Image API, you can determine whether the content falls into one or more of several categories in the material it scans or provide a custom image list for scanning. In this case, the service is looking for images of an adult nature, detects and runs OCR against text in images to see whether it falls into one of the categories listed under text, and detects faces. The ability to provide a custom list of images helps us in situations where an image manually needs to be allowed or denied repeatedly. In these cases, you can add the image to the list to avoid repetition.

- **Video**: The **Video Moderator** service helps you scan for adult or other inappropriate content from the video you are reviewing. The service will also return a timestamp for when the content appears as part of its output. However, as we will discuss later in the chapter, you must use the Azure Media Services to leverage the Video Moderator.

The Content Moderator service offers support for various languages, depending on what function you are attempting to use, so be sure to check out the documentation to get the most current list. For the **Language Detection**, **OCR**, and **Profanity** features, the service supports dozens of languages, but the **Auto-Correction** service currently supports only around 20. Now, let's take a quick look at pricing considerations for when you build your solution.

## Pricing considerations when deploying the service

As with all our solutions, we want to evaluate costs, and as part of the example in the previous section, we may be comparing against a different style of solution, so any additional development and service costs incurred by using the APIs should be part of your overall **Total Cost of Ownership** (**TCO**). The service provides two pricing tiers, but one small difference is that the free tier has a limit of 5,000 free transactions per month in some regions, while in other regions, there is no limit. I assume this has something to do with capacity issues in certain Azure datacenter regions around the world as, at the time of writing, there is a global shortage of microchips and specialty chips used for AI. Take a look at the service before choosing your region to ensure availability and potential limitations. Currently, the Free Tier only allows for one transaction per second, and each Text API call, which is considered a transaction, can contain only up to 1,024 characters. Images must be a minimum of 128 pixels and a maximum size of 4 MB.

The Standard Tier allows up to 10 transactions per second and they are billed on a tiered pricing basis, as per the number of transactions per month based on 1,000 transactions. This is a little confusing to explain, so the following table provides a snapshot of the current pricing for the East US 2 region:

| Number of Transactions | Price per 1,000 |
|---|---|
| 0-1M transactions | $1 |
| 1-5M transactions | $0.75 |
| 5-10M transactions | $0.60 |
| Over 10M transactions | $0.40 |

Table 11.1 – Sample prices per transaction while using the service

See? Isn't it easier to understand all this through an image/table than just simple text? Also, I know it is repetitive, but I cannot stress enough that this is just for the API call and does not include costs for other services you'll likely need, such as Networking, Azure Functions, Storage, and so on. Take your time and design your solution fully and capture all related costs, or better yet, contact your favorite Azure expert and ask them to help you out!

Next, we will dig into more detailed features for each of the APIs. So, let's go!

# Applying the service to text moderation

When discussing the options for text moderation while using the Content Moderation service, we want to look at the way our users interact internally and externally to identify the use cases for using the service. If you have a company blog site that is open for users to add content to, or perhaps even comment on, as many companies are starting to do, this might be a good starting place. As more companies deploy content management systems such as SharePoint, Joomla, Drupal, and WordPress, there is a growing need to ensure inappropriate content doesn't appear in a public forum, external or internal.

Systems like this offer a rich ecosystem of integrated widgets that can be deployed and configured as either free or paid, and this may be a better option depending on your individual needs, so be sure to evaluate what is available. Other areas where we could use the service might be mediums such as chat rooms, discussion boards, chatbots, company websites, and, potentially, internal documents. All these venues are areas where misusing these tools can lead to an uncomfortable work environment or corporate embarrassment, which companies would like to avoid. With the abundance of government policy being pushed forward, protecting the personal information of employees is also becoming much more prevalent. A feature such as this may not be available in some of these other services and may be a factor to look closer at in terms of the API.

Think of a customer service scenario where a representative should never ask a customer for their personal information or a person offer their personal information unprompted. In an interface such as a chat, this service could prevent that personal information from ever being seen by the customer service representative. In this context, whether you have experienced this type of situation or not, many organizations can benefit from this type of protection. I am using this as an example to illustrate that there may be peripheral situations within your organization where deploying a content moderator in non-traditional applications can protect the company as much as the users using the tools.

Another benefit beyond detecting personal data is the ability to autocorrect spelling within text. This is a nice feature when using an input form from a user for common, simple spelling mistakes to ensure cleaner data. However, this function is a mixed blessing of sorts because you run the risk of autocorrecting something that might be specific to a user or that is an uncommon spelling. I suggest that you implement this capability with a somewhat discerning approach based on each of the fields the service might be used for. This may save potentially significant cleanup for when many words are filtered for needing autocorrection or populating your database with bad data if a word is autocorrected unnecessarily.

As you look to deploy the service in the Azure portal, you will find a familiar set of options for many of the other Cognitive Services deployments. As with many of the other services, the bulk of the configuration and activity for the service will happen with the code we write and the API call we make, so the portal deployment is fairly basic, as shown in the following screenshot:

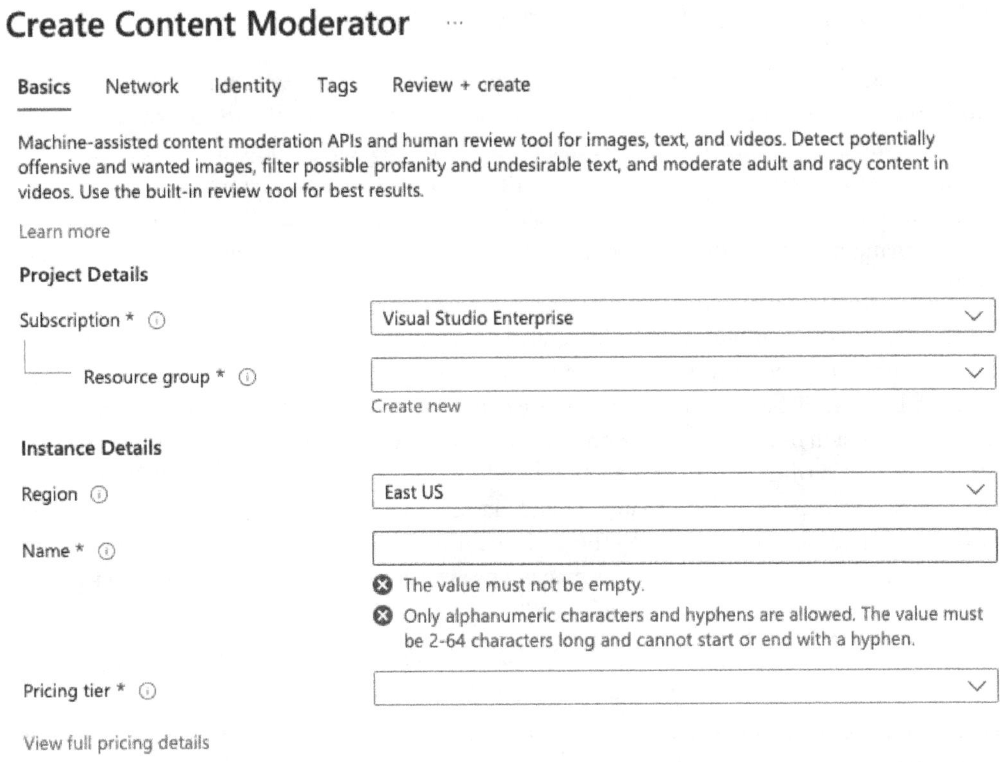

# Create Content Moderator ...

**Basics**    Network    Identity    Tags    Review + create

Machine-assisted content moderation APIs and human review tool for images, text, and videos. Detect potentially offensive and wanted images, filter possible profanity and undesirable text, and moderate adult and racy content in videos. Use the built-in review tool for best results.

Learn more

**Project Details**

Subscription * ⓘ

    Visual Studio Enterprise                                                          ⌄

└──── Resource group * ⓘ

                                                                                      ⌄
    Create new

**Instance Details**

Region ⓘ

    East US                                                                           ⌄

Name * ⓘ


    ✖ The value must not be empty.
    ✖ Only alphanumeric characters and hyphens are allowed. The value must
       be 2-64 characters long and cannot start or end with a hyphen.

Pricing tier * ⓘ

                                                                                      ⌄

View full pricing details

Figure 11.1 – The Basics pane of the Content Moderator deployment wizard in the Azure portal

Here, you will need to specify your **Subscription**, **Resource group**, **Region**, **Name**, and **Pricing tier** details, as well as any of the optional settings from the **Network**, **Identity**, **Tags**, and **Review + create** panes; that's all that's involved. As mentioned in previous chapters, this process is used to reserve the compute that will be used for your workload and doesn't cost anything to have sitting idle.

When we call the API, we point to this subscription and the service key, which will be established upon deployment so that we can use the necessary compute and leverage the API. When calling the API, you must specify which of the services you want to use as part of the **Request URL** string, as shown in the following code snippet:

```
https://{endpoint}/contentmoderator/moderate/v1.0/ProcessText/
Screen[?autocorrect][&PII][&listId][&classify][&language]
```

Note that all the parameters, or filter types, are considered optional as part of the API call. As with our other API calls for services, you must include your `Content-Type` and `Ocp-Apim-Subscription-Key` within **Request headers**. When sending your **Request Body**, you can send raw requests with **MIME** types such as HTML, XML, markdown, or plain-text alongside the API call. If we use the example outlined previously, providing such unwanted information might look like this:

> *"These chat systems don't work for crap. My social security number is 123121234, please call me at 5551235678"*

Now, who can't imagine their parents typing something just like this into a chatbot? So, this is what would be passed to the service, and we would want to filter out the word "crap" if it was considered offensive. Also, we would want to filter the social security and phone numbers before the customer service representative sees them. Using this example, the service would return with a 200 response code in JSON format, like so:

```json
{
    "OriginalText": "These chat systesm don't work for crap. My social
security number is 123121234, please call me at 5551235678",
    "NormalizedText": "These chat systems don't work for crap. My social
security number is 123121234, please call me at 5551235678",
    "AutoCorrectedText": "These chat systems don't work for crap. My
social security number is 123121234, please call me at 5551235678"
,
    "Misrepresentation": null,
```

Here, we have the items that were returned as possible PII:

```json
"PII": {
    "SocialSecurity": [
        {
            "Detected": "123121234",
            "SubType": "Regular",
            "Text": "123121234",
            "Index": 21
        }
    ],
    "Phone": [
        {
            "CountryCode": "US",
            "Text": "5551235678",
            "Index": 45
        }
    ]
},
```

The `Classification` feature currently only supports English as a language and tells us which category the detected word falls into. The service also tries to take the word in the context it is being used as it determines whether it falls into one of the following category types:

- **Category 1**: This category means that the filtered text could potentially be sexually explicit or adult language

- **Category 2**: In this category, the language could be considered sexually suggestive or mature

- **Category 3**: This category refers to language that could potentially be considered offensive in certain situations

As you can see, these categories attempt to discern the content of the phrase that's being analyzed before it assigns a score from 0 to 1, with 1 being the most likely to be filtered.

Here is how the system feels about the word `crap`:

```
"Classification": {
   "Category1":
   {
      "Score": 0.5
   },
   "Category2":
   {
      "Score": 0.6
   },
   "Category3":
   {
      "Score": 0.5
   },
```

Based on the results, the API suggests that the word be reviewed manually for action:

```
      "ReviewRecommended": true
   },
   "Language": "eng",
   "Terms": [
      {
         "Index": 10,
         "OriginalIndex": 10,
         "ListId": 0,
         "Term": "crap"
      }
   ],
   "Status": {
      "Code": 3000,
      "Description": "OK",
```

```
        "Exception": null
    },
    "TrackingId": "1717c837-cfb5-4fc0-9adc-24859bfd7fac"
}
```

The Python code to make this call would look something like the following, with {body} being the text we want to analyze with the service:

```
import http.client, urllib.request, urllib.parse, urllib.error, base64
```

Here, we pass our `header` information:

```
headers = {
    # Request headers
    'Content-Type': 'text/plain',
    'Ocp-Apim-Subscription-Key': '{subscription key}',
}
```

Next, we define the parameters, or filters, we want to use:

```
params = urllib.parse.urlencode({
    # Request parameters
    'autocorrect': '{boolean}',
    'PII': '{boolean}',
    'listId': '{string}',
    'classify': 'True',
    'language': '{string}',
})
```

Then, we send the information as part of the API call, along with the text for analysis:

```
try:
    conn = http.client.HTTPSConnection('westus.api.cognitive.
microsoft.com')
    conn.request("POST", "/contentmoderator/moderate/v1.0/ProcessText/
Screen?%s" % params, "{body}", headers)
    response = conn.getresponse()
    data = response.read()
    print(data)
    conn.close()
except Exception as e:
```

Finally, we get the response from the JSON we reviewed as part of the returned **200 response**:

```
    print("[Errno {0}] {1}".format(e.errno, e.strerror))
```

From here, we have the option to send the output to a database containing the details or an application of some sort where we can make adjustments to the text. Some options would be to obfuscate some of the PII details or suggest a replacement for a potentially offensive term with functionality to make the change to the original text. Now, let's look at how to create a custom list of terms for occasions where the default moderation model isn't sufficient.

## Using a custom text list

For the most part, the model that's provided by default for the text moderation service is sufficient for filtering inappropriate or unwanted material, among the other material previously described. However, there will be occasions where there is a particular business lexicon or words that might relate to items organizations use as early indicators of an employee leaving the company or sharing confidential information. In these situations, you will want to implement a custom list of terms that can be filtered and alerted to, should it be necessary. In this case, you will need to create a custom list of terms to test the input from whatever source you are using it against.

To create a new custom list of terms, you must leverage the same previously created Cognitive Service compute node with an API call similar to the following:

```
https://{endpoint-url}/contentmoderator/lists/v1.0/termlists
```

As with our previous calls, our header will contain our `Content-type` and `Ocp-Apim-Subscription-Key` for specifying our media type – in this case, text – and our subscription key. Finally, we will specify the terms we want to add to our new list, along with naming the list and adding a description, as shown in the following example:

```
{
  "Name": "<List Name>",
  "Description": "<List Description>",
  "Metadata": {
    "<Key>": "<Value>",
    "<Key>": "<Value>"
  }
}
```

The custom terms list allows you to perform the following actions, with most commands being self-explanatory:

- **Bulk Update**
- **Delete**
- **Get All**
- **Get Details**
- **Refresh Search Index**: You are required to refresh after your list is updated with a new term

- **Update Details**
- **Add Term**
- **Delete**
- **Delete All Terms**
- **Get All Terms**

To understand more about how to develop and maintain custom lists, check out this handy source: https://learn.microsoft.com/en-us/azure/cognitive-services/content-moderator/term-lists-quickstart-dotnet.

Depending on the function you would like to perform on the list, the Python code would resemble the following:

```python
import http.client, urllib.request, urllib.parse, urllib.error, base64
```

Specify the headers:

```python
headers = {
    # Request headers
    'Content-Type': 'application/json',
    'Ocp-Apim-Subscription-Key': '{subscription key}',
}
```

Specify the parameters:

```python
params = urllib.parse.urlencode({
})
try:
    conn = http.client.HTTPSConnection('westus.api.cognitive.
microsoft.com')
    conn.request("POST", "/contentmoderator/lists/v1.0/termlists?%s" %
params, "{body}", headers)
    response = conn.getresponse()
    data = response.read()
    print(data)
    conn.close()
```

Handle any errors and return an error message for investigation:

```python
except Exception as e:
    print("[Errno {0}] {1}".format(e.errno, e.strerror))
```

With that, we have deployed our custom term list and can check for any terms that aren't covered by the default model by creating our own. This example illustrates another reason we should build a simple web application or some other input screen – so that whoever is deemed the list maintainer has an easier way to maintain the list by leveraging the commands outlined in this section. Next, we'll look at how to use the API for image moderation.

## Applying the service to image moderation

There are three primary functions for the image moderation feature of the Content Moderator service:

- **Adult or racy content**: For detecting whether the content is sexual or suggestive in terms of mature material.

- **OCR on text**: For detecting and identifying whether text within an image being scanned contains any of the content listed earlier in the text filtering section.

- **Facial recognition**: For detecting how many faces appear in an image and where they are located within the image. This can be used for counting how many people are gathered – for instance, where capacity limitations are present or in other situations of that type.

Because this feature of the service is built similarly for the Text API, we will only provide brief examples and descriptions of how the service works.

For our API request, we will send our URL in the following, familiar format:

```
https://{endpoint}/contentmoderator/moderate/v1.0/ProcessImage/
Evaluate[?CacheImage]
```

The `CacheImage` parameter allows you to cache the image in the memory of the service for use post-detection. The `Evaluate` command at the end of the URL signifies that we are using the sexual or racy content filter. For facial detection, the command is `FindFaces`, while for OCR, we must specify OCR, followed by the language we are detecting if it's something other than the default language, English. The Request headers are also in the same format as the previous text example. Here, you need to dictate the content type, along with the following supported options, for file types to be scanned:

- GIF
- JPEG
- PNG
- BMP
- TIFF

A JSON document that includes the URL of the file in question would also be acceptable.

The result that's returned depends on the type of detection being performed. Let's summarize what results we should expect:

- **Adult or racy content**: Scanning for adult or racy content will yield a score between 0 and 1 for each category, and whether the service believes the content should be filtered as the score gets closer to 1. The results will look something like the following:

```
{
    "AdultClassificationScore": x.xxx,
    "IsImageAdultClassified": <Bool>,
    "RacyClassificationScore": x.xxx,
    "IsImageRacyClassified": <Bool>,
    "AdvancedInfo": [],
    "Result": false,
    "Status": {
      "Code": 3000,
      "Description": "OK",
      "Exception": null
    },
    "TrackingId": "<Request Tracking Id>"
}
```

- **Face detection**: When we want to detect how many faces are found and where they are located within the image, we can use the FindFaces feature. This feature will count the number of faces found in an image, as well as where they are located. This will return a result like the following:

```
{
    "TrackingId": "xxxx_xxxxxxxxxxxxxxxxxxxxxxxxxx_xxxxxxxx-xxxx-
xxxx-xxxx-xxxxxxxxxxxx",
    "CacheId": "xxxxxxxxxxxx",
    "Result": true,
    "Count": 1,
    "Faces": [
      {
        "Bottom": xxx,
        "Left": xxx,
        "Right": xxx,
        "Top": xxx
      }
    ]
}
```

More details on how to use the API, along with other features, can be found here: https://github.com/MicrosoftDocs/azure-docs/blob/main/articles/cognitive-services/Content-Moderator/image-moderation-api.md#detecting-faces.

- **OCR on text**: When we want to detect and filter text within images, we can leverage the **OCR** feature. For this option, we can specify the language the text is in. After doing this, we will be provided with a new enhanced parameter, which allows for more detailed scanning and additional operations. All the same image formats can be scanned with the exception that if you use the enhanced parameter, the .tiff file format is not supported. Also, using the enhanced service requires more compute and it takes longer to process the files for deeper recognition. The service can then look for similar content as the text content moderator does, such as inappropriate language and phraseology, by taking the OCR output and passing it to the Text API. Upon a successful request to the service, we get a **200 response** result, as shown here:

```
{
    "TrackingId":"xxxx_xxxxxxxxxxxxxxxxxxxxxxxx_xxxxxxxx-xxxx-
xxxx-xxxx-xxxxxxxxxxxx",
    "CacheId": "xxxxxxxxxxxx",
    "Language": "eng",
    "Text": "The quick brown fox jumped over the lazy dog",
    "Candidates": [
        {"Text": "The quick brown fox jumped over the lazy dog",
"Confidence": 1234},
        {"Text": "The qu1ck brawn fox iumped over the 1azy d0g",
"Confidence": 0.001},
    ]
}
```

To elaborate on what we are seeing with this result, the service detected text within an image and returned a couple of candidates for what the text could be with a confidence score assigned. This example doesn't contain any profanity or other types of offensive content; however, if desired, we could pass the results to the Text API for further analysis by chaining the functions together within our code. We will cover a more detailed example in the complete solution toward the end of this chapter.

Finally, as with the Text API, we can build a custom list of images to be used within the service to remove the image being posted and filtered repeatedly. Imagine a scenario where an image gets posted in a forum, then copied to other threads in the forum repeatedly. With a custom list, valuable processing power and time can be saved, as well as costs of course, by adding that image to the custom list so that it is blocked immediately. The service allows for five custom lists and up to 10,000 images per custom list. The image custom list API has the same features and commands as the text custom list; refer to the previous section for more details on available commands. Now, let's look at the Video Moderation API for filtering inappropriate content in video posts.

# Applying the service to video moderation

So far, we have covered the Text and Image APIs for scanning content as it is added to a variety of mediums, including blogs, forums, chats, and more. As we review the Video Moderator API, you'll find it is quite a departure from the Image and Text APIs. This departure takes the form of a completely different way of working with the service altogether and isn't currently designed to work like the other two services. In this case, it would make sense to have the service be advertised completely separately from Content Moderator because of the requirements to use the service. I'll get more into this in a minute, so bear with me, but it is important to note that similar to the previous two moderation services, you can use this service for video moderation. I won't elaborate any further on the capabilities of the service because of the nature of how it is used and because it doesn't warrant the same attention as the other services.

So, why do I think it should be separate, you ask? Well, to use the service, you are required to do so using the broader **Azure Media Services** (**AMS**), load your videos in there, and then scan for adult or racy content. At the time of writing, there is no other way to use video moderation, but it comes at no cost as part of the wider AMS umbrella, so that's a nice feature to have.

AMS is aptly named as it allows users to centralize the processing of video and audio media and enrich that content with enhanced metadata. The service bolsters capabilities such as the following:

- Extracting text (using the underlying Speech-to-text Cognitive Service)
- Detecting celebrities
- Detecting text in video
- Moderating adult or racy content
- Creating timestamps
- Facial recognition, including speaker recognition and emotion

With these capabilities and more, AMS is geared toward professional video production, which allows videos to be processed and serves as a basis for the Microsoft Stream services, part of the Microsoft Office suite of tools. The service allows you to host your video content and encrypt it, as well as apply **digital rights management** (**DRM**) using some of the most popular techniques for doing so. In the next section, we are going to look at how to operationalize a solution and deploy a system for reviewing and notifying others of flagged content.

# Flagging and reviewing inappropriate content

Now that we have provided a complete overview of each of the Content Moderator APIs, let's look at what it will take to make use of the service in production. As mentioned previously, turning on the Content Moderator itself follows the same process, regardless of whether you are using images or text. If you're asking why I didn't include video, read the last section, *Applying the service for video moderation*, to understand the state of **Video Content Moderation**. By creating the service in the Azure portal, you are simply enabling the compute that will be used to process the work required by the APIs, so looking at the particular settings of the service itself is relatively innocuous. What will be important is how you intend to deploy the service as a larger architecture, and what security, networking, tagging, and other considerations you need to make. The following diagram is a sample Azure Deployment to give you an idea of how you might leverage the service:

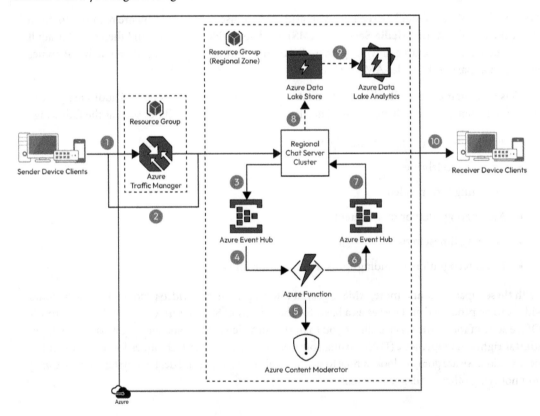

Figure 11.2 – Content Moderator API sample reference architecture

With this example architecture provided by Microsoft, the solution was built to monitor the interaction between players using the chat function of a gaming platform. To ensure fair play and respectful communication, messages may need to be filtered, and offending players may need to be held accountable for inappropriate content being shared. In this example, only text is being moderated for users, but similar steps could be taken to moderate images as well. The following list provides an overview of why the services involved will be useful when you receive content, find inappropriate material, and activities are taken downstream as a result:

- **Azure Traffic Manager** can be used to direct traffic to various servers, depending on which region the user is closest to, assuming resources are deployed to multiple regions. This can be helpful to ensure better performance for the user experience since the traffic needs to be routed for moderation, then back to wherever it is being posted.

- **Azure Event Hubs** is being used here to receive the incoming text from the client and will send the captured text to an **Azure function**.

- When the **Azure function** captures the input from the **event hub**, we begin the process of moderating the content by sending the data to the **Content Moderator** service, leveraging the API for the scenario we have. When there is an offense, we can notify the user with various message routing techniques via email or by sending them a notification in the application directly. Azure Functions can be deployed for many operations where Azure may not have a dedicated service, or a small code block is required for performing some operation.

- Given the scenario, if a user has multiple offenses, they will likely have their account suspended or possibly terminated. For this purpose, this example captures data about the user and their offense in an **Azure Data Lake Storage (ADLS)** account to track the necessary details.

- In this example, **Azure Data Lake Analytics** was provided as the tool for analyzing the data that was being stored in ADLS. However, this feature is no longer maintained, and best practices dictate using a similar data processing service such as **Azure Databricks** or **Azure Synapse Analytics**. These tools can process large amounts of data, so if there is a massive user base that is impossible to track manually, we can process this data quickly and trigger activities based on user history.

- Not pictured in the preceding diagram are the networking services that will be required, such as **Virtual Networks (vNets)** for encapsulating our deployed services and ensuring connectivity between them. Also, certain features such as firewalls, **private endpoints**, **Azure Key Vault**, and other services may be used to design a secure and isolated tenant deployment.

By using this example and the descriptions of how to use each of the services for your deployments, pieces will be stitched together to fit your performance and availability requirements, as specified in your initial business definitions, TCO, and ROI analyses. For more details about this example and the code related to the services, go to https://docs.microsoft.com/en-us/gaming/azure/reference-architectures/cognitive-content-moderation. Finally, now that you know about Content Moderator and the associated services you will need, let's look at Ocean Smart's implementation.

# Building the complete solution

With the many capabilities of the Content Moderator service, we are afforded many opportunities to implement moderation across several mediums. When Ocean Smart deployed a chatbot for helping with the customer experience on their website, they wanted to ensure they could keep their customers protected. They did so by implementing the Content Moderator service to help ensure that customers' PII was protected in situations where customers shared this information in chats.

We also want to ensure that the conversations with the bot remain appropriate and are not offensive, so we also make sure offensive language is filtered. Using a chatbot is just one example, and throughout this chapter, we have discussed several other mediums where the service can be leveraged. Most services will call the API in the same way as we'll show throughout the rest of this chapter.

In *Chapter 14*, we will discuss **Language Understanding** services and how to leverage them using a chatbot, so for detailed instructions on how to deploy the bot we will use for this example, jump ahead and review the process mentioned there. To moderate a chat, whether that involves interfacing with a bot or through a live operator, we will call the Content Moderator API using the method described in this section. For the purpose of this example, we are making the assumption we are connecting to the service through the chatbot.

Depending on how you intend to use the bot service, you may or may not be doing much with the user input. What if the user input was used as the basis for generating a frequently asked questions page or stored in a database for later reference? We might want to scrub that input before we connect it to any backend systems to avoid storing any user information or inappropriate language. We can do this by passing the user input through the Content Moderator service and using that as a filter so that inappropriate content or PII is not stored in backend systems.

> **Note**
> At the time of writing, the Bot Framework will still log user input for telemetry purposes. You cannot suppress this logging based on your detection of PII or objectionable content but can choose to remove the content before publishing or storing the information.

To start deploying the service, you can run the following command in the Azure CLI:

```
az cognitiveservices account create \
--name OceanSmartCh14ContentModerator \
--resource-group Chapter14 \
--kind ContentModerator \
--location eastus \
--sku F0
```

After you have created the service, you will need to retrieve the keys from the account using the following command:

```
az cognitiveservices account keys list \
--name OceanSmartCh14ContentModerator \
--resource-group Chapter14
```

When creating the bot with LUIS services, we give our user the ability to check the status of their order, called `CheckOrderDialog`. While using `CheckOrderDialog` in Bot Framework Composer, add a new activity between **User input (Text)** and **Send a response**. Select **Access external resources** → **Send an HTTP request**.

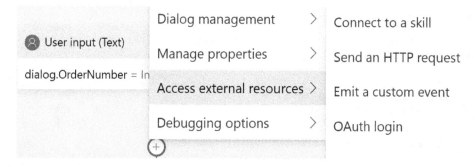

Figure 11.3 – Configuring Bot Framework Composer to call the Content Moderator service

As previously discussed, we make an API call to the service, so, in the properties of the activity, specify the following:

```
HTTP Method: GET
URL: https://eastus.cognitiveservices.azure.
com/contentmoderator/moderate/v1.0/ProcessText/
Screen?autocorrect=false&PII=true&classify=True
```

*If you deployed your Content Moderator service to a region other than eastus, then substitute eastus with the region to which you deployed*:

```
Body: =dialog.OrderNumber
Headers:
Key: Ocp-Apim-Subscription-Key
Value: <The value from "Key1" when you listed the cognitive service
keys>
Result Property: dialog.OrderContentReview
Content Type: text/plain
Response Type: json
```

The basic process that will occur here is as follows:

1.  The bot will take `OrderNumber` and pass it to the Content Moderator service as a request body.

2.  The response will be a JSON document, which we will send to a variable called `OrderContentReview`.

3.  If you would like to test your parameters, try this call in **Postman** or another API development or testing tool to make sure that your URL and keys are correct.

4.  As a debugging step, you could return the JSON body as a bot response to see what it looks like.

5.  Our first check will be for objectionable content as we cannot have anyone cursing at our bot! Below your HTTP request activity, add an if/else conditional activity, click on the + icon, and select **Create a condition** ➔ **Branch: If/else**.

6.  The response from the content moderator might look something like the following code block. Pretend `!#$%!` is some word you were told as a child not to repeat:

```
{
"OriginalText": "you !#$%!^"
"NormalizedText": " you !#$%!",
"Misrepresentation": null,
"Classification": {
```

Here, you can see that the `Category3` score is higher than `.5`, so it is recommended that the content be reviewed:

```
"ReviewRecommended": true,
"Category1": {
"Score": 0.020908381789922714
},
"Category2": {
"Score": 0.217061847448349
},
"Category3": {
"Score": 0.9879999756813049
}
},
```

7.  Finally, here are some of the other details that were returned, such as the language, status, and tracking ID that were logged for this particular activity:

```
"Language": "eng",
"Terms": null,
"Status": {
"Code": 3000,
"Description": "OK",
```

```
"Exception": null
},
"TrackingId": "01aebca7-5972-4a9d-9c93-0e7335736159"
}
```

The property we are interested in here is `ReviewRecommended`. Remember that the response is a JSON document and that you can reach that property through the following path:

```
dialog.OrderContentReview.content.Classification.
ReviewRecommended
```

For the condition property of the new activity, specify the following:

```
"=dialog.OrderContentReview.content.Classification.
ReviewRecommended"
```

8. Under the true branch of the if/else statement, add an activity to send a dialog response. Set the text to something like, "Hmmm... It looks like you included some harmful or offensive words. Let's stick to the order number so we can check that status for you."

9. After reminding the user to be nice, let's restart the dialog. Add an activity under your response (still in the `true` branch of the if/else statement): **Dialog Management → Repeat this dialog**.

Under the `false` branch of the if/else statement, we are going to add another if/else conditional.

1. This time, we are going to check the PII property of the response. If there is anything in that section of the document, the condition on this new if/else statement should be `"=dialog. ordercontentreview.content.PII != null"`.

2. Under the true branch of the PII response, add an activity to send a response similar to *"It looks like you may have included some personal information. All we need to check on your order is the order number."*

3. After you remind the user not to send personal information to a bot, repeat the dialog by adding the **Dialog Management → Repeat this dialog** activity.

4. Under the false branch of the PII check, we know there is no objectionable content and no PII, so we will check on the user's order status. Add an activity to tell the user their order is on the way! This should be like the bot response at the end of this dialog.

At this point, you can delete the **Send a response** action that is at the bottom of your dialog.

Your final dialog flow, from the HTTP request to the end, should look something like the following:

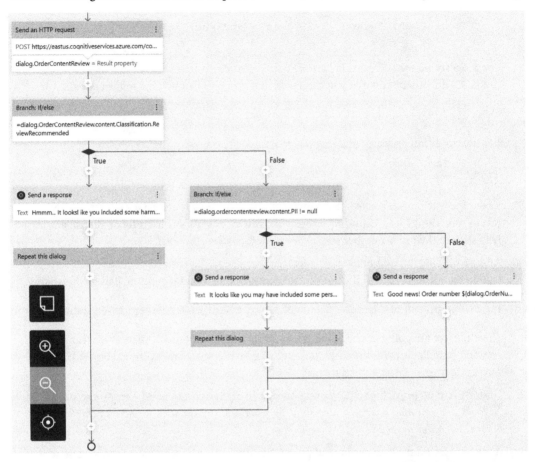

Figure 11.4 – Flow of decisions from the if/then tree configuration in the Bot Framework Composer

If you've gotten this far and want to try it out, go ahead and run your bot locally to test and deploy it to Azure! For PII content, try typing an email address or saying "*My IP address is…*" followed by something like an IP address. For objectionable content, I am not going to give you any suggestions. If you are unsure of what to type, then ask a friend!

Again, this is just one type of deployment that can be done to leverage the Content Moderator service for all the moderation types discussed throughout this chapter. You should now understand how to leverage the API and use the service with other mediums, whichever way they allow for the API call from within the app.

# Summary

With the proliferation of digital media and mediums, we are adding more and more outlets for malicious or inappropriate content online for those individuals who want to behave in such a manner. Significant efforts are being made to ensure the safety of the innocent in broader forums such as social media outlets, video-sharing sites, and large online forums, but rarely does that effort trickle down to smaller corporate outlets and the like. Typically, these services are proprietary to their developers and unfortunately, this leaves many smaller organizations to fend for themselves. For those organizations, I believe this chapter will be very useful. Here, you have the opportunity to deploy services to protect your organization, employees, and customers alike from some of the most popular attack surfaces and can do so at a metered and scalable cost.

As with all the other Cognitive Services that we've covered in this book, you will need to evaluate the TCO and ROI to ensure the efforts in development, as well as whether recurring costs will be worth the price of using the service. Each organization values the concerns we've established when it comes to content moderation at different levels, so those aspects should also be considered. If your organization doesn't mind having curse words come through to the company intranet, then that is the culture that is being dictated, and it is likely not worth your investment.

In this chapter, we covered how to begin using the Content Moderator service and how it enables us to protect users from being exposed to unwanted language and images, as well as your options for videos. We also dug into the expected API calls and responses, as well as how to handle different scenarios for configurations and optimizing the service. Each situation will vary, of course, depending on the requirements of your organization, but the extensive capabilities of the serivce should satisfy most of your corporate needs. In the next chapter, we will look at the next Decision Category service: Personalizer. Personalizer offers the next generation of surfacing the best and most used content for a variety of applications. Enjoy!

# 12
# Using Personalizer to Cater to Your Audience

Shopping cart personalization and website features of that ilk are commonplace for many of our everyday uses. This ranges from a movie or show selection on Netflix, based on a variety you have previously watched, to recommendations of additional items in an online shopping cart that align with your order. Many organizations are also exploring ways to accompany services with products and other services they offer, to provide customers with options and, of course, increase revenue opportunities.

The Personalizer Cognitive Service in Azure was developed with these uses in mind to provide customers with a simple API capable of learning patterns, based on the existing decision logic in your application. In this chapter, we will give an overview of how Ocean Smart was able to use the Personalizer service to build those capabilities into their sales portal. We will go through the development process, discuss **reinforcement learning** (**RL**), configure the Personalizer loop, and make improvements to the service deployed. Throughout this chapter, you will learn the following:

- The Personalizer service and its origins
- Receiving and scoring consumer feedback
- Using RL for recommendations
- Configure Content, Actions, and Context to make recommendations
- Using Evaluations to increase the effectiveness of your Personalizer service
- Building a completed solution

All these learning points will help you to understand how recommendation engines work, perform a review of the performance of the model, and improve the effectiveness of the models we build. Finally, we will show you some examples of how Ocean Smart was able to leverage the Personalizer service, with its online shopping portal for ordering fresh and frozen seafood products. We will also show how they increased sales of accompanying products by simply matching them with products added to a customer shopping cart. First, though, let's look at the technical requirements you will need to complete this chapter most effectively.

# Technical requirements

To show how Ocean Smart built its Personalizer pilot in our example, we will require several familiar tools, many of which you've used in previous examples from this book. As with all the examples, you will need access to the Azure portal with at least Contributor rights. Along with this, to use the service and build the example, you will need the following tools:

- Azure's Personalizer service

- The Azure Functions app

- Python version 3.9.6

- Azure Functions Core Tools

- **Visual Studio Code (VS Code)**

- The Python extension for VS Code

- The Azure Functions extension for Visual Studio Code

Before we start to build though, let's begin by discussing the history and details of the Personalizer service.

# The Personalizer service and its origins

Personalization engines have been used across many web retailers for decades to make some rudimentary recommendations as a user completes their online order. This type of recommendation became prevalent, as organizations could see that they were able to add to the overall sales by making these recommendations to accompany what the user purchased. As the personalization of web assets has proliferated beyond traditional shopping cart recommendations, Microsoft saw an opportunity to provide services that could cover several required solutions. Some of the solutions seen were as follows:

- A customized user experience that includes where to best place advertisements within a web page

- Having key content highlighted for a consumer that they might enjoy reading, based on previous articles they've read on common topics or themes

- Personalized product recommendations based on previous purchases or items already placed in a shopping cart

- Determining the appropriate time to send a notification to a subscriber where the maximum availability of that person is predicted, increasing the chances of a response from that user

- Any other situation where a user is working on an application and a list of options is provided for them, which you want to be displayed to provide recommendations, based on prior activity by the user or other factors

The Personalizer service uses **Reinforcement Learning**, which is a machine learning process where a model is improved by learning behaviors, based on feedback received. This can be feedback based on direct information provided by a user, known as the **inferenced model**, serving as a basis for user preferences. Alternatively, the **exploration policy** can be set to use information gathered about other input methods and responses received to provide an estimate of a user's preference, based on these other factors. Reinforcement learning can be enacted through a variety of methods, but by using the Personalizer service, we can gather direct feedback from users and the environment they are in. These variables are then used in ad hoc learning rather than directly controlled learning, which we will discuss in greater detail later in the chapter.

As with the other Cognitive Services, when you deploy the Personalizer service within the Azure subscription, you are deploying compute for which the API can be called and processing API requests. To facilitate the various workload types listed previously, the Personalizer service includes the following features:

- **Ranks** and **rewards** are a systematic way of providing a list of options, **ranked** in the order of what is most likely to be chosen from the list by a user. These options are ranked based on the prior experience of a given user and environment to present the best option. Depending on the option chosen, the **reward** will determine whether the choice provides additional value to the existing reinforcement learning model and retrain the model if so.

- **Learning modes** offer us the ability to begin learning patterns about an application, by using the Personalizer service to passively understand what choices are being made and not influencing the options provided, or ranking options based on a developed model. In **Apprentice mode**, the service will run without influencing the choices being offered to the user. When the model has been trained, the service can be run in **Online mode**, which will return the best action based on what the model suggests for results from prior learning. Further, we have the **offline evaluation** method, which allows us to test the developed model for results without impacting the deployed service or making any changes to the code. In essence, this mode is used for testing with the **Rank** and **Reward** APIs to look at the performance of a model that took place over a specified period, as you pick a date range for the evaluation.

- **Multi-slot personalization** allows the service to be used in multiple locations or with multiple concepts to track, rank, and reward various user behaviors in the application the API is being used by. Tests can be performed, such as tracking a sequence of rotating content and seeing how it impacts users or the effectiveness of various shapes within a page to draw attention to it.

- The **local inference SDK** allows a model to be downloaded and accessed on the local web client to return rewards faster and reduce latency for recommendations.

As the service has evolved, multi-slot, local inference, and offline evaluations have all been added as capabilities, and continued investment is expected based on the popularity of the service. We will take a deeper look at the features throughout the rest of the chapter, as they are interlaced with the core capabilities of the Personalization experience. First, we'll discuss how to receive and score feedback received within our app from the service.

# Receiving and scoring consumer feedback

When a user interacts with a web application or similar medium, they likely have the intention of being as efficient as possible in accomplishing the task they are using the application for. Unfortunately, sometimes, the applications that are provided don't necessarily provide an interface that helps the user to be as efficient as possible. Web interfaces that require users to hunt for their desired resource and aren't customized for the user the application is servicing have improved in recent years, but they are still lacking oftentimes. Further, with the passing of the GDPR a few years back, it's becoming more and more difficult to handle all the user session information in a simple cookie. Because of the requirement for users to opt in to allow cookies on their browser, previous settings and interactions may be lost or become unavailable, rendering traditional methods of storing information about users limited.

This evolution of how user data is managed and application adjustments are being made as a result of common activities has left a gap in our ability to simply track data and present recommendations based on user history. The Azure Personalizer service, using a machine learning model to make predictions when offering choices to users, provides a way to close that gap in a different way. With the environment information of a user, an existing trained machine learning model can now be leveraged to help provide better options to those users, based on predictions from the environment variables. If the user activity can specifically be logged, the service can provide even more precise details and recommendations. Also, because an API can be leveraged with most applications and the model is already trained for consumers, a client who would have typically needed to train their own model and manage the required infrastructure no longer has any of that overhead. This frees up team members or financial resources for use in other projects within an organization. An example of the effectiveness of the service is that when it was used with the Xbox home screen, Microsoft saw a 40% increase in user engagement (Need to cite: Azure Personalizer – Deliver smarter, more precise customer experience. (`valoremreply.com`)).

To get started with the Personalizer service, you will create the Cognitive Services resource in the Azure portal. As with most other Cognitive Services, the configuration options are relatively basic and designed to provide the compute needed for the service, with only a few required settings.

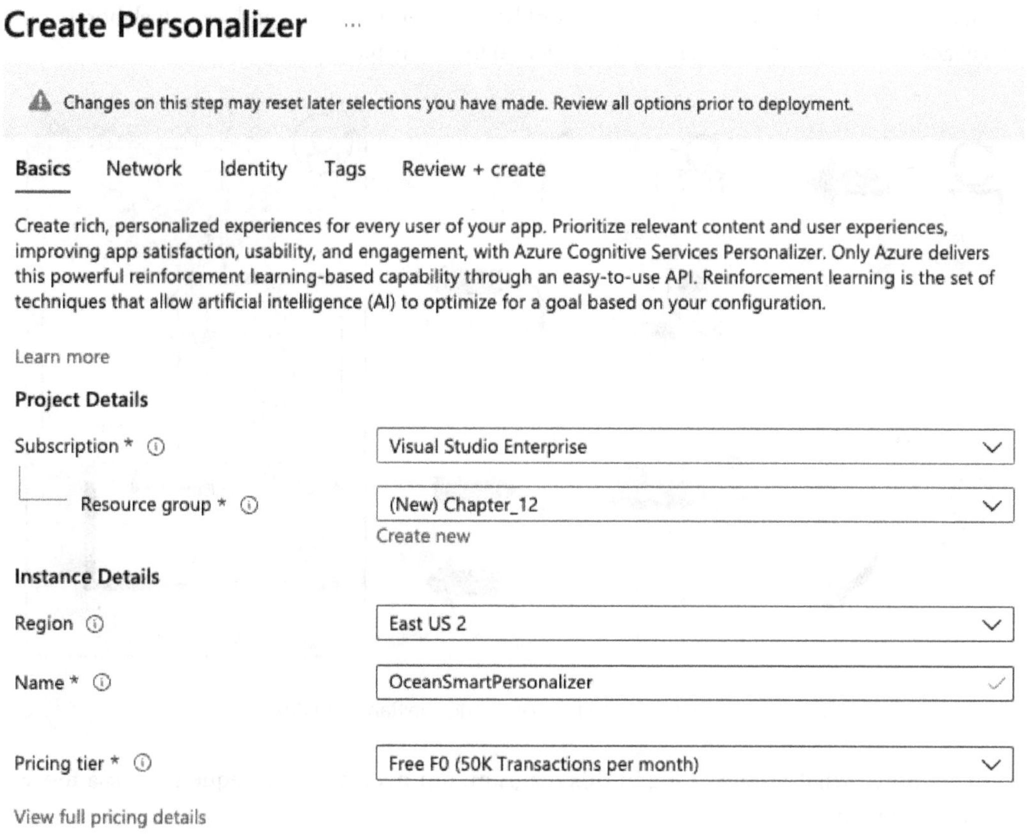

# Create Personalizer ...

⚠ Changes on this step may reset later selections you have made. Review all options prior to deployment.

**Basics**    Network    Identity    Tags    Review + create

Create rich, personalized experiences for every user of your app. Prioritize relevant content and user experiences, improving app satisfaction, usability, and engagement, with Azure Cognitive Services Personalizer. Only Azure delivers this powerful reinforcement learning-based capability through an easy-to-use API. Reinforcement learning is the set of techniques that allow artificial intelligence (AI) to optimize for a goal based on your configuration.

Learn more

**Project Details**

Subscription * ⓘ

| Visual Studio Enterprise | ⌄ |
|---|---|

Resource group * ⓘ

| (New) Chapter_12 | ⌄ |
|---|---|
Create new

**Instance Details**

Region ⓘ

| East US 2 | ⌄ |
|---|---|

Name * ⓘ

| OceanSmartPersonalizer | ✓ |
|---|---|

Pricing tier * ⓘ

| Free F0 (50K Transactions per month) | ⌄ |
|---|---|

View full pricing details

Figure 12.1 – The Azure portal configuration options to deploy the Personalizer service

We have the options of the Free and Standard tiers, with the Free tier having a transaction limit and a monthly storage quota. More details about current pricing and limits can be found here: `https://azure.microsoft.com/en-us/pricing/details/cognitive-services/personalizer/`. After the service has been deployed, you are provided with a REST API, which you can call from your application, and you can begin training the model that will be deployed for your data by interacting with the site calling the API. In other words, as you add more data about the environments of the users interfacing with the application, it will automatically improve, using the reinforcement learning technique to provide better options for the users.

This handy diagram gives a high-level overview of how the service works, and we will elaborate on the feedback portion and additional details further on in the chapter:

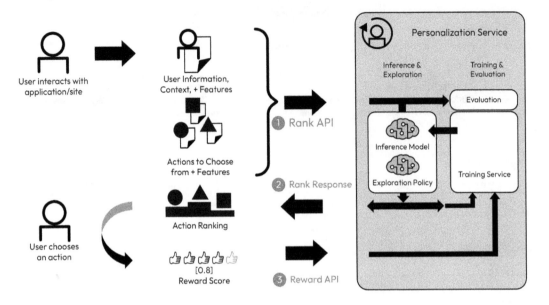

Figure 12.2 – The architectural flow of calling the Rank and Reward calls

Let's break down what is happening in this diagram, not necessarily in sequence, for a more detailed explanation:

- When a user interacts with a site that uses the Personalizer service, the API call is made, and the first Rank call is made with related Actions and Context, called an **Event.**

- When discussing Context, we are referring to the variables that can be captured about the user who interfaces with the API. This can be information about the user themselves, a profile describing the type of user, the location of the user, the type of device they are using, and other similar details that can be identified.

- The Actions are a list of items that are presented to the user for them to choose from. For instance, if a user selects from a drop-down list in the application, the Actions would be the full list of options.

- Our Event is provided with an ID for tracking, and a response is provided back to the user with the best options as predicted, based on the machine learning model:

  - This process leverages the **inference model**, referenced in the previous architecture, to identify the top choice, based on the results of the model created.

  - For secondary options, or in a case where a model doesn't have good options to match with the Context provided, the exploration policy will be leveraged.

- The policy is set as a percentage value, configurable in the Azure portal, which will return the percentage of the Rank calls to be used for exploration, or what the system predicts will be the best remaining options.

- As the user makes their choice, the **Reward** API is triggered, capturing the details of what the user chose.

- The rank and reward results are then coupled and associated as the model is retrained, helping to improve the existing model's accuracy.

- As part of the configuration of the service, you can determine how frequently to retrain the model, based on the model frequency update settings in the portal.

- You are also able to determine how long you would like to store the data that is being captured for use with the model. Be mindful that your frequency and retention configurations will require more or less compute and storage, which will result in a cost evaluation to determine the mix of frequency requirements and related costs.

- If any configuration changes are made to the **Reward** or **Exploration** settings in the portal, the model will be reset to capture new data, so it is advisable to consider this when changing those settings.

Now that we have provided some context on how the rank and reward system works in Personalizer, let's dive in deeper to understand how the service leverages Reinforcement Learning to provide the best possible options to users.

## Using Reinforcement Learning for recommendations

The core machine learning concept that is the basis for the Personalizer service is **Reinforcement Learning**. Along with Supervised Learning and Unsupervised Learning, it makes up the basic foundational pillars of machine learning. As discussed previously in the chapter, **RL** is a mix of the **exploration** of options and **exploitation** of an existing model. This concept differs from **Supervised Learning** because, with this pillar, we are expected to provide feedback for each activity, such as a labeled input/output pair for presentation or feedback when an incorrect option is presented and there's a need for feedback for correction. With **Unsupervised Learning**, patterns are learned from untagged data, which will mimic what is extrapolated from the data to build expected predictions.

So, as this method is applied to the service, we take our reward feedback from the application we're using to better train the model for the exploitation aspect, and present other options using the exploration option. This creates a continuous loop of both learning methods to provide known options, based on our user context, and still allows exploration based on the previously discussed **Exploration** setting from the service. One difference between the Personalizer application of Reinforcement Learning and other similar approaches to personalization is that Personalizer doesn't require a simulation environment to provide results. It was designed to react to external forces that are outside of the service's control and collect each data point for learning, with the understanding that there can be a negative experience for a user if a sub-optimal option is presented.

There are four core RL algorithms that the Personalizer service leverages to help make this happen:

- **Contextual bandits**: A term originally coined in 2007 by John Langford, contextual bandits refers to looking at a specific situation and making a choice between presented options, based on that situation. The algorithm allows us to provide a reward for the most applicable choice after the decision has been made and strengthens predictability.

- **Decision memory**: The decision memory algorithm allows us to provide a list of choices based on the presented environment variables and the model that has been built, using a set of linear models to align correlations.

- **Epsilon greedy**: Used by the Personalizer service, the epsilon greedy algorithm is used to provide randomly generated decisions that we can choose to exploit or explore. When we set the exploration percentage, we weigh the algorithm to favor what will be explored. So, if the setting is 10%, theoretically, 1 in 10 choices will be explored and not exploited.

The machine learning framework that the Personalizer service uses is **Vowpal Wabbit**. Vowpal Wabbit (`https://vowpalwabbit.org/`) was started by Yahoo Research and has since been largely contributed to by Microsoft Research. The algorithms listed previously are contained within the Vowpal Wabbit machine learning libraries and applications.

Now that we understand a little better what happens "behind the scenes" by exploring the algorithms, let's look at how to configure the service to make recommendations based on what happens around and with the user.

## Configuring Content, Actions, and Context to make recommendations

So far in the chapter, we have given you a pretty good idea of what the Personalizer service does for its audience, and we looked at what happens in the background with the machine learning algorithms and libraries that were used to develop the service. Now, we're going to start to dig into the service itself to look at how it is configured, and what the details that go into the environment variables we've mentioned a few times are by looking at **Features**. Note the capital "F" in that last sentence for Features. Yes, that was intentional, because when we talk about Features, we are talking about an actual concept in the Personalizer service, not just the features of the service. Get it? Sometimes, the naming decisions for these things make me laugh.

When we discuss Features, we refer to a unit or grouping of Actions or Context. Features provides all the information needed to help improve the reward system and increase reward effectiveness. When specifying features, you have the choice to use string, numeric, or Boolean as your data type; however, most of your features will be specified as strings, even when they are numbers. The numeric data type should only be used for situations where you want to use numbers to express magnitude – for instance, where multiple items are owned by a user and it would change how they respond to options. If a user had three children in their household, that would shape the Personalizer results differently than if they had only one child. The recommendation for situations where numbers are used to represent non-linear events, such as age and distance, is to provide a range of options rather than individual values. Features can be grouped based on similarities, and these groups are called **namespaces**.

When developing your use case for best performance, the **density** of your features will affect the performance of the service. A **dense** feature is something that has only a few categories of options. Using the prior example, if we have two Features describing the number of children in our household, less than two and two or more, this would be considered very dense. However, if we were listing possible iterations of Icelandic children's names, around 1,200, this would be considered a **sparse** feature. With so many options and combinations available, it would be less effective for our rank and reward process to provide options to a user. There is a fine balance between density and effectiveness, so when applicable, find the right mix of density that will capture the essence of what you need for your application and provide details, without causing inefficiencies with features that are too sparse.

**Context** features provide details about a user's environment variables, such as the operating system, browser, type of device, physical location or region, and chronological information.

The following is an example of the JSON you would use when you capture details about a user interacting with the site, captured within the feature namespaces, starting with the "user" Context:

```json
{
    "contextFeatures": [
        {
            "user": {
                "profileType":"AnonymousUser",
                "latlong": ["47.6,-122.1"]
            }
        },
```

Next, we have the "environment" and "device" Contexts:

```json
{
            "environment": {
                "dayOfMonth": "28",
                "monthOfYear": "8",
                "timeOfDay": "13:00",
                "weather": "sunny"
            }
        },
        {
            "device": {
                "mobile":true,
                "Windows":true
            }
        },
```

Finally, we have the `"activity"` Context:

```
{
    "activity" : {
        "itemsInCart": 3,
        "cartValue": 250,
        "appliedCoupon": true
    }
  }
 ]
}
```

Next, let's discuss **Actions**.

Actions are the list of choices we present to a user of an application, website, or similar interface. Actions may or may not have any relationship with the Context being captured; however, both will impact the Rank and Reward APIs, how effective they are, and how they are impacted. Some examples of Actions might be a recommendation of reports a user might want to run, a list of movies a user might want to watch, a set of products that might accompany an item in a user's shopping cart, and similar suggestions during an interaction.

The following JSON represents Actions in the form of food items and some of their properties, starting with `"pasta"` and its features:

```
{
    "actions": [
    {
      "id": "pasta",
      "features": [
        {
           "taste": "salty",
           "spiceLevel": "medium",
           "grams": [400,800]
        },
        {
           "nutritionLevel": 5,
           "cuisine": "italian"
        }
      ]
    },
```

Here, we can see the `"ice cream"` food item, including its features:

```
{
    "id": "ice cream",
    "features": [
        {
            "taste": "sweet",
            "spiceLevel": "none",
            "grams": [150, 300, 450]
        },
        {
            "nutritionalLevel": 2
        }
    ]
},
```

Next, we can see the `"juice"` menu item:

```
{
    "id": "juice",
    "features": [
        {
            "taste": "sweet",
            "spiceLevel": "none",
            "grams": [300, 600, 900]
        },
        {
            "nutritionLevel": 5
        },
        {
            "drink": true
        }
    ]
},
```

Finally, we include the `"salad"` menu item with its details:

```
{
    "id": "salad",
    "features": [
        {
            "taste": "salty",
            "spiceLevel": "low",
            "grams": [300, 600]
        },
        {
```

```
        "nutritionLevel": 8
    }
  ]
 }
 ]
}
```

In this example, we provide our list of foods – pasta, ice cream, juice, and salad, along with some features about those foods. When the selection is chosen by the user, the ID of the Action along with the Context details are sent to the Reward API, with a score between 1 and -1. Those details are used as part of retraining the machine learning model in the next **Learning Loop** that is performed. A Learning Loop is a Personalizer resource that provides benefits to whichever portion of your application you want to use the service for, and it has an associated model that is created and improved with more use. Multiple Learning Loops can be applied to your application, depending on how you want to deploy the Personalizer service – for instance, multiple drop-down lists within the application, with multiple lists of Actions. Learning Loops are enhanced over time as more data is added and more rewards are provided.

Many factors will affect the performance of the Personalizer service, some of which we have covered in this section. Microsoft provides a significant amount of these recommendations in their documentation, and they should be part of your analysis when building requirements for your Personalizer service. These details and options for scalability can be found at the following link: `https://learn.microsoft.com/en-us/azure/cognitive-services/personalizer/concepts-scalability-performance`. Another feature of the service to enhance effectiveness is the capability to perform offline evaluations. We will discuss this topic in the next section.

## Using evaluations to increase the effectiveness of your Personalized Service

After you have deployed the service and are collecting data about user interactions and using the rank and reward system, you may want to assess ways to enhance your model, Actions, Context, or Features. Rather than making changes to the current configurations, Microsoft gives you the option to assess these options by using **offline evaluations**, assuming that enough data has been captured to do so. Offline evaluations allow you to test your features and how effective they've been over the span of your learning loop. With this option, you can specify a date range for your testing through the current time without affecting the existing model or the performance of the model for users interfacing with the application. As discussed previously in the chapter, if you make changes to certain configurations, it will redeploy your model, and you will need to build it from scratch and lose all the history amassed. Remember that we talked about the data retention feature earlier in the chapter, and of course, you will only be able to do an offline evaluation up to the point when the retention setting removed data. When deciding to use an offline evaluation, be sure to have at least 50,000 optimized experiences, giving you enough data points to test against and evaluate performance. Ideally, doing these evaluations will allow you to better understand what is most effective for your audience and inspire additional ways to make better predictions.

It also should go without saying that the data that is contained within a model should be relevant to normal behavior. If you've recently had a **denial of service (DdoS)** attack or performed a large application load test, you are not going to get a representative set of data to test on, so it would be a waste of time. Also, it's important to evaluate the confidence bounds of the existing learning policy, ensuring that they are not too wide because you haven't received enough reward detail to make for an effective evaluation.

An offline evaluation not only evaluates the ranking data but also provides comparisons against not having the service implemented at all. Further, the offline evaluation will provide the following:

- The average rewards achieved

- Comparative effectiveness of random choices

- Comparative effectiveness of different learning policies

- Context contributions to increased or decreased success

- Action contributions to increased or decreased success

- Opportunities to discover new and more effective learning policies

After the completion of the offline evaluation, the user (tester) will have the option to swap the existing learning policy with a newer and theoretically better-performing policy, based on the evaluation. The user can also download the policy for future implementation if desired. The result of your offline evaluation will provide you with details on whether to add new features or remove ineffective features, or whether features might be providing undesirable or irresponsible content. These features among other capabilities offer the ability to regularly enhance your audience's experience.

Another type of evaluation is a **feature evaluation**, which is performed while a model is deployed and the service is online. This type of evaluation takes place within the Azure portal and allows for a subset of evaluations that are performed using offline mode. By running the feature evaluation online, there is some risk of causing performance issues for users interfacing with the application while the evaluation is being performed. With offline mode, you can evaluate which features of Actions and Context are the most and least effective, as well as provide feedback to design teams about potential issues with deployments and user choices.

Depending on what you need for analysis and whether you want to potentially impact users, determine which evaluation is most appropriate for your solution, or run them both and see what results you can leverage to make your application more effective. Now that we have provided a full overview of the service and its features, let's look at what a complete solution would look like and how Ocean Smart was able to leverage the service.

# Building a completed solution

For the first proof of concept, we decided to use the Ocean Smart seafood catering business unit to display additional recommendations to accompany selected items and present a user with a list of platters to select from. The goal is for the first item in the list to be the selection that the user is most likely to purchase. To accomplish this, we create a function app with two functions – `GetRankedActions` and `RewardAction`. The `GetRankedActions` action presents the list of possible Actions for the user, ordered by the probability that the user will purchase that item. `RewardAction` tells the Personalizer service whether that item was purchased or not. To train the model, we have a test script that selects a user at random, presents that user with choices from the Personalizer, and lets the Personalizer know whether the first choice presented was one the user would purchase. Here is a basic diagram of the flow:

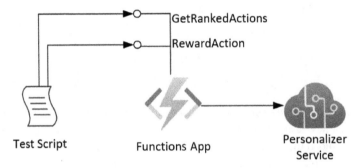

Figure 12.3 – A sample flow of data to triggers the Functions app to use the Personalizer service

Note that to keep this example straightforward, we have selected a small sample of catering options and users that we keep in code, as opposed to reaching out to a data store.

To support this process, we create the following:

- An Azure Personalizer service

- A Functions app with two functions:

  - `GetRankedActions`

  - `RewardAction`:

    ```
    az login
    az account set --subscription <your-subscription-id>
    az group create --location eastus2 --name <your-resource-group>
    az cognitiveservices account create \
    --name ch12-personalizer \
    --resource-group <your-resource-group> \
    --kind Personalizer \
    --sku F0 \
    ```

```
--location eastus2 \
--yes
```

You will need to retrieve the keys from the deployed service to call it from the Functions app:

```
az cognitiveservices account keys list \
    --name your-personalizer-learning-loop \
    --resource-group your-personalizer-resource-group
az cognitiveservices account keys list \
    --name ch12-personalizer \
    --resource-group <your-resource_group>
```

Now we have the resources needed to create our Azure Functions. As mentioned in the technical requirements, to follow this example, you will need the following:

- Python Version 3.9.6
- Azure Functions Core Tools
- Visual Studio Code
- The Python extension for Visual Studio Code
- The Azure Functions extension for Visual Studio Code

If you open the \Chapter 12\Code Snippets\functionapp folder in Visual Studio Code, you should see the following folder structure:

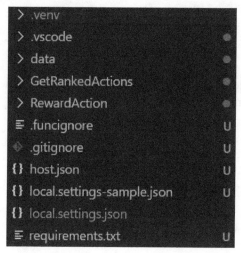

Figure 12.4 – The files and folders listed from the Personalizer project in Visual Studio Code

A couple of files/folders that are important to the function runtime are as follows:

- The `GetRankedActions` and `RewardAction` folders are our two functions in this Function app. We will dig into these later in this section.

- `local.settings-sample.json`: This contains the settings that the functions will need in order to execute properly. Note that the key values are not specified.

- `local.settings.json`: This is not yet present in your repo. You will create this file shortly.

- `requirements.txt`: When you deploy your function app, the function app runtime `pip` installs any packages listed in `requirements.txt`.

To follow the best practices from a security perspective, the `local.settings.json` file is not checked into GitHub, as it contains secrets. We use `local.settings-sample.json` to store the setting names that the function app requires.

Make a copy of `local.settings-sample.json` and name it `local.settings.json`.

You should see the following:

```
{
  "IsEncrypted": false,
  "Values": {
    "AzureWebJobsStorage": "",
    "FUNCTIONS_WORKER_RUNTIME": "python",
    "PERSONALIZER_KEY" : "",
    "PERSONALIZER_ENDPOINT" : ""
  }
}
```

The Personalizer key and endpoint settings are the values seen when you deployed the Personalizer service in the steps earlier in this section.

## Data used for this example

In a production environment, you would likely have a database or an API to retrieve lists of catering platters, lists of users, and so on. For simplicity, we have just crafted some JSON collections to hold the data for this example.

Open the `data` folder, as shown in the following screenshot:

Figure 12.5 – The files listed in the data folder in Visual Studio Code

For starters, we will work with the `platters.py` configuration.

The output of an API call to retrieve a list of catering platters might return something like this:

```python
actions_and_features = {
    'pasta_with_shellfish': {
        'attributes': {
            'qty':10,
            'cuisine':'italian',
            'price':8
        },
        'dietary_attributes': {
            'vegan': False,
            'low_carb': False,
            'high_protein': False,
            'vegetarian': False,
            'low_fat': True,
            'low_sodium': True
        }
    },
```

Here, we provide additional examples that can be returned. You get more elaborate details on each item, as displayed with `pasta with shellfish`, outlined in the previous example:

```python
'sushi': {...},
'seafood_salad': {...},
'lobster_rolls': {...},
'vegetable_platter': {...},
...
}
```

This list of catering platters is the actions that we present to the user, and each platter has a set of features associated with it.

The `rewards.py` file defines the reward we give to Personalizer for supplying us with the best platter. If the user purchases the platter, that is a reward of 1; if the user does not do anything with the suggestion, that is a reward of 0. Clicking and adding to the cart are intermediate rewards with lesser values of 0.2 and 0.4 respectively:

```
rewards = {
            'abandon': 0,
            'click': 0.2,
            'add_to_cart': 0.4,
            'purchase': 1
}
```

You will define the reward definitions based on what makes sense in your application – for example, tracking likes or when a user adds a platter to a favorites list. These could have associated reward values also included in the file.

The `users.py` file contains a list of users and attributes about these users that Personalizer uses to make recommendations:

```
user_profiles = {
    'Andy': {
        'company_size': 'large',
        'avg_order_size': '0-20',
        'orders_per_month': '10-20',
        'allergies': 'none'
    },
    'Tim': {…}
    'Paul': {…}
    'Scott': {…}
    'Chris': {…}
}
```

Next, let's look at the `GetRankedActions` folder for additional configurations.

### GetRankedActions

The `GetRankedActions` folder contains the files necessary to create the Azure Functions' `GetRankedActions` function, as shown here:

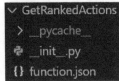

Figure 12.6 – The contents of the GetRankedActions function, as shown in Visual Studio Code

Looking at `function.json`, we can see the structure of the function we are deploying:

```json
{
  "scriptFile": "__init__.py",
  "bindings": [
    {
      "authLevel": "function",
      "type": "httpTrigger",
      "direction": "in",
      "name": "req",
      "methods": [
        "get"
      ]
    },
    {
      "type": "http",
      "direction": "out",
      "name": "$return"
    }
  ]
}
```

Some additional details about the previous code block are as follows:

- `scriptfile`: This shows that `__init__.py` contains the code that is called when the Azure function is invoked.

- The bindings declare the trigger, input, and output of the function:

  - This function will be invoked when an http request is made.

  - The function runtime passes the http request information to a parameter called `req`.

  - The return of the function is the http response that the function runtime passes back to the caller.

As indicated in the bindings, `__init__.py` contains the code for this function:

1. Let's start with some functions to access the data defined earlier:

   ```python
   def get_platters():
       res = []
       for platter_id, feat in actions_and_features.items():
           action = RankableAction(id=platter_id, features=[feat])
           res.append(action)
       return res
   ```

2.  The `get_platters` function iterates over the catering platter information and creates an array of `RankableAction` objects that the Personalizer service uses to make its recommendation:

    ```
    def get_user_context(user):
        location_context = {'location': \
            random.choice(['west', 'east', 'midwest'])}
        season = {'season': \
            random.choice(['spring', 'summer', 'fall', 'winter'])}
        cuisine_searched = {'cuisine_searched': \
            random.choice(['italian', 'mexican', 'asian',
    'american'])}
        result = [user_profiles.get(user, ''), \
            location_context, season, cuisine_searched]
        return result
    ```

    `get_user_context` returns information about the user to whom Personalizer recommends a catering platter. We augment the static user profile with information about the context of the user's request. This context could be anything that you can glean from the user's interaction with your system.

3.  The main function is the function invoked by the Azure Function runtime. As per the bindings, it accepts `HttpRequest` as input and returns `HttpResponse`:

    ```
    def main(req: func.HttpRequest) -> func.HttpResponse:
    ```

4.  We start testing the service by setting up our data. We retrieve the user from the query string parameters of the http request. We call `get_user_context` to look up the user in our data store and augment the profile with the calling context that we are interested in. We also load the list of platters from our data store:

    ```
    user = req.params.get('user', '')
    user_context = get_user_context(user)
    platters = get_platters()
    ```

5.  Next, we load the environment variables needed to connect to the Personalizer service. This key and endpoint are the values we entered earlier in `local.settings.json`:

    ```
    key = os.getenv("PERSONALIZER_KEY", "")
    endpoint = os.getenv("PERSONALIZER_ENDPOINT", "")
    ```

6.  Using the configured key and endpoint, we set up a connection to the Personalizer service:

    ```
    client = PersonalizerClient(endpoint,
                                CognitiveServicesCreden-
    tials(key))
    ```

7. The `RankRequest` class puts our actions and user context into a format that the Personalizer service can use to rank the platters in the appropriate order for the user:

```
rank_request = RankRequest(actions=platters,
                           context_features=user_context)
```

8. We now call the `rank` method of the Personalizer service to provide us with the ranked list:

```
rank_response = client.rank(rank_request=rank_request)
```

9. We format this response for the output of our function, pulling out the attributes that will be important to our caller. The body of our response is a JSON object. At the top level, we include the user, `event_id` (which we will use to supply a reward value back to the Personalizer), and the overall rankings identified by the service:

```
platter_list = {'user':user,
                'event_id':rank_response.event_id,
                'best_action': rank_response.reward_action_
id,
                'rankings':[]}
for ranking in enumerate(rank_response.ranking):
    recipe_list['rankings'].append(
                    {
                    'rank' : ranking[0],
                    'id' : ranking[1].id,
                    'probability' : ranking[1].
probability
                    }
                )
```

10. Next, we return the result to the caller:

```
return func.HttpResponse(
        json.dumps(recipe_list),
        mimetype="application/json"
        )
```

Next, let's look at the `RewardAction` function.

## RewardAction

The `RewardAction` function supplies the reward value back to the Personalizer. We let the Personalizer determine whether the action it selected was acted upon by the user, and thus, the service learns from the rewards to improve its recommendation.

Figure 12.7 – The contents of the RewardAction function in Visual Studio Code

Similar to our other function, function.json contains the information that the Azure Functions runtime will use to host the function. This bindings file is identical to our GetRankedActions. The function.json function is declared in in __init__.py, triggered by an http request, which the runtime will pass as an input parameter. The runtime will then return an http response as output:

```
{
  "scriptFile": "__init__.py",
  "bindings": [
    {
      "authLevel": "function",
      "type": "httpTrigger",
      "direction": "in",
      "name": "req",
      "methods": [
        "get"
      ]
    },
    {
      "type": "http",
      "direction": "out",
      "name": "$return"
    }
  ]
}
```

The main function in __init__.py contains the code for this function. Like GetRankedAction, we can see that the function runtime passes us the request object as an http input, and the response object is our function output:

```
def main(req: func.HttpRequest) -> func.HttpResponse:
```

We pull the event ID and reward from the request query string. event_id is the one provided by the Personalizer service in GetRankedAction:

```
event_id = req.params.get('event_id', '')
reward = float(req.params.get('reward', '-1'))
```

As previously discussed, we pull the Personalizer service endpoint information from the environment variables created from `local.settings.json` and create an instance of the Personalizer client with this information:

```
key = os.getenv("PERSONALIZER_KEY", "")
endpoint = os.getenv("PERSONALIZER_ENDPOINT", "")
client = PersonalizerClient(endpoint,
    CognitiveServicesCredentials(key))
```

In this function, we simply pass the reward directly to the Personalizer service and return an http success status code:

```
client.events.reward(event_id=event_id, value = reward)

return func.HttpResponse(
    "Reward {0} was applied to event id {1}".format(
    reward, event_id), status_code=200
)
```

At this point, we have an API that will rank platters for our users and accept rewards. In the next section, we will look at the test script to test out the API.

## Testing and deploying the functions

You can test the functions locally in the Python project by running the `func start` command in the `Chapter 12\Code Snippets\functionapp\`directory.

You should see the following in the terminal:

```
Azure Functions Core Tools
Core Tools Version:       4.0.4915 Commit hash: N/A  (64-bit)
Function Runtime Version: 4.14.0.19631

Functions:

    GetRankedActions: [GET] http://localhost:7071/api/GetRankedActions

    RewardAction: [GET] http://localhost:7071/api/RewardAction
```

Figure 12.8 – The results of running the func startcommand in the Visual Studio Code terminal

To call `GetRankedActions` in the terminal, use the following URL: `http://localhost:7071/api/GetRankedActions?user=<username>`.

Replacing the `<username>` parameter at the end of the URL with a name in the datafile.

To call `RewardAction` in the terminal, use the following URL: `http://localhost:7071/api/RewardAction?event_id=<event_id from previous call>&reward=<some reward score>`.

The following test script uses the `localhost` URLs for testing, but you can substitute this with actual deployed URLs to test deployed functions:

1. To create a function app through **VS Code**, navigate to the Azure icon (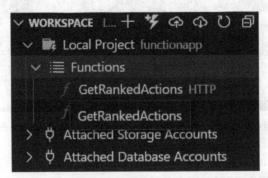) in the **VS Code navigation** panel. Find your subscription and open the **Function App** note. Right-click on **Function App** and select **Create New Function App in Azure… (Advanced)**. In the wizard, do the following:

   I.    Enter a name for your function app

   II.   Under **Runtime Stack**, select `Python 3.9`.

   III.  Select the resource group to which you deployed the Personalizer service.

   IV.   Select **Consumption plan**.

   V.    Create a new storage account – use the default name or specify a new name.

2. You can skip the **Application Insights** deployment unless this is for a production deployment where details provided by Application Insights would be valuable to your organization.

The deployment will create a storage account used for status and monitoring, an Azure App Service plan to host the functions, and the Functions app resource.

To deploy the functions to your subscription, follow these steps:

1. Navigate to the Azure extension in VS Code and then **WORKSPACE** | `Local Project` | the **Functions** node.

Figure 12.9 – Displaying details from the Azure extension in VS Code when deploying a local function

2. Click on the **deploy** icon ( ) and select **Deploy to Function App…**.

3.  In the wizard, do the following:

    I.    Select the subscription to which you are deploying the Functions app.

    II.   Select the Functions app that you just created in the previous section.

    III.  Accept the warning that you are about to overwrite anything in the Functions app.

4.  When the deployment is completed, you will have a Functions app running in Azure!

5.  The last step is to upload the settings from your `local.settings.json`. In VS Code, note that there are some default settings loaded but not the Personalizer endpoint and access key that we configured in the previous section.

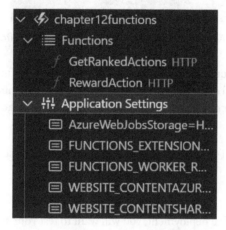

Figure 12.10 – The default settings when loading your Functions app in Azure using VS Code

6.  Right-click on **Application Settings** and select **Upload Local Settings….**

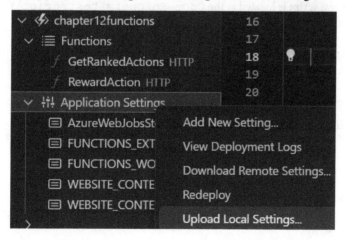

Figure 12.11 – The VS Code Azure extension menu option to upload local settings for your project

You should now see that the settings include the Personalizer endpoint and key settings.

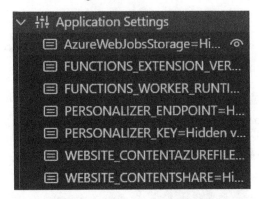

Figure 12.12 – The VS Code Azure extension after loading local settings from your Function app

7.  If you right-click on the function name, you can select and copy the function URL and test it, just like you did with the local deployment. The URL should look something like this: `https://<-functionapp>.azurewebsites.net/api/getrankedactions?code=<func-tion-access-key>`.

This URL can be used as part of your testing, as we will show in the test script in the next section.

## Using a test script

Naturally, before completing a full deployment, you will want to test your solution to get some idea of how successful it will be with your ranks and rewards. Here, we will discuss the initial connection to the service, then reward platter sizes based on the size of the company, which will improve our ranks, depending on the correlation between a large platter for a large company and a small platter for a small company. Our test script is located at the `Code Snippets\testscript\testscript.py` path in the GitHub repository:

1.  The `get_ranked_actions` function calls the `GetRankedActions` Azure function that the user passed into the `user` parameter:

    ```
    def get_ranked_actions_for_user(user:str) -> dict:
    ```

2.  We open an http connection to our app service with the following code:

    ```
    conn = http.client.HTTPConnection("localhost:7071")
    ```

3.  We execute a `GET` request on the URL for our function and pass the user as a `querystring` parameter:

    ```
    conn.request("GET", "/api/GetRankedActions?user={0}".
    format(user))
    ```

4. The response of this function is a JSON document. We decode the response and load it into a JSON document, which we return to the caller:

```
response = conn.getresponse()
data = response.read()
return json.loads(data.decode("utf-8"))
```

5. Next, the `send_reward_for_action` function calls our `RewardAction` Azure function. The `event_id` parameter is the ID of the event captured from `get_ranked_actions`. The reward indicates whether the user purchased or not. This function will return `True` if the http call returned a success and `False` otherwise:

```
def send_reward_for_action(event_id:str, reward:int) -> bool:
```

6. Again, we start by opening the http connection to our app service:

```
conn = http.client.HTTPConnection("localhost:7071")
```

7. Then, we execute a GET request on our function and pass `event_id` and `reward` as query string parameters:

```
conn.request("GET",
    "/api/RewardAction? event_id={0}&reward={1}".format(
        event_id, reward))
```

8. Finally, we return `True` or `False`, indicating whether or not the function call succeeded:

```
res = conn.getresponse()
return res.status == 200
```

9. In `calculate_reward`, we return 1 if, in our simulation, the user purchases the platter, and 0 otherwise. The logic we implement here is very rudimentary, where large companies purchase large platters and small companies purchase small platters:

```
def calculate_reward(user_name:str, platter_name:str) -> int:
```

10. To get the attributes of the user and platter whose names were supplied as parameters, we use this code:

```
user = get_users().get(user_name)
platter = get_platters().get(platter_name)
```

11. If the user or platter was not found, we return 0:

```
if (user == None or platter == None):
    return 0
```

12. If `company_size` is large and the platter is 50 or greater, purchase. Otherwise, do not purchase:

```
if user["company_size"] == "large":
    if platter["attributes"]["qty"] >= 50:
        return 1
    else:
        return 0
```

13. If `company_size` is small and the platter is less than or equal to 10, purchase. Otherwise, do not purchase:

```
if user["company_size"] == "small":
    if platter["attributes"]["qty"] <= 10:
        return 1
    else:
        return 0
```

14. If `company_size` is medium and the platter is between 10 and 50, purchase. Otherwise, do not purchase:

```
if user["company_size"] == "medium":
    if platter["attributes"]["qty"] >= 10
            and platter["attributes"]["qty"] <= 50:
        return 1
    else:
        return 0
return 0
```

15. Now that we have the building blocks, `get_rankings`, `calculate_reward`, and `send_reward_for_action`, we can enter the test script. Our test script will run until we terminate the program:

```
while(True):
```

16. Select a random user from our list of users:

```
user = random.choice(["Andy", "Tim", "Chris", "Paul",
"Scott"])
```

17. Get a recommended platter for the selected user:

```
rankings = get_ranked_actions_for_user(user)
```

18. Keep track of `event_id`, as this will be needed to submit the rewards to Personalizer. Also, keep track of `best_action`, which will be needed to calculate the reward:

```
event_id = rankings.get("event_id", "")
best_action = rankings.get("best_action", "")
```

19. Calculate the reward for this recommendation:

```
reward = calculateReward(user, best_action)
```

20. Submit the reward to the personalization service:

```
send_reward_for_action(event_id, best_action, reward)
```

21. Print the results in the console:

```
print("User: {0}, Platter: {1}, Reward: {2}".format(
    user, rankings.get("best_action"), reward))
```

22. Wait one second:

```
time.sleep(1)
```

With that, the process will start again until we stop the script from running.

As you run this example, you will see that, initially, the recommendations are randomized, and the rewards are almost all 0s. As we see from the purchase activity, Personalizer learns which attributes of the user match the attributes of the item purchased, but this never gets to a 100% success rate. Personalizer will still make some random recommendations if the attributes change for the users or items. This randomized behavior also helps Personalizer make good recommendations for new items and new users. This can also be configured, as discussed earlier in the chapter, when we set the percentage based on requirements.

In this example, you can see the basic workings of the Personalizer service. We looked here at a very simplistic set of attributes and reward calculations. How simplistic a set is depends on the content you recommend, such as the following:

- Social media likes
- Subscriptions
- Add to cart actions
- Send to a friend actions
- Other options you define

These are other examples of items with reward weights as well. You will also have many more user and item attributes for Personalizer to use when making its recommendations.

It is important to note that you reward Personalizer for the selected best action. The service includes other items in a ranked list, so you can suggest other items to the user; however, it is only the best action that is rewarded. In this example, if the user purchased the second item in the list and not the first, that is still a reward of 0 as far as Personalizer is concerned, but you can assign weighted rewards based on the rank as you see fit.

Well, as you can see, this isn't a traditional shopping cart helper service just designed to get people to buy more stuff. With the Personalizer service, you can rank just about any interface where a user makes a choice, and with time, those choices will become more and more accurate, based on popular choices and other factors we've discussed in this chapter.

You have now deployed your first Personalizer, albeit rudimentary, so let's close this chapter and head on to the next.

## Summary

In this chapter, we discussed the various configurations of the Personalizer Cognitive Service and some examples of where Personalizer can be used to benefit your organization. Rank and reward configurations will help you to better provide the most relevant options to your users, and with the exploration capability, you can offer less popular choices if they happen to be the best. We also discussed the various machine learning algorithms that are used to help with Reinforcement Learning, to improve the deployed machine learning models built for Personalizer. Finally, we were able to provide an end-to-end solution to customize how items will be ranked and rewarded. Using this logic, you can leverage an API with a simple web interface or Power Apps deployed to your organization, or embed the logic into an existing application to offer better suggestions.

In the next chapter, we will look at how you can improve your customer service team with the Azure Speech service.

# 13

# Improving Customer Experience with Speech to Text

When a customer calls the Ocean Smart customer service line, they are anticipating a friendly and helpful associate who will solve their current challenge. With years of exceptional service and quality being provided to customers, this is the expectation that has been built. However, with massive growth and global expansion, monitoring this quality is not as easy as it once was. Ocean Smart hoped that AI could help provide a solution and a way to track the quality of the customer service that was being provided.

A great customer experience is becoming more and more critical for successful businesses in this climate of on-demand everything. If a person has a not-so-great experience with a company, they're sure to let the world know as quickly as possible using as many social media outlets as possible. Because of this, Ocean Smart wanted a better system for improving how customer calls were handled and wanted to set a precedent for training customer service representatives. This chapter will describe how, by using Azure Speech services to capture customer call transcripts, Ocean Smart was able to dramatically improve the experience for its customers.

In this chapter, we will cover the following:

- Overview of Azure Speech services
- Working with real-time audio and batch speech-to-text data
- Improving speech-to-text accuracy with Custom Speech
- Working with different languages
- Building a completed batch solution

As with previous chapters, we will discuss decision points where you will choose between quality and service based on the cost of services, as well as how to understand the scaling of resources depending on requirements. The example gives a demonstration of batching audio recordings and transcribing the audio to a text document, scoring the overall sentiment of the document, and discussing options for tracking scores received by customer service representatives. With that, let's discuss what you need in the way of technical requirements.

# Technical requirements

As with previous chapters and deployments, there are some requirements you'll need in order to build any example for your use. First is an Azure account with a minimum of contributor rights if you're not an owner of the subscription to be able to deploy resources. To help reduce costs for development, oftentimes, developers can use Visual Studio Code. You can download it for Windows, Linux, or macOS platforms here: `https://code.visualstudio.com/download`. For the examples we will display later in the chapter, you will need several extensions in Visual Studio Code, which can be downloaded directly within the tool. These extensions are as follows:

- Python as an extension:

  - You'll also need to install the Python tools on your workstation, found here: `https://www.python.org/downloads/`

  - Speech SDK for Python (`https://pypi.org/project/azure-cognitiveser-vices-speech/`)

- Azure account

- Azure Functions

- Azure CLI Tools (not required, but helpful)

Other tools and extensions may be required, depending on your specific deployment requirements.

# Overview of Azure Speech services

The Azure Speech services are a collection of APIs surrounding various ways to convert speech to text, convert text to speech, translate speech, and other related services. When we consider the importance of speech in any business, and the ability to improve communications for accessibility and cultural reasons, it is easy to position these capabilities as transformative. As organizations become globalized and it is an everyday occurrence that language translation services can be used to improve internal and external communications, Microsoft has made significant effort and investment to support the most popular languages worldwide. In this chapter, you will learn how those investments have evolved to offer many solutions where the communication gaps have been closed significantly, which has led to an enhanced customer service experience for Ocean Smart customers.

In the Ocean Smart example, we are taking audio recordings from voice messages and customer service calls and transcribing those calls to a document. We are also using the translation service to translate Spanish audio to English text. From there, we could apply the Sentiment service to capture a general sense of customer satisfaction in calls based on the words used within the calls. As we provide satisfaction scores for these calls, customer service managers can then go directly to customers whose experience is less than spectacular and make the best effort to make their experience better going forward. We are also able to alert our sales team of the concerns around the customer experience to ensure they know when a customer is unhappy and can be mindful as they interact with individuals from that customer. Customer acquisition costs for Ocean Smart are significant, and competition is high, so it is much more efficient to keep existing customers happy than to acquire new ones. If the audio quality of a call is poor, and a call is difficult to extract a transcript from, or a sentiment score is relatively even (not overly good or bad), we want to ensure the right members of the team are able to review the calls manually to provide their own score.

Other capabilities of the Speech services have applications that could be implemented later for Ocean Smart as more and more AI capabilities are adopted by the organization. The following list provides some use cases where the services can be appropriately leveraged:

- **Captioning** – This Speech service allows the transcription of audio to text in real time and batches. Using these services, Microsoft has embedded the ability to transcribe audio and provide captions in real time in applications such as PowerPoint, Teams, and more. This capability is especially useful in cases where a hearing-impaired person is attending a presentation or, combined with translation, we can translate a presentation to the native language of the audience.

- **Audio Content Creation** – The Creation capability gives us the option to create new audio content with a more natural voice from text, removing the classic "robot" voice. This can be used for synthetic audiobooks, personal digital assistants, and any other content we want to read aloud from text.

- **Call center transcription** – We will focus on this capability in this chapter and, as you will find, the strength and value of being able to capture, review, and react to audio content being captured in the call center provide great visibility. With the ability to transcribe audio in real time or batches, we have the flexibility to build a comprehensive solution and provide tremendous value to the organizations we work for.

- **Voice assistant** – As with the Captioning service, we can use the Speech services to build custom voice assistants for our organizations with business-domain-specific lexicons to provide assistance in a voice that understands normal business operations.

These scenarios and more can be produced with the various capabilities of the Speech service by using the following capabilities currently offered by Microsoft:

- **Speech-to-text** – With the speech-to-text service, we can offer real-time or batch processing of audio from a variety of audio input sources. By default, we use the Microsoft machine learning model to provide this capability; however, if you find that the model provided isn't sufficient for your specific use cases, you can also explore the custom speech model development process. A custom model will allow you to develop a model of terminology specific to your organization.

- **Text-to-speech** – With the text-to-speech service, you can use various voice options for speaking digitized text in human-like voice. These could be used for a wide range of options, such as a digital assistant or call center voice messages. There is a dedicated **Speech Synthesis Markup Language** (**SSML**) that will help you make appropriate alterations to the voice you have chosen for options such as rate of speech and pitch of voice. This service also uses a Microsoft-provided machine learning model as a baseline for the service; however, a custom neural voice machine learning model can also be developed using the service.

- **Speech translation** – With the speech translation service, you can develop applications that carry out real-time audio translation. This can be used within an application, for instance, where you want to translate audio while having a conversation with a person speaking in a different language. We will use this service for an example of how to translate audio recorded in one language to text output in a different language.

- **Language identification** – The language identification service can be used to specify what language is being spoken within an audio recording or similar example. This is used for identifying the input language and then specifying what to translate the language to. Currently, there are dozens of languages with many dialects within each language supported by the service. An up-to-date list can be found at the following URL: `https://learn.microsoft.com/en-us/azure/cognitive-services/language-service/language-detection/language-support`.

- **Speaker recognition** – The speaker recognition service allows us to recognize a speaker in an audio file based on voice patterns in a person's speech. This helps when building transcripts from audio and video files to help identify the person who is speaking. A useful example would be having a video of an event where several speakers are involved, and we want to give our consumers the option to jump directly to the speaker of choice.

- **Pronunciation assessment** – The pronunciation assessment feature allows us to help consumers improve their pronunciation. For instance, a language learning app could use several services developed together to offer a listening and feedback system to help with improving a person's pronunciation when learning a new language.

- **Intent recognition** – The intent recognition service can be coupled with **Language Understanding** services to use audible commands on what action to be taken when interacting with an interface such as a chatbot. These commands will then be used to perform some task in the application where the service is being used, as voice command inputs can be more efficient than traditional input devices such as a keyboard and mouse.

Hopefully, the previous descriptions help you to understand the intent and capabilities of the Speech services offered. Within the services themselves, options will vary for the development languages available, whether the service can be containerized for local deployments, and various ways of interacting with the SDKs, from GUIs to CLIs. Next, we will explore the various elements required to determine whether real-time or batch operations are a better option for your application.

# Working with real-time audio and batch speech-to-text data

Now that we have provided an overview of the various services you can leverage and use cases you can expect to deploy using the Speech services, we will start to explore deeper to better position our example of building a customer service feedback system. Due to the nature of our example, we will focus on how to use batch audio transcription services; however, with so many applications for real-time transcription, we will explore both options in this section, as the approaches are vastly different.

In the case of a call center, and improving the customer service process, there could be applications for real-time feedback to be provided to the customer service agent. This could provide a sentiment score as the conversation is happening based on the words being used within the conversation; however, with the nature of any conversation, the tone could change very quickly from positive to negative and could cause a distraction to the agent during the call. This is a challenge with AI systems universally. When the AI cannot recognize the context or tone, using sarcasm for example, the intent of a word or phrase could be misinterpreted.

For this reason, Ocean Smart thought it was a better option to analyze calls and messages after the fact for assistance with enhancing training opportunities. This gives them the ability to analyze the whole of the conversation, as well as look at trends over time. If an agent is having an off day or a particularly difficult customer but is generally very effective in their role, a single negative call wouldn't be a problem. However, if a pattern of several calls were to emerge, or the overall sentiment score of a particular agent was low, it could be an opportunity for training, a discussion, or, potentially, a separation from the company. This could also help to identify a potentially difficult customer or a customer who has had several bad calls in a short amount of time, which could lead to a lost customer. A use case for this type of situation could be to have a notification sent to a manager giving them some context and allowing them to join the call. As previously discussed, customer retention is significantly less costly than customer acquisition, so the management team would like to be warned early of potential lost customer events to resolve the issues as quickly as possible.

With those things in mind, we will discuss the approaches of real-time and batch speech-to-text transcription in the following sections.

## Real-time speech-to-text

Many use cases have been defined over the years for speech-to-text, including common services such as closed captions for television programming. With enhancements in technology, this has also become more prevalent in common applications being used and even specific applications for capturing speech in a digitized text format. Most computer operating systems have some capability for rudimentary speech-to-text in a document of some sort, and even running rudimentary processes on the computer. Speech-to-text, in an example like this, is just the basis for capturing what is being said, and a text-related document may not be created. The speech aspect is captured and then used in a downstream process such as language understanding to trigger another downstream activity.

With the advancement of AI and digital assistants such as Amazon's Alexa, Apple's Siri, and Microsoft's Cortana, we're using these digital assistants as a faster means of performing an activity on our devices, such as creating a calendar event or new task, calling someone, or sending a message, usually. There are certainly some challenges with these systems, even today, as other factors can cause less than optimal results when attempting to perform one of these tasks with our devices. This can be caused by ambient or otherwise background noise, or hardware and software issues that might distort the voice input of these devices, such as a bad hardware driver running, or other unrelated issues occurring. Personally, when Siri is not working efficiently for me, after getting frustrated with the device, I typically realize it has probably been a while since I last rebooted the device, and after going through that process, the experience tends to be much better.

Along those lines, we are still seeing significant adoption of "smart" home devices from Amazon, Google, and Apple that will work with other IoT devices for home automation, controlling an increasing number of devices within our homes. Currently, it is common for people to have garage door openers, lighting, electric outlets, temperature control, cameras, irrigation, and window shades that can all be controlled by voice using these home automation controllers as the central hub. For quite some time, there has been the legend of the ultimate smart home where everything is automated, from controlling the items listed previously to laundry, toasting, refrigeration, baking, and more with connected devices providing such automation. At the time of this writing, however, these more peripheral options of home automation seem to be less desirable, as market demand is low and proper development of these types of solutions for the home is lacking. As major developers of these systems emerge and more standardized ecosystems accompany these home hub solutions, time will tell how much adoption is experienced going forward.

Stepping away from the personal context and capabilities brought by our own devices, from a business perspective, there are many areas where speech-to-text can be used as a basis for optimizing operations. Voice-controlled machinery and computer systems can be run more efficiently using speech, as well as some of the applications from a home automation perspective listed previously. The application you choose for speech-to-text will largely depend on the value you can perceive from said deployment. As we said at the start of the book, and a recurring theme throughout, it is important to evaluate what will help you bring the most value to your organization and best understand how long it will take to realize the return on investment as a result. The complexity behind a complete deployment will depend on the application requirements but, in general, a real-time speech-to-text application will have defined services required to meet a minimum goal.

In developing a real-time speech-to-text solution to provide a sentiment score of a call, translation of text, or similar application, it is good to first understand the limitations of the Cognitive Services service to ensure the incoming audio can be processed efficiently. The bitrate of the audio, stereo or mono audio, and even things such as background noise can all be factors in how effectively the solution will work. What is the phone system you are using? Does it have an easy way to feed your audio into your application, or will it require more investment for compatibility? After you have built your application for converting the audio, what will the downstream application do, or where will your audience look at the results of the conversation? Again, these are just some of the considerations you'll need to make when building a complete solution. Here, we will provide an overview of what you'll need to acquire your audio, then process the output:

- For starters, regardless of your input type, you will be required to create an Azure Cognitive Services Speech service. From the Azure portal, search for this and you will be provided with a wizard similar to the following:

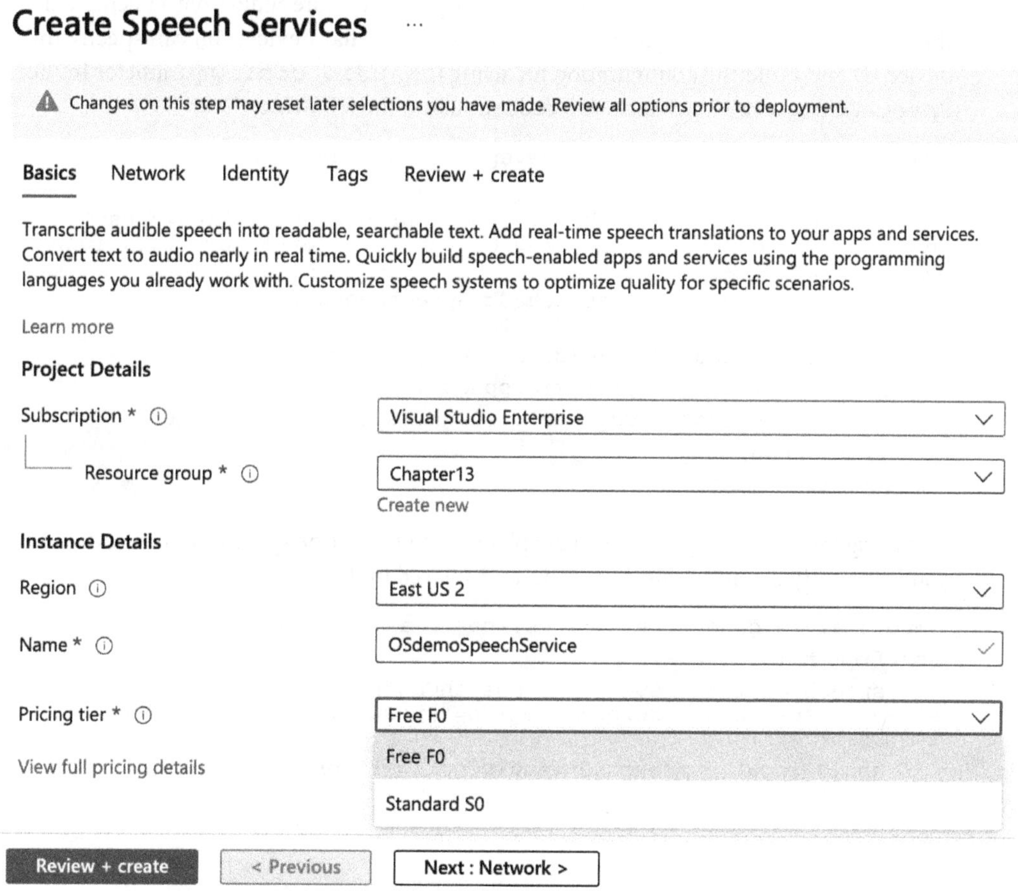

## Create Speech Services   ⋯

⚠ Changes on this step may reset later selections you have made. Review all options prior to deployment.

**Basics**    Network    Identity    Tags    Review + create

Transcribe audible speech into readable, searchable text. Add real-time speech translations to your apps and services. Convert text to audio nearly in real time. Quickly build speech-enabled apps and services using the programming languages you already work with. Customize speech systems to optimize quality for specific scenarios.

Learn more

**Project Details**

Subscription * ⓘ

| Visual Studio Enterprise | ⌄ |

Resource group * ⓘ

| Chapter13 | ⌄ |

Create new

**Instance Details**

Region ⓘ

| East US 2 | ⌄ |

Name * ⓘ

| OSdemoSpeechService | ✓ |

Pricing tier * ⓘ

| Free F0 | ⌄ |

View full pricing details

Free F0

Standard S0

| Review + create | | < Previous | | Next : Network > |

Figure 13.1 – Create Speech Services wizard

- For simplicity, we have included the **Pricing tier** options in the previous image, but we'll look at those options and applied costs later in the chapter. The service itself is fairly straightforward to set up, and other than **Network** and **Tags** considerations, there is not much to configure. When the deployment is complete, the service will provide a way for us to begin the transcription process.

- You also have the ability to create the Speech service inside of your Python code, as the following demonstrates:

```
speech_config = speechsdk.SpeechConfig(subscription="<paste-
your-speech-key-here>", region="<paste-your-speech-location/
region-here>")
```

- When initially acquiring audio, you will have to dictate the source the audio will come from using the Speech SDK and apply the appropriate service for receiving the audio from the following choices:

    - *Capturing from a microphone device* – If you are looking to capture audio from a microphone, there is no need to specify your audio device. For a similar device, you can specify the device ID and build the configuration file using the `audio_config` parameter in the `SpeechRecognizer` instance with code similar to the following:

```
import azure.cognitiveservices.speech as speechsdk
def from_mic():
    speech_config = speechsdk.SpeechConfig(subscription="<pa
ste-your-speech-key-here>", region="<paste-your-speech-location/
region-here>")
    speech_recognizer = speechsdk.SpeechRecognizer(speech_
config=speech_config)
audio_config = AudioConfig(device_name="<device id>");
    print("Speak into your microphone.")
    result = speech_recognizer.recognize_once_async().get()
    print(result.text)
from_mic()
```

    - *Capturing from an audio file* – If you are planning to transcribe speech from an audio file, you will specify the file within your code, as displayed in the following:

```
import azure.cognitiveservices.speech as speechsdk
def from_file():
    speech_config = speechsdk.SpeechConfig(subscription="<pa
ste-your-speech-key-here>", region="<paste-your-speech-location/
region-here>")
    audio_input = speechsdk.AudioConfig(filename="your_file_
name.wav")
```

```
    speech_recognizer = speechsdk.SpeechRecognizer(speech_
config=speech_config, audio_config=audio_input)
    result = speech_recognizer.recognize_once_async().get()
    print(result.text)
from_file()
```

- *Continuous audio streaming* – Finally, if you are planning to have an application that is listening for audio and will stop listening only when the operator of the application tells the application to stop, your deployment will be different. This option gives us the ability to enable dictation, such as including punctuation as part of the speech. This is handled differently than a microphone or file since those options are listening for audio silence as files are processed, as you will instead use the `speech_recognizer.start_continuous_recognition()` and `speech_recognizer.stop_continuous_recognition()` events in your code. Some examples where this would be useful would be in an application that adds closed captions, or for transcribing the audio coming from a video feed. For a more detailed list of service limitations, please visit this URL: `https://learn.microsoft.com/en-us/azure/cognitive-services/speech-service/speech-services-quotas-and-limits`.

Now that we can capture speech from audio, we need to determine what to do with the output of the transcription for further processing. An example scenario where this would be useful, as we will display later in the chapter, is to transcribe a conversation. To do this, we will use the **Conversation Transcription** feature of the Speech service, which is designed to provide key details about the conversation being transcribed. Using the service, we can capture details such as the following:

- **Timestamps** – Timestamps are used for specifying at which point audio occurs in a recording. They can also be used to match the timing of the transcript for use with video transcripts, for instance.

- **Readable transcripts** – Readable transcripts provide the output of the service in a paragraph-like format for structured sentences, with punctuation and so on.

- **User profiles** – To recognize the speaker who is speaking, a user profile must be created using an audio sample and validation.

- **Speaker identification** – Speakers can be identified within a recording if a user profile with an accompanying voice signature has been created prior to audio transcription.

- **Multi-speaker diarization** – If multiple speakers appear in audio, multi-speaker diarization can be used to separate each speaker and identify that speaker if a user profile has been created, or to identify them as a guest.

- **Real-time transcription** – Real-time transcription provides a stream of text as it is being recognized and the speaker is speaking, including speaker identification as recognized or a guest.

- **Asynchronous transcription** – Asynchronous transcription allows more accurate captures of speech within an audio file or similar application. Because the service can take longer to process and uses a larger machine learning model than the real-time transcription service, it will have better accuracy.

- **Real-time plus asynchronous transcription** – In the case where you want to have a real-time transcript, such as closed captions during a presentation, and a future transcript to be provided afterward, you can combine both features using the API.

The following gives a high-level overview of how the service works and the flow of data from audio input to file output:

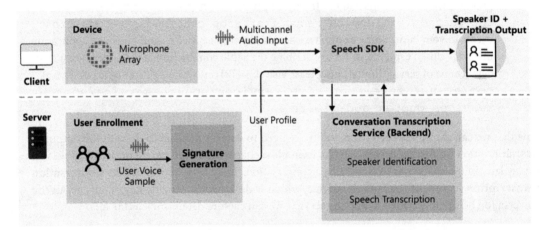

Figure 13.2 – Conversation Transcription service overview

As displayed in the lower left of the figure, to recognize a speaker specifically, a user would have to submit a voice sample, and a signature of their voice would have to be generated for recognition. If the speaker isn't previously identified, the service will simply classify speakers as guests, and each voice will get a guest identifier, such as Guest_0, Guest_1, and so on. The service that provides the signatures is called the Signature Generation service and will validate the sample audio as well as generate a user profile. More detail on the service can be found here: https://aka.ms/cts/signaturegenservice.

When we consider a scenario for real-time conversation transcription, let's look at having a senior leadership meeting at Ocean Smart. If meeting minutes needed to be captured without having a note-taker, we could use the service to do so. If we provide user profiles for each individual in the meeting and even had guests providing additional voices, we could easily provide a full transcript of the meeting. Further, consider a place in the future where this type of technology is used in law enforcement to predict the potential escalation of a situation, or in a courtroom where exact transcripts of the proceedings can be captured without the need for a stenographer. These are just a few examples of where the technology can be used to provide efficient and accurate records of events that are easily searchable as well.

The previous overview provides a high-level idea of what is possible with the real-time Conversation Transcription service. Next, we will take a deeper look at the batch Speech service, as we march toward the complete example of how Ocean Smart was able to take advantage and improve customer service and employee training as a result. We will also look at the option for **Asynchronous Conversation Transcription** capabilities.

## Batch speech-to-text

When we start to talk about how to really derive value from our latent data, as we did in the second part of this book focused on a knowledge mining solution, it cannot be overlooked how much latent data can be embedded within audio files – historical recordings for all types of purposes, from board of director meetings to company announcements and other recorded content, which just gets put into a file server somewhere, are highly unlikely to ever be used. Now, with the ability to perform batch speech-to-text operations on all those files, supporting .wav, .mp3, and .ogg formats, there is an easy way to extract potentially significant value from those files lying dormant. This section of the chapter will provide an overview of how the service works, hopefully setting the stage for the full-blown example at the end of the chapter.

As with the other Cognitive Services, the batch transcription service is a REST API that can be called to perform speech recognition services on audio files by pointing the service at a storage container with the files, assuming appropriate permissions, in Azure. A few important items to note about the service follow:

- Currently, when a batch job is triggered with the service, there is no way to prioritize when your job will be run, so be mindful of this when you create your application, and set expectations accordingly.

- Another thing to note is that the batch services require a Standard tier Speech service resource, as the Free tier is not supported for these operations.

- For your audio input, the current formats supported are listed previously, and each of the formats can be in either 8- or 16-kHz bit rates for both stereo and mono recordings. When the transcript is performed, the output will separate the stereo channel within the JSON provided. This may create some confusion with the output file, so refer to the timestamps provided for appropriate ordering of conversation in whatever mechanism you plan to use for providing an interface.

- The batch service will process individual audio files or a group of files stored in a public location or Azure Storage account by pointing the service at the URI of the location. However, as we will demonstrate, after a file has been processed, if you intend to store the file long-term or delete the file, that would be handled by a separate activity with an Azure Functions function or similar operation. There are no workflows or similar operations with the service, and this should be considered when designing your overall solution.

- At this time, the diarization feature can only recognize two speakers from mono-recorded audio, and stereo isn't currently supported. The output JSON will identify the speaker as 1 or 2, and each line of text will distinguish which speaker the line came from.

A simple example of the JSON that will be passed by the REST API call follows:

```
{
  "contentUrls": [
    "<URL to an audio file 1 to transcribe>"
  ],
  "properties": {
    "wordLevelTimestampsEnabled": true
  },
  "locale": "en-US",
  "displayName": "Transcription of file using default model for en-US"
}
```

As displayed in the previous code, you first pass the URLs of where the audio files are located. Next, you define the properties of the call you are making and want to pass when doing the operation, discussed further in the following. Finally, you set your locale of what you would like the output file language to be in.

When considering optional properties for what can additionally be performed as part of the batch transcription operation, the following commands can be included in the `"properties"` section of your code:

- `profanityFilterMode` – `Masked` (default), `None`, `Removed`, or `Tags` are the properties for handling profanity in the transcribed audio.

- `punctuationMode` – `DictatedAutomatic` (default), `None`, `Dictated`, or `Automatic` are acceptable options for how the transcript will be written concerning punctuation within the text.

- `wordLevelTimestampsEnabled` – `false` (default) or `true` are the options to enable timestamps at a word level. This will help with retrieving where a word is specifically said within the audio if required.

- `diarizationEnabled` – `false` (default) or `true` are the options if you intend to use the diarization feature for detecting audio from multiple voices. This option also requires the `wordLevelTimestampsEnabled` option to be `true`.

- `channels` – If your audio file contains multiple channels, you can specify which channel you'd like to capture content from for transcription. The default is to capture channels 0 and 1; however, this is optional and should only be specified if your audio resides in a different channel.

- `timeToLive` – This option allows you to determine whether a transcription will be deleted after a certain amount of time after processing. By default, transcripts aren't deleted; however, if you are using the transcript after processing and will no longer require it, you can clean it up by designating how long after transcription to delete it. For instance, using `PT6H` would delete the transcript 6 hours after processing.

- `destinationContainerUrl` – This option can be used to send the output JSON to a file in a specified storage container. If a storage container is not specified, Microsoft stores the file in a storage container that is managed by the service.

As mentioned previously, these properties are all optional when passing the details to the REST API and should be considered as best suits the solution you are building.

When the service is run, for each audio file that is processed, a resulting output JSON document is produced. Each document contains information about the details we have specified so far in this chapter. Details such as the source audio file, timestamps, recording duration, words captured with corresponding confidence scores, inverse-text-normalized forms of words, plus any other properties specified will all be captured within the JSON for processing as needed downstream in operations.

Now that we have provided the details needed for configuration and the logic behind building an application using the standard machine learning models provided by Microsoft, with implementation steps later in the chapter, let's take a look at what is required to use a Custom Speech model in your application.

# Improving speech-to-text accuracy with Custom Speech

Even though the Microsoft research and development teams have received tremendous acclaim for all their work in developing groundbreaking machine learning technology for transcribing speech-to-text, they are aware that not all business domain-specific details can be captured. For this reason, they have provided the ability for customers to augment the base machine learning model with domain-specific terms directly related to the customer business. This portion of the chapter will focus on how to work with and deploy these custom models for use in your organization.

To build your augmented model, you will use the Speech Studio, which can be found at `https://speech.microsoft.com/portal`. After you have logged in with your Azure account, you will be presented with several options for working with various speech operations, including the following:

- Speech-to-text
- Text-to-speech
- Voice assistant
- Additional resources

For the purposes of this section, we will be focusing on the Custom Speech operation, but you will find many more options for working with the service, as shown in the following figure:

**Speech-to-text**

Quickly and accurately transcribe in more than 100 languages and dialects. Enhance the accuracy of your transcriptions by creating a custom speech model that can handle domain-specific terminology, background noise, and accents. Learn more about Speech-to-text

**Real-time Speech-to-text**

Quickly test live transcription capabilities on your own audio without writing any code.

Try out Real-time Speech-to-text

**Custom Speech**

Add your own data and adapt to specific speaking styles, vocabulary, and more with a customized speech-to-text model.

Start a Custom Speech project

**Pronunciation Assessment**

Get instant feedback on pronunciation accuracy and fluency by reading a script aloud.

Try out Pronunciation Assessment

**Text-to-speech**

Build apps and services that speak naturally with more than 400 voices across 138 languages and dialects. Create a customized voice to differentiate your brand and use various speaking styles bring a sense of emotion to your spoken content. Learn more about Text-to-speech

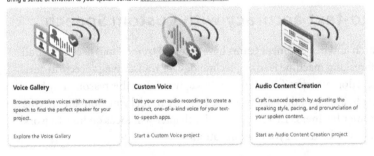

**Voice Gallery**

Browse expressive voices with humanlike speech to find the perfect speaker for your project.

Explore the Voice Gallery

**Custom Voice**

Use your own audio recordings to create a distinct, one-of-a-kind voice for your text-to-speech apps.

Start a Custom Voice project

**Audio Content Creation**

Craft nuanced speech by adjusting the speaking style, pacing, and pronunciation of your spoken content.

Start an Audio Content Creation project

Figure 13.3 – Azure Speech Studio landing page displaying some project options

Similar to how we used the Custom Vision model tool in *Chapter 10*, this portal is designed to give a GUI for working with and building your custom model augmentation, as well as testing the model, and more. You will still need to deploy a Speech resource to your Azure subscription, which will provide the compute required for training and, subsequently, testing against your model after it has been developed and deployed. The following graphic provides an overview of expected capabilities and actions when building your own custom models:

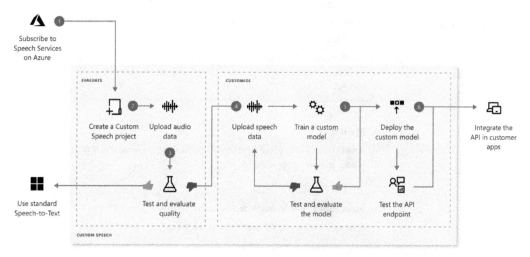

Figure 13.4 – Typical Custom Speech model build and deployment
steps using the Speech Studio and Azure

As we can see from the visual, there are several up-front activities that need to be accomplished prior to actually training your custom model. The first activity you'll encounter when you create a project in the Speech Studio for building a custom model is to upload some data for training and testing your model, where you will be prompted for the type of data, as displayed in the following figure:

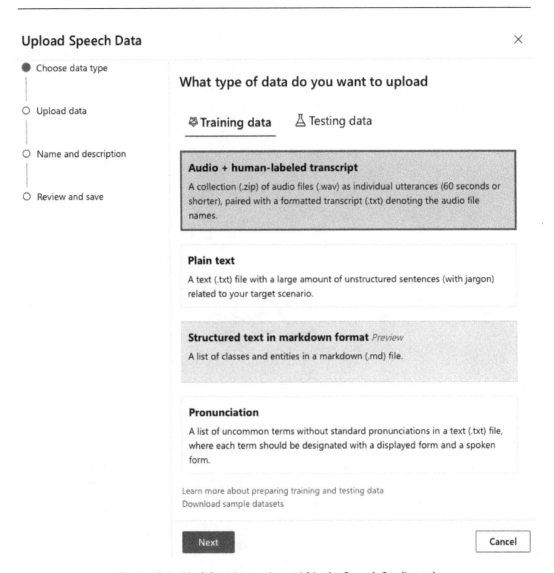

Figure 13.5 – Model testing options within the Speech Studio tool

As displayed, you are presented with the type of scenario you have for building a custom speech model and the data type you're uploading. However, also note that you have the ability to do some testing within this same tool. Using this option, you can upload files for testing the quality of your model or transcript, depending on what assets you have to test with. The currently supported testing scenarios are listed in the following capture:

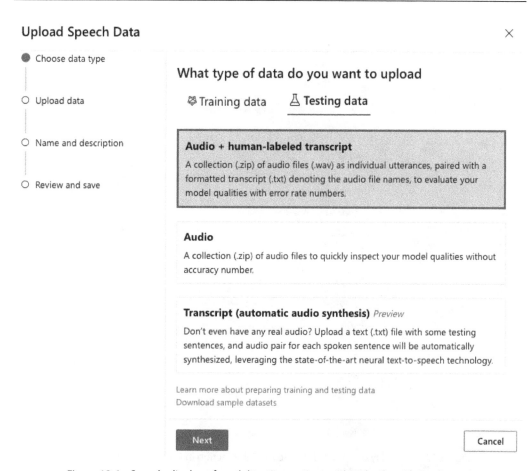

Figure 13.6 – Sample display of model testing options within the Speech Studio tool

Again, the scenarios are pointed out asking you to direct the studio to where your files are stored. As you choose your desired option, next, you will be prompted to upload your file(s) from either a local file or Azure blob, or other shared web locations. Examples provided for links are URL, SAS, or another web link providing the files. You can then name the upload and give a description and, finally, the files are uploaded into the service waiting for your preferred next option. From there, you will test your audio model and any other activities for preparing the model for production.

The other main capability is to be able to train your own Custom Speech model as an augmentation to a **base model** that Microsoft provides and maintains, including revisions for using specific models, as displayed in the following capture:

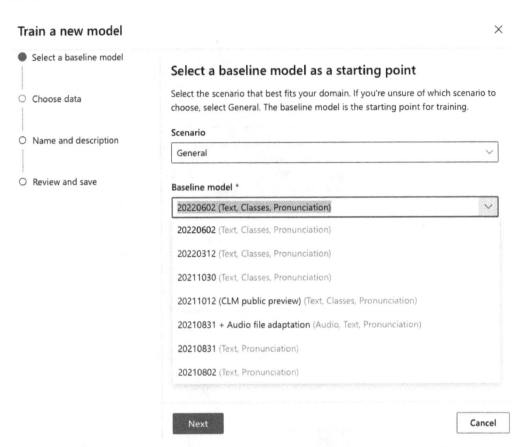

Figure 13.7 – Display of options for base model selection in the Speech Studio

As shown, there are several versions of models previously deployed and types of models provided for use. Currently, the only scenario offered is **General**, but based on their note at the top, one can assume more specific scenarios will be provided for use of different base model types. After you choose your base model, you will be directed to select one of your uploaded Speech datasets to accompany the model, and name and describe the newly created Speech model.

From there, you can build your model test for inspecting the recognition quality and accuracy of the model, measured in the **Word Error Rate (WER)**. The WER is a good indicator of whether you need to train a custom model on top of a base model or use the Microsoft base model for your project. You can obtain this score by uploading your audio file with the accompanying transcript file, then testing the transcript against the audio using the Speech Studio interface. More details about the WER can be found here: `https://learn.microsoft.com/en-us/azure/cognitive-services/speech-service/how-to-custom-speech-evaluate-data?pivots=speech-studio`. After all of your testing is complete and you are satisfied with however you plan to proceed with your model, you can deploy it using the tool to an endpoint that can be consumed by your application.

Again, I want to stress that the Speech Studio is just an interface for working with your models. When you deploy your model, you are using the Speech service you created in the Azure portal and deploying it to the endpoint of your choosing. These are the services that will cost money in Azure, so be sure to keep an eye on limits and operations, as they can get pricey as a volume of transactions is added. You will need to make sure you evaluate the costs of the services you will use based on the type of operation you are performing, such as **speech-to-text**, **text-to-speech**, **speech translation**, and **speaker recognition**. There are Free and Standard tiers with concurrency requests limited by tier (one concurrent request in the Free tier), then a mix of audio hours per month, characters recognized, and other transactions. For a more in-depth understanding of costs, you can use the Speech services pricing page, found here: `https://azure.microsoft.com/en-us/pricing/details/cognitive-services/speech-services/`.

This provides a high-level overview of how you can build a Custom Speech model using the **Speech Studio**. There are significant capabilities also available using the **Azure CLI** and scripting options such as **PowerShell**. With the investment Microsoft has made in its Speech Cognitive Services offerings, we anticipate seeing continued significant investments due to their popularity. In the next section, we will look at the Speech Translation features of the Speech service.

# Working with different languages

As we have previously discussed in this book, the globalization of the planet Earth over the past 30-50 years has created an evolution in technology unlike ever imagined. Moore's law observes that the number of transistors in a dense integrated circuit doubles about every two years, and this has roughly held true since his initial prediction back in 1975 until when, very recently, it was declared no longer considered possible (Wikipedia, `https://en.wikipedia.org/wiki/Moore%27s_law`). As one result, we have seen a massive proliferation of technology to help humans adapt to the challenges of globalization, and we cannot look past the language barriers faced by international travelers and companies. What's more compelling when we can do more than simply text translation using a search engine is the ability to be able to translate the spoken word on the fly using that technology. For this reason and many more, Microsoft has made significant investments in the Speech Translation Cognitive Service.

In Microsoft's terms, the basic capabilities of the service are to serve four core services for its customers:

- Speech-to-text translation with recognition results
- Speech-to-speech translation
- Support for translation to multiple target languages
- Interim recognition and translation results

We are seeing these applications in many uses for companies and consumers alike to help with breaking down communications barriers. These examples exist for real-time translation for two people speaking different languages, and applications for learning new languages and having the ability to provide feedback on pronunciation similar to that of a foreign language teacher in primary schools. Applications such as Microsoft's PowerPoint and Teams can do real-time translation of speech and translate captions to text in a different language for a foreign audience, and there are many other examples that are available and popular.

For the Ocean Smart customer experience improvement, being a global company, they first wanted to tackle the challenge of customers who call customer support and don't speak the core language of the company, English. In years past, they would have to hire an individual who did speak the language of their most popular customers in a region of the world, or at least understood it to a certain extent. In other situations, they might need to have a local intermediary who could work with the company for a fee. By being able to implement the speech-to-text translation service for real-time translation, and translation for recorded messages, Ocean Smart can implement technology to solve a human labor challenge and save some expenses.

For building a custom machine learning model, Microsoft has built a reasonably comprehensive interface for most of the activities performed, as we saw in the previous section, but in the case of translation services, it's much more code driven. In this next section, we are going to discuss what is required to build a translation application.

## Using the translation services

As we are seeing with many of the Cognitive Services discussed throughout the book, there are a plethora of options for which programming language when accessing a Cognitive Services API, depending on the service. For the purposes of this book, we have tried to standardize that language as Python, wherever possible, because of its popularity amongst the services and consistency. In the case of Speech, this remains to be the case, and we get started by defining our Azure region and subscription information, which are defined in the environment variables and will be defined at the global scope with the following code:

```
speech_key, service_region = os.environ['SPEECH__SUBSCRIPTION__KEY'],
os.environ['SPEECH__SERVICE__REGION']
```

When using the Speech SDK for all speech activities, there is an accompanying config file that is created that will include the type of service you are using, subscription information, and whatever mechanism you are using to call the Speech service, such as endpoint, host, or authorization token. Depending on the services or activities you will be performing, you will use code to call various functions for performing operations.

In the case of translation, we will call `SpeechTranslationConfig` by using a method of your choosing from the following:

- *With a subscription* – Pass in a key and the associated region.
- *With an endpoint* – Pass in a Speech service endpoint. A key or authorization token is optional.
- *With a host* – Pass in a host address. A key or authorization token is optional.
- *With an authorization token* – Pass in an authorization token and the associated region.

The following steps define the process of listening to, translating, and outputting speech from one language to another at a high level:

1. To define the languages you are translating from and to, you will first define the language to be listening for and then define the language you want to translate to. This is performed by calling the `TranslationRecognizer` class and passing it your `translation_config` details. This will require an `audioConfig` parameter for defining the source of audio to be listening from, such as a microphone or audio file, as previously discussed.

2. After the system has "listened" and translated the audio, you will put the results to text files for other downstream operations. The service will allow you to capture the recognized audio and the translated audio.

3. Finally, if you would like to perform a speech-to-speech translation type and output the translation to a synthesized voice, define the `voice_name` parameter.

An example of the completed code follows.

This is for defining your environment variables and languages for source and translation:

```
import os
import azure.cognitiveservices.speech as speechsdk
speech_key, service_region = os.environ['SPEECH__SERVICE__KEY'],
os.environ['SPEECH__SERVICE__REGION']
from_language, to_language = 'en-US', 'de'
```

This is for building your translation method:

```
def translate_speech_to_text():
    translation_config = speechsdk.translation.
SpeechTranslationConfig(
            subscription=speech_key, region=service_region)
    translation_config.speech_recognition_language = from_language
    translation_config.add_target_language(to_language)
    translation_config.voice_name = "de-DE-Hedda" #Definition for
voice and language
    recognizer = speechsdk.translation.TranslationRecognizer(
            translation_config=translation_config)
```

This is for defining your synthesizing details and ensuring audio exists in the file:

```
def synthesis_callback(evt):
    size = len(evt.result.audio)
    print(f'Audio synthesized: {size} byte(s) {"(COMPLETED)" if
size == 0 else ""}')
    if size > 0:
        file = open('translation.wav', 'wb+')
        file.write(evt.result.audio)
        file.close()
```

Here, we are prompting the user to say something in the source language to be translated into the destination language:

```
recognizer.synthesizing.connect(synthesis_callback)
print(f'Say something in "{from_language}" and we\'ll translate
into "{to_language}".')
result = recognizer.recognize_once()
print(get_result_text(reason=result.reason, result=result))
```

And finally, this is for capturing the audio and converting it to text:

```
def get_result_text(reason, result):
    reason_format = {
        speechsdk.ResultReason.TranslatedSpeech:
            f'Recognized "{from_language}": {result.text}\n' +
            f'Translated into "{to_language}"": {result.
translations[to_language]}',
        speechsdk.ResultReason.RecognizedSpeech: f'Recognized:
"{result.text}"',
        speechsdk.ResultReason.NoMatch: f'No speech could be
recognized: {result.no_match_details}',
        speechsdk.ResultReason.Canceled: f'Speech Recognition
canceled: {result.cancellation_details}'
    }
    return reason_format.get(reason, 'Unable to recognize speech')
translate_speech_to_text()
```

As discussed, this code will be formed and functions and parameters will be included, depending on the requirements of the application you are building. More details about the Speech Translation service module using Python can be found here: https://docs.microsoft.com/en-us/python/api/azure-cognitiveservices-speech/azure.cognitiveservices.speech.translation?view=azure-python.

With that, you now have the details required to understand what is necessary to build a Speech application for speech-to-text recognition, build a custom machine learning model if the provided base models aren't sufficient, and finally, translate text or speech. We will now put the complete batch solution together in the following section.

# Building a complete batch solution

In this chapter, we use the Speech service to translate audio files that are sent into Azure Blob Storage. When the file is created, we can then choose to perform other downstream activities – for example, extracting a sentiment from the document and tracking the results. The following diagram shows the process that we follow to monitor the storage account, begin the async request to start the transcription, and once the transcription is complete, write the results file to Azure Blob Storage:

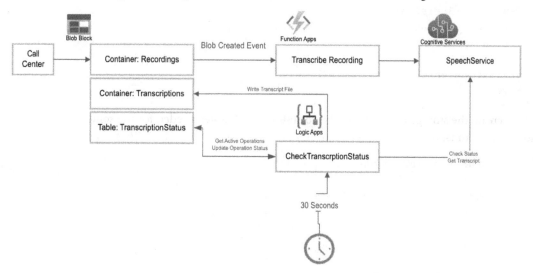

Figure 13.8 – Process outline for creating a transcript from an audio file

To support this process, we create the following:

- **Azure Cognitive Speech service** to perform the transcription activity.

- **Azure Storage account**:

  - Blob container to store audio files.

  - Blob container to store transcription results.

  - Storage table to track transcription job progress.

- **Azure Functions App**:

  - One function to monitor the audio file container and start the transcription job.

- **Azure Logic App**:

  - If there are any queued jobs, check their status with the speech service, and once the job is complete, write the results to the appropriate storage container.

You can use the following Azure CLI commands to create the Cognitive Services service and storage account used for this chapter.

First, create the Speech service using the following commands:

```
az login
az account set --subscription <enter your-subscription-id>
az cognitiveservices account create \
--name ch13-training \
--resource-group <enter your-resource-group> \
--kind SpeechServices \
--sku F0 \
--location eastus2 \
--yes
```

Next, create the storage account and the **containers** and **tables** needed for the solution with the following commands:

```
az storage account create \
--name ch13storage \
--resource-group Chapter13 \
--location eastus2

az storage container create \
--name recordings \
--account-name ch13storage
az storage container create \
--name transcriptions \
--account-name ch13storage
az storage table create \
--name transcriptionStatus\
--account-name ch13storage
```

Now, we have the resources needed to create our **Azure functions**. To follow this example, you will need the following:

- Python version 3.9.6
- Azure Functions Core Tools
- Visual Studio Code
- Python extension for Visual Studio Code
- Azure Functions extension for Visual Studio Code

If you open the \Chapter 13\Code Snippets\TranscribeAudioFunction folder in Visual Studio Code, you should see the following folder structure:

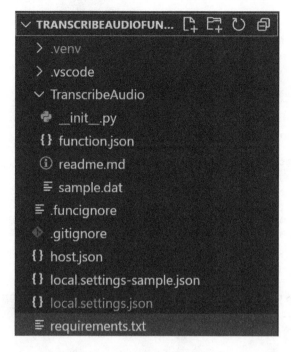

Figure 13.9 – Files and folders listed in the solution for transcribing audio

A few files/folders that are important to the function runtime are as follows:

- The `ProcessNewImage`, `PublishLatestIteration`, and `TrainNewModel` folders are our three functions in this function app. We will dig into these next.

- `local.settings-sample.json` – Contains the settings that the functions will need in order to execute properly. Notice that the key values are not specified.

- `local.settings.json` – This is not present in your repo; you will create this file shortly.

- `requirements.txt` – When you deploy your function app, the Functions app runtime pip installs any packages listed in `requirements.txt`.

Let's take a look at the `local.settings-sample.json` file and create a copy that is configured to your environment.

Make a copy of `local.settings-sample.json` and name it `local.settings.json`. You should see the following in the file:

```
{
  "IsEncrypted": false,
  "Values": {
    "AzureWebJobsStorage": "",
    "FUNCTIONS_WORKER_RUNTIME": "python",
```

```
    "ch13_STORAGE": "<storage_connection_string>",
    "speech_key" : "<speech_key>",
    "service_region" : "eastus2"
  }
}
```

The ch13_STORAGE value is the connection string to the storage account created previously. You can retrieve this connection string with the following:

```
az storage account show-connection-string -name ch13storage
```

For the speech key, use the following:

```
az cognitiveservices account keys list \
--name ch13-speech-cog \
--resource-group <your-resource-group-name> \
--query "key1"
```

When the function app is deployed, we publish this local.settings.json file to the function app. The Functions app creates environment variables for each of these settings for use by the function app code.

At this point, we have the services deployed and the configuration set. We can look at the code in each of the functions and get ready to deploy the function app and code.

## TranscribeAudio function

The TranscribeAudio function is triggered when a new file is placed in the Recordings container of the specified storage account. The function reads the file and passes it to the transcription endpoint of our Speech service. The transcription service is an asynchronous service. Instead of waiting for the transcription to complete, we will track the status of transcriptions in a **storage table** and use an **Azure Logic Apps app** to monitor in-process transcriptions and store the results in storage.

The function contains two main files:

- __init__.py contains the code for the function.
- function.json contains the configuration and bindings for the function.

Let's look at function.json first.

We see that "scriptFile" points to "__init__.py"; this tells the runtime that the code to execute when this file is called is located in the file:

```
{
  "scriptFile": "__init__.py",
```

The "bindings" section lists input and output parameters that the function runtime will supply to the function. The first binding here is our **trigger**. This binding tells the runtime to listen to events raised by the Blob Storage account located at the **connection string** specified in the ch13_STORAGE configuration variable in the recordings path and execute when files are created or updated:

```
"bindings": [
  {
    "name": "newRecording",
    "type": "blobTrigger",
    "direction": "in",
    "path": "recordings/{name}",
    "connection": "ch13_STORAGE"
  },
```

Our next binding is the output binding. The function runtime will supply us with output parameters where we can write our results. The output binding points to our Azure storage table:

```
  {
    "name": "outTable",
    "type": "table",
    "tableName": "transcriptionStatus",
    "partitionKey": "result",
    "connection": "ch13_STORAGE",
    "direction": "out"
  }
]
```

In the __init__.py file, we find the code that will be executed when a new file lands in this storage container.

The entry point to the function is called main. Note that we have three parameters to this function that map to the bindings in function.json

```
def main(newRecording: func.InputStream,
         outTable: func.Out[str]
        ):
```

These settings are uploaded to the function configuration from local.settings.json when the function app is created. When the runtime starts, it pushes these values into environment variables accessible to the code:

```
speech_key = os.environ["speech_key"]
service_region = os.environ["service_region"]
```

We have wrapped the call to transcribe the audio in a Python function, which we will review next:

```
transcription_id = transcribe_file(newRecording.name,
                                    service_region,
                                    speech_key)
```

Once we have queued the transcription job, we write a row to our output table so we can track the job's status:

```
data = {
  "rowKey" : str(uuid.uuid4())
  , "partitionKey" : "result"
  , "fileName" : newRecording.name
  , "transcriptionId" : transcription_id
  , "status" : "new"
  , "statusCheckCount" : "0"
}
outTable.set(json.dumps(data))
```

The `transcribe_file` Python function makes the call to our Speech service. There is no Python API to perform this operation so we will call the REST APIs directly. The function takes three parameters:

- `file_name` is the name of the file that was passed to our blob trigger.

- The `service_region` and `speech_key` settings came from our `local.settings.json` file:

```
def transcribe_file(file_name,
                    service_region,
                    speech_key
                    ):
```

The body of our rest API call is a JSON document that tells the Speech service where to find our audio file and includes some properties that control details of how we would like the transcription service to behave:

```
payload = json.dumps({
    "contentUrls": [
        f"https://ch13storage.blob.core.windows.net/{file_name}"
    ],
    "properties": {
        "diarizationEnabled": False,
        "wordLevelTimestampsEnabled": False,
        "punctuationMode": "DictatedAndAutomatic",
        "profanityFilterMode": "Masked"
    },
    "locale": "en-US",
```

```
        "displayName": "Transcription using default model for en-US"
    })
```

Along with the payload, our request to the service requires authentication information, the API key for our Speech service, which we will include as a header to our REST API call:

```
headers = {
        'Ocp-Apim-Subscription-Key': f'{speech_key}',
        'Content-Type': 'application/json'
        }
```

Once we have created our payload, we use the `http.client` library to create an `HTTPSConnection` object pointing to our instance of the Speech service and execute a `POST` request with our payload in the body of the request:

```
service_connection = http.client.HTTPSConnection(
                f"{service_region}.api.cognitive.microsoft.com")
service_connection.request(
                "POST",
                "/speechtotext/v3.0/transcriptions",
                payload,
                headers)
```

The response from this request contains the `transcription ID` that we use to later track the status of this transcription operation. The body of the response is a JSON document. First, we load the document into a Python dictionary, and then we extract the transcription ID:

```
response_string =
            service_connection.getresponse()
                            .read()
                            .decode("utf-8")
dataDict = json.loads(response_string)
transcription_id = dataDict['self'].split('/').pop()
return transcription_id
```

## Retrieve transcription results Logic Apps app

For this example, the process of checking transcription operation status, retrieving the results, and writing completed transcriptions to storage has been encapsulated into an Azure Logic Apps workflow.

The `Chapter 13\Code Snippets\RetrieveTranscriptionLogicApp` directory contains the definition for this Azure Logic Apps app.

We chose Logic Apps for this portion of the solution to show another way to glue together some of the operations that you generally perform when working with Cognitive Services. As you are experimenting with different API calls, sometimes, working in a low-code environment gives you slightly more scope to test individual changes and iterate your solution very quickly.

Just like an Azure function, Logic Apps are executed based on various types of triggers. Here, we will execute this workflow every 30 seconds on a trigger called the **Recurrence** trigger:

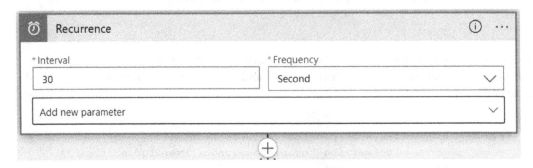

Figure 13.10 – Capture of the configuration for the Recurrence trigger in a Logic Apps app

Next, we initialize variables that will be used in this workflow. There are some areas of Logic Apps that work a little differently than you may be used to when writing code in Python or C#. One of those differences is that variables cannot be defined inside of a loop. As we will be executing a `for each` loop to check the status of multiple transcription operations, we will initialize the variables at the top of this workflow. The variables are as follows:

- `speechKey` – string – This is the key used to access the Speech service. We are hardcoding the key in this example, but you could store this value in Azure Key Vault and retrieve the key at runtime.

- `statusCheckCount` – integer – We are checking the transcription status for each request every 30 seconds. If the request takes longer than five status checks, we will mark the operation as timed out.

- `newEntity` – string – The variable to hold the details of updated data to place in our `transcriptionStatus` table, initialized to an empty string.

- `transcriptFileUrl` – string – The variable to hold the URL of our transcribed audio results, initialized to an empty string.

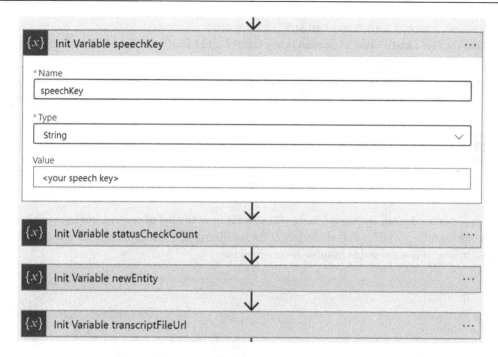

Figure 13.11 – Screen capture displaying details of specified variables

Once we have initialized our variables, we will use the Azure storage table connector's **Get Entities** operation to retrieve the **entities** that we would like to review. We set the table to **transcriptionStatus** and add a filter to only look at new entities:

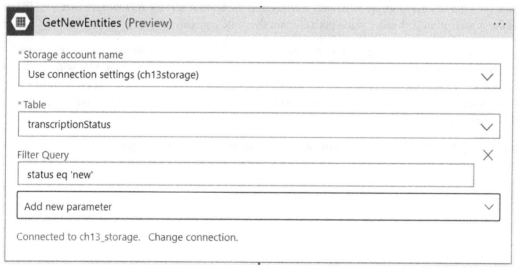

Figure 13.12 – Configuration of the Entities feature of the Azure storage table

The call to `Get entities` returns an array that we can loop through in the `for each` loop. Notice that the **Get Entities res..** collection is highlighted and has an icon next to it. In Logic Apps, this is called **dynamic content**.

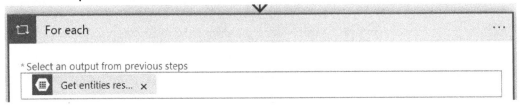

Figure 13.13 – Example of the for each loop within Logic Apps connecting to Get entities

When we set that value, all we needed to do was select it from the list of content from the previous steps. Aside from the variables that we declare at the beginning of this workflow, each operation has its own output that is addressable in subsequent operations.

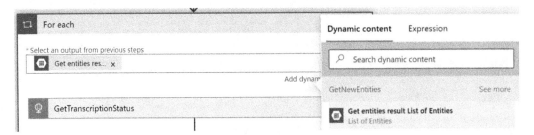

Figure 13.14 – Example of adding dynamic content based on previously built steps

Inside the `for each` loop, we will make a request to the Speech service API. Notice that the URI and the subscription ID header value both contain dynamic content.

The URI concatenates the base URL with `transcriptionId`, which we pull from the current item in our for each loop. If you hover over the `transcriptionId` content, you will see the `items('For_each')['transcriptionId'].items('For_each')` expression, giving us the current item of the loop named `For_each`, and `['transcriptionId']` pulls the value from the current entity.

`speechKey` is pulled directly from our variable initialized previously in *Figure 13.11*.

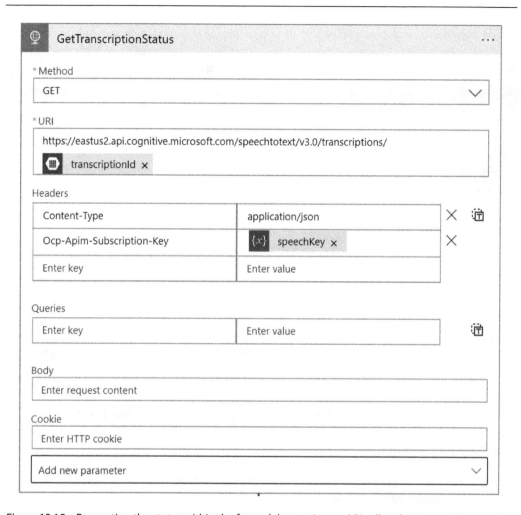

Figure 13.15 – Requesting the status within the for each loop using an API call to the transcription service

Now that we have checked the transcription status, we can check the status of the request and take appropriate action. We have three possible outcomes, which we will choose from here:

- The transcription succeeded
- The transcription failed
- The transcription is still in progress

We use a `switch` operation and evaluate the status field of the body of our response from the `GetTranscriptionStatus` operation. The expression we are evaluating is `body('GetTranscriptionStatus')['status']`.

Note that this is not the status code of the HTTPS request. We are assuming there has been a successful HTTPS call to the service. This is a status value that is in the body of the response, which indicates whether the asynchronous transcription activity has completed successfully.

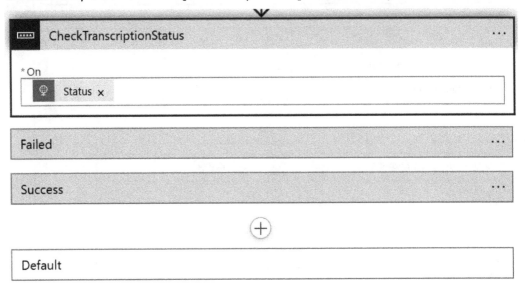

Figure 13.16 – Checking the status of our transcription service

Now, we can handle each of the options as we receive the results with the following approaches.

## Failed transcription result

Let's look at the **Failed** case first. The service might not be able to transcribe the speech if, for example, the audio file is corrupt, or the URL is incorrect.

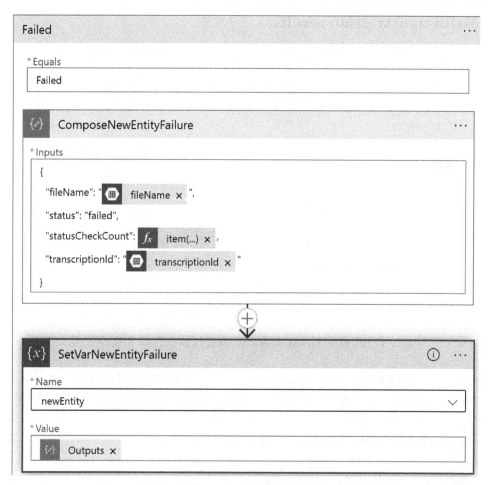

Figure 13.17 – Configuration for failed transcription results

When a transcription operation fails, we update the `transcriptionStatus` storage table to record a status of `failed`. At this point, we compose the new JSON document and store it in a variable. We will update the table in a subsequent operation. Some examples of errors are along the lines of the following:

- **Response 400** – In cases where the operation cannot be performed successfully with the specified values

- **Response 401** – In cases where the user isn't authorize

Additional error response details can be found in the API documentation found here: `https://eastus.dev.cognitive.microsoft.com/docs/services/speech-to-text-api-v3-0/`

## Successful transcription results

If the operation succeeds, there is a little more work to do; let's look at the following figure:

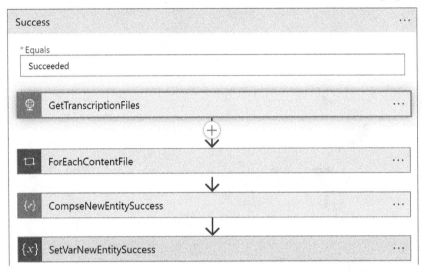

Figure 13.18 – Steps for handling a successful transcription request

First, we make a call back to the service to get the transcription results. This call returns two URLs: one that contains the transcription and another that contains metadata about the transcription operation. All we care about in this scenario is the transcription results.

First, we make a call to the Speech API to retrieve the content URLs.

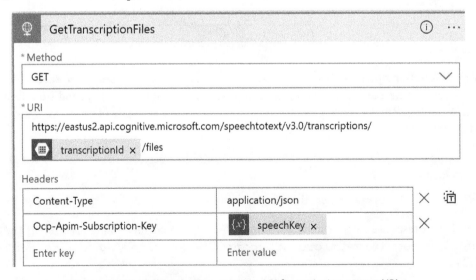

Figure 13.19 – Calling the Transcription API for retrieving output URLs

The body of the response to this call is a JSON document. This document contains an attribute named `values`. The `values` attribute is an array of objects that contain a `kind` field and a `url` field. This next step loops through the `values` array and checks the `kind` field. If the `kind` field results in `Transcription`, then we take action; if the `kind` field is anything else, we ignore that element.

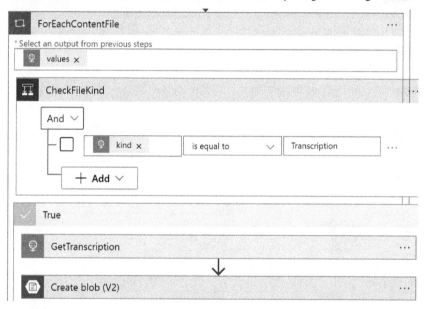

Figure 13.20 – Steps for handling "kind" results from successful transcription

If this is a Transcription URL, then make a request to the referenced URL using the following expression in the request URI: `items('ForEachContentFile')['links']['contentUrl']`. Notice that there are no headers specified here.

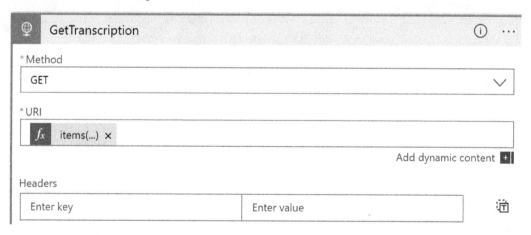

Figure 13.21 – Configuration for requesting the Transcription URL

Finally, we record the results of the transcription to our output container:

- **Folder path** is our `transcriptions` container

- **Blob name** is an expression based on the table entity that is the current item of the outer for each loop. The blob name containers the path to the `recordings` container, which we will remove, and we will write this file as a JSON file instead of a `.wav` file. This expression accomplishes this task: `replace(replace(items('For_each').fileName, 'recordings/', ''), '.wav', '.json')`.

- **Blob content** is the body of the previous HTTP request.

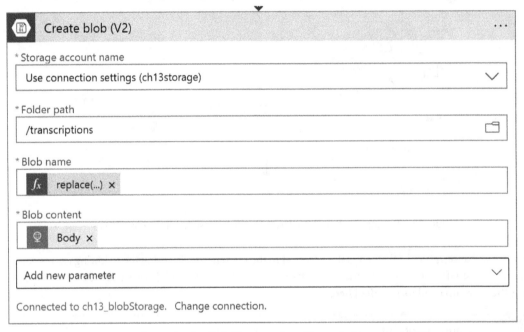

Figure 13.22 – Configuration for Blob Storage where Transcription output will be stored

Once we have written the file, we can update the storage table entity with a new status of `"processed"` so it does not appear in our subsequent queries.

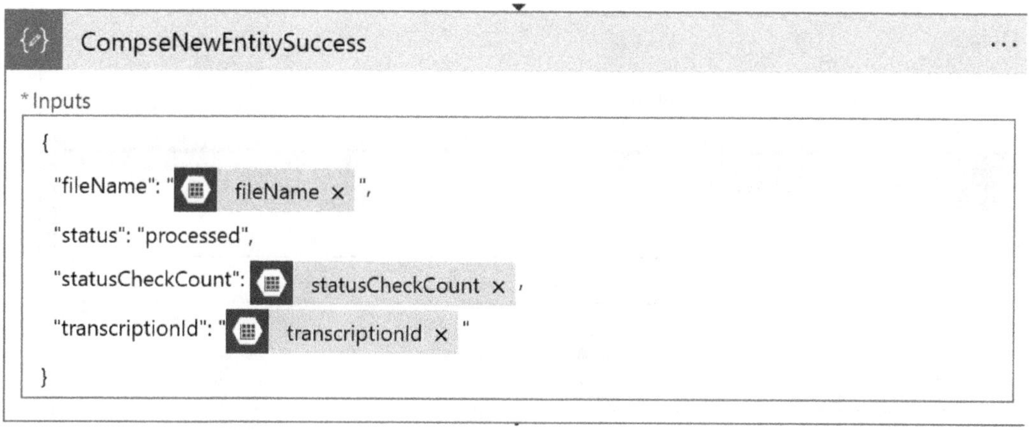

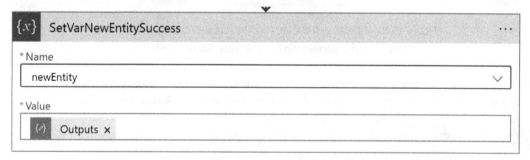

Figure 13.23 – Updating status of transcription processing as processed

And we set the variable to represent the successful transcription:

Figure 13.24 – Setting the variable using Logic Apps

### Transcription still processing

The last condition that we check is the default condition. We hit this condition if the status is neither `"Failed"` or `"Succeeded"`. Basically, this is the case for an operation that is still queued or in progress. The first thing we will do is check to see whether we have exceeded our maximum retries.

We pull the current item's existing retry count and add one with the following expression: `add(items('For_each').statusCheckCount, 1)`:

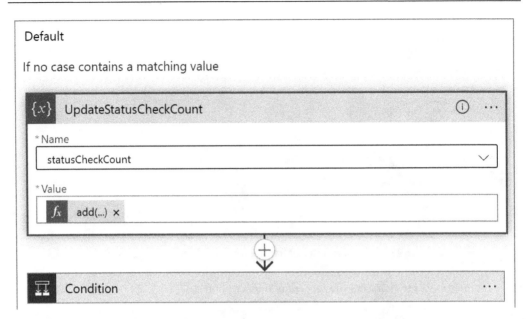

Figure 13.25 – Checking the status and incrementing the count of
checks if the transaction is  not succeeded or failed

Now, we can check the number of retries and determine whether to keep trying or mark the operation as timed out. We have already incremented the counter, so if we are at **6**, then we need to time out.

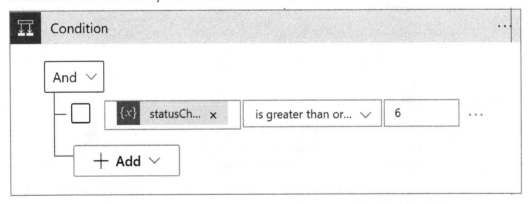

Figure 13.26 – Checking the count of tries for incomplete transcription

Since we've met our initial condition of five checks, we want to show a status of a `timedOut` operation:

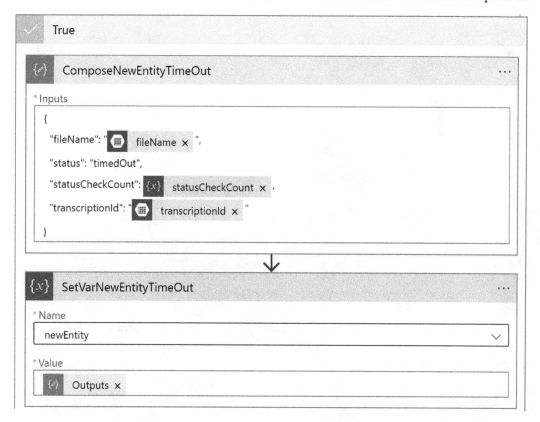

Figure 13.27 – Setting our status as timed out per hitting our threshold of five tests

If we haven't hit our threshold yet, we should continue with our checking until we hit that threshold:

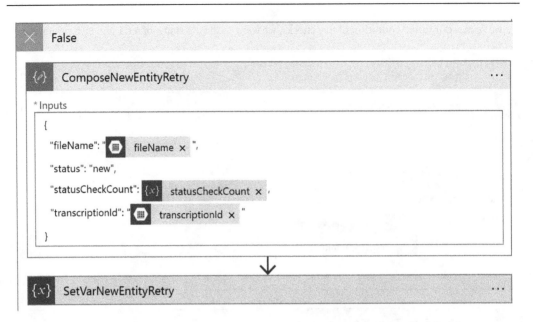

Figure 13.28 – Showing that the threshold of five checks has not yet occurred

The last check we have is really an exception handler. If there were any failures while looking at this entity, such as writing the blob, making an HTTP request, or any other failure that we have not accounted for, we will mark the entity as failed.

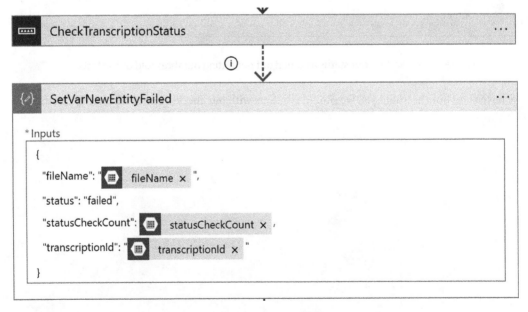

Figure 13.29 – Logic Apps app representing the entity as "failed"

Notice the red arrow between `CheckTranscriptionStatus` and `SetVarNewEntityFailed`. This indicates that the `SetVarNewEntityFailed` operation should only be called if `CheckTranscriptionStatus` ends in a failed status. You can specify this by selecting the **Configure run after** from the ellipsis menu on the `SetVarNewEntityFailed` operation.

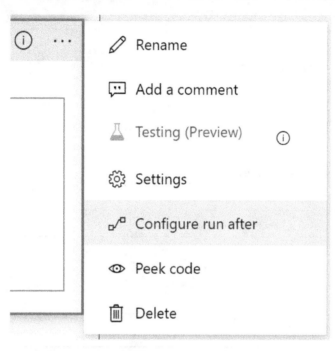

Figure 13.30 – Menu options for setting variable dialog

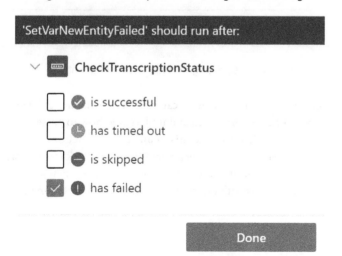

Figure 13.31 – Options for "Configure run after" option in the menu

The last step in the workflow is to update our storage entity with the final status. Here, we use the **Replace Entity** operation from Azure storage tables and specify the `newEntity` variable, which will hold the new status and update the count from our workflow's logic.

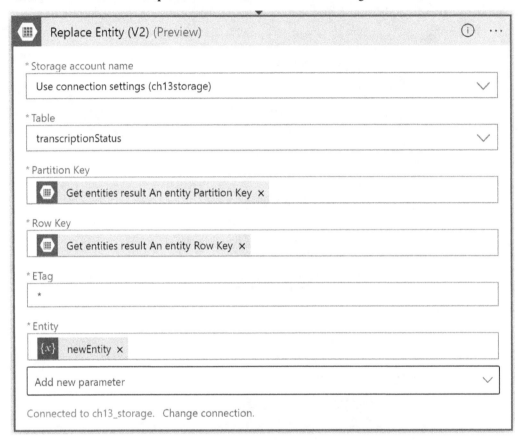

Figure 13.32 – Updating the final status of our entity

Looking at the completed workflow in this manner can seem a little daunting. If you were well-versed in Python or C# and knew your REST APIs well and understood how to parse the results by writing code, it would likely be more efficient to code this in an Azure Function. However, Azure Logic Apps is a great tool that allows you to iterate quickly and test your workflow one step at a time very efficiently. It is also great for exploring and understanding how to use a new set of REST APIs. Now, let's look at some options for working with our outputted document containing the transcribed text.

## Capturing sentiment and reporting

Now that we have transcribed the contents of the audio file that we fed into the Speech service and are ultimately working with a text document, we can examine the options provided by Azure Cognitive Service for Language.

As described earlier in the chapter, Ocean Smart determined that if they could extract sentiment from conversations, it could provide a basis for employee training and enhancing customer service. In this case, the **Natural Language Understanding** (NLU) service can detect a language or classify the sentiment of text provided. A feature of sentiment analysis known as **opinion mining** can go one step deeper and provide additional context about words found in the text to provide even more detail. An example of this would be if a product name were found within the text, opinion mining could provide some of the details or related information about that product from the internet.

When developing the sentiment capability as a follow-on activity, similar to leveraging the Speech service, you will deploy a Language resource in the Azure portal. In the following screenshot, you'll note that you are prompted to select the type of project you are developing to help determine the right resources for deployment:

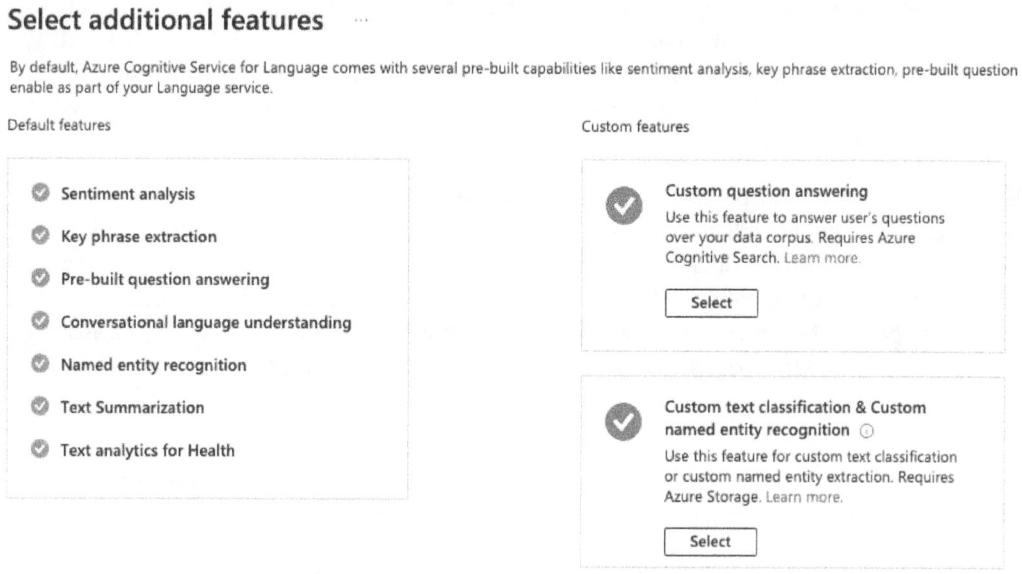

### Select additional features  ...

By default, Azure Cognitive Service for Language comes with several pre-built capabilities like sentiment analysis, key phrase extraction, pre-built question enable as part of your Language service.

Default features

- ✓ Sentiment analysis
- ✓ Key phrase extraction
- ✓ Pre-built question answering
- ✓ Conversational language understanding
- ✓ Named entity recognition
- ✓ Text Summarization
- ✓ Text analytics for Health

Custom features

✓ **Custom question answering**
Use this feature to answer user's questions over your data corpus. Requires Azure Cognitive Search. Learn more.

[ Select ]

✓ **Custom text classification & Custom named entity recognition** ⓘ
Use this feature for custom text classification or custom named entity extraction. Requires Azure Storage. Learn more.

[ Select ]

Figure 13.33 – Dialog provided when first deploying a Language service in the Azure portal

Since our project is looking to use the sentiment service, we will choose the latter option: **Custom text classifications & Custom named entity recognition**. The deployment process, again, is like that of the Speech service in that you are simply deploying resources for compute to run your operations. One difference is a recent addition to some of the Cognitive Services when being deployed, and that is the acknowledgment of using the service responsibly:

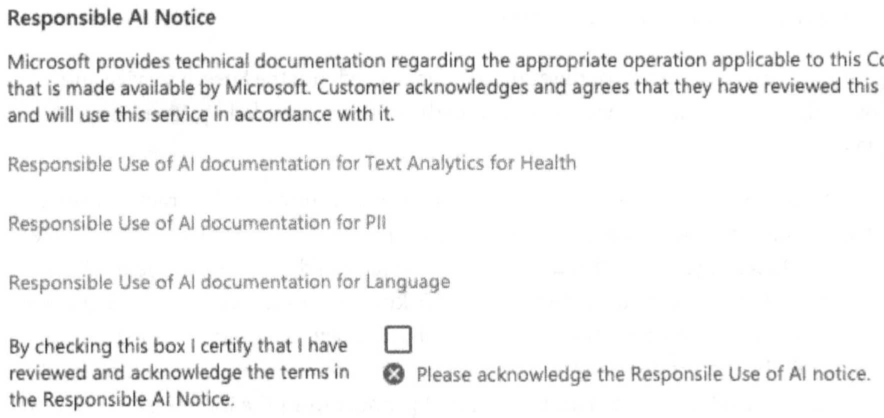

**Responsible AI Notice**

Microsoft provides technical documentation regarding the appropriate operation applicable to this Cognitive Service that is made available by Microsoft. Customer acknowledges and agrees that they have reviewed this documentation and will use this service in accordance with it.

Responsible Use of AI documentation for Text Analytics for Health

Responsible Use of AI documentation for PII

Responsible Use of AI documentation for Language

By checking this box I certify that I have    ☐
reviewed and acknowledge the terms in    ⊗ Please acknowledge the Responsile Use of AI notice.
the Responsible AI Notice.

Figure 13.34 – Responsible use of AI notice found at the bottom of the
Basic page when deploying many Cognitive Services

There are many discussions about how to use AI responsibly and the provided guidelines by Microsoft on doing so; we will discuss this topic in more detail in *Chapter 15*. For now, it is required to select this acknowledgment to be able to proceed. Beyond that, the configuration will be for **Network**, **Identity**, and **Tags** as standard questions when deploying. After the service deployment is complete, you will access the service with an API call for using the machine learning model and compute required to run your workload.

When using the service, the primary interface is code, with no GUI available for processing your text. In this case, again, we will use Python to continue being as consistent as possible through the book where available. There is a Free and Standard tier of the service, as with many others, and we recommend the Free tier for PoCs and Standard for production deployments. Because we have already discussed the process for setting up the environment with Python and other tools, we can start by grabbing the `textanalytics` client library with the following command:

```
pip install azure-ai-textanalytics==5.1.0
```

Now that your environment is ready, the following is some sample code for using various options of the Language service for gathering sentiment and opinion mining:

- First, grab the key and endpoint from the Language service in the Azure portal:

```
key = "paste-your-key-here"
endpoint = "paste-your-endpoint-here"
```

- Next, import the libraries needed for using these services:

```
from azure.ai.textanalytics import TextAnalyticsClient
from azure.core.credentials import AzureKeyCredential
```

- Authenticate the client using your key and endpoint:

```
def authenticate_client():
    ta_credential = AzureKeyCredential(key)
    text_analytics_client = TextAnalyticsClient(
            endpoint=endpoint,
            credential=ta_credential)
    return text_analytics_client
client = authenticate_client()
```

- Here is an example method for detecting sentiment and opinions in text:

```
def sentiment_analysis_with_opinion_mining_example(client):
    documents = [
        "The quality of the Lobster meat was inconsistent and
mushy in some parts. Usually, we get much better quality when we
order from Ocean Smart."
    ]
```

- Here, we specify that we're looking for opinions from the document level:

```
    result = client.analyze_sentiment(documents, show_opinion_
mining=True)
    doc_result = [doc for doc in result if not doc.is_error]
    positive_reviews = [doc for doc in doc_result if doc.
sentiment == "positive"]
    negative_reviews = [doc for doc in doc_result if doc.
sentiment == "negative"]
    positive_mined_opinions = []
    mixed_mined_opinions = []
    negative_mined_opinions = []
```

- Here, we provide our overall scores for when feedback is positive, negative, and neutral:

```
    for document in doc_result:
        print("Document Sentiment: {}".format(document.
sentiment))
        print("Overall scores: positive={0:.2f};
neutral={1:.2f}; negative={2:.2f} \n".format(
            document.confidence_scores.positive,
            document.confidence_scores.neutral,
            document.confidence_scores.negative,
        ))
        for sentence in document.sentences:
            print("Sentence: {}".format(sentence.text))
            print("Sentence sentiment: {}".format(sentence.
sentiment))
            print("Sentence score:\nPositive={0:.2f}\
nNeutral={1:.2f}\nNegative={2:.2f}\n".format(
```

```
                    sentence.confidence_scores.positive,
                    sentence.confidence_scores.neutral,
                    sentence.confidence_scores.negative,
        ))
```

- Here, we provide ranges for positive and negative mined opinions:

```
        for mined_opinion in sentence.mined_opinions:
            target = mined_opinion.target
            print("......'{}' target '{}'".format(target.
sentiment, target.text))
            print("......Target score:\n......
Positive={0:.2f}\n......Negative={1:.2f}\n".format(
                target.confidence_scores.positive,
                target.confidence_scores.negative,
            ))
            for assessment in mined_opinion.assessments:
                print("......'{}' assessment '{}'".
format(assessment.sentiment, assessment.text))
                print("......Assessment score:\n......
Positive={0:.2f}\n......Negative={1:.2f}\n".format(
                    assessment.confidence_scores.positive,
                    assessment.confidence_scores.negative,
                ))
        print("\n")
    print("\n")

sentiment_analysis_with_opinion_mining_example(client)
```

Now that we have established our ranges for what our scores should reflect as we analyze the text we are using for our example, we will provide the output of the text passed into the service. As you will see with the output provided, keywords from the text are extracted and scored from each of the sentences, and then each sentence will also receive a score. The output for our previous example is provided in the following:

```
Document Sentiment: mixed
Overall scores: positive=0.47; neutral=0.00; negative=0.52
Sentence: The quality of the Lobster meat was inconsistent and mushy
in some parts.
Sentence sentiment: negative
Sentence score:
Positive=0.00
Neutral=0.00
Negative=0.99
......'negative' target 'lobster'
......Target score:
......Positive=0.00
```

```
......Negative=1.00
......'negative' assessment 'meat'
......Assessment score:
......Positive=0.00
......Negative=1.00
......'negative' target 'inconsistent'
......Target score:
......Positive=0.00
......Negative=1.00
......'negative' assessment 'mushy'
......Assessment score:
......Positive=0.00
......Negative=1.00
......'negative' assessment 'parts'
......Assessment score:
......Positive=0.00
......Negative=1.00
Sentence: Usually, we get much better quality when we order from Ocean
Smart.
Sentence sentiment: positive
Sentence score:
Positive=0.94
Neutral=0.01
Negative=0.05
......'positive' target 'better'
......Target score:
......Positive=1.00
......Negative=0.00
......'positive' assessment 'quality'
......Assessment score:
......Positive=1.00
......Negative=0.00
```

So, in this case, we have negative sentiment for the quality of the lobster, but positive sentiment for typical quality. We can capture the detail of this output in a JSON document or, even better, we can put the key information into a database such as SQL Server or CosmosDB to capture all the details. These details then can all be related back to the original audio file for assigning an overall sentiment for the service. From there, you can use your business intelligence or reporting tool of choice to display the results. These tools can be used for making comparisons for customers and customer service representatives alike, as well as showing trend information over time. You can also use them as a way of alerting for a situation where a service representative is having consecutive bad calls or voice messages being left, which should improve the customer service experience and employee training over time.

# Summary

With that, you now have the ability to use the Speech service for creating a transcript from an audio conversation or capturing a live audio transcript and displaying it in real time for captioning and other uses. From there, you have the opportunity to track the quality of calls using the sentiment skill available with Language services and provide the ability for your organization to greatly enhance the customer service experience, as well as training tools. These capabilities are some of the more prevalent examples where the Cognitive Services tools are applied to real-world scenarios, but just a small portion of the overall capabilities from both the Speech and Language services. Be sure to use examples such as the one laid out in this chapter and apply critical thinking around what other skills are offered within the services, as well as enhancements applied over time, for what might be beneficial to your organization. Be mindful of the limitations of the service we discussed throughout the chapter as you plan your deployment. Additional steps outside of what is available with the service, such as audio conversions or quality degradation, to adhere to the limitations may be necessary as part of your process. These items should be easily identified through the planning phase as you gather requirements and help paint a picture of what a successful deployment will look like.

For Ocean Smart, this set of tools has provided a great way to measure customer satisfaction and to have even more assets for determining the overall health of customer relationships. It also provides a constant feedback loop for customer service and sales representatives regarding how customers are experiencing working with the Ocean Smart team. Finally, it provides another tool for the management team to determine who the top performers are and which team members need more guidance. Our next chapter explores how to complement these services with Language Understanding services and the Azure Bot Service to provide a different form of customer service. Let's go!

# 14

# Using Language Services in Chat Bots and Beyond

Are chat bots a function of corporate America, stripping out costs and assuming humans are content interacting with anyone, human or synthetic? Are they a way to remove initial barriers and understand customers' requirements without requiring interaction by humans? Because Ocean Smart puts such a focus on customer service, there was significant hesitation in deploying a chat bot as the initial interaction point for their customers. However, with the potential cost savings and the ability to include translation and content moderation by combining multiple Azure Cognitive Services, the benefits of deploying the technology outweighed the negative aspects.

In this chapter, we will explore how Ocean Smart was able to leverage and combine these Cognitive Services to enhance the global customer experience and save some costs by no longer using human beings as the initial point of contact for customer service. To further improve the customer experience, Ocean Smart has deployed a chat bot on its website to help customers get support or find what they need. To make the chat bot more effective, they deployed Language Understanding and Translator Cognitive Services, which helps any customer enter a question in any of the supported languages and receive logical answers and support for their questions. All this, without any human intervention, only being directed to a human if necessary.

In this chapter, we will review the following:

- Using a chat bot for enhanced customer service
- Tying the Cognitive Service for Language to the chat bot for natural language processing
- Using translator services for worldwide solutions
- The advanced capabilities of Language Understanding
- Building a bot using Language Understanding and Content Moderator

This is, of course, just the beginning of the capabilities we can leverage using a chat bot. Whether we take the services further for uses such as **Robotic Process Automation (RPA)** or enhancing internal communication and process, this collection of services can really enhance an organization by minimizing inefficiencies. So, let's get started by discussing some of the benefits of deploying a chat bot, and then move on to some of the capabilities of the Language Services.

## Technical requirements

To build our bot, we will use Bot Framework Composer version 2.x, which you can download from `https://learn.microsoft.com/en-us/composer/install-composer?tabs=windows#download-composer`.

Bot Framework Composer is available on Windows, Mac, and Linux and has two pre-requisites:

- Node.js 14.x: `https://nodejs.org/en`
- .NET Code SDK 3.1 or later: `https://dotnet.microsoft.com/en-us/download/dotnet/3.1`

Bot Framework Composer will build a C# project behind the scenes and deploy it to our Azure subscription. If you would like to view the C# project, you can use Visual Studio Code or Visual Studio 2022 Community Edition, which you can find at `https://visualstudio.microsoft.com/vs/community`.

## Using a chat bot for enhanced customer service

In the past, various organizations prided themselves on providing the utmost satisfaction possible when talking about customer service for their products or services. Of course, the old adage "the customer is always right" came into play for some of these organizations, but whether they make the investments necessary to truly embody that statement is a whole other discussion. You see, the drawback to investments in customer service representatives and all other investments relating to this area is that they don't have tangible revenue increases that can be directly tied to a good customer experience.

The value provided is often peripheral, and it is difficult to measure exactly how much investment should be made to positively impact revenue without overspending in this area, where the investment becomes wasted. Organizations that don't put quite as much of an investment in this area intentionally are deciding to value their customers less and reduce their own costs. This may be a valid strategy in the case of a volume supplier, or other similar business models where customer satisfaction would be less of a premium. I think it is fair to assume that the greater volume of customers an organization services, especially if the bulk of those customers are evenly related to what they spend, the fewer expectations they have of quality service. The opposite would be true of a pure services company that specializes in an area, so they can charge a premium for their services and customers would have higher expectations of them. Regardless of the type of organization you own or work for, this discussion is an ongoing one, and it constantly requires fine-tuning to ensure the waste-to-benefit ratio is cost-effective.

Some time back, however, organizations began to look at different ways to cut those costs, and still attempt to provide reasonably good quality customer service, so changes began to be made. In the modern era of technology, prior to the explosion of the web as the main way customers interacted with the organization they purchased from, phone and email were the first tools used. Implemented technologies such as auto-responsive email and auto-attended phone systems were deployed, with the intent of satisfying some of the more mundane aspects of customer service. Oftentimes, these technologies actually made it more difficult for customers to get service, if they didn't fall into one of the simplified activities these technologies were designed to assist with. For the organizations implementing the technologies, it helped them to save on recurring costs on active customer service reps. All this as a relatively inexpensive option was only paid for once and was fairly simple to implement.

However, as we moved toward an online portal being the main face of a company, expectations from customers led them toward the web for their customer service. We saw technologies such as online forms for gathering details of customers' concerns, and even chats with a live operator when web pages became dynamic enough to support such options. We have also seen other ways to service customers. As touchscreens became popular and cost-effective, we have seen an explosion of kiosks where cashiers and customer service reps alike are no longer necessary. The largest retail and grocery chains in the US have made significant investments in automated checkout stations, for example. These can come at a price, as we have to consider the feelings of a customer when they must wait longer in a store because the price didn't come up correctly, or a barcode couldn't be read. Also, the amount of technology required to help prevent shoplifting or ensure a customer is old enough to purchase alcohol must be evaluated, compared to the costs of staffing personnel at every register. Regardless of the evaluation steps, every organization needs to determine what technology is best to deploy to serve its customers' needs.

Initially, chat bots were unsophisticated and could only respond to specific questions with an accurate answer. There was no interpretation, and if the question asked wasn't part of the script, the best you could hope for would be how to contact customer service by phone or email, and most of the time you'd get a response like, "*I don't understand.*" The latest innovation in chat bots has really targeted addressing these challenges when appropriately responding to requests by customers and a bunch of other use cases, from internal helpdesk requests and HR questions to placing a lunch order at a cafeteria. These enhancements have all made the organizations they serve more efficient, and none of it would be possible without being able to interpret what is being typed into a chat. The piece that was missing is now provided by Language Understanding on the interpretation layer, helping us understand what is being asked and logical responses providing options to a user.

However, before we get ahead of ourselves, let's look at the layers of a bot and the components used to implement these more sophisticated capabilities. The way a bot is developed in the Microsoft ecosystem is by using the Bot Framework SDK to create the structure of the bot, as well as adding any external features, such as some of the AI services we've discussed in this book. This chapter will focus on Language Services, but you can browse the different options when you start using the Bot Framework for your own projects. Microsoft provides the following diagram that represents a high-level flow of information between a person and a bot:

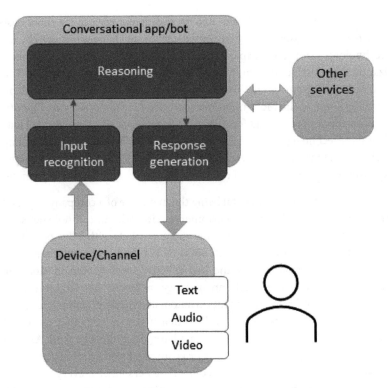

Figure 14.1 – A high-level representation of a bot conversation using the Bot Framework SDK

The SDK was designed to simplify things and help the builder to configure and deploy components of a bot to the supported destination of choice, quickly. The currently supported languages are C#, JavaScript, Python, and Java; however, Python and Java support are set to be deprecated in November 2023. The kit also includes CLI tools to help with the development process, the bot connector service, which relays messages, and related Azure resources for ongoing configuration. On top of the native capabilities, as mentioned, you can connect various Cognitive Services, Azure Storage for logging, and transcripts with native connectivity. Developing the tool is a prescriptive process, where you follow six steps to ensure success:

1. **Plan**: There needs to be some homework done prior to starting to build the bot. What are you trying to accomplish? What is the benefit? What are the associated costs? Have you done a complete ROI and TCO assessment? Just make sure you have done your homework prior to spending a bunch of time on a project that could be doomed to fail without the right capabilities and buy-in from users. Microsoft has provided design guidelines to help ensure success, which can be found here: `https://learn.microsoft.com/en-us/azure/bot-service/bot-service-design-principles?view=azure-bot-service-4.0`. This resource will help you by providing details of past lessons learned and what it takes to build a great chat bot that everyone will love!

2. **Build**: When discussing the build step of creating a bot, we should focus on the construction of the flow of chat between a consumer and the bot, and the services that will be leveraged as a result. When considering the ability to employ Cognitive Services, for instance, there are many other aspects of bot construction that come into account. Determining where the bot will be hosted (probably Azure, but not necessarily), the number of consumers that are expected to use the bot, and how the resources required to run the bot will be managed are all aspects of the build process. The capabilities don't end with a simple chat interface either. Bot Framework can use menus of images, called cards, to create a graphic representation of what is being shown. Consider a use case where you want to order lunch from a cafeteria – wouldn't it be so much more helpful to load sample images of what a dish looks like to help with the process of choosing what to order?

3. **Test**: When building a bot, depending on how complex the build is, you may need to perform extensive testing to ensure the desired results are achieved. Because bots have become so powerful in the actions they can take, there are three recommended testing options provided by Microsoft:

   • **Bot Framework Emulator**: This tool gives you the ability to test the bot and gain a full understanding of the actions taken, based on the commands you send. The Emulator can be installed locally in your development environment for complete offline testing and debugging.

   • **Publishing to a web app**: To perform **user acceptance testing** (**UAT**), you could deploy the bot to an Azure web app and give the address to testers, prior to publishing the bot to a live environment. This will allow the full functionality to be explored by remote testers and help gain feedback from multiple vectors.

   • **Unit testing**: Within the SDK development environment, you can perform unit testing for each element of the statement and response dialog. This method is different from the other two because you don't interface directly with the bot. The unit test tool works with the `DialogTestClient` class, which was specifically designed to test inline code to track responses to specific activities. This helps to narrow in on specific activities and ensure they perform appropriately.

4. **Publish**: So, now that you have fully tested your bot and are happy that the flow works perfectly, it's time to publish your bot to the location of your choice. Of course, in step 1, we plan out the details of our bot. Following that logic indicates that you've predetermined where you will publish the bot to – perhaps an Azure web service, or embedded on your own website. You'll also need to decide how you will manage the identities of your bot for a user-assigned managed identity, a single-tenant app, or a multi-tenant app. You'll also have to decide whether the bot will be used regionally or globally. As a result, if you decide to go global, you'll need to keep in mind the multilingual aspects of making that decision.

5. **Connect**: Great, now you have deployed your bot, and now you just need to make sure that the site is accessible from the outside for interaction from consumers. This is also the time when you decide whether you want to extend the bot to any of the additional **channels** to run on. Channels allow you to have direct communication with your bot and other communication applications your customers may interact with, such as Facebook, Alexa, and Slack. Depending on the application, you can expect various experiences, as not all platforms support all capabilities, so assume further testing will be necessary after you tie the bot using channels. For the most current list of channels, navigate to the following page: `https://learn.microsoft.com/en-us/azure/bot-service/bot-service-manage-channels?view=azure-bot-service-4.0`.

6. **Evaluate**: To maximize the value of your bot, you will want to monitor a multitude of aspects, such as who is using the bot and how it is being used. Perhaps you've built in a feature that is never used or have far too many users abandoning the bot after a short amount of time, without getting what they need from it. In situations such as these, it's possible you've built too much complexity into the bot or misunderstood some of the main reasons users will interact with the bot to begin with. All these details can be analyzed in the Azure portal, along with all the other management capabilities of Azure Bot Service.

So, there you have it – a foundation in bot building, at least in the Azure world. Microsoft provides tutorials online (`https://learn.microsoft.com/en-us/azure/bot-service/bot-service-quickstart-create-bot?view=azure-bot-service-4.0&tabs=csharp%2Cvs`), as well as "Bot in a Day" workshops (to gain more hands-on experience with bots). Since the focus of this book is more on the AI components that Azure provides, we're going to look more deeply at the Language Cognitive Services available to integrate within your bot.

## Tying the Cognitive Service for Language to the chat bot for NLP

One of the first ways we can enhance our bot experience is by changing the conversation, literally, to interpretation, enabling us to shift from a contextual understanding to a conversational understanding. As we will display later in the chapter with our working example from Ocean Smart, this can apply to a customer checking on the status of an order, or a whole other host of options. To understand what challenge our customer is having, we ask for the order number to check on the status, but without the **Conversational Language Understanding** (CLU) capability of the Cognitive Service for Language, the bot would just see a sequence of numbers and letters. Of course, with no other understanding, the bot would be stuck without knowing what the number was or how to handle it.

Initially, these Language Understanding capabilities were handled by the Azure **Language Understanding Service** (**LUIS**), but it was announced that this service would be retired on October 1, 2025, to make way for the newer CLU. As of April 1, 2023, you are no longer able to deploy the LUIS service, and only security and patches will be applied to the existing services, so just start with CLU and the Cognitive Service for Language service to save any migration headaches down the road. The CLU enables developers to build their own custom natural Language Understanding models to set expected responses from a consumer, and shows how to handle the details of the response. Referring back to our Ocean Smart example, we would expect an order number back from the consumer when prompted, so we can use that number to search the ERP system for details.

Using the CLU integrated with a bot is only one of the ways that it can be useful. Other types of deployments would also apply, where the CLU can understand the intent of the consumer and take some action or provide information as a reaction to some dialogue. Some examples of where this can also be useful are as simple as the basic commands for a voice-to-text system, where voice commands are recognized. Phrases such as *"Turn the lights off"* or *"Play the next track"* are basic examples, but much more sophisticated interactions can also be implemented to navigate a labyrinth of challenges and responses, getting very detailed information from your human resources systems.

When getting started with the CLU, you will need to have a good understanding of what you intend to use the service for, and what the expected actions you will take are. To start, you will define **intents** and **entities** as they relate to your actions:

- **Intents**: Intents are the tasks or actions that the user consuming your CLU (through your bot in this instance) wants to take. This is where you provide a command for the bot, with our example being *"Check on order,"* for instance. In this case, our intent would likely be `CheckOrder` or something similar, as defined by what you want the action to be.

- **Entities**: When you define your intent, you tell the CLU that there is an action you want to take ultimately, and when you define your entities, they will be aligned with your intent. In this case, the CLU will expect the consumer to provide an order number, thus responding with *"What order number would you like to check on?"*

Combining your intents and entities will begin the process of defining your schema for a project. The schema-defining process should be collaborative for all the stakeholders of this project, as it will require significant discussion and planning to understand all the intents and entities you want to be defined. In other words, defining the schema will help you outline all the functions you want the CLU to be able to interpret and perform. With our example, there are many actions you might want to take, all related to the order process, or you can just simply give the CLU the ability to check status. The option is up to the developer but can be provided with great capabilities, such as canceling or updating an order with the right configuration and integration with your ERP. All these elements are part of planning out how you want to build your bot and how deep you want to go with its capabilities, ultimately defining the flow of the conversation the consumer will have with the bot.

> **Important note**
> Although our example at the end of the chapter displays the direct integration of the LUIS service with the Bot Framework, we are discussing Language Services because it is the evolution of LUIS, and eventually, support will be direct for it instead of LUIS.

To get your CLU integrated with the bot you plan to use, you will need to create a resource in the Azure portal by searching for the `Cognitive Services Language service`. When you start to create the service, you will be presented with the following options:

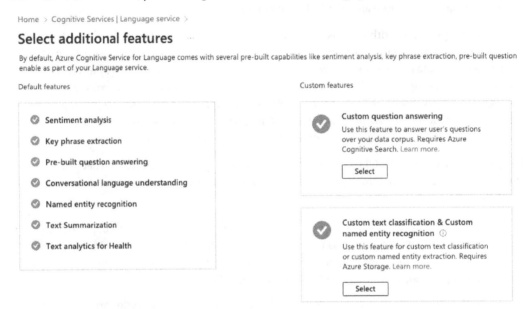

Home > Cognitive Services | Language service >

**Select additional features**

By default, Azure Cognitive Service for Language comes with several pre-built capabilities like sentiment analysis, key phrase extraction, pre-built question enable as part of your Language service.

Default features

- Sentiment analysis
- Key phrase extraction
- Pre-built question answering
- Conversational language understanding
- Named entity recognition
- Text Summarization
- Text analytics for Health

Custom features

**Custom question answering**
Use this feature to answer user's questions over your data corpus. Requires Azure Cognitive Search. Learn more.

Select

**Custom text classification & Custom named entity recognition** ⓘ
Use this feature for custom text classification or custom named entity extraction. Requires Azure Storage. Learn more.

Select

Figure 14.2 – The Language service configuration page in the Azure portal

Depending on your example, you can choose which services you want to add, and you will be brought to a standard resource creation page, where you will be asked for standard details such as name, subscription, region, pricing tier, and so on. When your service is deployed, you can then work in Language Studio by navigating to `https://language.cognitive.azure.com/`. At this stage in the book, you should be somewhat familiar with a few of the auxiliary portals Microsoft provides to work with some of their Cognitive Services, such as the Custom Vision portal and the Forms Recognizer tool to build solutions. These portals help to simplify the development process by getting away from having to build all your solutions with code. In this case, Language Studio is a relatively new portal that has some functionality, but much more to come. When logging in with your Azure account, you are presented with some of the following options:

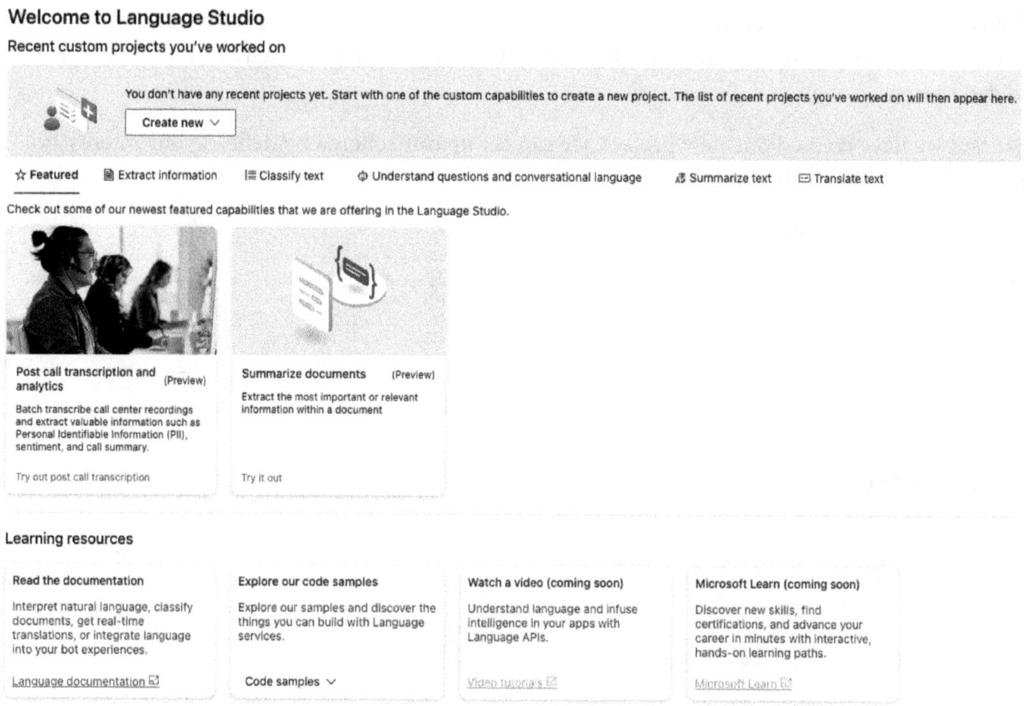

**Welcome to Language Studio**

Recent custom projects you've worked on

You don't have any recent projects yet. Start with one of the custom capabilities to create a new project. The list of recent projects you've worked on will then appear here.

Create new ∨

☆ Featured     📄 Extract information     ≔ Classify text     ⊕ Understand questions and conversational language     ⅍ Summarize text     ▭ Translate text

Check out some of our newest featured capabilities that we are offering in the Language Studio.

**Post call transcription and analytics**     (Preview)

Batch transcribe call center recordings and extract valuable information such as Personal Identifiable Information (PII), sentiment, and call summary.

Try out post call transcription

**Summarize documents**     (Preview)

Extract the most important or relevant information within a document

Try it out

**Learning resources**

**Read the documentation**

Interpret natural language, classify documents, get real-time translations, or integrate language into your bot experiences.

Language documentation ↗

**Explore our code samples**

Explore our samples and discover the things you can build with Language services.

Code samples ∨

**Watch a video (coming soon)**

Understand language and infuse intelligence in your apps with Language APIs.

Video tutorials ↗

**Microsoft Learn (coming soon)**

Discover new skills, find certifications, and advance your career in minutes with interactive, hands-on learning paths.

Microsoft Learn ↗

Figure 14.3 – The Language Studio landing page to create various Language Services projects

Upon clicking **Create new**, you get the following options:

- **Conversational Language Understanding**: Build natural language into apps, bots, and IoT devices. Coincidentally, we will want to choose this for integration with the bot for our project.

- **Orchestration workflow**: Connect and orchestrate CLU and custom question and answer LUIS projects together in one single project.

- **Custom question answering**: Customize the list of questions and answers extracted from your content corpus to provide a conversational experience that suits your needs.

- **Custom text classification**: Train a classification model to classify text using your own data.

- **Custom-named entity recognition**: Train an extraction model to identify your domain categories using your own data.

When creating a new project, you are asked which Azure resource you will use, which is what we created in the previous process, and some basic details about your project, such as name, language(s), and description.

Now that we have created our new project, we can set up our schema by defining our intents and entities. First, we start with intents:

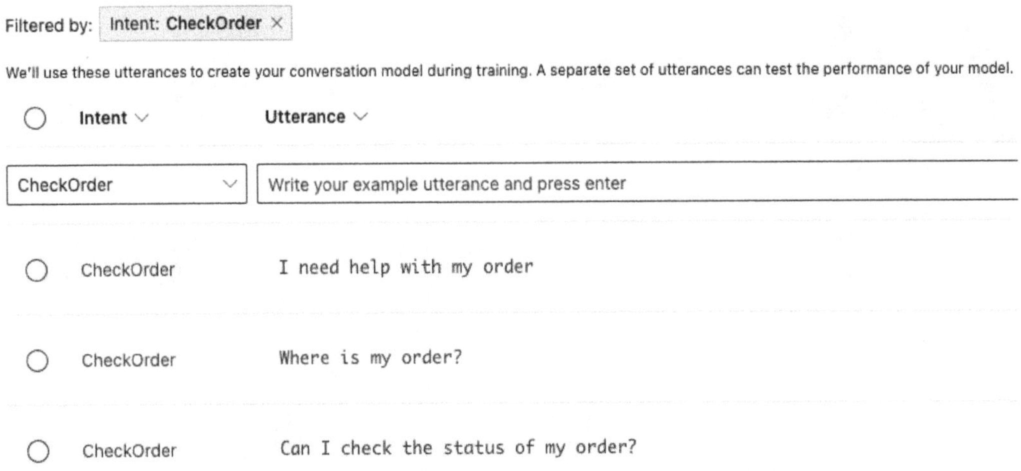

Filtered by:    Intent: CheckOrder ✕

We'll use these utterances to create your conversation model during training. A separate set of utterances can test the performance of your model.

| ○ | Intent ⌄ | Utterance ⌄ |
|---|---|---|
| | CheckOrder ⌄ | Write your example utterance and press enter |
| ○ | CheckOrder | I need help with my order |
| ○ | CheckOrder | Where is my order? |
| ○ | CheckOrder | Can I check the status of my order? |

Figure 14.4 – Sample utterances aligned to the CheckOrder intent in Language Studio

Here, you can see we have added a few utterances, or an example of a question a consumer might ask of our bot, to be aligned with the intent we created, **CheckOrder**. Next, we will make our entities able to extract details from the user's request. For instance, if our user were to ask, "*Check order status on invoice number S023876*," we want to be able to set up an **entity** for our invoice number to offer a more direct response to our user. Some additional for entities are provided in the portal, and sometimes a picture says it best – the following screenshot is the current guidance:

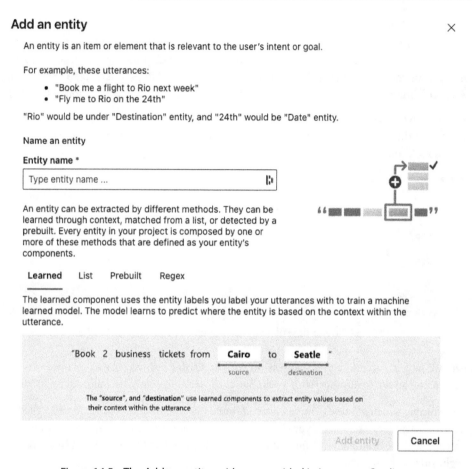

Figure 14.5 – The Add an entity guidance provided in Language Studio

So, in our case, we would want to add context to look up some other action with our order. As shown in the screenshot, entity components are made up of learned, prebuilt, regular expression, and listed values. The components and functions are as follows:

- **Learned**: This component is the true nature of the book and AI functionality, as it uses the entity labels you provide to train the machine learning model. As the model is trained, this component helps to predict where the entity exists, based on the context of the utterance.

- **Prebuilt**: The prebuilt component provides pre-built options to extract the most popular types of responses, such as numbers, dates, and personal information. These components are automatically detected in the utterance. The complete list of prebuilt components can be found here: https://learn.microsoft.com/en-us/azure/cognitive-services/ language-service/conversational-language-understanding/prebuilt- component-reference.

- **List**: The **List** component is a set of exact-match words you can specify as related to the entity, including their synonyms. This function can be used when there might be different ways to express the same item. The example Microsoft provides is mapping an airport code to its full name using their "Booking airline tickets" examples, such as "BOS" referring to "Boston Logan Airport." Either term could be used by the consumer for the origin or destination of their tickets.

- **Regular expressions**: The final component, **Regex**, matches a regular expression with the pattern of the expression. In the case of the order number previously listed, our expression would look something like the following:

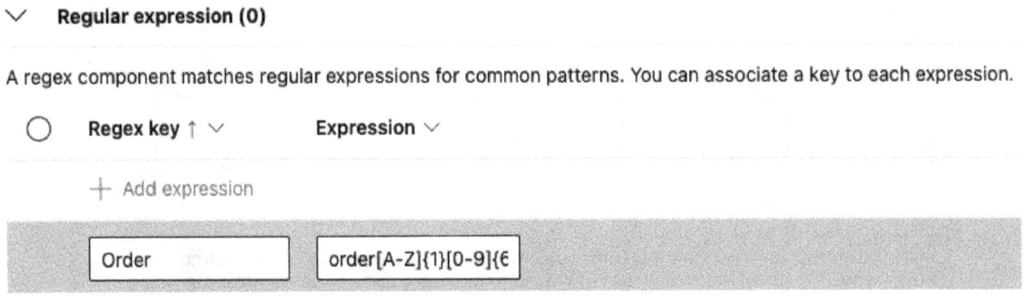

∨    **Regular expression (0)**

A regex component matches regular expressions for common patterns. You can associate a key to each expression.

○    **Regex key** ↑ ∨        **Expression** ∨

+  Add expression

| Order | order[A-Z]{1}[0-9]{6 |

Figure 14.6 – An example of a regular expression in Language Studio

As shown, we have created a regular expression with an **Order** key and the pattern we can expect when referencing an order number, with a number as the leading character followed by six digits.

When determining which of these components you would like to leverage, you will have a well-defined schema for your Language service. If you decide that it is imperative for the entity you are looking for to be matched with or predicted by one of the components, you can toggle the **Not Required** slider on the right side of the screen.

> **Important note**
> There is another point to consider from a cost scrutiny perspective. The more components that are involved and the more that data processing services do, the more costs you are going to incur. Be mindful of these options when considering what is really required.

As you work your way down the menu to your project in language studio on the left-hand side of the screen, there are several more features you can apply to the project and model you are developing:

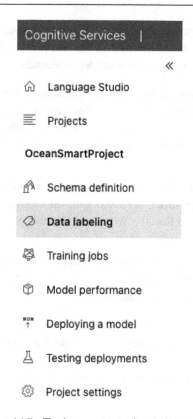

Figure 14.7 – The Language studio options menu

The details of the preceding menu items are pretty self-explanatory, but we will go through them, just in case something isn't quite clear to you:

- **Data labeling**: When you added the intents and utterances to those intents, you've already created your own **data labels**. From here, you can create two sets of labels, one for training and one for testing. By default, you add the intents and utterances to the training model set, but you can also create a testing model set as well. When you create a testing model, you can test the performance of the model with different intents and utterances versus the performance of the current training model.

- **Training jobs**: After your intents with utterances and entities are all set up, it is time to create a training job to build your custom model, based on the details you've entered. Another important item to note is that there are costs associated with the training of your model, based on the level of training, **standard** or **advanced**. You will also determine how your data will be split between training and testing. With the training, you will be paying for compute by the hour. More details can be found here: https://azure.microsoft.com/en-us/pricing/details/cognitive-services/language-service/.

- **Model performance**: After you have trained your model, of course, you can view the performance of the model you just trained. The model performance is evaluated on three criteria for each intent and entity separately, and the entire model collectively:

  - **Precision**: The **precision** of your model is a measure of how accurate it is in comparing correctly identified positives and all identified positives expressed in a percentage. The higher your precision score is, the more accurate and effective the model is. The ratio is calculated as follows Precision = `#True_Positive / (#True_Positive + #False_Positive)`

  - **Recall**: The **recall** score is calculated by the number of **predicted positives** compared to the **tagged positives**. This measure is used to display the number of correctly predicted classes and is expressed as follows Recall = `#True_Positive / (#True_Positive + #False_Negatives)`

  - **F1 score**: The **F1 score** is used to finely tune your model, comparing precision to recall to provide the optimum results. The score is calculated with the following method F1 Score = 2 * Precision * Recall / (Precision + Recall)

- **Deploying a model**: In order to leverage the model we have trained from our application, be it a bot or otherwise, we need to deploy the model for use with the service. By deploying the model, we are provided with a **prediction URL** that we will call from our application for use. You can leverage the Language SDK to consume the model here: `https://aka.ms/use-sdk-clu`.

- **Testing deployments**: Language Studio also gives you the ability to do some ad hoc testing of your model as well. Here, you can select your deployment and either provide a sample utterance to see which of your entities and intents are recognized, similar to making an API call to the service. You can either enter a single utterance or upload a text document to test and view the results.

Language Studio is a nice tool that provides a clean interface for all your model development, deployment, testing, and maintenance. This section provided an overview of the features and capabilities when creating a custom language model for use with a bot. However, this is just the beginning of what you can do with Language Studio and its services. As described earlier, there are many custom capabilities and services you can develop to create elaborate scenarios with the Language Cognitive Services. One of those scenarios is being able to work with multiple languages, a common challenge for global organizations such as Ocean Smart. In the next section, we are going to further explore these capabilities within the CLU and Language Studio.

# Using the translator services for worldwide solutions

As we discussed in the previous section, we have significant capabilities within Language Services to create a custom model with entities and intents, to respond to our consumers in an intelligent fashion. It is a complicated process to plan and deploy a bot with this intelligence because you need to be able to predict what a consumer might ask for help with, or else divert them to customer service via email or the phone. That can be an arduous process, but what happens when your bot or other application needs to interact with consumers who are not using the primary language that you have developed? Well, the CLU has options for handling just these scenarios by providing **multilingual projects**.

With multilingual projects, we can work with several languages by providing utterances in different languages, associated with entities and intents for each of those languages. However, the real value of using multilingual projects is that you can choose the primary language you will use, and let the tool complete the translation for you with the various supported languages. If, for some reason, the translation capabilities aren't sufficient, perhaps because of an accent or dialect, you can also add utterances specifically for that language for a more accurate response. In fact, the recommendation from Microsoft on how to best use the translation component is to test against the languages you intend to use, and only add a few utterances that don't perform well for the specific language that is not used. This can be done on the **Tag utterances** page in Language Studio, and it is recommended to start with just a few utterances to see some improvement in that language. To use the service, simply check the box labeled **Enable multiple languages in project?** when creating a new project, as shown in the following screenshot:

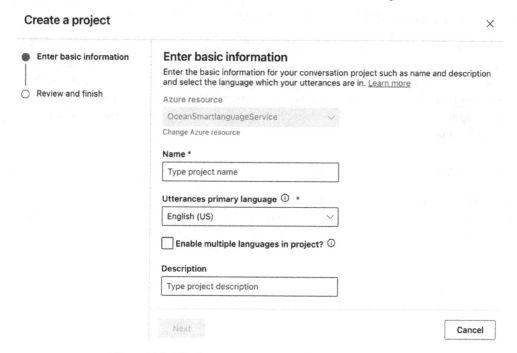

Figure 14.8 – The Create a project wizard in Language Studio

Currently, there are dozens of languages supported by the CLU, and you can always reference an up-to-date list here: `https://learn.microsoft.com/en-us/azure/cognitive-services/language-service/conversational-language-understanding/language-support#languages-supported-by-conversational-language-understanding`. There is also multilingual support for prebuilt components; however, each of the prebuilt options has its own supportability, so make sure to check the documentation before assuming a language is supported by a prebuilt component. If the specific language you are using with the prebuilt option is not supported, it will default to the selected language of the project you are working in.

Ocean Smart is a global company with offices in North America, South America, Europe, and Asia, but even though we have multilingual support, if each of these locations had to access resources in only one region, inefficiency would be created. For this reason, CLU supports each of these regions, and it is suggested as a best practice that you create resources in each of these regions for improved responsiveness. So, each of the resources would be deployed to each of the regions required by the Azure portal, then you can point your CLU project to each of the regions when deploying your project. Each of these deployment resources requires its own language resource to provide the prediction engine. After each is deployed, the model you have trained is replicated in each of the regions as well. Now, you have created a multilingual, multi-region CLU, resulting in global support. Next, we are going to look at a few more of the more advanced features of Language Services before building the complete solution.

# Advanced capabilities of Language Understanding

Since the LUIS service has transitioned to the CLU and the broader Language Services under the Cognitive Services umbrella, Microsoft has been able to ascertain a better understanding of how customers use the service for quite some time. The result of these details has given Microsoft the ability to add advanced features that customers can leverage, adding more capability to their projects as well as additional features. Here, we will briefly discuss some of the advanced features that may be beneficial for your project as well.

## Orchestration workflow

In the previous section, we discussed how the CLU can support multilingual projects as well as deploy them to multiple regions, and these options have evolved significantly over time. Another key element developed is the ability to work with multiple projects in sequence with the orchestration workflow tools, adding the ability to tie projects together for more advanced capabilities. With the various project types described previously in the chapter within the language studio, you can create a project using these different types but use them for the same application. For instance, if you wanted to use Language Understanding alongside the translation service, and then trigger a different activity leveraging RPA with an Azure logic app, these skills can be chained together using the project workflows.

## Question answering

The native capability of **Natural Language Processing (NLP)** is for your trained model to translate the statement or question you are making and respond or do something actionable with it. We commonly see NLP used by smartphone and desktop assistants, and it is also used in social media and chat bot enhancements. With question answering, there are two options:

- **Custom**: When implementing custom question answering, you can manage a knowledge base of question-and-answer pairs, as well as assign metadata and synonyms and allow feedback in specific areas. When you load your source document into the service, content is extracted from the source that creates these pairs, which can then be modified as needed to better answer the questions asked. The custom option provides more features than the prebuilt option but requires more training and management.

- **Prebuilt**: The prebuilt question-answering option is an evolution of the former **QnA Maker** service, where your document is loaded into the service. From there, the service will simply answer a query that relates to the document with the most relevant passage. There is no need to manage the knowledge base, but it will offer less accurate answers to the users of the service.

Whichever route you choose to go down with the question-answering service, it will help you to deploy services more quickly, such as a frequently asked questions chat bot and similar applications, likely enhancing the consumer's experience.

## None intents

When building our projects with intents and entities, it would be close to impossible to assign every utterance that could be used by a consumer of our application. For this reason, we have the concept of **none intents**. These are something of a catch-all for utterances that don't match an existing intent and can help save some confusion in the application if a completely unrelated utterance is introduced to the model.

An example of where this might be used in the Ocean Smart case could be something such as an utterance of "*I want to order fish.*" Because the word "order" is contained in the utterance, the system could be confused and look for details on an order that is already in the system. By simply reading the statement, we know that the intention of the user is to create a new order, but the model likely will not. A new order may or may not be a capability that has been built into the bot. In this example, however, we're assuming it is not, and we want to ensure a loop isn't created where the user is continually being asked for their order number when they want to create a new one.

The result is a comparison of the scores for the existing intents against the score of the none intents. Depending on the score, the service will determine what is the intent of the user of the system. Within the **CLU project** settings, the **none score threshold** is a set based on your observations of the score of the existing intents in the model. The higher your threshold is set, the more closely the utterances you have entered need to match. As a result, you may need to change the threshold occasionally as the model becomes more finely trained and accurate. Utterances that align with the none intents can also be added, as you begin to find questions frequently asked of the model that don't align with the purposes of your application, bot, and so on.

Some of the advanced configurations may or may not be used when using these solutions, but it is good to be aware of what these capabilities are. With that, you now should have all the information needed to build your own bot, leveraging Cognitive Services for Language, so let's look at how to do that with our Ocean Smart example.

## Building a bot using language Understanding

One area where we see Language Services used frequently is chat bots. In this chapter, we will use **Bot Framework Composer** to build a chat that calls LUIS. We will use this solution as the application for our previous example of the **Content Moderator** service from *Chapter 11*.

LUIS is the precursor to the Language Service described in this chapter. At the time of writing, Bot Framework still uses LUIS, and there should be a new version of Bot Framework that supports the Language Service in the coming months.

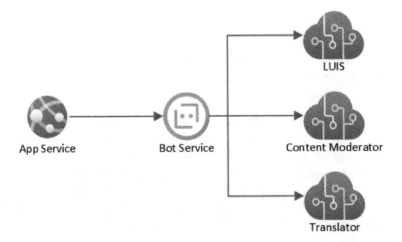

Figure 14.9 – A diagram of the services and data flow that use Bot Framework and LUIS

So, let's jump in and get started on creating the project to build our bot.

## Creating our bot project

When you launch the Bot Framework Composer application, you will come to a welcome page:

1.  Let's start by creating a new project, as shown in the following screenshot:

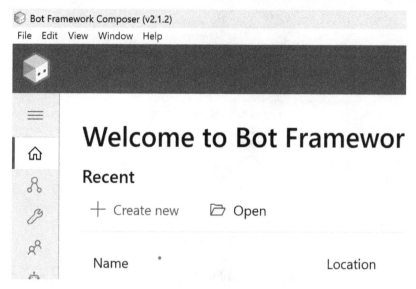

Figure 14.10 – Bot Framework Composer – the Create new project dialog

2.  **Create new** launches a dialog with a list of bot templates to choose from:

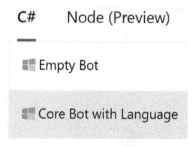

Figure 14.11 – Bot Framework Composer template choices

3. We will use the **Code Bot with Language** template. After selecting the template, give your project a name and a location to store the files associated with this project. In the runtime app for this project, we use **Azure Web App**.

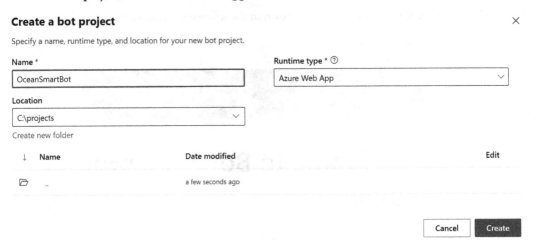

*Figure 14.12 – The Create a bot project dialog box*

4. Once you click **Create**, Bot Framework will download the selected template, create a C# solution, and perform an initial build.

5. There is an outstanding task on the right-hand side to connect our Bot Framework to the LUIS service.

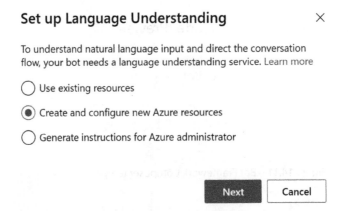

*Figure 14.13 – Adding the LUIS service to the bot within Bot Framework Composer*

6. For this example, we will use Bot Framework Composer to create our services. Log into the Azure portal and select your subscription. Next, select the resource group where your LUIS service will be deployed, select a region to run LUIS, and give it a name:

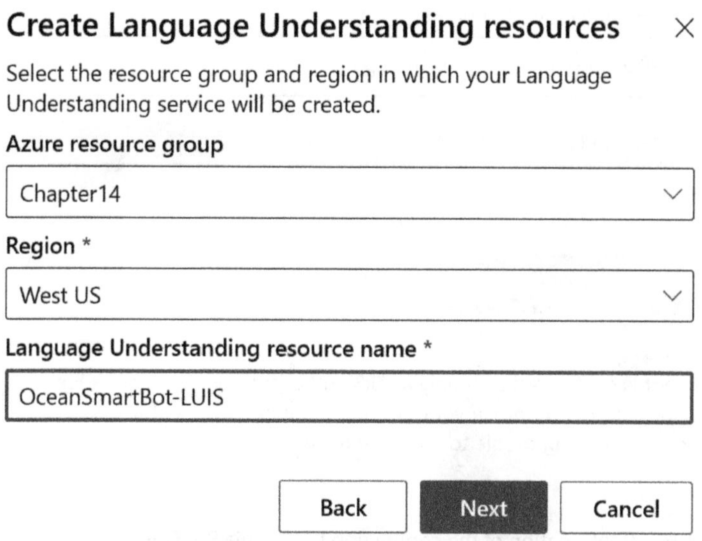

**Create Language Understanding resources**    ✕

Select the resource group and region in which your Language Understanding service will be created.

**Azure resource group**

| Chapter14 | ⌄ |

**Region ***

| West US | ⌄ |

**Language Understanding resource name ***

| OceanSmartBot-LUIS |

| Back | Next | Cancel |

Figure 14.14 – Selections for where the LUIS resources will be deployed

7.  Composer will present a dialog for you to review your selections:

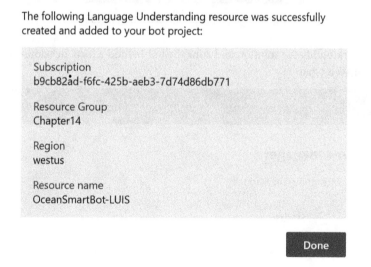

Create Language Understanding resources    ✕

The following Language Understanding resource was successfully created and added to your bot project:

Subscription
b9cb82ad-f6fc-425b-aeb3-7d74d86db771

Resource Group
Chapter14

Region
westus

Resource name
OceanSmartBot-LUIS

Done

Figure 14.15 – Validation of the settings for where the LUIS resources will be deployed

8.  Once the service is provisioned, Bot Framework Composer takes you to the bot settings page, where you can review your connection to LUIS.

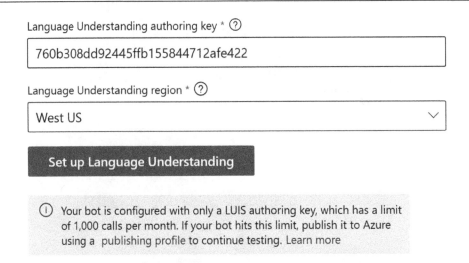

Figure 14.16 – Confirmation of the connection to LUIS via Bot Framework Composer

9.   We now have a bot project where we can start building our bot for Ocean Smart. To test the framework and configuration locally, click **Start bot**.

Figure 14.17 – The Start bot button to begin testing

10.  Bot Framework builds the solution and runs the bot behind a local development web server. Select **Open Web Chat**:

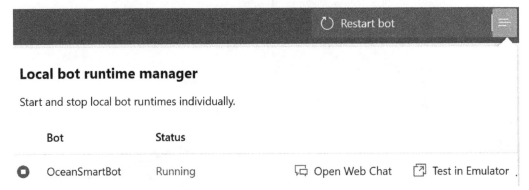

Figure 14.18 – Options to test the bot in the Bot Framework Composer tool

Now we have configured the basic bot capabilities prior to adding any skills.

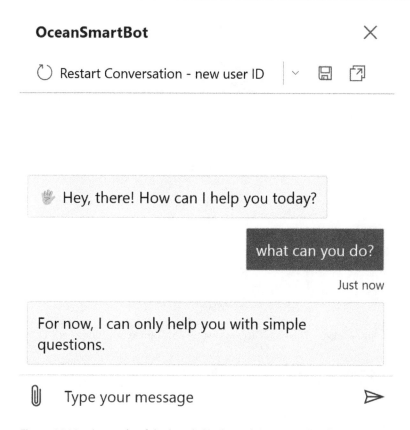

Figure 14.19 – A sample of the bot dialog box when testing locally in the SDK

Right now, the bot doesn't do much, as we haven't added any skills yet. To test it, try asking a few questions and see what responses the bot gives you.

## A quick tour of Bot Framework Composer

As displayed throughout the chapter, there are many things to consider when developing a bot solution. Further, there are other sources that will help you develop a bot with a personality that engages users, connects to various backend systems, performs tasks on behalf of the user, presents knowledge base content, and so on. For demonstration purposes, our bot will be very simple and is used here just to demonstrate the interaction between the Bot Framework and the LUIS service.

On the left-hand side of your screen, you should see a menu:

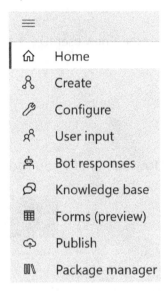

Figure 14.20 – The menu options within Bot Framework Composer

In this chapter, we spend most of our time in **Create**, where we create dialog flows, and **User input**, where we express the intents that we expect from our users and bot responses, and the text we wish the bot to respond to under various conditions.

Figure 14.21 – The options within the Create menu item

In the **Create** view, you see three icons, representing different types of resources in the project:

- ⬠: This is the project or bot you are working on currently.
- ⬚: The flowchart icon represents a dialog flow.
- ⚡: The lightning bolt represents various triggers to the bot.

Click on the **Help** trigger under the bot's main dialog flow. This is the dialog flow with the same name as your project.

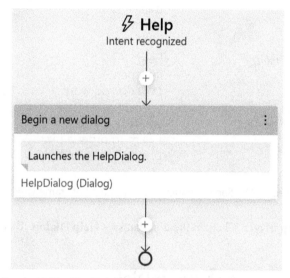

Figure 14.22 – The Help dialog option from the Create menu

You can read this flow as "*When a phrase is recognized that the bot understands as 'help,' launch the* **Help** *dialog flow.*" The following are some examples of phrases that indicate the *help* intent.

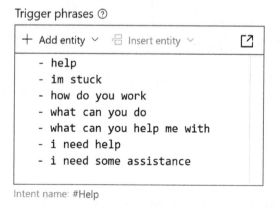

Figure 14.23 – Example utterances to use the Help dialog

We can augment this list to add utterances that might be common to our users. You can see below this list a **#Help** link. If you click **#Help**, it takes you to the **User Input** section of Bot Framework Composer. Here, you will see the various intents that the bot recognizes and the utterances that will be sent to LUIS for training:

| Intent | Sample Phrases |
| --- | --- |
| #Cancel | - cancel<br>- quit<br>- abort |
| #Help | - help<br>- im stuck<br>- how do you work |
| #None | - where is my car?<br>- I want to order a pizza<br>- place an item on hold |

Figure 14.24 – Sample phrases built into the Bot Framework

Navigate back to the **Help** trigger. Click on the link that says **Help Dialog**. This launches the editor for the **Help** dialog flow:

Figure 14.25 – The Help dialog conversation workflow

Currently, the **Help** dialog has one activity, which is to send a response. The bot framework will choose from the following list. You can view this list by clicking on the **Send a response** activity.

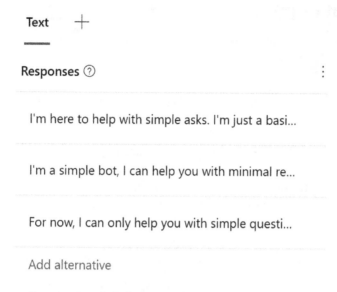

Figure 14.26 – Sample responses to the Help dialog action

You can add alternative outputs here or navigate to the **Bot Responses** section of Bot Framework Composer. Note that the **Help Dialog** section has two entries:

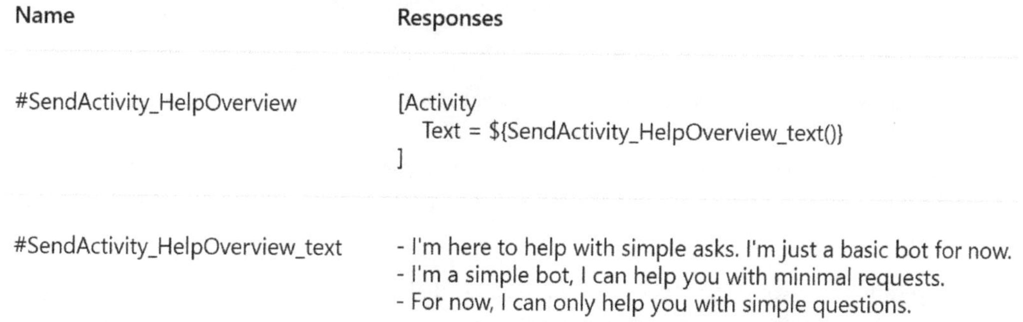

| Name | Responses |
| --- | --- |
| #SendActivity_HelpOverview | [Activity<br>    Text = ${SendActivity_HelpOverview_text()}<br>] |
| #SendActivity_HelpOverview_text | - I'm here to help with simple asks. I'm just a basic bot for now.<br>- I'm a simple bot, I can help you with minimal requests.<br>- For now, I can only help you with simple questions. |

Figure 14.27 – A sample of bot responses in Bot Framework Composer

The first entry is a code snippet that sets the text of an activity to $\{$SendActivity_HelpOverview_text()$\}$ The second entry is the list of text outputs to choose from. To see how this is used, navigate back to the dialog flow.

Next to **Bot responses,** click **Show Code.**

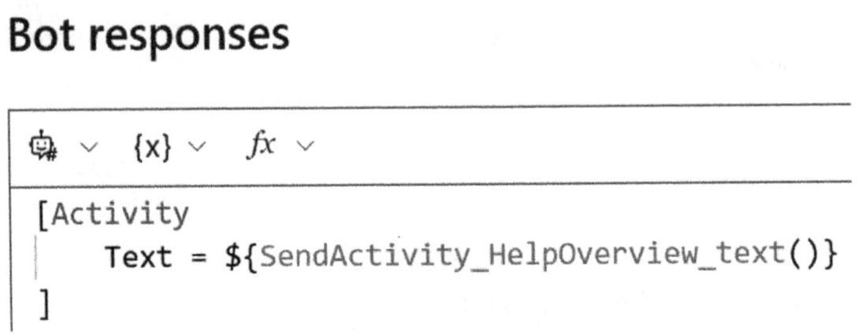

## Bot responses

```
[Activity
    Text = ${SendActivity_HelpOverview_text()}
]
```

Figure 14.28 – The Bot responses code editing window in Bot Composer Framework

In this dialog, if you click the **Bot responses** dialog, you can choose from any bot response templates for this dialog. Right now, we only have one defined for the **Help** dialog.

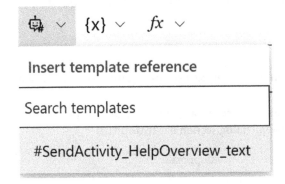

Figure 14.29 – A list of available templates created in Bot Framework Composer

If you just start adding responses to a bot response, Bot Framework Composer will either add those responses to the existing template if it is defined, or add a new template if one has not been defined for the specified activity.

Dialogs can be arbitrarily complex; the following is a dialog that greets a user with a different message, depending on whether they are a returning user or a new user.

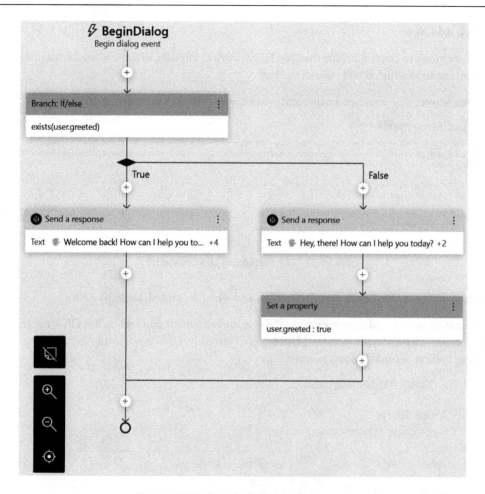

Figure 14.30 – Sample dialog to greet a user

As we construct the dialog for a user to check their order status, we will use similar branching constructs and show basic variable handling.

Select **Publish** from the menu, and under **Publish Target**, select **Manage Profiles**.

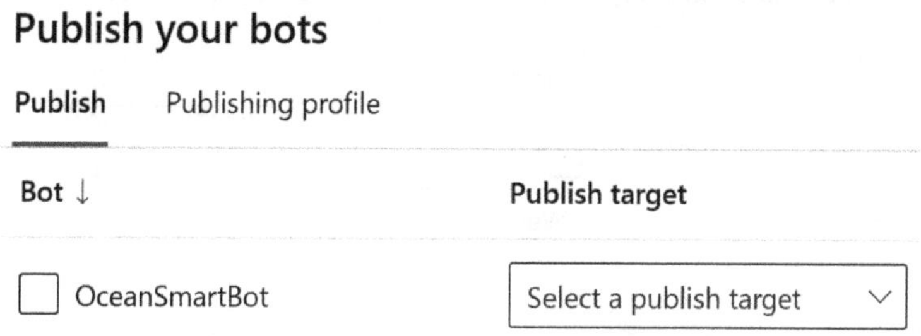

## Publish your bots

**Publish**    Publishing profile

_____

**Bot** ↓                              **Publish target**

☐  OceanSmartBot              | Select a publish target        ∨ |

Figure 14.31 – The Publish target window

Then, click **Add New**.

Here, we are going to create a profile that Bot Framework Composer will use to create resources in our environment, in which it will publish the bot.

On the first screen, give your bot a name and select the **Publish bot to Azure** option:

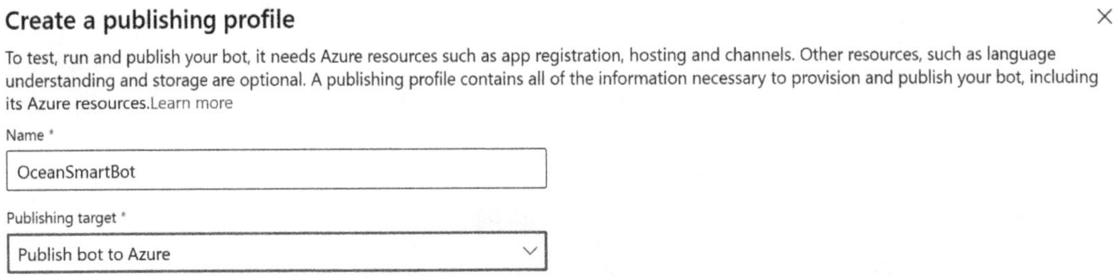

### Create a publishing profile                                                    ✕

To test, run and publish your bot, it needs Azure resources such as app registration, hosting and channels. Other resources, such as language understanding and storage are optional. A publishing profile contains all of the information necessary to provision and publish your bot, including its Azure resources.Learn more

Name *

| OceanSmartBot |

Publishing target *

| Publish bot to Azure                                    ⌄ |

Figure 14.32 – The publishing profile window

On the next screen, select **Create new Resources**, and when prompted, log in to Azure.

Select your subscription and resource group, and give the bot a name and region. It is OK if the region for the App Service is different than the LUIS region. Currently, LUIS is not in all Azure regions. For **Operating System**, leave **Windows** selected.

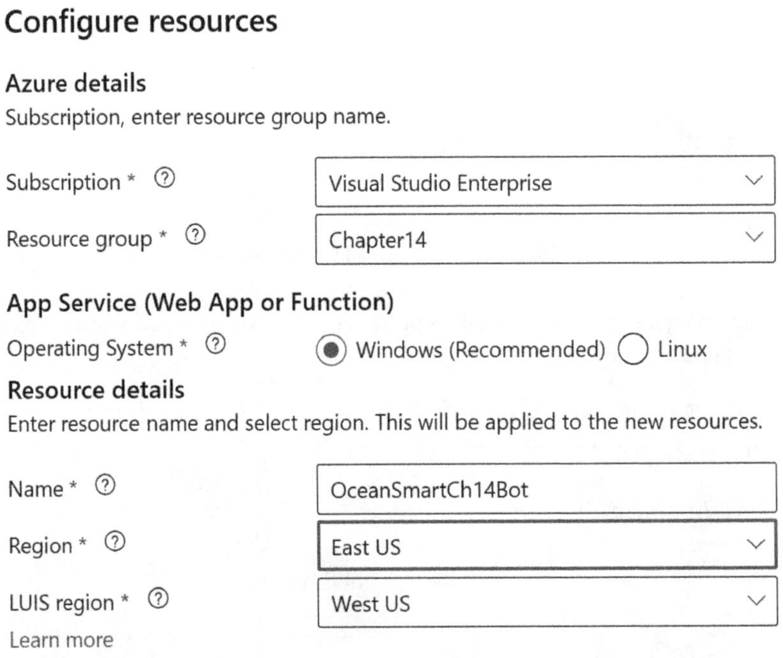

## Configure resources

### Azure details
Subscription, enter resource group name.

Subscription * ⑦          | Visual Studio Enterprise          ⌄ |

Resource group * ⑦        | Chapter14                         ⌄ |

### App Service (Web App or Function)
Operating System * ⑦     ⦿ Windows (Recommended)  ◯ Linux

### Resource details
Enter resource name and select region. This will be applied to the new resources.

Name * ⑦                  | OceanSmartCh14Bot                   |

Region * ⑦                | East US                           ⌄ |

LUIS region * ⑦           | West US                           ⌄ |
Learn more

Figure 14.33 – Deploying new resources for bot publishing

On the **Add resources** screen, you will see a number of resources that will be deployed to host the bot. You can scroll to the bottom and uncheck the optional resources, as we will not need them for this example.

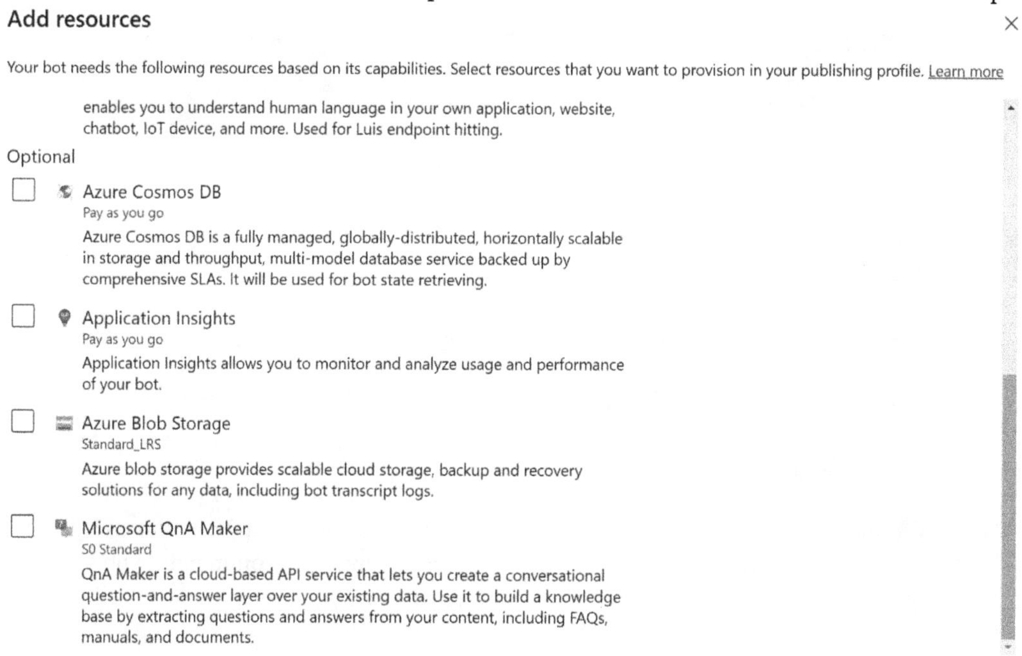

Add resources
Your bot needs the following resources based on its capabilities. Select resources that you want to provision in your publishing profile. Learn more
enables you to understand human language in your own application, website, chatbot, IoT device, and more. Used for Luis endpoint hitting.
Optional
Azure Cosmos DB
Pay as you go
Azure Cosmos DB is a fully managed, globally-distributed, horizontally scalable in storage and throughput, multi-model database service backed up by comprehensive SLAs. It will be used for bot state retrieving.
Application Insights
Pay as you go
Application Insights allows you to monitor and analyze usage and performance of your bot.
Azure Blob Storage
Standard_LRS
Azure blob storage provides scalable cloud storage, backup and recovery solutions for any data, including bot transcript logs.
Microsoft QnA Maker
S0 Standard
QnA Maker is a cloud-based API service that lets you create a conversational question-and-answer layer over your existing data. Use it to build a knowledge base by extracting questions and answers from your content, including FAQs, manuals, and documents.

Figure 14.34 – The optional resource choices when deploying the bot to Azure

After the **Review** screen, Bot Framework Composer will deploy the initial resources that are part of the publishing profile that you just created.

Go back to the **Publish** tab, select the publishing profile that you just created, then select the bot you want to publish and click **Publish selected bots** at the top of the screen.

Publish selected bots
Pull from selected profile
Publish your bots
Publish
Publishing profile
Bot ↓
Publish target
OceanSmartBot
OceanSmartBot

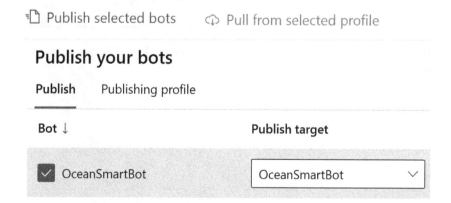

Figure 14.35 – The bot publishing window after adding a new profile

Once the publishing has completed, open the Azure portal and navigate to the resource group you selected.

You should see five resources that were deployed by Bot Framework Composer.

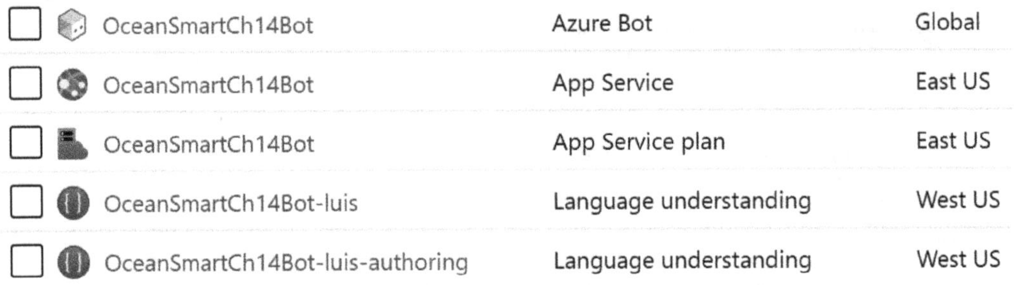

| | OceanSmartCh14Bot | Azure Bot | Global |
|---|---|---|---|
| | OceanSmartCh14Bot | App Service | East US |
| | OceanSmartCh14Bot | App Service plan | East US |
| | OceanSmartCh14Bot-luis | Language understanding | West US |
| | OceanSmartCh14Bot-luis-authoring | Language understanding | West US |

Figure 14.36 – The resources deployed to Azure as part of publishing a bot

A quick description of each of the deployed services follows:

- **Azure Bot**: This resource is the guts of the bot you have deployed. It understands how to take inputs, execute the various triggers and dialogs configured, and communicate on several channels. It is basically an app connected through an API, and you expose these APIs through various frontends or "channels."

- **App Service**: The App Service is a web frontend to the bot service and hosts the user interface to the Web Chat channel.

- **App Service plan**: The hosting plan for the App Service. This is a definition of the compute used to host the App Service.

- There are two **Language Understanding** resources deployed:

  - The **LUIS prediction** endpoint, called by the running bot

  - The **LUIS authoring** endpoint, used to author language models while developing your bot

Let's look at the LUIS authoring resource. Click on the resource in the Azure portal, and then click on **Go to portal**.

Custom Portal
Go to our custom portal to build, train, test and publish your domain specific custom LUIS applications.
Go to portal

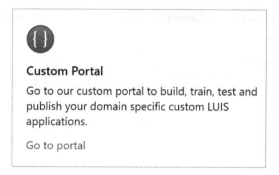

Figure 14.37 – The Custom Portal description to publish LUIS applications

This will take you to the LUIS portal, where you can select the conversation app that was deployed by Bot Framework Composer:

Conversation apps
Azure subscription: Visual Studio Enterprise / Authoring resource: OceanSmartCh14Bot-luis-authoring
Choose a different authoring resource.
New app
Import
Export
Import logs
Export logs
Rename
Delete
Migrate
Name
Last modified
OceanSmartBot(composer)-OceanSmartBot.en-us.lu
14/11/2022

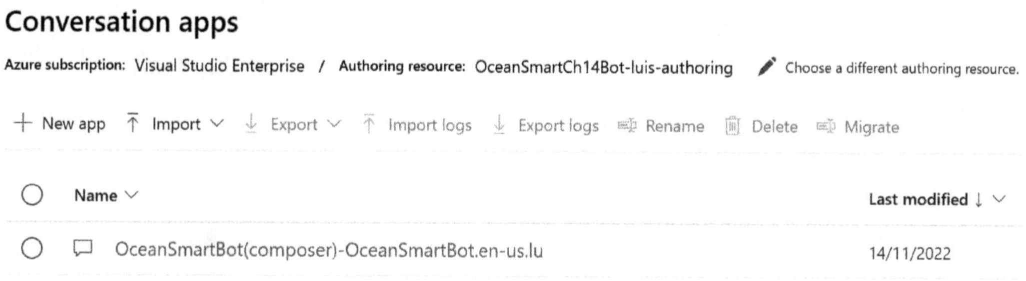

Figure 14.38 – A view of the deployed conversation apps in the LUIS portal

Note that the intents created are the intents from Bot Framework Composer.

Intents
Create
Add prebuilt domain intent
Rename
Delete
Name
Cancel
Help
None

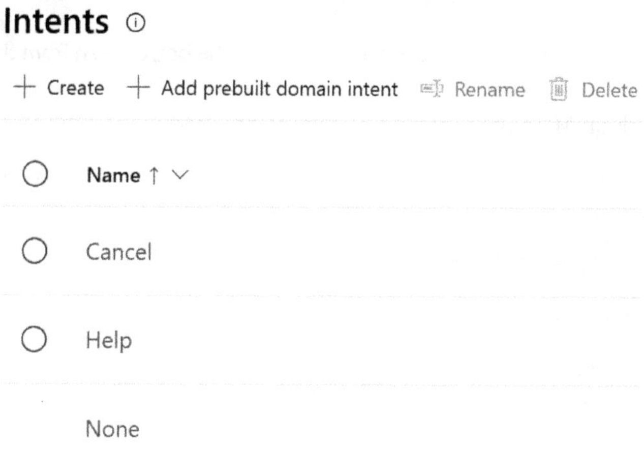

Figure 14.39 – A list of intents created for the bot as seen from the LUIS portal

If you click on the **Help** intent, the **Examples** screen shows the examples provided by Bot Framework Composer.

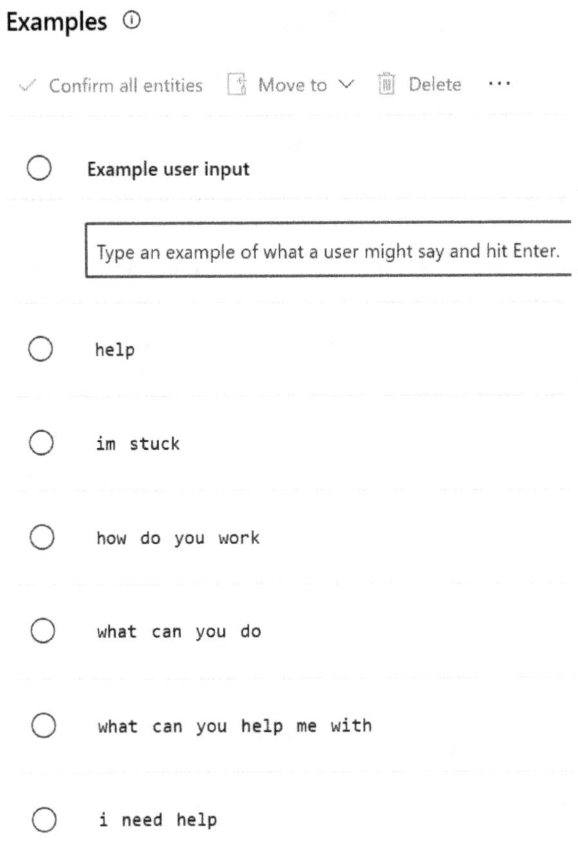

Examples ⓘ

  ✓ Confirm all entities   📝 Move to ∨   🗑 Delete   ···

○   **Example user input**

      | Type an example of what a user might say and hit Enter. |

○   help

○   im stuck

○   how do you work

○   what can you do

○   what can you help me with

○   i need help

Figure 14.40 – A list of utterances created when configuring the bot, as seen from the LUIS portal

In the LUIS portal, click on **MANAGE** and then **Azure Resources**:

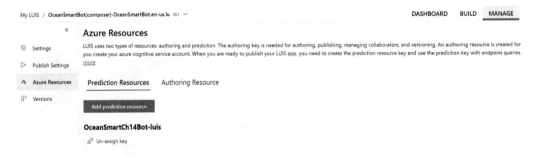

Figure 14.41 – A list of Azure resources available in the LUIS portal

Note that the **Prediction Resource** is the LUIS prediction resource in your resource group.

Back in the Azure portal, navigate to your resource group and select the **Azure Bot** resource. In the navigation menu for the Azure Bot resource, select **Test in Web Chat**.

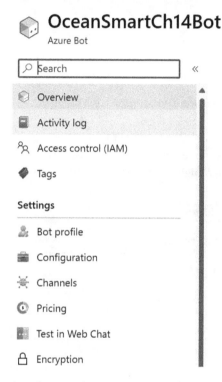

Figure 14.42 – A list of options for the Azure Bot resource in the Azure portal

You should be greeted by the bot and be able to engage in the same limited conversation as you were able to in Bot Framework Composer.

At this point, we have a running bot in Azure and a way to deploy updates to both the bot dialog flow and the LUIS authoring resource. As we publish new versions of the bot, new versions of the language model will be trained and made available to the LUIS prediction resource.

## Adding the check my order flow

In this section, we will add a flow that checks an order status. We do not have a backend system that we can check against, but since Ocean Smart is incredibly quick and efficient, we will just let the user know that their order is on the way!

Return to Bot Framework Composer and then select the **Create** item from the menu.

Click on the ellipses next to the main bot dialog and select **Add new trigger**.

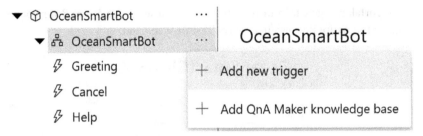

Figure 14.43 – Adding a new trigger in Bot Composer Framework

This will be an **Intent recognized** trigger. We expect the user to ask to check the status of their order. Name your trigger CheckOrder and add some examples, such as those shown in the following screenshot, which are things a user might say to a seafood distributor to ask about their order status.

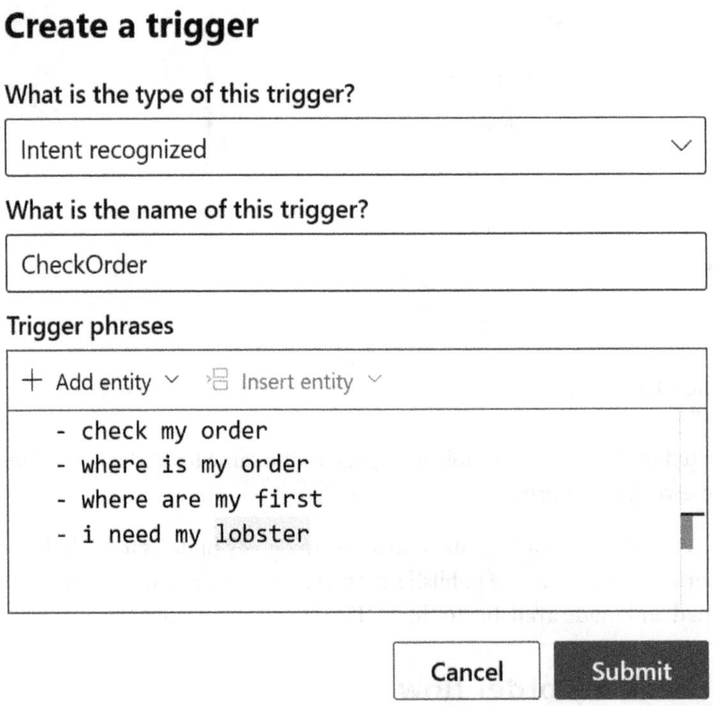

## Create a trigger

**What is the type of this trigger?**

Intent recognized                                                          ∨

**What is the name of this trigger?**

CheckOrder

**Trigger phrases**

+ Add entity ∨    Insert entity ∨

    - check my order
    - where is my order
    - where are my first
    - i need my lobster

Cancel        Submit

Figure 14.44 – Creating a trigger dialog window in Bot Composer Framework

Once you click **Submit**, you are presented with an empty dialog flow. If you navigate to **User Input** from the main menu, you should see a new #**CheckOrder** intent with the utterances supplied.

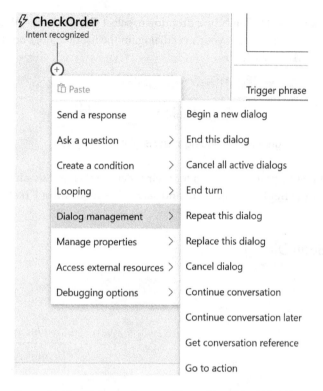

Figure 14.45 – Options when working with a new dialog flow

Click on the **Begin a new dialog** activity:

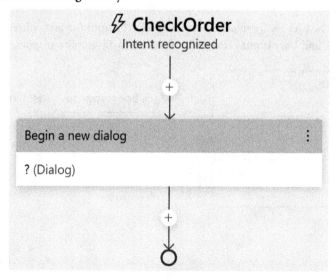

Figure 14.46 – Begin a new dialog for CheckOrder intent

In the properties, click on the **Dialog Name** dropdown, select **Create a new Dialog**, and name it `CheckOrderDialog`. After creating your new dialog, in the list of dialogs on the left, select the new dialog and the **BeginDialog** trigger.

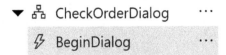

Figure 14.47 – Adding a new BeginDialog trigger

Let's engage the consumer by prompting them for their order number and sending a response. Click the plus button under the **BeginDialog** event and select **Ask a question | Text**, as shown in the following screenshot:

Figure 14.48 – An example of user engagement by asking a question in the dialog

Note that prompting the user for input adds two activities – **Prompt for text**, where the bot will ask something of the user, and **User input (Text)**, where the user will supply a response.

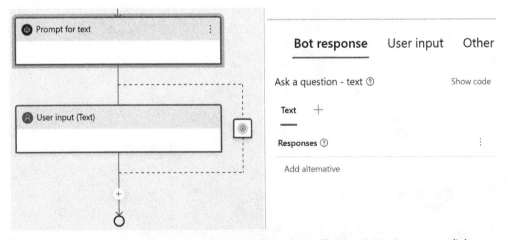

Figure 14.49 – Displaying the Prompt for text and User input (Text) activities in our new dialog

In the **Ask a question - text** property you can add prompts, allowing the bot to look up the user's order status if they supply their order number.

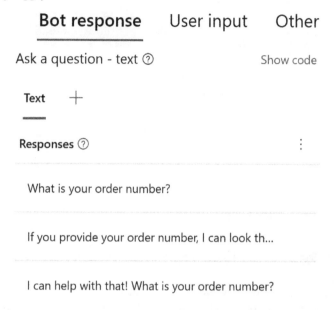

Figure 14.50 – Sample responses added to ask the user for input

In the user input, set the output property to dialog.OrderNumber. This will store the response in a variable, scoped to this dialog.

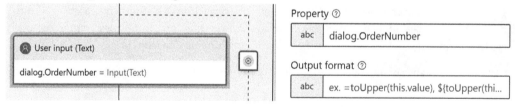

Figure 14.51 – Adding an output property to capture the user response

We have asked the user for their order number and stored the order number in a variable scope to this dialog. Now, we can output a message. Click on the plus button underneath **User Unput** and select **Send a Response**.

In the text property of this new activity, enter Good news! Order number ${dialog.OrderNumber} is on the way!. You can also add alternative outputs if you want.

Go ahead and run your bot and start the web chat to test out the new dialog.

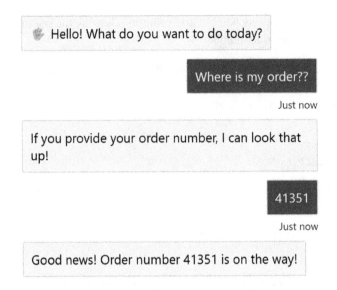

Figure 14.52 – Sample dialog between the user and the bot, checking on order status

At this point, you may want to add a new welcome message that introduces yourself as an order-checking bot or tailor the help messages to indicate that checking orders is something you can help with. Next, let's look at how to handle conversations that may be in another language as default.

## Allowing a user to add shipping notes – language translation

Bot Framework Composer allows for the localization and translation of standard responses, and you can create LUIS language models in multiple languages. However, in this example, we want to capture a user's free-form text and translate it into English for our shipping department.

First, let's add an instance of the translator service to our resource group using the following commands in the Azure CLI:

```
az cognitiveservices account create \
--name OceanSmartCh14Translator \
--resource-group Chapter14 \
--kind Translator \
--location eastus \
--sku F0
```

You will need the keys for use later, so retrieve the keys from the newly created account by running the following command:

```
az cognitiveservices account keys list \
--name OceanSmartCh14Translator \
--resource-group Chapter14
```

After we have added the Cognitive Service and retrieved the keys, return to Bot Framework Composer and add a new prompt for the user. After we notify them that their order is being prepared, let's ask them whether they have any notes for the shipping department. We will capture these notes in whatever supported language the user prefers and translate the notes to English for the shipping department.

Add a new **Prompt with Multi-Choice** step after our order status notification.

The prompt will say something like, *"Do you have any notes for the shipping department?"* In the user input section, enter yes and no as the expected responses, and store the result in a dialog variable called hasNotes.

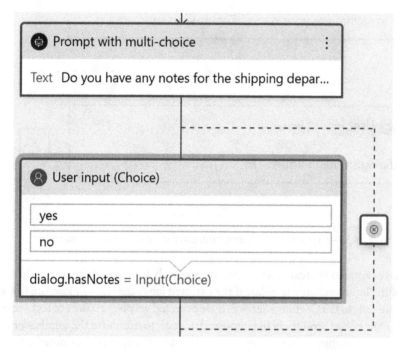

Figure 14.53 – Adding a multi-choice prompt with user input options

After we have collected the input, check to see whether they said "yes" with a new conditional.

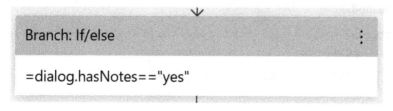

Figure 14.54 – Displaying the "yes" branch conditional

On the `true` branch, add a prompt for their notes. The prompt text should be something like, "*Do you have any notes for the shipping department? Feel free to add notes in the language you prefer, and we will translate them for our shipping department.*"

As with the previous variable example, we will capture the response in a dialog variable, `dialog.shippingNotes`:

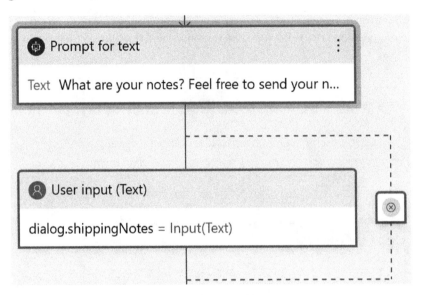

Figure 14.55 – Capturing a response from the user about any shipping notes

Now that we have captured the text in a variable, we are ready to translate the notes. First, we detect the language of the input and only translate if the detected language was not English; however, that would require two calls to the Cognitive Service. If we expected very large blocks of text, we could take the first couple of lines and send them to language detection to minimize the number of characters we translate. In this case, however, we only expect a couple of sentences per order, so we will just translate them into English if required.

Add a new HTTP request action to calls the **Translator API** and set the following properties:

- **HTTP method**: `Post`
- **URL**: `https://api.cognitive.microsofttranslator.com/translate?api-version=3.0&to=en`
- **Body**: `="[{'Text':'" + dialog.shippingNotes +" '}]"`

- **Headers**:

  - **Key**: `Ocp-Apim-Subscription-Key`
  - **Value**: The key you retrieved from the Cognitive Service
  - **Key**: `Ocp-Apim-Subscription-Region`
  - **Value**: `eastus` (or whichever region you deployed to)

- **Result property**: `dialog.translatedNotes`
- **Content type**: `application/json`
- **Response type**: `json`

After we call the **Translator** service, we will note that we have sent the messages to shipping and display the translated notes. In an actual implementation, we might store this text in a database or call an API for our shipping application to capture these notes. Here, we will just show the user that we captured them.

First, add a response to show the user what we captured.

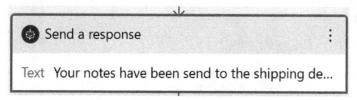

Figure 14.56 – A sample Send a response dialog window

The response will look something like this:

```
We translated your notes to English for our shipping department:
${dialog.translatedNotes.content[0].translations[0].text}
```

> **Important note**
> Note that if you want to add a line break to your response, hit *Shift + Enter* in the response **Text** field.

If we performed a translation, we would show the English version of the notes by adding a new conditional to include our detected language and translated text variable, which should be the following:

```
=dialog.translatedNotes.content[0].detectedLanguage.language != 'en'
```

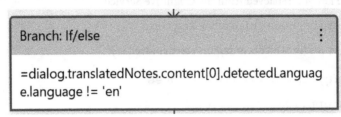

Figure 14.57 – Creating a new branch to display the language and text translated with a variable

Remember that the response is a JSON document, and we can navigate the response using property syntax. The translator accepts an array of strings to translate. We know that we just submitted one string, so we will look at the first response only. If we detect a language other than English, we provide the English translation. On the `true` branch of the conditional, add the following response:

```
We translated your notes to English for our shipping department:
${dialog.translatedNotes.content[0].translations[0].text}
```

Note there are two arrays that we reference here:

- First, `content[0]`, as before, indicates the first string that we wish to translate, but we can also translate to multiple languages simultaneously

- Second, we know that we only have one translation, so we can just reference the first item in the array with `translations[0]`

For this example, we can now complete the dialog! The dialog flow to capture and translate the shipping notes should look something like the following:

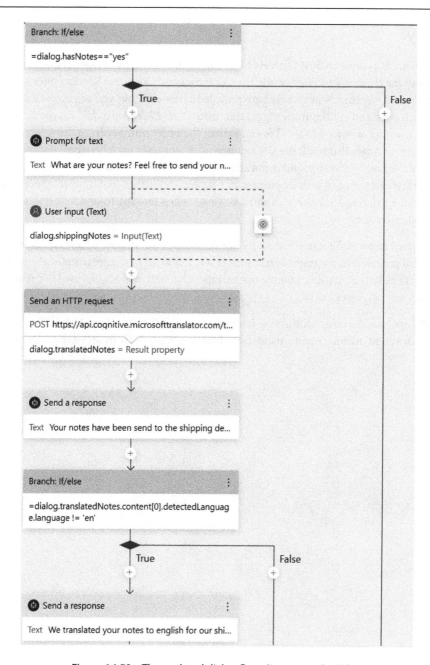

Figure 14.58 – The updated dialog flow diagram with added

That about covers what you need to get started with a dialog workflow. Now, it's time to test and make your own customizations. To get started with testing your bot, go ahead and run your bot locally to test and deploy it to Azure when you are satisfied with the results!

# Summary

The bot framework is a common host to access LUIS and, in the future, Language Services. As we have seen throughout the chapter, Bot Framework, the Composer and Cognitive Services offer a powerful solution when paired together. Now that we have provided a base example, you can evolve this solution to do things such as extract entities from trigger text. Instead of *"Check my order,"* maybe the user will say, *"What is the status of order 12345?"* We can extract the order number from the utterance using language entities. You can also hook the Bot Framework Composer up to external data sources, as we did with the Content Moderator, and communicate on various channels such as Microsoft Teams, Facebook, and text messaging, which we covered in *Chapter 11*. Further, as described, there are many other use cases the Language Services can assist you with when looking to optimize operations and improve customer service.

Here, we've covered many of the features of Azure Bot Service and working with Language Services with LUIS. We've also provided an overview of translation services to serve the greater global community. These options can be leveraged using a bot, or several other channels or mediums used to communicate with customers and employees alike.

Next, we will conclude the book with some discussion around the direction AI is taking currently and some major recent advancements, using large language models from services such as OpenAI and ChatGPT.

# 15
# Surveying Our Progress

So, what do you think? Will AI be the technological panacea, where everything is just done for us with a simple command and all the low-skill processes are replaced with robots, or will it lead to the destruction of planet Earth? Before opening the "chaos theory" can of worms, let's take a look at all the positive outcomes we are now seeing because of AI.

AI is a rapidly growing field that affects a wide range of industries in various ways. From manufacturing to healthcare, AI is being used to automate processes, improve efficiency, and generate new insights. You probably can't name an industry where AI has not made an incredible impact. We are detecting medical ailments, automating rudimentary processes such as driving, predicting more accurate weather, projecting sales numbers with alarmingly accurate results, and so many more applications. Clearly, AI has many positive impacts, but what about the conversation about how many people will lose jobs because of AI? True, some of the more basic tasks that can be performed with intelligent equipment or bots or applications may require less human intervention, but humans live longer and work longer; with the rate of change due to technology, shouldn't more be expected of us humans?

Let's be honest though, you didn't buy this book to have a philosophical discussion on how AI will impact the human race, did you? No, I think you'd rather look at what has been accomplished in totality, and what exciting innovations we can look forward to.

In this chapter, we'll be covering the following topics:

- Highlighting recent advancements in AI
- The lessons learned and returns on investments
- Evaluating future opportunities for optimization

# Highlighting recent advancements in AI

At the time of writing, OpenAI LP, the organization that created ChatGPT has been valued at $29 billion based on its latest round of funding. OpenAI LP is a for-profit AI research company created by OpenAI, a non-profit company founded in 2015 with the *"stated goal of promoting and developing friendly AI in a way that benefits humanity as a whole"* (`https://en.wikipedia.org/wiki/OpenAI`).

The developed model was built on top of the popular GPT-3.5 language model family and leverages both supervised learning and reinforcement learning for its model refinement, which is continuously evolving. Microsoft has invested over $1 billion and has pledged to invest another $10 billion in the next round. Microsoft, along with many other influential technology companies and executives, makes up the majority of the ownership of OpenAI LP. This is with very little revenue being recognized compared to its valuation, but simply a light demonstration believed in by many investors, both individual and corporate alike. Because this technology is able to so accurately and thoroughly answer a user's question about so many topics, we're seeing a significant enhancement in the internet search and reference process. The value of this advanced technology doesn't currently have much in the way of monetization, other than simple API-related revenue for the research company, but the power of its capability has made it currently the highest-ever valued start-up company. The technology is now known for the fastest-ever growth of users, reaching over 1 million unique users in just 5 days, as well as monthly records for the number of users accessing the service.

Understandably, this advancement in the areas of language, text, and logic is causing quite an uproar in the broader technical community. Google is reported to have called an internal "code red" because of how concisely ChatGPT has been able to answer questions, although there has been some debate as to how accurate the service is. With that in mind though, if ChatGPT became accurate enough to be considered the "definitive answer," search engines would be rendered useless for any type of reference discussion. In another context, the education community is very concerned, due to how eloquent the presentation of the information is, as an entire essay can be answered on a given topic, with a well-structured answer leaving educators with the question, *"Did ChatGPT write this paper, or did my student?"* The disruptive nature of AI is being seen every day in new ways, and these advancements make for an exciting future – hopefully, without killer robots!

When you consider what ChatGPT is, it is not too far from the Cognitive Services that we have covered in this book. The ChatGPT service is used by connecting to it via an API, and the expertly trained GPT-3.5 large language model is used to answer a question. This model has been refined over and over for several years to provide answers in the needed capacity. Given that the Cognitive Services APIs are trained in a similar capacity, with constant enhancement, and offer a valuable service to many customers, it will be great to see what strides are made in the coming years. Next, we will discuss all that Ocean Smart accomplished by implementing the various Cognitive Services examples provided throughout the book.

# The lessons learned and returns on investments

The book you have just finished reading is chock-full of discussions about how to ensure you maximize your return on investment and total cost of ownership when it comes to deploying Cognitive Services. We have also attempted to be as transparent as possible when discussing some of the limitations of the technologies as well. The intention of this transparency is to hopefully save you some time, money, and energy on a project that would ultimately fail, due to a technological gap or lack of valid reasoning. We have also provided you with some of the decision points Ocean Smart faced when evaluating the total cost of ownership. Think of these points as your "buyer beware" guidance. The last thing you want is to provide an inaccurate estimate for what a service will actually cost to deploy and maintain to your boss, so be sure to pay attention to these sections and start slow. Starting slow, measuring results, and estimating monthly costs will help you budget for the full workload and evaluate those critical measurements – ROI and TCO.

With this in mind, much of this book has covered the technical details and implementation guidance for the various Azure Cognitive Services. When deciding how to conclude the book, we wanted to give some examples of success stories where customers have deployed Cognitive Services, fulfilled the goals of this book, and implemented these services – helping organizations, optimizing operations, enchancing customer service, and increasing revenue. The various examples were developed with Cognitive Services and have evolved over time, and hopefully, it will be clear what value the deployments brought to their organizations. If we were asked for one piece of guidance about how to get started with AI, as discussed throughout this book, it would be to start small and grow as you need. Follow a true project life cycle to ensure that technology, requirements, and costs are equally regarded with your analysis, and rely on the Azure cloud to provide the needed scaling resources. Staying on top of the changes to the various services can be quite a job, but if you are looking for the latest and greatest information about Azure Cognitive Services, we recommend checking out the *Azure updates* blog, which can be found at the following URL: `https://azure.microsoft.com/en-us/updates/`. This, along with many of the other related blogs for each of the services, appears on a list in the appendix of this book.

## Industry ripples

One of the most significant ways that AI affects industry is through automation. In manufacturing, for example, robots and other forms of automation have been used for decades to perform repetitive tasks such as assembly line work. However, with the advent of AI, these robots are becoming increasingly sophisticated and capable. They can now learn from their experiences, adapt to new situations, and even make decisions on their own. This leads to increased productivity, improved quality control, and reduced labor costs.

Another way that AI affects industry is through improved efficiency, a recurring theme in this book, chapter after chapter. In the logistics and transportation industry, for example, companies use AI to optimize routes, predict demand, and reduce downtime. This has resulted in more efficient use of resources and lower costs for businesses.

A great example of this is Choice Aviation Services, which used Power Apps and Cognitive Services to greatly enhance its logistics operations. Customers arriving at the company's warehouse now enter their delivery information in a Power Apps application, displayed on a touchscreen kiosk in the waiting area of the warehouse. The company knew that language barriers had been a challenge in the past, so they integrated Azure Translator into the app, using an out-of-the-box connector. This enables the app to display text in over 90 languages and dialects. You can read more about this success story here: `https://customers.microsoft.com/en-us/story/1386301470305506070-choice-aviation-services-travel-and-transportation-power-platform`.

In the retail industry, AI is used to personalize shopping experiences for customers, resulting in improved customer satisfaction and increased sales. A good example of this is the Walgreens Boots Alliance digital transformation project, where a bot was quickly deployed to help with rudimentary tasks such as refilling prescriptions, general store questions, and even providing guidance on levels of risk during the COVID-19 pandemic, with advice on what actions to take. You can read more about this use case here: `https://customers.microsoft.com/en-us/story/792290-walgreens-boots-alliance-retailers-digital-transformation-azure`.

AI also affects industries in new ways, such as generating new insights and discoveries. In the healthcare industry, for example, AI is used to analyze large amounts of patient data and identify patterns that would be impossible for humans to detect. This leads to new treatments and therapies, as well as improved diagnostics. A Microsoft partner, Xoriant, works with medical companies to help deploy Cognitive Services and AI for a whole host of applications. Many organizations capture data with handwritten documents; oftentimes, they are stored as unstructured data, usually called "dark data." Xoriant works with these organizations to digitize those records and add structure to that data, and then provide insights into what those records contain. Read more about all the great work Xoriant does in the healthcare space here: `https://customers.microsoft.com/en-us/story/1351712794075425995-xoriant-partner-professional-services-azure-cognitive-services`.

In the finance industry, AI is used to detect fraud and analyze financial data, resulting in improved risk management and increased profits. Another strong Microsoft partner, KPMG, works with its customers to help identify and prevent financial crime and even insider trading misconduct. Using Cognitive Services, KPMG helps customers to transcribe conversations into digital form, extract and sort text from troves of documents, and analyze images and videos, including OCR, to search for any kind of fraud that may be happening. Read more about how KPMG is helping financial institutions here: `https://customers.microsoft.com/en-us/story/1554364202574065104-kpmg-professional-services-azure-ai`.

It's worth mentioning again that while the potential benefits of Azure Cognitive Services and AI are significant, it's important for organizations to adopt these technologies with a strategic, responsible, and well-planned approach. Next, let's look at considerations for the future and ways to approach areas beyond simple cost.

# Evaluating future opportunities for optimization

When building a business case, typically, most organizations are looking to solve an operational challenge or provide added value to the company by building a cost analysis. However, sometimes, these evaluations are focused on greater societal drivers, such as sustainability and other initiatives benefitting the greater good. Most organizations are supporters of one or more causes, and they might ask employees to volunteer their time or orchestrate fundraisers. With some of these initiatives, AI is used to help make them more efficient, or surface data that provides better information for decision-making. This involves the company understanding the specific challenges they are trying to solve, selecting the most appropriate services and tools, and working closely with their development and deployment teams to ensure that the AI solution is integrated seamlessly into existing systems and processes.

A few examples of these initiatives are as follows:

- **Education**: AI is used to develop intelligent tutoring systems that can help students learn more effectively, personalize educational content based on students' individual learning styles and abilities, and analyze student performance data to identify areas for improvement.

- **Environment**: AI is used to monitor and protect wildlife, track and analyze weather patterns and climate change, and improve the efficiency of energy systems to reduce carbon emissions.

- **Agriculture**: AI is used to develop precision agriculture techniques that can help farmers optimize their crop yields while minimizing the use of resources, such as water and fertilizer.

There are many other areas that are being explored, but hopefully, this provides some perspective on what is possible and being done with AI. These initiatives are run by corporations and non-profit organizations alike, all the while done in an ethical and responsible way. In the next section, we will explore the ethical considerations of AI as these tools are developed.

## The ethics of AI

We have focused on many of the features and configuration aspects of the technology along with how we can improve our organizations, while helping to justify the associated costs. What we haven't talked about much are the ethics associated with any AI project. As AI continues to become more integrated into our daily lives, it's important for organizations to ensure that they are using these technologies in responsible and ethical ways. For example, when using Azure's Natural Language Processing services to analyze customer feedback, organizations must be mindful of privacy and security, ensuring that customer data is protected and not used for any malicious purposes. Additionally, organizations must be transparent about how they are using AI, and they should take steps to educate their customers and employees about how these technologies are being used and the benefits they bring.

Another important consideration is the potential for AI to perpetuate bias and reinforce existing inequalities. For example, a biased training dataset can result in an AI system that produces unfair or inaccurate results. Organizations must take care to ensure that the training datasets they use are representative and diverse and should regularly test and monitor their AI systems for bias.

For these reasons and more, Microsoft created their own Responsible AI guidance and framework for being able to ensure AI deployments adhere to specific standards. In fact, Microsoft is intensely committed to having AI be deployed responsibly to the point of hold its employees and partners for the same standards.

If you are interested to learn more about their approach, you can find more details here: `https://www.microsoft.com/en-us/ai/responsible-ai?activetab=pivot1%3aprimaryr6`

In summary, as organizations adopt Azure Cognitive Services and AI, it's important that they approach these technologies with an ethical and responsible mindset. This includes considering the privacy and security of customer data, being transparent about how AI is used, and taking steps to mitigate any potential biases or inequalities. By doing so, organizations can ensure that they use these powerful technologies in ways that benefit both their businesses and society as a whole.

## Summary

Azure Cognitive Services and AI are powerful tools that transform the way businesses and organizations operate in today's data-driven world. With a wide range of services covering areas such as speech recognition, natural language processing, and computer vision, Azure offers businesses the ability to integrate cutting-edge AI technologies into their existing systems and processes, driving innovation and growth.

The ease of integration and scalability of Azure Cognitive Services, combined with its reliability and security, make it an attractive choice for organizations of all sizes, regardless of their technical expertise or resources. Additionally, the Azure platform provides businesses with the ability to quickly and easily experiment with new AI-powered solutions, reducing the risk and complexity associated with traditional software development.

In this book, we have explored the various components of Azure Cognitive Services, detailing the specific capabilities of each service and providing examples of real-world applications. We have also discussed the benefits of using Azure Cognitive Services and AI, including increased efficiency, improved customer experiences, and a competitive edge in the marketplace.

Overall, Azure Cognitive Services and AI are poised to play a significant role in the future of technology and business, and organizations that embrace this technology now will be well-positioned for success in the years to come.

However, with the growth of AI, there are also implications to consider. One of the major concerns is job displacement. As AI takes over more tasks and functions, it is likely that some jobs will become obsolete. This could result in widespread unemployment, particularly in industries that are heavily dependent on automation. Additionally, there are concerns about the potential for AI to be used in ways that are harmful to society, such as in the development of autonomous weapons or the violation of privacy rights.

Another implication is the potential for AI to be biased, particularly in the use of algorithms for decision-making. These biases could be due to the data that is used to train the AI models, which may be skewed or incomplete. This could lead to unfair decisions, particularly in areas such as hiring, lending, and criminal justice.

The rise of Azure Cognitive Services and AI marks a major turning point for organizations seeking to leverage cutting-edge technology to improve their operations and gain a competitive edge. With its comprehensive suite of services and tools, organizations of all sizes and across all industries can harness the power of AI and take their business to the next level. Thank you for reading this book. Hopefully, we have provided the insight to help you and your organization embrace these great technologies to gain the efficiencies and improvements we've tried to provide throughout.

# 16
# Appendix – Azure OpenAI Overview

The timing of the publication of this book couldn't be more pivotal, as we are seeing first-hand the impact AI is having across the globe with the release of ChatGPT by OpenAI LP, a for-profit subsidiary of the non-profit OpenAI. OpenAI is a research organization founded in 2015, with the goal of promoting and developing friendly AI that benefits humanity. OpenAI has become one of the leading organizations in the field of AI, with a focus on advancing the state of AI research and deployment. The organization is made up of a team of leading AI researchers and engineers and is dedicated to advancing AI research and deployment.

One of OpenAI's most notable contributions to the field of AI is its work on **large language models (LLMs)**. A language model is a type of machine learning model that is trained on large amounts of text data. The success of these models has been attributed to their ability to capture patterns in training data and use these patterns to generate new text that is similar to the input. LLMs such as OpenAI's **Generative Pre-trained Transformer (GPT-3)** have achieved remarkable results in a wide range of **natural language processing (NLP)** tasks, including text generation, translation, and summarization. In addition to its work on language models, OpenAI has also made important contributions to other areas of AI, such as reinforcement learning and computer vision.

The first major success of OpenAI LP is ChatGPT, a specific instantiation of OpenAI's GPT-3 (or GPT-3.5 depending who you ask) language model that is optimized to generate human-like responses in a conversational setting. ChatGPT can understand and respond to a wide variety of questions, covering a wide range of topics and styles of conversation. This makes it an ideal platform to build conversational AI applications, such as chatbots and virtual assistants. Consumers of ChatGPT are able to leverage the technology through an API, similar to how customers use Azure Cognitive Services.

Despite the remarkable progress that has been made in the development of LLM interfaces such as ChatGPT, there are still many challenges and limitations that need to be addressed. For example, while LLMs have been trained on vast amounts of text data, they can still make mistakes and generate responses that are inconsistent with human beliefs and values. There is also ongoing work to address issues of bias in LLMs, as they can lead to and amplify harmful stereotypes and prejudices present in the training data they are trained on. Additionally, these models consume a large number of computational resources, making it difficult to deploy them in real-world applications.

## Reviewing industry trends

In this book, we have covered many topics surrounding the implementation of AI in many scenarios where organizations can benefit from improving operations. Here are a few trends and developments that are likely to shape the future of these systems:

- **Increased capabilities**: As AI research continues to advance, we can expect LLMs such as ChatGPT to become even more capable, with improved accuracy and the ability to handle a wider range of NLP tasks. This will likely lead to the development of new applications and use cases for these models.

- **Greater efficiency**: LLMs such as ChatGPT are currently trained on vast amounts of data, require substantial computational resources, and can take significant time to process and train. As we have discussed several times throughout the book, there is always a trade-off between cost and time, and we are certainly seeing this same paradigm with ChatGPT. In the future, we can expect to see advances in AI algorithms and hardware that will allow these models to be trained more efficiently, making it easier to deploy them in real-world applications.

- **More focused models**: Currently, LLMs such as ChatGPT are trained to perform a wide range of NLP tasks. In the future, we can expect to see the development of more focused models that are optimized for specific applications, such as customer service or content creation.

- **Interdisciplinary collaboration**: The development of AI systems such as ChatGPT requires collaboration between researchers and engineers from a wide range of disciplines, including computer science, linguistics, psychology, and philosophy. In the future, we can expect to see continued interdisciplinary collaboration as AI systems continue to evolve and become increasingly integrated into our lives.

So, maybe you're asking the question, "*What exactly has OpenAI provided that makes you think all of these world-changing events will occur?*", so I figured we might as well provide some examples of some of those services here.

# Understanding what Azure OpenAI services are

Through the lens of Azure, there are several APIs available through a "gated preview," which essentially means you must assure Microsoft that you aren't going to use these tools for nefarious purposes. OpenAI services currently available in Microsoft Azure, allowing users to take advantage of the scalability, security, and global reach of the Azure platform, are as follows:

- **OpenAI GPT-3**: OpenAI's **GPT-3** is a state-of-the-art language model that can generate human-like text. Consumers can leverage GPT-3 by making API calls to the OpenAI API using a supported programming language of choice (such as Python and JavaScript). You can use the API to generate text, translate text from one language to another, summarize text, and perform other NLP tasks.

- **OpenAI ChatGPT**: After initially just providing the **GPT-3** and **Playground** APIs, the ChatGPT API has recently been added to the list of available services through the Azure platform. This API has support for multiple languages, can generate natural language responses to natural language questions, and excels in **conversational AI** for use cases such as customer service. The API allows you to customize the language model, enabling users to fine-tune it to their specific use cases. Because the service is built on Azure's cloud infrastructure, customers are provided a highly scalable and reliable platform to run AI workloads, something that has been a challenge for customers using the service directly from OpenAI. In healthcare, the ChatGPT API has been used to develop conversational agents that can help patients to book appointments, provide medical advice, and answer frequently asked questions.

- **OpenAI Codex**: OpenAI Codex is an AI-powered recommendation engine that provides personalized recommendations for users. To use OpenAI Codex, you can send API requests with information about your audience, such as their interests and preferences, and receive personalized recommendations in return.

- **OpenAI DALL-E**: OpenAI DALL-E is a powerful generative model that can create unique, high-quality images from textual descriptions. To interact with OpenAI DALL-E, you can send API requests with textual descriptions of the images you would like to generate and receive the generated images in return. An example would be how Adobe has integrated the DALL-E API into its popular image editing software, Photoshop, allowing users to generate unique and realistic images from textual descriptions within the application.

- **OpenAI Ada**: OpenAI Ada is a virtual writing assistant that can help users write emails, reports, and other documents more efficiently. To interact with OpenAI Ada, you can send API requests with the text you would like Ada to help you write and receive suggestions and recommendations for improvement in return.

- **OpenAI GPT-3 Playground**: The OpenAI GPT-3 Playground is a web-based interface that allows developers and data scientists to experiment and interact with the GPT-3 model. For access to the OpenAI GPT-3 Playground, you can simply go to the website and type a message in a prompt. The Playground will then generate text based on the prompt, and you can continue to interact with the model by adding more text or changing the prompt.

> **Important note**
>
> Note that these are just examples, and the exact implementation of each service may vary, depending on your specific use case and the platform you are using. If you have any specific questions about using these services, contact Microsoft or an authorized partner for support.

Commonly customers of Microsoft are wondering what security and privacy implications are due to the open nature of ChatGPT and in contrast the Azure OpenAI APIs. The Azure OpenAI APIs are private to the tenant where they are deployed, and the data resides in that tenant only, unless the customer sends the model or data elsewhere. As more services are rolled out, and features added to Microsoft product, such as the recently announced Co-Pilot in many products, these are good questions to be asking. Before using any of the services, make sure you are compliant in your own requirements as you consider your own deployments.

How and where customers will use these APIs for use within their organization will also evolve over time, and due to the nature of the excitement around the services being launched, there can be some misconceptions, which we will cover next.

# Clarifying common misconceptions

The pure nature of AI, doomsday or otherwise, is challenging for the majority of people to conceptualize. Attempting to simplify these advanced technical concepts can prove to be challenging, especially with the whirlwind of "fake news" plaguing our world. For that reason, I think it's a great idea to acknowledge that there are several misconceptions about ChatGPT and OpenAI that are worth addressing:

- **ChatGPT is fully autonomous**: ChatGPT is not a fully autonomous AI system but, instead, a machine learning model that generates text based on the input it receives. It is not capable of independent thought or decision-making and can only generate responses based on the information it has been trained on.

- **ChatGPT is perfect**: Despite its impressive capabilities, ChatGPT is still prone to making mistakes and generating responses that are inconsistent with human beliefs and values. It is important to understand that ChatGPT is not a perfect AI system and that its responses should be critically evaluated before being used in real-world applications.

- **OpenAI only works on language models**: OpenAI is a research organization that is focused on advancing the state of AI research and deployment, with a focus on LLMss such as ChatGPT. However, OpenAI also works on a wide range of other AI projects and applications, including computer vision, reinforcement learning, and robotics.

- **OpenAI is a commercial organization**: While OpenAI has received funding from a number of commercial organizations, it is a non-profit research organization that is dedicated to advancing AI in a way that benefits humanity as a whole. Its primary goal is not to generate commercial profit but to advance the state of AI research and deployment.

- **ChatGPT is biased**: As with all machine learning models, ChatGPT is trained on data and can perpetuate and amplify harmful biases and stereotypes present in the training data. OpenAI actively works to address these issues and develop AI models that are fair and unbiased.

It is important to understand that ChatGPT and OpenAI are complex and powerful AI systems and that there are many misconceptions and misunderstandings about their capabilities and limitations. By continuing to critically evaluate these systems and address the challenges and limitations they face, we can ensure that they are developed and deployed in a responsible and ethical manner.

## Summary

The future of OpenAI, ChatGPT, and LLMs is likely to be shaped by continued advances in AI research and technology, as well as by ongoing efforts to address ethical and moral considerations. By continuing to advance the state of AI research and deployment, organizations such as OpenAI will play a critical role in shaping the future of AI. We will also see various iterations of additional APIs, as various organizations identify gaps in the current offerings and other large tech companies make investments in similar projects.

OpenAI, LLMs, and ChatGPT represent a significant advance in the field of AI and have the potential to transform a wide range of industries and applications. Microsoft has already begun to name where they will integrate ChatGPT into some of their existing products, such as the Bing search engine, Microsoft Teams, and Microsoft Office products, just for starters. Over time, more products will take advantage of the power of the LLMs and further enhance productivity in certain activities. There are many great uses of these technologies when used responsibly. However, it is important to continue to address the challenges and limitations of these systems, in order to ensure that they are developed and deployed ethically.

# Index

# E

# F

# G

Packtpub.com

Subscribe to our online digital library for full access to over 7,000 books and videos, as well as industry leading tools to help you plan your personal development and advance your career. For more information, please visit our website.

## Why subscribe?

- Spend less time learning and more time coding with practical eBooks and Videos from over 4,000 industry professionals

- Improve your learning with Skill Plans built especially for you

- Get a free eBook or video every month

- Fully searchable for easy access to vital information

- Copy and paste, print, and bookmark content

Did you know that Packt offers eBook versions of every book published, with PDF and ePub files available? You can upgrade to the eBook version at packtpub.com and as a print book customer, you are entitled to a discount on the eBook copy. Get in touch with us at customercare@packtpub.com for more details.

At www.packtpub.com, you can also read a collection of free technical articles, sign up for a range of free newsletters, and receive exclusive discounts and offers on Packt books and eBooks.

# Other Books You May Enjoy

If you enjoyed this book, you may be interested in these other books by Packt:

**Azure Machine Learning Engineering**

Sina Fakhraee, Balamurugan Balakreshnan, Megan Masanz

ISBN: 9781803239309

- Train ML models in the Azure Machine Learning service
- Build end-to-end ML pipelines
- Host ML models on real-time scoring endpoints
- Mitigate bias in ML models
- Get the hang of using an MLOps framework to productionize models
- Simplify ML model explainability using the Azure Machine Learning service and Azure Interpret

**Machine Learning in Microservices**

Mohamed Abouahmed, Omar Ahmed

ISBN: 9781804617748

- Recognize the importance of MSA and ML and deploy both technologies in enterprise systems
- Explore MSA enterprise systems and their general practical challenges
- Discover how to design and develop microservices architecture
- Understand the different AI algorithms, types, and models and how they can be applied to MSA
- Identify and overcome common MSA deployment challenges using AI and ML algorithms
- Explore general open source and commercial tools commonly used in MSA enterprise systems

## Packt is searching for authors like you

If you're interested in becoming an author for Packt, please visit `authors.packtpub.com` and apply today. We have worked with thousands of developers and tech professionals, just like you, to help them share their insight with the global tech community. You can make a general application, apply for a specific hot topic that we are recruiting an author for, or submit your own idea.

## Share Your Thoughts

Now you've finished *Practical Guide to Azure Cognitive Services*, we'd love to hear your thoughts! Scan the QR code below to go straight to the Amazon review page for this book and share your feedback or leave a review on the site that you purchased it from.

https://packt.link/r/1-801-81291-8

Your review is important to us and the tech community and will help us make sure we're delivering excellent quality content.

# Download a free PDF copy of this book

Thanks for purchasing this book!

Do you like to read on the go but are unable to carry your print books everywhere?

Is your eBook purchase not compatible with the device of your choice?

Don't worry, now with every Packt book you get a DRM-free PDF version of that book at no cost.

Read anywhere, any place, on any device. Search, copy, and paste code from your favorite technical books directly into your application.

The perks don't stop there, you can get exclusive access to discounts, newsletters, and great free content in your inbox daily

Follow these simple steps to get the benefits:

1. Scan the QR code or visit the link below

https://packt.link/free-ebook/9781801812917

2. Submit your proof of purchase
3. That's it! We'll send your free PDF and other benefits to your email directly

CPSIA information can be obtained
at www.ICGtesting.com
Printed in the USA
JSHW050244200523
41983JS00002B/28